WORKING THE RUINS

Feminist
Poststructural
Theory and
Methods in
Education

Edited by
Elizabeth A. St.Pierre
and Wanda S. Pillow

ROUTLEDGE
New York and London

Published in 2000 by
Routledge
29 West 35th Street
New York, New York 10001

Published in Great Britain by
Routledge
11 New Fetter Lane
London EC4P 4EE

Copyright © 2000 by Routledge

Printed in the United States of America on acid-free paper.

Library of Congress Cataloging-in-Publication Data

Working the ruins: feminist poststructural theory and methods in education / Elizabeth A. St.Pierre and Wanda S. Pillow, eds.
       p.   cm.
    Includes bibliographical references and index.
    ISBN 0–415–92275–5 — ISBN 0–415–92276–3
      1. Feminism and education. 2. Poststructuralism.
  3. Postmodernism and education. 4. Education—Research.   I. St.Pierre,
Elizabeth.   II. Pillow, Wanda S.
LC197.W67   1999
370.11′5—dc21
                                      99-30799
                                          CIP

CONTENTS

ACKNOWLEDGMENTS

None of us are lone scholars, and we have found this to be especially true during the genesis and production of this book. Many people have supported us in this project and in all the others that led to it. So, lest we forget someone, we extend a warm thank you to everyone we've ever worked with. In particular, we thank Ilene Kalish, our editor at Routledge, who helped conceptualize and guide our work; Heather Lee and Guadalupe Martinez for their typing assistance; and Kate McCoy for her careful reading of our introduction.

Wanda thanks Bettie for suggesting this project and for her support as colleague, co-theorist, and special *amiga*. Wanda also thanks Laurence Parker for his advice and support. And to Jeremy and Kimberle, who kept a watchful and curious eye on her work patterns, and to Pretinha, who warmed her lap on all the late nights, Wanda says *muchas gracias*.

Bettie thanks Wanda for sharing her fine mind, generous patience, and sweet friendship, and Patti Lather who suggested she and Wanda "get that book out!" She is also most grateful to Rowena Adams and George St.Pierre for their loving and ongoing support of all the projects in her life.

Several chapters, edited to varying degrees, have been previously published; we express our appreciation to Sage Publications, Taylor & Francis, and the University of Minnesota Press for permission to reprint the following:

Britzman, Deborah. (1995). "The question of belief": Writing poststructural ethnography. *International Journal of Qualitative Studies in Education, 8*(3), 229–38. [Taylor & Francis]

Chaudhry, Lubna Nazir. (1997). Researching "my people," researching myself: Fragments of a reflexive tale. *International Journal of Qualitative Studies in Education, 10*(4), 441–53. [Taylor & Francis]

Collins, Patricia Hill. (1998). What's going on? Black feminist thought and the politics of postmodernism. In *Fighting words: Black women and the search for social justice*. Minneapolis, MN: University of Minnesota Press. [University of Minnesota Press]

Lather, Patti. (1997). Drawing the line at angels: Working the ruins of feminist ethnography. *International Journal of Qualitative Studies in Education, 10*(3), 285–304. [Taylor & Francis]

Leach, Mary. (1997). Feminist figurations: Gossip as a counterdiscourse. *International Journal of Qualitative Studies in Education, 10*(3), 305–14. [Taylor & Francis]

McCoy, Kate. (1997). White noise—the sound of epidemic: Reading/writing a climate of intelligibility around the "crisis" of difference. *International Journal of Qualitative Studies in Education, 10*(3), 333–47. [Taylor & Francis]

Pillow, Wanda S. (1997). Exposed methodology: The body as a deconstructive practice. *International Journal of Qualitative Studies in Education, 10*(3), 349–63. [Taylor & Francis]

Richardson, Laurel. (1997). Skirting a pleated text: De-disciplining an academic life. *Qualitative Inquiry, 3*(3), 295–303. [Reprinted by permission of Sage Publications]

St.Pierre, Elizabeth A. (1997). Nomadic inquiry in the smooth space of the field: A preface. *International Journal of Qualitative Studies in Education, 10*(3), 365–83. [Taylor & Francis]

Introduction

Inquiry among the Ruins

Elizabeth A. St.Pierre
and Wanda S. Pillow

The feminist educators writing for this volume acknowledge in various ways that they are working in the "twilight of foundationalism" (Nicholson, 1999, p. 117), after the crises of representation and legitimation, and through and out of a restless "post" period that troubles all those things we assumed were solid, substantial, and whole—knowledge, truth, reality, reason, science, progress, the subject, and so forth. During the last half of the twentieth century, poststructuralism[2] in all its manifestations, along with other "posts"[3] that describe continuing skepticism about regimes of truth that have failed us, has worked the ruins[4] of humanism's version of those concepts. Rather than finding despair, paralysis, nihilism, apoliticism, irresponsibility, or immorality in the decay and devastation of the ruins (charges such as these are often used to dismiss poststructuralism, but some believe they describe the foundational world),[5] these feminists have found possibilities for different worlds that might, perhaps, not be so cruel to so many people.

Their task as educators[6] is to "look awry" (Žižek, 1991) and ask questions that produce different knowledge and produce knowledge differently, thereby producing different ways of living in the world. What might such reinscriptions look like? And, importantly, how do those of us who have been privileged by the authority of foundationalism, those who have begun to understand their complicity in perpetuating its indignities, proceed? "How does one act knowing what one does?" (Visweswaran, 1994, p. 80).

These are the questions that frame this collection of essays, questions that neither produce nor desire another clear, consensual, and whole alternative. Rather they encourage a lusty, rigorous, enabling confusion that deterritorializes ontological reckonings, epistemological conditions and justifications, and methodological striations. Out of the radical open-ness produced by troubling "an established way of thinking" under which "a prevailing system of representation is naturalized and seen as the only truthful and 'correct' way" (Trinh, 1992, p. 125), these feminists produce different structures of intelligibility that, in turn, produce differ-ent epistemologies, ontologies, and methodologies that may make edu-cation unintelligible to itself,[7] a condition which, they might add, is a consummation devoutly to be wished.

Feminists and poststructuralists have worked together and sepa-rately during the last half of this century to facilitate structural failures in some of foundationalism's most heinous formations—racism, patri-archy, homophobia, ageism, and so forth—the ruins out of which they now work. Feminism as a Western social movement[8] has had a pro-found influence on the daily lives of women and men by challenging patriarchy at every turn. Feminist theory has worked to achieve legiti-macy in the academy with acknowledged epistemologies and method-ologies that reflect a broad range of "feminisms"[9] that do not necessarily agree with one another. Poststructuralism, though largely academic in nature, has also had an effect on everyday living, because its critiques, formed in response to the very material complications of living *in medias res*, circulate back through public discourse, which con-tinually reconstructs it. The title of this collection of essays refers to a certain relationship between feminism and poststructuralism, yet the book is neither about the marriage of feminism and poststructuralism nor about the pros and cons of such a union. Rather, it illustrates how the two theories/movements work similarly and differently to trouble foundational ontologies, methodologies, and epistemologies, in gen-eral, and education, in particular.

The uneasy tension that was evident in the initial juxtaposition of feminism and poststructuralism has abated somewhat since the refer-ents of these terms have proliferated to such an extent that a certain exhaustion with trying to fix their meanings has set in. Furthermore, it is evident from the recent increase in feminist work informed by post-structuralism that the relationship of the two bodies of thought and practice is not inimical, but rather invigorating and fruitful (for work specific to education, see Britzman, 1991; Davies, 1993; Elam & Wieg-man, 1995; Lather, 1991; Luke & Gore, 1992; Munro, 1998; Thorne, 1993; Walkerdine, 1990; Weiner, 1994). Still, we should not assume that feminism and poststructuralism have worked together to produce a felicitous synthesis that can solve the problems of living in the new mil-lennium. Rather, the authors of the essays in this book work out of Diane Elam's (1994) question about the relationship between feminism and poststructuralism, "How are they *beside* each other?" (p. 1). What is it that these two theories/movements share, not in terms of their convergence, but rather in their "divergence from (or dislocation of) politics and philosophy" (p. 1)? How do they work similarly to critique, interrupt, and reinscribe normative, hegemonic, and exclusionary ideologies and practices?

The essays in this collection provide some answers to these questions, answers that emerge from their authors' specific curiosities; that focus on their situated engagements in relationships, teaching, and research; and that employ diverse methodologies to investigate what Foucault (cited in Rajchman, 1985) describes as "something cracked, dully jarring, or disfunctioning in things I saw, in the institutions with which I dealt, in my relations with others" (p. 36).

Although the categories "feminist," "poststructural," "feminist poststructuralism," or "poststructural feminism" are insufficient for describing the complex ways the authors work with, within, and against these theories as well as their reasons (ethical and political) for doing so, they are the categories available to us at this time, and so we use them in our book title and in this introduction, just as the authors do in their essays. However, we prefer to think of the relationship we are working in and out of as feminist *and* poststructural, a relationship that gestures toward fluid and multiple dislocations and alliances.

We caution that this collection should not be read as a cohesive statement about poststructural feminism since we know that even its contributors disagree on many points. The range of topics they address is broad: narrative knowing; the use of autobiography and fiction in research; attention to women's gossip as well as to their bodies; the place of women's pleasure in the academy; the use of hypertext as a poststructural feminist epistemology; the use of figurations as epistemological and methodological tools; the usefulness of a rhizoanalysis of data; the "crisis" of multiculturalism; the problems of feminist and poststructural ethnography, including the meaning of the "field"; and the continuing problem of subjects denied subjectivity (black feminists, Latina mothers, women with HIV/AIDS, older women, teen mothers, women in the academy).

These scholars do not claim to have found solutions to the issues they engage, e.g., the "perfect counter-hegemonic story" (Villenas, 1998). Neither do they evidence the "paralysis" (Kemmis, 1995) so often attributed to poststructuralism, nor, in contrast, have they written "victory narratives" (Pillow, 1997). What is evident in this multiplicity is that poststructural feminism is indeed useful for women and for education. Instead of realizing Rosenau's (1992) fear that the social sciences might become "casualties of its [postmodernism's] excesses," (p. 3), their work moves toward a reconfigured social science, a "less comfortable social science"

(Lather, chapter 14 in this volume), one that tries to be "accountable to complexity."

As an entrée to the individual chapters in this collection, we provide in what follows more detailed discussions of working the ruins of (a) humanism, (b) education, and (c) methodology in order to describe the limits these scholars work within and against as they reconceptualize education and educational research.

Working the Ruins of Humanism

We begin this section with a disclaimer: Neither we nor the scholars whose work is represented in this volume intend to set up a binary opposition between poststructuralism and humanism that privileges poststructuralism. This would, in any case, be almost impossible to accomplish since each has proliferated along multiple trajectories, producing very different theoretical frameworks and material realities that cannot easily be grouped together, except, perhaps, to more easily dismiss them (Butler, 1992). However, we must point out that this sort of structural mistake is difficult to avoid since we are always speaking within the language of humanism, our mother tongue, a discourse that spawns structure after structure after structure—binaries, categories, hierarchies, and other grids of regularity that are not only linguistic but also very material.

Within the discourse of humanism, it makes sense to say and think only certain things, and poststructural feminists are interested in different discourses in which different statements and different material and political conditions might be possible. They work toward the not-yet-thought, what Derrida (1978/1966) calls the "as-yet unnamable which begins to proclaim itself" (p. 293). Such spaces, gaps, and interstices in humanism's structures are seductive; poststructural feminists have indeed shown that discourses are not closed systems and that shifts in historical thought and material conditions are possible. Still, they worry that such free spaces might be yet another fiction and are suspicious of the emancipatory impulses of humanism that presume we can "get it right" once and for all. We have never "gotten it right." This is not to say that revolution is not possible or desirable but that, often, one regime of truth simply replaces another.

The good news for postrevolutionaries is that more modest resistance and freedoms are offered to us on a daily basis and that accepting those invitations can indeed produce changes for the better. In fact, the authors of the essays in this book believe we are obliged to accept such invitations, to practice a "constant 'civil disobedience' within our constituted experience" (Rajchman, 1985, p. 6). Thus, in the face of overwhelming domination, we may be "freer than we feel" (Foucault, 1988, p. 10). The women who write here, privileged as they are, are well aware of such everyday practices of resistance.

With the preceding caveat in mind, we return to the topic at hand, humanism, a grand theory with a long and varied history that has described the truth of things for centuries. An amazingly supple philosophy, it has produced a diverse range of knowledge projects since man (a specific Western, Enlightened male) first began to believe that he, as well as God, could, through the right use of reason, produce truth and knowledge. As Foucault (1984) points out, humanism "is a theme or, rather, a set of themes that have reappeared on several occasions, over time, in European societies; those themes, always tied to value judgments, have obviously varied greatly in their content, as well as in the values they have preserved" (p. 44). Humanism has, in fact, been used by liberals, Nazis, feminists, Marxists, Protestants, Catholics, and others in the production of truth, knowledge, norms, and policies.

Jane Flax (1990) describes some of the themes, the foundations, of humanism as follows: that there is "a stable, coherent self"; that "language is in some sense transparent"; that "reason and its 'science'—philosophy—can provide an objective, reliable, and universal foundation of knowledge"; that "knowledge acquired from the right use of reason will be 'true'"; that "by grounding claims to authority in reason, the conflicts between truth, knowledge, and power can be overcome"; and that "freedom consists of obedience to laws that conform to the necessary results of the right use of reason" (pp. 41–42). If these are the themes that structure humanism, then Butler (1992) reminds us that the task of postfoundationalism is "to interrogate what the theoretical move that establishes foundations authorizes, and what precisely it excludes or forecloses" (p. 7).

To this end, postfoundational theoretical and political positions, including feminist, race, critical, queer, and postcolonial theories (theories that work against humanism's authorizations and its exclusions) take issue with these themes of humanism since they are clearly not in everyone's best interests. In fact, their effects have been devastating to many people on the wrong side of humanism's subject/object binaries—male/female, white/black, rich/poor, heterosexual/homosexual, healthy/ill, and so on. Those oppressed by humanism's structures have struggled to reclaim and rewrite untold histories, to subvert what counts as knowledge and truth, and to challenge those who claim the authority to speak for them (see, for example, Alcoff, 1991). Patricia Hill Collins (chapter 2 in this volume) states that "redefining marginality as a potential source of strength [has] fostered a powerful oppositional knowledge."

Yet this work at the margins is still within reach of the center, which, even though it cannot hold, forms and re-forms within relations of power, stretching to assimilate and contain whatever and whoever is too different, ergo, the "suppleness" of humanism (see Spanos, 1993, for a discussion of how this has worked in education). At some point, even oppositional theories, like liberal feminism, must face their own limits, and poststructuralism challenges them to consider how they participate in the failures of humanism—how their seemingly oppositional stances might be false triumphs.

Still, poststructural feminism and all the other "posts" (postfeminism, postmodernism, postfoundationalism, postcolonialism, postemancipatory and postrevolutionary discourses, and so on) do not offer a corrective to humanism. Rather, they offer opportunities for limit-work, work that operates at the boundaries of the possibilities of humanism.

Poststructuralism, then, does not assume that humanism is an error that must be replaced—i.e., humanism is evil because it has gotten us into this fix; poststructuralism is good since it will save us. It does not offer an alternative, successor regime of truth, it does not claim to have "gotten it right," nor does it believe that such an emancipatory outcome is possible or even desirable. Rather, it offers critiques and methods for examining the functions and effects of any structure or grid of regularity that we put into place, including those poststructuralism itself might create. Gayatri Spivak (1993) identifies several of these deconstructive analyses as follows: power/knowledge readings (Hekman, 1990; Marshall, 1997; Singer, 1993), archaeology (Scheurich, 1997), genealogy (Ferguson, 1991; Lenzo [McCoy], 1995; Pillow & McCoy, 1995), and rhizoanalysis (see Alvermann, chapter 5 in this volume).

Poststructural feminist educators use these analyses and the epistemologies that enable them to critique Cartesian, Hegelian, and positivist epistemologies that assume the historical progress of man toward absolute knowledge and freedom; that assume it is possible to measure, represent, predict, and control knowledge of the social world; that assume metaphysics can rise above the level of human activity; that assume a knowing, disinterested, rational subject who can uncover "objective" knowledge; that assume the scientific method is the path to true knowledge, and so on.

Significantly, poststructural feminism continues to trouble the subject of humanism—the rational, conscious, stable, unified, knowing individual whose morality allows atrocities beyond imagining but still claims inalienable "rights" that protect it from responsibility to the Other it destroys. The subject of poststructuralism is generally described as one constituted, not in advance of, but within discourse and cultural practice. Some critics believe that such a subject is also determined, but Butler

(1992) explains that the agency of this subject lies precisely in its ongoing constitution—the "subject is neither a ground nor a product, but the permanent possibility of a certain resignifying process" (p. 13). Indeed, poststructural feminists are troubled by the very category "woman" and work to keep that category unstable and undefined, open to the reconfiguration Butler describes. They agree with Derrida (1995), who says that this loosening of the category does not imply the "liquidation of the subject" but rather a "subject [that] can be reinterpreted, re-stored, re-inscribed" (p. 256).

There have been several complications with this revisioning of the subject with which feminists continue to struggle (e.g., Alcoff, 1997; Nicholson, 1990). In the 1980s, poststructuralism provided a necessary and useful critique of practices of essentialism within feminism (Fuss, 1989) by offering theories to work against feminism's tendency to generalize from the experiences of white, Western, middle-class women. These theories focused on the intersection of the identity categories: race, class, gender, sexual orientation, ethnicity, nationality, age, wellness, etc. (e.g., Crenshaw, 1995). However, even this acknowledgment of the complexity of women's subjectivities has not gone unchallenged, and women like Sara Suleri (1992) continue to ask, "how can feminist discourse represent the categories 'woman' and 'race' at the same time?" (p. 760).

To complicate matters further, other feminists have questioned the timing of the popularity of poststructural theory in Western academia, pointing out that they prefer not to be decentered and, therefore, silenced once again (see, for example, race theorists and Latina and Black feminists, Anzaldúa, 1987; Astin, 1992; Asante, 1998; Collins, 1990, 1998, chapter 2 in this volume). In this regard, Varadharajan (1995) refers to the "failure of poststructuralism to appeal to the dispossessed" (p. xiii). Nancy Hartsock (1990) summarizes this position as follows: "Why is it that just at the moment when so many of us who have been silenced begin to demand the right to name ourselves, to act as subjects rather than objects of history, that just then the concept of subjecthood becomes problematic?" (p. 163). Finally, along with these two critiques comes a third from Marxist feminists who take issue with what Teresa Ebert (1996) calls "ludic feminism"—a form of poststructural feminism that prioritizes discourse over material political transformation.

Many feminists believe poststructural feminism is more concerned with language and discourse than with working to improve the everyday oppressions women suffer. The conversation around the poststructural subject in feminism is complex, and no resolution is in sight or, according to poststructural feminists, even desirable. After all, keeping the subject in play is their desire. While some fear the dissolution of the subject and consequent political paralysis, others, to the contrary, believe that a subject-in-process is in the best interests of women. Their argument is that if "woman" is defined once and for all, then there is no hope of a reconfiguration that might offer different, strategic possibilities for ethical, political, and relational work. What kind of women and what kinds of feminism might we fail to produce if we define "woman" and "feminism" once and for all? At any rate, the impulse to regulate and normalize these categories has not been successful. There are many feminisms, and one of the strengths of this proliferating category is that it continues to reinvent itself strategically, shifting and mutating given existing political agendas, power relations, and identity strategies.

Working the Ruins of Education

The category "education," like the categories "woman" and "feminism," has certainly been troubled by the feminist educators writing for this collection. Their curiosities—their pedagogical and research interests—have not been contained within the normalized and regulated categories "teaching" or "educational research," nor has the site of their research been confined to the classroom or school. Unlike some who might worry about this loosening of "education," we are happy to follow their "lines of flight" (Deleuze & Parnet, 1987/1980) and are, in fact, reminded of Shulamit Reinharz's (1992) dilemma when trying to define feminist research methods for her wonderful book, *Feminist Research Methods in Social Research*. She writes, "My solution to the practical problem of a working definition is to use people's self-definition. . . . A person did not have to identify her research methods as 'feminist research methods,' but rather had to identify herself as a feminist doing research" (pp. 6–7).

In the spirit of feminism and, consistent with poststructuralism's wariness about the disciplinary impulse of categorization, we support Reinharz's solution of self-definition. We maintain that the poststructural feminist educators in this volume do not have to prove that their work is "educational research." Rather it is up to us, their readers, to rethink that category as we carefully consider the provocative work they have accomplished. At any rate, education has always been a loose category, one whose content we educators, in our attempts to prove that education is a legitimate discipline, struggle to describe to outsiders. Rather than trying to locate and define education, however, we might ask different questions of it, questions that Bové (1990) explains poststructuralists ask of any discourse or cultural practice: "How does it [education] function? Where is it to be found? How does it get produced and regulated? What are its social effects? How does it exist?" (p. 54).

Asking these questions has led the scholars writing for this collection to the following issues identified by Peters (1997) as problems poststructural educators might consider:

> "more complex notions of student and teacher subjectivities [Alvermann, Chaudhry, McWilliam, McCoy, Pillow, Richardson, Villenas]; the challenge to simpleminded accounts of autonomy and agency [Britzman, Collins, Lather, Pillow, Richardson, Villenas]; the reassessment of and consequent richer notions of "reading" and "writing" [Alvermann, Britzman, Chaudhry, Davies, Leach, Morgan, Richardson, St.Pierre]; greater attention paid to the discursive power of the "languages of education" in the constitution of education in the broadest sense [Britzman, Lather, Leach, McWilliam, St.Pierre]; the emphasis on notions and principles of becoming and process over questions of being and ontology [Collins, Lather, St.Pierre]; the critique of binary modes of thinking per se [Lather, McCoy, Morgan, Pillow, St.Pierre]; the rehabilitation of desire as a set of cultural and educational forces [Davies, McWilliam, Pillow]; and the investigation and acknowledgment of the notion of difference [Chaudhry, Collins, McCoy, Villenas]." (pp. 10–11)

Responding to the call of concerns such as these enlarges education, multiplies it across disciplinary boundaries, encourages it to examine its attachments and limits, and reinvigorates it to such an extent that it might, indeed, become unrecognizable. We believe that it must if it intends to address the issues that Peters summarizes and that these educators explore.

Working the Ruins of Methodology

As stated earlier, certain feminists have found poststructural critiques useful because humanism's ontology and epistemology have failed women on many occasions. Reinventing itself after the "postmodern turn" (Hassan, 1987), feminism, as well as other oppositional discourses and practices, has theorized and put to work different ontologies to live and to describe living in a postmodern world and different epistemologies to make sense of that world (e.g., Black feminist thought—Collins, 1990; Dillard, 1997; hooks, 1994; critical race theory—Crenshaw et al., 1995; Parker, Deyhle, Villenas, & Nebeker, 1988; Parker, Deyhle, & Villenas, 1999; critical race feminism—Wing, 1997; queer studies—Britzman, 1995; Tanaka & Cruz, 1998; Tierney, in press; Sears, 1992; pissed criticism—Pillow, 1996; Quinby, 1994; Chicana epistemology—Delgado Bernal, 1998; Delgado-Gaitan, 1993; Gonzáles, 1998; Villenas, 1996). It follows, then, that once those philosophical categories have shifted, methodology will shift as well. If humanism's inscription of reality, knowledge, truth, rationality, and the subject are dangerous fictions, then its "science" also becomes problematic. If this is the case, what might a different science look like? What kind of science can address questions such as the following: "As researchers, what can we be certain about; if we're researching things that defy categorization, how do we constitute data; how do we avoid getting frozen by uncertainty; if we're not doing realist, modernist research, what systems do we employ?" (McWilliam, Lather, & Morgan, 1997, p. 2).

Other questions also become obvious. Do we wish to continue to use the categories of research that humanism's science has defined? The research process is so complex that much of what happens is unintelligible either because the existing categories no longer work or because we simply have no category—no language—with which to describe what is happening either theoretically or in the "field" (a troublesome category, see St.Pierre, chapter 13 in this volume). For example, what counts as data? Can the category "data" be enlarged to include "sensual data," "dream data," and "response data"? (St.Pierre, 1997a). If so, what exactly are the "methods" that produce such data? And if, as Richardson (1994) suggests, "writing" is a method of inquiry, what kind of data does it produce—only words on a page? If we believe writing is a research method, are we then obliged to analyze the data it produces—everything we write during the course of a project? If we do that, can we ever complete a project? And how do we account for the thinking that writing produces?

The questions proliferate once the structure, the foundations of methodology, fails. When does research begin and end if one gives up a linear concept of time? Does it make sense to continue to describe and prescribe a step-by-step, linear research process? If time shifts in poststructural research, then place and space must shift as well. Where, when is research? If we resist the impulse to normalize and regulate research (now we have it right!), will it be acceptable for each researcher to define her own categories, her own process—to define "research" and "science?" Can research be so situated (hasn't it always been?) and, if so, how will we know it's valid? How will we even know whether it's "research?"

Do concepts like "triangulation" and "audit trail" and the "constant comparison method" of data analysis make sense in poststructural research? As Scheurich (1997) explains, "Even radical researchers, who have questioned the deep rules and assumptions in education still audiotape, systematically code, and do pattern or thematic analysis of data. These latter practices are the practices of reason and they are assumed to accord with a researcher-trained mind" (pp. 171–72). Several recent volumes in education propose other ways of thinking about our research (Gitlin, 1994; McLaren & Giarelli, 1995; Stronach & MacLure, 1997), suggesting different "rational" practices of data analysis and "training" for researchers.

Interestingly, these provocative questions are posed within the framework of humanism. Wouldn't their answers also be bound within its limits? Is it possible to think outside those structures of intelligibility? Is there a "language for the thought of the limit" (Foucault, 1977, p. 40), a language of the ruins, that is outside the serenity of the metaphysical subject, the comforting closure of dialectics, and the easy logic of foundational rationality? How does praxis work in a postmodern world as we struggle in the vortex of being and thinking and doing? The contributors to this volume, lost in the ruins of the "old" science, gesture toward this kind of transgressive work that is not only different from what has come before but also different from itself. Without the "lure of a transcendental guarantee, the promise of philosophy to 'correct existence'" (Butler, 1995, p. 131), or the consolation of the universal, these poststructural feminist educators work on, strategically assembling and then reassembling feminism, education, and science.

Introducing the Chapters

Working the Ruins: Feminist Poststructural Theory and Methods in Education is divided into three parts: "Interruptions," "Disciplines and Pleasures," and "Figurations." Part I, "Interruptions," includes six chapters that interrupt and challenge traditional research practices as they work the ruins of ethnography. By studying both the doing and the effects of such work, we can see how poststructural feminism troubles and opens up traditional ways of knowing (Collins); of doing ethnography, both the fieldwork and the text (Britzman); of analyzing and representing our research (Alvermann, Morgan); and of thinking about our relationships with our subjects and ourselves (Chaudhry, Villenas).

In chapter 1, "'The Question of Belief': Writing Poststructural Ethnography," Deborah P. Britzman explores the question of whether poststructural ethnography in education is possible. Her questions are intriguing. For example, she asks whether there is a knowledge that ethnography cannot tolerate knowing, and can there, then, be an educational ethnography that exceeds the constraints of humanism? Britzman troubles and rethinks the category of "the real," asking what might be possible if we render ethnography unintelligible. How would we perform our ethnographies, and what would our "reports" look like under such questioning?

Conversely, in chapter 2, "What's Going On? Black Feminist Thought and the Politics of Postmodernism," Patricia Hill Collins is troubled by the goal of poststructural feminists to pursue the possibilities of unintelligibility. She asks whom and what such interests serve. While not dismissing postmodernism, Collins focuses on the politics of postmodernism from the theoretical and material position of Black feminist thought, which is concerned with women whose work and lives continue to require legitimization because of their marginalization. Collins troubles and interrupts the "rubrics of deconstruction" that she believes has become a gatekeeper in the academy and raises important questions about whom postmodern theories and methods serve, benefit, privilege.

Sofia Villenas continues this line of critique in chapter 3, "This Ethnography Called My Back: Writings of the Exotic Gaze, 'Othering' Latina, and Recuperating Xicanisma," by questioning the role of the "native" woman anthropologist and analyzing her own complicit relationship with the traditional "good" anthropological tale. Villenas explains that women of color in the academy find that being "officially" sanctioned to do critical ethnography is a bittersweet triumph—how, where, and when can the colonized anthropologist go home after being the subject rather than the object of anthropology? Continuing her earlier work (Villenas, 1996) that describes her embeddedness in the colonizer/colonized opposition in her study with Latina mothers, she describes both the limits of anthropological traditions and the effects of the "posts" on those traditions in her own work.

Similarly, in chapter 4, "Researching 'My People,' Researching Myself: Fragments of a Reflexive Tale," Lubna Nazir Chaudhry foregrounds the limits of how we think about doing ethnography, data analysis, and written representation. Chaudhry investigates her positionality as a Pakistani Muslim researcher affiliated with a U.S. institution conducting ethnographic research with Pakistani Muslim immigrants in California. Interrupting the linear narrative of the ethnographic tale, Chaudhry's presentation of three vignettes reconstructed from field notes and a reflexive journal illustrates the tensions and contradictions that trouble both what counts as data and, like Villenas, the ethics of postcolonial research.

Donna E. Alvermann's work in chapter 5, "Researching Libraries, Literacies, and Lives: A Rhizoanalysis" focuses on poststructural practices of data analysis. Like Britzman and Villenas, Alvermann returns to previous studies of adolescents' conversations about books to deconstruct her own work, and, in this case, to use rhizoanalysis, a poststructural analytic theorized by Deleuze and Guattari (1988/1980), and "implicated reading," a feminist reading analytic theorized by Lynn Pearce (1997), to rethink data she had coded, analyzed, and storied according to traditional qualitative research practices. Rhizoanalysis allowed her to map disparate phenomena—the data from her study, a mother's interview with her son about his reading practices, a popabilly hip-hop recording, a *Newsweek* article featuring TV's comedy hit *South Park,* and a critique of an advertisement for cyberculture software. This poststructural practice of data analysis allows her to consider how "texts function outside themselves" and reveals discontinuities "unmarked" in her original analysis.

Chapter 6, Wendy Morgan's essay, "Electronic Tools for Dismantling the Master's House: Poststructuralist Feminist Research and Hypertext Poetics," describes Morgan's project of using hypertext to loosen up the text of Patti Lather's (1997) provocative representation of her study, with Chris Smithies, of women with HIV/AIDS, *Troubling the Angels: Women Living with HIV/AIDS.* Making different connections across Lather's text and adding new data, Morgan has produced a new text, "Monstrous Angels," that demonstrates the unruliness, fragmentation, mutations, and unfinished nature of hypertext representations. Morgan's essay illustrates how, even though hypertext is not, in itself, liberatory, it can serve the purposes of poststructural feminists who seek a different agency and a different field of operations. Morgan's work sets an agenda for a poetics of a poststructuralist feminist research hypertextuality for subsequent elaboration and is especially important, given the potential of technology to change and "rediscipline" our practices.

The chapters in Part II, "Disciplines and Pleasures," explore how women's bodies, both materially and figuratively, are sites of discipline and pleasure. They explore how women are intelligible to themselves and to others; how we live, work, love, and laugh within structures that we cannot and do not necessarily want to escape—home, schools, academia, and nation—and within the identity categories that inscribe us—gender, race, class, age, sexuality, and so forth. In addition to examining how women are disciplined by others as well as themselves, these scholars examine resistance and further inscription.

In chapter 7, "Skirting a Pleated Text: De-Disciplining an Academic Life," Laurel Richardson describes her book, *Fields of Play: Constructing an Academic Life* (1997), that surveys her own academic history by re-presenting several of her academic papers framed by "writing stories" that situate that academic work within her personal life. In both the book and this essay, Richardson continues to explore "writing as a method of inquiry," illustrating how she has used writing throughout her rich career to construct and deconstruct her self and to resist the disciplinary, patriarchal nature of her discipline, sociology, and the academy itself.

Erica McWilliam in chapter 8, "Laughing within Reason: On Pleasure, Women, and Academic Performance," continues to explore the situation of academic feminists by surveying (using Foucault, Bakhtin, Mary Russo, and Camille Paglia) the social and historical construction of the pleasure that is available to them in this site, a pleasure that must be "within reason." She argues that pleasure and desire are the products of training, phenomena shaped and disciplined by patterns of language that become intelligible in particular times and places, and suggests that we learn to be pleasured by certain pedagogical practices and not others. She asks us to consider the value of irony, a more private pleasure, since it unsettles what it means for women to behave properly in the academy and, at the same time, acknowledges feminists' complicity in academic disciplinary practices.

With Bronwyn Davies's contribution in chapter 9, "Eclipsing the Constitutive Power of Discourse: The Writing of Janette Turner Hospital," we again examine how different kinds of writing, in this case, fiction writing, produce different knowledge. Davies has both studied the work of and interviewed Janette Turner Hospital, an Australian novelist, who troubles the modernist human/inhuman, entity/environment, body/landscape binaries that have disciplined us to live in the world in certain ways and not others. Hospital's writing fuses body and landscape in ways that foreground the relations among discourse, subjection, and desire and allows the writing/reading subject to eclipse her own enabling conditions—the ways she has been disciplined and subjected—and to establish volatile new linkages that refuse oppressive and controlling forces.

The last essay in Part II, Wanda S. Pillow's "Exposed Methodology: The Body as a Deconstructive Practice," continues the focus on the body of women as a site of disciplinary power and resistance. Pillow recognizes that the body may be a troublesome site for women to work from, a site that can be both silenced and proliferated as well as celebrated and marginalized. However, she moves beyond these conceptions and explores what is exposed when we pay attention to the body in our research. Pillow cites her own embodied collusion with the teen mothers she was "researching." She discusses how this embodiment was a point of departure and a site of return influencing how and what she paid attention to in her research and provides in an embodied tale the literal story of the embodied experiences of teen mothers in public schools.

Part III, "Figurations," includes four essays in which the authors employ figurations (gossip, white noise, the nomad, and angels) to help them think against the prescribed narratives of humanist science. Explaining that figurations are not graceful metaphors that provide coherency and unity to contradiction and disjunction, but rather are cartographic weapons, "splitting analytics" (McCoy, 1997), that propel them into the turbulence masked by coherence, these feminists use figurations as practices of failure, tools of "rigorous confusion that jettison clarity in favor of the unintelligible" (St.Pierre, 1997b, p. 281) in an effort to move toward different realities.

Mary Leach, in chapter 11, "Feminist Figurations: Gossip as a Counterdiscourse," suggests that "serious gossip" is a productive practice of meaning-making, one that disrupts the valorized concept of dialogue, which is often inadequate when difference collides in discourse. Leach considers how gossip, as a counterdiscourse, offers a subject-in-process points of exit from the normative and regulating logocentric discourses that ground scientific knowledge, since it circulates on the margins of institutional discourses. Difficult to control, rhizomatic, fluid, and always incomplete, gossip redistributes, disperses, and frees thought from a dialectic that would fix difference in dialogue.

In chapter 12, "White Noise—the Sound of Epidemic: Reading/Writing a Climate of Intelligibility around the 'Crisis' of Difference," Kate McCoy examines how cultural difference has been constructed as a crisis of epidemic proportions. In her study of preservice teachers' analyses of the discourse of multiculturalism as it is represented both in the popular media and in education, she uses the figuration "white noise" as a conceptual tool to examine the ways preservice teachers' media analyses make use of available discourses to construct a network of intelligibility around cultural difference. Data gathered from assignments in a five-week course are represented in the form of poems constructed from student journals and papers. McCoy challenges educators to consider what is opened up when critical pedagogy shifts its emphasis from examinations of reproduction and student resistance to explorations of intelligibility.

Elizabeth A. St.Pierre uses Deleuze and Guattari's (1987/1980) figuration of the "nomad" in chapter 13, "Nomadic Inquiry in the Smooth Spaces of the Field: A Preface." Nomads deterritorialize space and refuse to settle into grids or categories and thus attempt to escape either side of humanist binaries. In her study of the older, white southern women of her hometown, she positions herself as a nomadic thinker and, by exploring this new mental space, learns that the nature of other spaces changes accordingly and new questions emerge. What and where is the space of the field in which the ethnographic method is employed in post-structural inquiry? Similarly, what does the space of the text, a different field, become for nomadic ethnographers who require alternative writing spaces in order to deterritorialize the linearity and coherence of the ethnographic text? Traditional notions of both the space of the field and the space of the text no longer serve nomadic ethnographers who sidle out of definitions that no longer obtain. She learns that the categories fail when figurations are employed but that their ruins become fruitful sites for thinking our way out of the deadlock of metaphysics.

Patti Lather concludes this collection in chapter 14, "Drawing the Line at Angels: Working the Ruins of Feminist Ethnography," by calling on the figuration "angels" to respond to the failure of feminist ethnography. Early on in a five-year study in which she and her co-researcher, Chris Smithies, worked with 25 women living with HIV/AIDS, Lather came upon the figuration, "angels," which helped her rethink the traditional limits of both humanist theory and traditional research methodology. In this essay, she describes an angel economy she has employed in both interpretive and textual strategies in her research as she works toward a "less comfortable social science" that troubles the desires of an innocent feminist ethnography to give voice to the voiceless. Terrible, trickster, excessive, and mourning angels refuse the comfort and consolation of habituated knowing in order to think the ruins of our ways of making sense of and writing about the devastation of AIDS.

Conclusion

We hope these examples of poststructural feminist theory and methods in education illustrate the diversity of the work that can be done amid the failure of humanism, feminism, education, and methodology. We find this work affirmative, heartening, and exciting and believe it exemplifies the rigorous scholarship that is possible once we attempt to put aside the grounding rules of humanism that burden educational inquiry and practice. As Foucault (1988/1982) reminds us, "there are more secrets, more possible freedoms, and more inventions in our future than we can imagine in humanism" (p. 15). Certainly, the researchers in this text are generous with their unfoldings, their challenges, their pleasures, their contingent methodologies, and their revitalization of education; and perhaps we should, once more following Reinharz (1992), go straight to their essays to see what is possible, theoretically and methodologically, in poststructural feminist research in education.

Notes

1. Our thanks to Kate McCoy for letting us use this title, which comes from her 1996 AERA presentation, "Inquiry Among the Ruins: (Un)Common Practices," and also for her careful reading of this introduction.

2. We have chosen to use the term *poststructuralism* to describe a theoretical shift under postmodernism that informs the work and critique of the essays in this book. The terms poststructuralism and postmodernism are commonly conflated and, while we acknowledge with Michael Peters (1996) that the use of either term "homogenizes the differences among poststructural thinkers" (p. 19), we employ the term *poststructural* to refer to the academic theorizing and cri-

tiques of discourse, knowledge, truth, reality, rationality, and the subject of the last half of the twentieth century, particularly those enabled by French philosophers such as Jean Baudrillard (1988), Gilles Deleuze (1994/1968), Gilles Deleuze and Felix Guattari (1983/1972, 1987/1980), Jacques Derrida (1974/1967, 1978/1966), Michel Foucault (1972/1969, 1978/1976, 1979/1975, 1980), and Jean-François Lyotard (1984/1979). The influence of Friedrich Nietzsche's (1992) work is, of course, evident in all of these scholars' work. We have been especially influenced by the work of feminists, whom we think of as "poststructural" but who might refuse that category, such as Rosi Braiddotti (1991, 1994), Judith Butler (1990, 1992, 1993), Jane Flax (1990), Elizabeth Grosz (1994, 1995), and Gayatri Chakravorty Spivak (1974, 1987, 1990, 1993). We believe, with Peters (1996), that postmodernism applies to a broader "set of cultural changes" (p. 19) brought about by critiques of colonialism, racism, patriarchy, homophobia, and ageism reflected in popular as well as "high" culture.

3. "Post" should not be associated with "past." The "post" in postcolonialism does not mean that colonialism no longer exists but rather that there is now a "continuous engagement with the effects of colonial occupation" (Thomas, 1993, p. 8). Ilter (1994) warns that some critics of postmodernism situate its "post" as "modernism's other" in order to domesticate it. In chapter 6 of this volume, Wendy Morgan describes postfeminism as "convergences between feminism and poststructuralism." See Ann Brooks (1997) for a discussion of postfeminism and keep in mind the "post"card Wanda Pillow displays prominently in her office that sums up her view of postfeminism (where "post" is used in the "after" sense): "I'll be a post-feminist in post-patriarchy."

4. We are grateful to Patti Lather for allowing us to use her phrase, "working the ruins," which appears in the subtitle of her chapter in this collection as the title of this book. Both Walter Benjamin (1977/1963) and Judith Butler (1992), in addition to Lather, write about the possibilities of working out of the failure of received knowledge.

5. Indeed, Linda Alcoff (1997) believes that the "first wave of political critiques of postmodernism is coming to a deserved close" (p. 6).

6. We use the term *education* broadly as is evidenced by the inclusion of the work of Patricia Hill Collins (1990, 1998) and Laurel Richardson (1990, 1993, with Verda Taylor, 1994, 1997). Although both are categorized in the academic discipline of sociology, they are surely educators and have had a profound influence on the work of the other "educators" in this book.

7. In an interactive symposium, "But Is It Research?," at the 1994 American Educational Research Association meeting in New Orleans, Louisiana, Deborah Britzman concluded her comments with the hope that educational research would become increasingly unintelligible to itself. Thanks to Patti Lather for sharing this reference with us.

8. Taking Linda Nicholson's (1999) caution that the accepted story of the progressive history of feminism is a "simple story" which like all simple stories

"leaves out a great deal" (p. 2), we offer this tracing of feminism as a map, which no doubt will continue to be challenged, complicated, and redrawn. The first wave of the women's movement began in the mid-1800s. Some find it convenient to say it began in 1848 with the Seneca Falls Women's Rights Convention. This wave is often said to have concluded about 1920, when the Suffrage Bill was passed. The second wave of the women's movement began in the 1960s, and its key writings are collected in a volume edited by Linda Nicholson (1997), *The Second Wave: A Reader in Feminist Theory*. A special issue of *Hypatia*, *12*(3), summer 1997, is devoted to third-wave feminism. In addition, two anthologies of work by young third-wave feminists that are frequently cited are *Listen Up: Voices from the Next Feminist Generation* (1995), edited by Barbara Findlen, and *To Be Real: Telling the Truth and Changing the Face of Feminism* (1995), edited by Rebecca Walker.

9. See Rosemary's Tong's (1998) book, *Feminist Thought: A More Comprehensive Introduction* for a discussion of some of the feminisms.

References

Alcoff, L. (1991). The problem of speaking for others. *Cultural Critique, 20*(Winter), 5–32.

Alcoff, L. (1997). The politics of postmodern feminism, revisited. *Cultural Critique, 36*, 5–27.

Anzaldúa, G. (1987). *Borderlands: The new mestiza=La frontera*. San Francisco: Aunt Lute Books.

Asante, M. K. (1998). *The Afrocentric idea*. Philadelphia: Temple University Press.

Astin, R. (1989). Left at the post: One take on blacks and postmodernism. *Law and Society, 26*, 751–54.

Baudrillard, J. (1988). *Jean Baudrillard: Selected writings* (M. Poster, Ed.). Stanford, CA: Stanford University Press.

Benjamin, W. (1977). *The origin of German tragic drama* (J. Osborne, Trans.). New York: Verso. (Original work published 1963)

Bové, P. (1990). Discourse. In F. Lentricchia & T. McLaughlin (Eds.), *Critical terms for literary study* (pp. 50–65). Chicago: University of Chicago Press.

Braidotti, R. (1991). *Patterns of dissonance: A study of women in contemporary philosophy*. New York: Routledge.

Braidotti, R. (1994). *Nomadic subjects: Embodiment and sexual difference in contemporary feminist theory*. New York: Columbia University Press.

Britzman, D. (1991). *Practice makes practice: A critical study of learning to teach*. Albany: State University of New York Press.

Britzman, D. (1995). Is there a queer pedagogy? Or, Stop reading straight. *Educational Theory, 45*(2), 151–65.

Brooks, A. (1997). *Postfeminisms: Feminism, cultural theory and cultural forms.* London: Routledge.

Butler, J. (1990). *Gender trouble: Feminism and the subversion of identity.* New York: Routledge.

Butler, J. (1992). Contingent foundations: Feminism and the question of "postmodernism." In J. Butler & J. W. Scott (Eds.), *Feminists theorize the political* (pp. 3–21). New York: Routledge.

Butler, J. (1993). *Bodies that matter: On the discursive limits of "sex."* New York: Routledge.

Butler, J. (1995). For a careful reading. In S. Benhabib, J. Butler, D. Cornell, & N. Fraser (Eds.), *Feminist contentions: A philosophical exchange* (pp. 127–43). New York: Routledge. (Essay dated 1994)

Collins, P. H. (1990). *Black feminist thought: Knowledge, consciousness, and the politics of empowerment.* New York: Routledge.

Collins, P. H. (1998). *Fighting words: Black women and the search for justice.* Minneapolis: University of Minnesota Press.

Crenshaw, K. (1995). Mapping the margins: Intersectionality, identity politics, and violence against women of color. In K. Crenshaw, N. Gotanda, G. Peller, & K. Thomas (Eds.), *Critical race theory: The key writings that formed the movement* (pp. 357–83). New York: New Press.

Crenshaw, K., Gotanda, N., Peller, G., & Thomas, K. (Eds.) (1995). *Critical race theory: The key writings that formed the movement.* New York: New Press.

Davies, B. (1993). *Shards of glass: Children reading and writing beyond gendered identities.* Cresskill, NJ: Hampton Press, Inc.

Deleuze, G. (1994). *Difference and repetition* (P. Patton, Trans.). New York: Columbia University Press. (Original work published 1968)

Deleuze, G., & Guattari, F. (1983). *Anti-Oedipus: Capitalism and schizophrenia.* (R. Hurley, M. Seem, & H. R. Lane, Trans.). Minneapolis: University of Minnesota Press. (Original work published 1972)

Deleuze, G., & Guattari, F. (1987). *A thousand plateaus: Capitalism and schizophrenia* (B. Massumi, Trans.). Minneapolis: University of Minnesota Press. (Original work published 1980)

Deleuze, G., & Parnet, C. (1987). Many politics. In *Dialogues* (H. Tomlinson & B. Habberjam, Trans.). New York: Columbia University Press. (Original work published 1977)

Delgado Bernal, D. (1998). Using a Chicana feminist epistemology in educational research. *Harvard Educational Review, 68*(4), 555–79.

Delgado-Gaitan, C. (1993). Researching change and changing the researcher. *Harvard Educational Review, 63,* 389–411.

Derrida, J. (1974). *Of grammatology* (G. C. Spivak, Trans.). Baltimore: Johns Hopkins University Press. (Original work published 1967)

Derrida, J. (1978). Structure, sign and play in the discourse of the human sciences. In *Writing and difference* (A. Bass, Trans.) (pp. 278–93). Chicago: University of Chicago Press. (Lecture delivered 1966)

Derrida, J. (1995). "Eating well," or the Calculation of the subject. In E. Weber (Ed.), *Points . . . Interviews, 1974–1994* (P. Kamuf, Trans.) (pp. 255–87). Stanford, CA: Stanford University Press.

Dillard, C. (1997, April). The substance of things hoped for, the evidence of things not seen: Towards an endarkened feminist ideology in research. Paper presented at the annual meeting of the American Educational Research Association, Chicago, IL.

Ebert, T. (1996). *Ludic feminism and after.* Ann Arbor: University of Michigan Press.

Elam, D. (1994). *Feminism and deconstruction: Ms. en abyme.* London: Routledge.

Elam, D., & Wiegman, R. (Eds.). (1995). *Feminism beside itself.* New York: Routledge.

Ferguson, K. E. (1991). Interpretation and genealogy in feminism. *Signs: Journal of Women in Culture and Society, 16*(21), 322–39.

Findlen, B. (Ed.). (1995). *Listen up: Voices from the next feminist generation.* Seattle, WA: Seal Press.

Flax, J. (1990). Postmodernism and gender relations in feminist theory. In L. J. Nicholson (Ed.), *Feminism/postmodernism* (pp. 39–62). New York: Routledge.

Foucault, M. (1972). *The archaeology of knowledge and the discourse on language* (A. M. Sheridan Smith, Trans.). New York: Pantheon Books. (Original work published 1969)

Foucault, M. (1977). Preface to transgression. In D. F. Bouchard (Ed.), *Language, counter-memory, practice* (D. F. Bouchard & S. Simon, Trans.) (pp. 29–52). Ithaca, NY: Cornell University Press.

Foucault, M. (1978). *The history of sexuality, Volume 1: An introduction* (R. Hurley, Trans.). New York: Vintage Books. (Original work published 1976)

Foucault, M. (1979). *Discipline and punish: The birth of the prison* (A. Sheridan, Trans.). New York: Vintage Books. (Original work published 1975)

Foucault, M. (1980). *Power/knowledge: Selected interviews and other writings, 1972–1977* (C. Gordon, Ed.; C. Gordon, L. Marshall, J. Mepham, & K. Soper, Trans.). New York: Pantheon Books.

Foucault, M. (1984). What is enlightenment? (C. Porter, Trans.). In P. Rabinow (Ed.), *The Foucault reader* (pp. 32–50). New York: Pantheon Books.

Foucault, M. (1988). Technologies of the self. In L. H. Martin, H. Gutman, & P. H. Hutton (Eds.), *Technologies of the self: A seminar with Michel Foucault* (pp. 16–49). Amherst: University of Massachusetts Press. (Text is a partial record of a 1982 seminar)

Fuss, D. (1989). *Essentially speaking: Feminism, nature and difference.* New York: Routledge.

Gitlin, A. (Ed.). (1994). *Power and method: Political activism and educational research.* New York: Routledge.

González, F. E. (1998). Formations of Mexicananess: Trenzas de identidades multiples/growing up Mexicana: Braids of multiple identities. *International Journal of Qualitative Studies in Education, 11*(1), 81–102.

Grosz, E. (1994). *Volatile bodies: Toward a corporeal feminism*. Bloomington: Indiana University Press.

Grosz, E. (1995). *Space, time, perversion*. New York: Routledge.

Hartsock, N. (1990). Foucault on power: A theory for women? In L. J. Nicholson (Ed.), *Feminism/postmodernism* (pp. 157–75). New York: Routledge.

Hassan, I. (1987). *The postmodern turn: Essays in postmodern theory and culture*. Columbus: Ohio State University Press.

Hekman, S. (1990). *Gender and knowledge: Elements of a postmodern feminism*. Boston: Northeastern University Press.

hooks, b. (1994). *Teaching to transgress: Education as the practice of freedom*. New York: Routledge.

Ilter, T. (1994). The unassimilable Otherness of the "post" of postmodernism and the radicality of radical sociology. *Critical Sociology, 20*(2), 51–80.

Kemmis, S. (1995). Emancipatory aspirations in a postmodern era. *Journal of Curriculum Studies, 3*(2), 133–68.

Lather, P. (1991). *Getting smart: Feminist research and pedagogy with/in the postmodern*. New York: Routledge.

Lather, P., & Smithies, C. (1997). *Troubling the angels: Women living with HIV/AIDS*. Boulder, CO: Westview Press.

Lenzo (McCoy), K. (1995). Looking awry: A genealogical study of pre-service teacher encounters with popular media and multicultural education. Unpublished doctoral dissertation, Ohio State University, Columbus.

Luke, C., & Gore, J. (Eds.). (1992). *Feminisms and critical pedagogy*. New York: Routledge.

Lyotard, J.-F. (1984). *The postmodern condition: A report on knowledge* (G. Bennington & B. Massumi, Trans.). Minneapolis: University of Minnesota Press. (Original work published 1979)

Marshall, C. (Ed.). (1997). *Feminist critical policy analysis I: A primary and secondary schooling perspective*. London: Falmer Press.

McCoy, K. (1996, April). Inquiry among the ruins: (Un)Common practices. Paper presented at the annual meeting of the American Educational Research Association, New York City.

McCoy, K. (1997). Killing the father/becoming uncomfortable with the mother tongue: Rethinking the performative contradiction. *Educational Theory, 47*(4), pp. 489–500.

McLaren, P. L., & Giarelli, J. M. (Eds.). (1995). *Critical theory and educational research*. Albany: State University of New York Press.

McWilliam, E., Lather, P., & Morgan, W., with McCoy, K., Pillow, W., & St.Pierre, E. A. (1997). *Head work, field work, text work: A textshop in new feminist research* (video and study guide). Queensland, Australia: Queensland University of Technology.

Munro, P. (1998). *Subject to fiction: Women teachers' life history narratives and the cultural politics of resistance.* Buckingham, UK: Open University Press.

Nicholson, L. J. (Ed.). (1990). *Feminism/postmodernism.* New York: Routledge.

Nicholson, L. J. (Ed.). (1997). *The second wave: A reader in feminist theory.* New York: Routledge.

Nicholson, L. J. (1999). *The play of reason: From the modern to the postmodern.* Ithaca, NY: Cornell University Press.

Nietzsche, F. (1992). *Basic writings of Nietzsche* (W. Kaufmann, Ed. & Trans.). New York: Modern Library.

Parker, L., Deyhle, D., & Villenas, S. (Eds.). (1999). *Race is . . . race isn't: Critical race theory and qualitative studies in education.* Boulder, CO: Westview Press.

Parker, L., Deyhle, D., Villenas, S., & Nebeker, K. C. (Eds). (1998). Critical race theory and qualitative studies in education. *International Journal of Qualitative Studies in Education, 11*(1). (Special issue on critical race theory)

Pearce, L. (1997). *Feminism and the politics of reading.* London: Arnold.

Peters, M. (1996). *Poststructuralism, politics and education.* Westport, CT: Bergin & Garvey.

Peters, M. (1997). Nietzsche, poststructuralism and education: After the subject. *Educational Philosophy and Theory, 29*(1), 1–19.

Pillow, W. S. (1996). Practices within and against: Ironic interventions and pissed criticism in policy theory. Paper presented at the annual meeting of the American Educational Studies Association, Montreal, Canada.

Pillow, W. S. (1997). Decentering silences/troubling irony: A feminist postmodern approach to policy analysis. In C. Marshall (Ed.), *Feminist critical policy analysis I: A primary and secondary schooling perspective* (pp. 134–52). London: Falmer Press.

Pillow, W. S., & Lenzo, K. (1995). *Genealogical inquiry.* The 1995 Volume, Qualitative Research. Athens: University of Georgia.

Quinby, L. (1994). *Anti-apocalypse: Exercises in genealogical criticism.* Minneapolis: University of Minnesota Press.

Rajchman, J. (1985). *Michel Foucault: The freedom of philosophy.* New York: Columbia University Press.

Reinharz, S. (1992). *Feminist methods in social research.* New York: Oxford University Press.

Richardson, L. (1990). *Writing strategies: Reaching diverse audiences.* Newbury Park, CA: Sage.

Richardson, L. (1994). Writing: A method of inquiry. In N. K. Denzin & Y. S. Lincoln (Eds.), *Handbook of qualitative research* (pp. 516–29). Thousand Oaks, CA: Sage.

Richardson, L. (1997). *Fields of play: Constructing an academic life.* New Brunswick, NJ: Rutgers University Press.

Richardson, L., & Taylor, V. (Eds.). (1993). *Feminist frontiers III.* New York: McGraw-Hill.

Rosenau, P. M. (1992). *Post-modernism and the social sciences: Insights, inroads, and intrusions*. Princeton, NJ: Princeton University Press.

Scheurich, J. J. (1997). An archaeological perspective, or is it turtles all the way down. In *Research method in the postmodern* (pp. 159–81). London: Falmer Press.

Sears, J. (Ed.). (1992). *Sexuality and the curriculum: The politics and practices of sexuality education*. New York: Teachers College Press.

Singer, L. (1993). *Erotic welfare: Sexual theory and politics in the age of epidemic*. New York: Routledge.

Spanos, W. V. (1993). *The end of education: Toward posthumanism*. Minneapolis: University of Minnesota Press.

Spivak, G. C. (1974). Translator's preface. In J. Derrida, *Of grammatology* (G. C. Spivak, Trans.) (pp. ix–xc). Baltimore: Johns Hopkins University Press.

Spivak, G. C. (1987). *In other worlds: Essays in cultural politics*. New York: Routledge.

Spivak, G. C. (1990). *The post-colonial critic: Interviews, strategies, dialogues*. New York: Routledge.

Spivak, G. C. (1993). *Outside in the teaching machine*. New York: Routledge.

St.Pierre, E. A. (1997a). Methodology in the fold and the irruption of transgressive data. *International Journal of Qualitative Studies in Education, 10*(2), 175–89.

St.Pierre, E. A. (1997b). An introduction to figuration—a poststructural practice of inquiry. *International Journal of Qualitative Studies in Education, 10*(3), 279–84.

Stronach, I., & MacLure, M. (1997). *Educational research undone: The postmodern embrace*. Buckingham, UK: Open University Press.

Suleri, S. (1992). Woman skin deep: Feminism and the postcolonial condition. *Critical Inquiry, 18*, 756–69.

Tanaka, G., & Cruz, C. (1998). The locker room: Eroticism and exoticism in a polyphonic text. *International Journal of Qualitative Studies in Education, 11*(1), 137–54.

Thomas, G. (1993). Post-colonial interrogations. *Social Alternatives, 12*(3), 8–11.

Thorne, B. (1993). *Gender play: Girls and boys in school*. New Brunswick, NJ: Rutgers University Press.

Tierney, W. G. (Ed.). (in press). Queer frontiers: Qualitative research and queer theory. *International Journal of Qualitative Studies in Education*. (Special issue)

Tong, R. (1998). *Feminist thought: A more comprehensive introduction*. New York: Westview Press.

Trinh, T. M-H. (1992). *Framer framed*. New York: Routledge.

Tyson, C. (1998). A response to "Coloring epistemologies:" Are our qualitative research epistemologies racially biased? *Educational Researcher, 27*(9), 21–22.

Varadharajan, A. (1995). *Exotic parodies: Subjectivity in Adorno, Said, and Spivak*. Minneapolis: University of Minnesota Press.

Villenas, S. (1996). The colonizer/colonized Chicana ethnographer: Identity, marginalization, and co-optation in the field. *Harvard Educational Review, 66*, 711–31.

Villenas, S. (1998, April). What's diversity got to do with qualitative research: An interactive conversation. Interactive symposium presented at the annual meeting of the American Educational Research Association, San Diego, CA.

Visweswaran, K. (1994). *Fictions of feminist ethnography*. Minneapolis: University of Minnesota Press.

Walker, R. (Ed.). (1995). *To be real: Telling the truth and changing the face of feminism*. New York: Anchor Books.

Walkerdine, V. (1990). *Schoolgirl fictions*. New York: Verso.

Weiner, G. (1994). *Feminisms in education: An introduction*. Buckingham, UK: Open University Press.

Wing, A. K. (Ed.). (1997). *Critical race feminism: A reader*. New York: New York University Press.

Žižek, S. (1991). *Looking awry: An introduction to Jacques Lacan through popular culture*. Cambridge, MA: MIT Press.

PART I

INTERRUPTIONS

Chapter 1

"The Question of Belief": Writing Poststructural Ethnography

Deborah P. Britzman

> The things to look at are styles, figures of speech, setting, narrative devices, historical and social circumstances, not the correctness of representation nor its fidelity to some great original.
>
> (Said, 1978, p. 21)

Edward Said advises readers encountering the texts of culture to consider both the structure of the narration and what it is that structures its modes of intelligibility. Such advice may seem strange when the text being examined is an educational ethnography. At first glance, ethnography seems to promise "fidelity to some great original," that is, to the original of culture. For those engaged in the doing and the reading of mainstream educational ethnography, more often than not, it is the "ethno" and not the "graphy" that seems to be the focus of attention. As a genre of research, I would note just three of its attractive and mythic "ethno" qualities. First, ethnography is both a process and a product; there are methods for how to go about narrating culture, and these social strategies promise a text. Second, good ethnographic texts tell stories that invariably embody qualities of a novel. Implicitly, ethnographies promise pleasure or at least new information to the reader. Third, an ethnography takes the reader into an actual world to reveal the cultural knowledge working in a particular place and time as it is lived through the subjectivities of its inhabitants. Such access persuades readers that they can imaginatively step into this world and act like a native, or, at the very least, understand the imperatives of cultural assimilation. These textualized qualities appear seamless because they blur traditional distinctions among the writer, the reader, the stories, and how the stories are told.

Such qualities are seductive in the power they bestow. There is a belief and expectation that the ethnographer is capable of producing truth from the experience of being there and that the reader is receptive to the truth of the text. In both instances, experience is "the great original." Ethnography assures us that there is both a "there" and "beings" who are there. Indeed, ethnographers claim to transpose their language onto something from "out there." In this way, the ethnographic text intends to translate, even as it is meant to stand in for, social life. The reader learns to expect cultural secrets and may well suppose that outsiders can become vicarious insiders. An ethnography offers moments of empathetic power in the ways it positions cultural knowledge and in the ways it positions readers of culture. Private moments are rendered public, and the goal of understanding—albeit through secondhand knowledge—is assumed to be within the reach of readers. In this mainstream and modernist version, ethnography depends upon the rationality and stability of writers and readers and upon noncontradictory subjects who say what they mean and mean what they say. This is the straight version of Ethnography 101.

With the advent of poststructuralist theories, these understandings need to be examined. The ground upon which ethnography is built turns out to be a contested and fictive geography. Those who populate and imagine it (every participant, including the author and the reader) are, in essence, textualized identities. Their voices create a cacophony and dialogic display of contradictory desires, fears, and literary tropes that, if carefully "read," suggest just how slippery speaking, writing, reading, and desiring subjectivity really are. In poststructuralist versions, "the real" of ethnography is taken as an effect of the discourses of the real; ethnography may construct the very materiality it attempts to represent. Poststructuralist critiques begin with assumptions of historicity and define ethnography as both a set of practices and a set of discourses. As an interpretive disturbance to the promise of representation, poststructuralists read the absent against the present. Thus, the ethnographic promise of a holistic account is betrayed by the slippage born from the partiality of language of what cannot be said precisely because of what is said, and of the impossible difference within what is said, what is intended, what is signified, what is repressed, what is taken, and what remains. From the unruly perspectives of poststructuralism, ethnography can only summon, in James Clifford's (1986) terms, "partial truths" and "fictions" (p. 5). In this ethnographic version, the authority of ethnography, the ethnographer, and the reader is always suspect.

Three kinds of ethnographic authority are being questioned here: the authority of empiricism, the authority of language, and the authority of reading or understanding. In the first case, what does it mean to disrupt what Paul Smith (1988) terms the "simple empiricism" (p. 86) of ethnography, that there is a real out there to narrate and to read? When it comes to considering the authority of language and the seeming stability of meaning from which it derives, what happens to writing and to reading if we take as our place of departure T. Minh-ha Trinh's (1989) warning about the effects of writing: "Words empty out with age. Die and rise again, accordingly invested with new meanings, and always equipped with a secondhand memory" (p. 79)? What happens to the authority of reading—the presumption that there is a direct relationship between the reader's reading and the text's telling—if we begin with Althusser's (cited in Rooney, 1989) refusal of textual innocence: "There is no such thing as an innocent reading, we must ask what reading we are guilty of" (p. 37)? Can ethnographic writing provoke textual and methodological doubt when, as Paul Atkinson (1990) argues, "The ethnographic text depends upon the plausibility of its account" (p. 2)? How does one believe the ethnographer, when, as Peggy Phelan (1993) theorizes, "In doubting the authenticity of the image, one questions as well the veracity of she who makes and describes it" (p. 1)? If ethnographic authority depends upon a tacit agreement among the participants, the ethnographer, and the reader (that the story is real, the discourse transparent, and only the names have been changed to protect the innocent) and that agreement is always betrayed, how is the ethnographic pact effectuated? How does one understand plausibility and persuasion? If the relationship between the real and the representational is always in doubt, what is the basis of belief and identification?

These difficult questions surround the doing and the reading of educational ethnography. Recent educational ethnographies and writing about this genre are pushing at normative disciplinary boundaries in terms of what it is that structures methodological imperatives, the ethnographer's stances, and the ethnographic voice; the kinds of theoretical traditions through which data are constructed, represented, and narrated; what are taken to be problems suitable for ethnographic research; and the problems of how one might read against the ethnographic grain (Brodkey, 1987; de Castell & Haig-Brown, 1993; Dippo, 1993; Fine, 1991; Lather, 1991). Questions of subjectivity move beyond the stance of knowing how others make sense and toward a consideration of how reflexivity can be practiced when making sense of oneself is understood as occurring through the construction of the other (Morrison, 1992; Phelan, 1993). Still other questions push against the very concept of reflexivity to consider the constitutive constraints of representation itself (Bakhtin, 1990; Butler, 1990; Owens, 1992). Ethnographic theorizing has become more tentative and less concerned with the old struggles of establishing authority as a way of research; it is more concerned with the archaeology of construction, the sedimentary grounds of ethnographic authority.

Poststructuralist theories raise critical concerns about what it is that structures meanings, practices, and bodies, about why certain practices become intelligible, valorized, or deemed as traditions, while other practices become discounted, impossible, or unimaginable. For poststructuralists, representation is always in crisis, knowledge is constitutive of power, and agency is the constitutive effect, and not the originator, of situated practices and histories (see, for example, Butler, 1993; Clifford & Dhareshwar, 1989; Feldman, 1991; Foucault, 1978; Ong, 1988; Pratt, 1992; Wolfe, 1992.) While it is beyond this essay to provide more than a sketchy account of poststructuralism, my purpose is to explore how particular poststructural considerations have challenged me to think differently about pinning "the real" onto the ethnographic account and to theorize, in explicit terms, the politics of recounting and being accountable. While it might be discomforting to leave a sentimental ethnography that desires to represent without looking back, because ethnography is always about a second glance, it is necessary to consider what precisely this second glance might imagine.

Given the ethnographic real as a contested territory, I examine what is at stake in writing and reading ethnography when one attempts to account for what Phelan (1993) terms "the question of belief" (p. 1) in the real and in the representational. Are there ways to think the unthought of ethnographic narratives? That is, is there an ethnographic unconscious that marks its constitutive limits? Is there a knowledge ethnography cannot tolerate knowing? My concern is with what reading with suspicion—for both writers and readers of ethnography—has to do with how one might imagine the construction of ethnographic narrative beyond the naive faith that seeing is believing. Rather than critiquing someone else's study, this essay is a form of speculative self-critique. I take the odd position of moving behind the scenes of my own ethnographic work to elaborate the theoretical and narrative decisions I made in producing my text. As a "hidden chapter" in my own ethnographic text, I offer thoughts about the narrative dilemmas unleashed when one attempts to write a poststructuralist ethnography or when one attempts to take seriously the problem of producing an account of social life that bothers the writer's and perhaps the reader's confidence in truth, in the visible, and in the real. While I retain the hope that ethnography can offer education a more complicated version of how life is lived, my concern is with the thorny issues unleashed when representation, however emancipatory, is acknowledged as crisis. Hence, I move back and forth between two related themes: conceptual issues in the study of the meanings of teaching and theoretical issues in the production of narratives structured within poststructuralist perspectives.

Poststructuralist concerns haunt my ethnographic research, writing, and reading. In my ethnographic study of secondary student teachers,

Practice Makes Practice: A Critical Study of Learning to Teach (1991), I began working poststructurally. With ethnographic data in hand, I decided to study these data (and hence the problem of learning to teach) as if I were reading a novel and, consequently, as if narratives of teaching were primarily a complex of contradictory interpretations and competing regimes of truth. I wondered what would it mean to read student teaching as if it were a text. Looking backward, my narrative desire was to write a "Rashomon" of student teaching, an ethnographic opera where voices argued, disrupted, and pleaded with one another; where the high drama of misunderstandings, deceit, and the conflicting desires made present and absent through language and through practice confound what is typically taken as the familiar story of learning to teach. I tried to write against the discourses that bind the disagreements, the embarrassments, the unsaid, and the odd moments of uncertainty in contexts overburdened with certain imperatives. I tried to do this by provoking and contradicting multiple voices: the ethnographic voice that promises to narrate experience as it unfolds, the hesitant voices of participants who kept refashioning their identities and investments as they were lived and rearranged in language, and poststructuralist voices that challenge a unitary and coherent narrative about experience.

In studying the lived experience of actual individuals but not wanting to individualize or render as a psychological problem the social disarray these individuals lived, I wanted to move beyond the impulse to represent "the real story of learning to teach" and attempt to get at how "the real" of teaching is produced as "the real story." Additionally, while the people in my study were actual persons, my intent was not to represent their actuality. Rather, taking the work of Foucault (1978) seriously, I wanted to trace how student teachers became an invention of the educational apparatus. Given the inordinate amount of research about this population, given the way the subject of student teacher is "an incitement to discourse," I became curious about how student teachers became a historical problem for education, how student teachers became constituted as a problem population. My interest, then, was to trace the "invention" of the student teacher, to explore how this invention became viewed as synonymous with "experience" in education; how the subject position of student teacher was lived and fashioned in education; and why certain modes of intelligibility, such as the binary of theory and practice, became a central problem.

The tension I felt given these approaches to the study of teaching was between working with these theories and still writing an ethnography. That is, while educational ethnography promises the narrative cohesiveness of experience and identity and the researcher's skill of representing the subject, poststructuralist theories disrupt any desire for a seamless narrative, a cohesive identity, or a mimetic representation. Poststructuralism disturbs the ethnographer's confidence in "knowing" experience or in possessing the writerly power to do anything else but borrow discourses and tack them onto other discourses. For the poststructuralist, "being there" does not guarantee access to truth. Thus, the tradition of ethnographic authority derived from participant observation becomes a site of doubt, rather than a confirmation of what exists prior to representation. These positions undermine the ethnographic belief that "reality" is somehow out there waiting to be captured by language.

In poststructuralist versions, subjects may well be the tellers of experience; but every telling is constrained, partial, and determined by the discourses and histories that prefigure, even as they might promise, representation. To fashion narration with the imperatives of poststructuralism means that the researcher must become overconcerned with experience as a discourse and with competing discourses of experience that traverse and structure any narrative. The ethnographic narrative must somehow acknowledge the differences within and among the stories of experience, how they are told, and what it is that structures the telling and the retelling (Brodkey, 1987). Borrowing poststructuralist theories that bothered my ethnographic confidence, then, required that I work with language differently, that I admit how my own telling is partial and governed by the discourses of my time and place. These recountings cannot, however, ease or resolve the contradictions born in language, the discourses that bind and unleash meanings, and the real made present and absent by my efforts. Given these discursive boundaries, my writing could only point to the contradictions that structure the uneasy dialogue between humanism and poststructuralism, between what is taken as lived experience and the afterthought of interpretive efforts, between the real subjects and their textual identities.

I confess that I still have difficulty uncoupling myself from the persuasive promises of ethnography. I desire to construct good stories filled with the stuff of rising and falling action, plots, themes, and denouement. And yet, within the narrative tropes I chose to employ, there is a contradictory point of no return, of having to abandon the impossible desire to portray the study's subjects as they would portray themselves. Thus, I positioned myself behind their backs to point out what they could not see, would not do, and could not have said even as I struggled against such omnipotence. I tried to hold tightly to the ethic of not producing these subjects as persons to blame or as heroes of resistance. Instead, my concern was one of questioning how the categories of blame and resistance became discursively produced and lived. In textualizing their identities, I held on to the hope that readers would be compelled to ask the dangerous questions: What is it that structures my own stories and my own intelligibility? What do my moral imperatives cost?

Here, then, were my contradictory desires: to textualize identities at their most vulnerable moments, to speak about and for individuals by juxtaposing their words with my own, to dramatize the ordinary days that make time seem like no time at all, *to narrate development as a creepy detour*, and to persuade readers of the credibility of my interpretive efforts. I wanted to warn them that all I could offer were partial truths and my own guilty readings of other people's dramas. The space I attempted to open was one where experience could not speak for itself but could be considered as a category that bracketed and even performed certain repetitions, certain problems, certain desires. Within such a space, experience, like representation, was already divided from itself. Much of my work as a reader of what others did, in fact, questioned how that experience was structured, how what was constituted as experience was reminiscent of education's available and normative discourses. I tried to study the cost of experience.

The secondhand stories that I attempted to narrate were grounded in the worlds and the words of those who live in teacher education. My first attempts to build an ethnography were quite traditional. Like the good fieldworker-*cum*-ethnographer, I "followed" student teachers throughout their high school internships. Working under the old assumptions of ethnography, I viewed student teaching as "ethnographically friendly" because it had a beginning, middle, and end, and *that*, I thought, was a significant quality in any ethnographic account. Yet I was naive in constructing such an expectation. It prevented an interested reading of both the competing stories working through and against the narration of experience and the conceptual orderings of everyone involved that seem to position experience as seamless even while it was lived as disorderly, discontinuous, and chaotic.

While student teaching was bounded by a specific commitment, there was no correspondence among how chronology was being constituted by the participants, how I was constituting the ethnographic present, and how everyone involved was fashioning narrative unity. These multiple and simultaneous notions of time fashioned the subject of student teaching in particular ways. That is, neither the idea nor the identity of the student teacher was finished by the conclusion of student teaching. Time did not clarify what it meant to learn to teach. Instead—and this is where poststructuralism allowed me to rethink the very category of time—time itself had become a discursive site of struggle. There was never enough time to do all that one wanted to do; student teaching went on for too long; it betrayed the promise of effective practices; the chronology of the curriculum could not account for existential time to think things through; and most discounted the time of student teaching as not quite real time. Working against such complexity was the construct of the "ethnographic present," a sense of time that is frozen in the immediate and refuses to admit either competing chronologies or even to recognize chronology itself as a normative construct.

Within this twilight zone were the student teachers. A significant amount of interview talk and observational field notes focused their perceptions of their experience as student teachers. But a different sense of time fashioned how they talked about their educational biographies in relation to learning to teach. I came to this study with clear ideas about how educational biography is reproduced in learning to teach but, again, had not considered chronology itself to be problematic. Thus, I could not make sense of the contradictory process whereby the past is reinvented and textualized through the discourses and practices of the present. A linear and literal sense of time could not account for the ways in which student teachers produce their identities. And they do produce them, not as if they moved through an orderly experiential continuum, but as if identities already constituted a cacophony of beckonings and involuntary returns. Could an ethnographic narrative present the "secondhand memories" of student teachers rather than the student teachers themselves as the site of struggle?

My dilemma was how to order but not normalize the stories of student teaching. In thinking about how to structure their narratives from interviews and field notes, knowing that I learned about their stories week by week, I decided not to mix their sense of time with the unfolding chronology that bound their own narrative truths. Doing so would give me too much power as an ethnographer. These student teachers built and rebuilt their identities with small and contradictory details because they were caught in an oxymoron called *student teacher*. Their first sense of chronology, however secondhand, was significant to them. Working under the old promise of representation, my first drafts of their stories detailed how they saw their world. But these early versions could not read how their very constitution of chronology impeded insight into who they thought they were becoming. The problem was that my first writing attempts represented traditional ethnographic structure, hence a humanistic ethnographic subject. My initial chapter titles said as much: "The Story of Jamie Owl" and "The Story of Jack August." Such phrases promised a unitary narrative, a noncontradictory and essentialized subject, and, of course, a cohesive account. The problem was that these narratives were traversed by competing story lines, contradictory representations of the meanings of learning to teach, and subjectivities that refused to stand still. In trying to write a traditional ethnographic narrative, I had affixed "Jack" and "Jamie" to the unified subjects' positions of humanistic discourse despite the fact that they were continually becoming undone by the slippage of this very discourse.

To disrupt my own retelling, I rewrote each chapter, constituting my narrative to form a kind of photographic negative to theirs. I followed the photographic technique of Walter Benjamin (1969): "The enlargement of the snapshot does not simply render more precise what in any case was visible, though unclear: it reveals new structural formations of the subject" (p. 263). The new chapters were retitled: "Narratives of Student Teaching: Stories from Jamie Owl" and "Narratives of Student Teaching: Stories from Jack August." My hope was to reposition the site of struggle from the individual to their narratives and to pluralize their retellings to account for the competing stories, "new structural formations," and the hesitations of chronology that were made present and absent through their language. These contradictions of chronology, knowledge, and identity, as expressed in their words, structured the subheadings of each chapter. Jamie Owl's subtitles include: "Grand questions," "Should I stay or should I go," "I'm not a teacher," "A world without people," "Taking note," "Being noted," "Give them what they want," "Maybe I should go out in a blaze of glory," and, "School, school, school!" Jack August's subtitles include: "Shouting out ideas," "Keeping them on their toes," "How do you sway people," "How am I supposed to judge class participation," "Not really a teacher," "Finding gimmicks," and, "I was kind of sad when I cleaned out my desk." These phrases suggest a tentativeness; they allude to, in ways my own words could not, the uncertainty that cannot be uncoupled from the teacher's identity.

To heighten the detours of experience and hence to gesture toward experience as an unstable construct may well agitate traditional ethnographic notions of agency and voice. One of the values that originally attracted me to ethnographic research was the commitment to the participant as a knowing, intentional being, or, at the very least, to the assumption that cultural knowledge is produced within culture. The method promises to deliver voices that have been previously shut out of normative educational research and to remedy the ways educational research normalizes populations through its imposition of categories that situate individuals as the site of the problem. For many who do ethnographic work in education, there is the political commitment to the right to speak, to represent oneself, however partially; in this version, the ethnographer must be committed to advocating subjugated knowledge. However, these necessary commitments need not preclude an approach to representation that situates narrative efforts, as opposed to the narrators themselves, as a site of crisis (Kennedy & Davis, 1993). Because representation cannot deliver what it promises, unmediated access to the real, ethnographers must think the categories of agency and voice beyond the humanist assumptions of a self capable of transcending history or a self that can somehow recover his or her authenticity from the unwieldy effects of discursive regimes of power and truth.

Whereas humanistic versions of agency and voice posit the subject as the originator and must, consequently, imagine the social, or the structural, or the historical as that which somehow distorts what should have been "there" all along, the version of agency and voice that I asserted began with the notion that as constructions they are provisional, nonunitary, and situated. Because in this version they are continually being fashioned in practices, agency and voice are the social effects and not the originators of history and of social relations. It is not the ethnographer's work to "bestow" or to "disavow" the verisimilitudes of others. Instead, the problem is to theorize the modes of intelligibility that constitute subjects. The problem is not one where the ethnographer authenticates a particular truth. Rather, the ethnographer traces, but not without argument, the circulation of competing regimes of truth.

In poststructuralist narratives, subjects cannot be uncoupled from the conscious and unconscious of discourses that fashion how subjects become recognized and misrecognized. Every discourse constitutes, even as it mobilizes and shuts out, imaginary communities, identity investments, and discursive practices. Discourses authorize what can and cannot be said; they produce relations of power and communities of consent and dissent, and thus discursive boundaries are always being redrawn around what constitutes the desirable and the undesirable and around what it is that makes possible particular structures of intelligibility and unintelligibility. Feminist poststructuralist theories have been particularly helpful in describing this drama. They argue that by assuming people to be effects of language, knowledge, power, and history, rather than their essential authors, a more provisional, historical, and ethical understanding of agency is possible (Butler, 1990, 1993; de Lauretis, 1987; Fuss, 1989). The point is that if discourses construct and incite the subject and produce contradictory investments, pleasures, and knowledge, then they can also be employed to deconstruct the kinds of naturalization that push one to take up the impossible moral imperatives of policing categories, ensuring boundaries, and attempting to live the promises of a noncontradictory, transcendental self. Precisely because one's conceptual ordering of experience structures intelligibility and unintelligibility and because one's conceptual ordering of experience is an effect of discourse, one might also be able to begin to employ more suspicious discourses that exceed practices of normalization.

With these poststructuralist insights, I could position the term *student teacher* as an oxymoron. I did this because those with whom I spoke were caught in a messy process of theorizing whom they were becoming when they were learning to teach. A word such as *teacher* is already overpopulated with other contexts; with other people; with competing forms of knowledge; and with desires, pleasures, and fears. Thus, the word itself constitutes both a set of discourses and a set of practices. Its contradictory meanings cannot be isolated from the speaker, the listener, or the histories and practices that overdetermined contexts of education and pedagogy. The problem is that, as a discourse and as a practice, the word *teacher* and the subject positions it produces always have the potential of producing disavowal within the subject who lives this discursive category as a crisis of representation.

Such theorizing, after all, may not make sense to the people behind my text. Indeed, there still remains the messy problem of whether the people in my text, if asked, would see themselves as inventions of discourses and as fragmented subjectivities. Most, if not all, of my participants were deeply invested in the humanistic notion of an essential self that had somehow been repressed by some condition, person, idea, or social structure. They all believed there was a real self to possess and to represent and yet, in a general sense, they viewed the context of education as a site that demanded they hold these real selves in abeyance. More particularly, the student teachers and those who surrounded them viewed the condition of student teaching as inhibiting "real" teaching. Like most people in teacher education, they were deeply invested in the idea that experience is telling, that one learns by experience, by being there, and not by theories. If this were not the case, why have such a long internship? If learning to teach does not come about through practice teaching, if schools are not the best places of teacher education, where does that leave us? I am getting at the inevitable tension, born from the theories that structured my narrations, that my interpretation will agonize what they take as their lived experience. And if ethnography authenticates representation, what does it mean to employ theories that call into question promises of representation and belief?

The only way I know around this teleology of "the real" without falling into arguments regarding true and false consciousness is to revision the project of ethnography beyond the structuring regulations of the true and the false, the objective and the subjective, and the valid and the invalid. At the very least, it means approaching ethnographic writing as an effect of a contest of discourses, even if the ethnographer has the power to suggest what is at stake when identities are at stake. There is something more at work here having to do with emptying out the signifier "Qualitative Research" and filling it with provocations that disturb the impulse to settle meanings. I now think of ethnography as a regulating fiction, as a particular narrative practice that produces textual identities and regimes of truth. Such an approach admits a significant problem ignored by traditional ethnographic narratives, namely the inevitable tensions of knowledge as partial, as interested, and as performative of relations of power. This returns us to the clashing investments in how stories are told and of the impossibility of telling everything. There is that excess, that difference within the story, informing how the story is told, the imperatives produced within its tellings, and the subject positions made possible and impossible there. These signifying "spaces" must be admitted as central to the structure and regulation of ethnographic work if readers are to participate in exceeding and informing the meanings ethnography might offer. The reason we might do ethnography, then, is to think the unthought in more complex ways, to trouble confidence in being able to "observe" behavior, "apply the correct technique," and "correct" what is taken as a mistake. Ethnographic narratives should trace how power circulates and surprises, theorize how subjects spring from the discourses that incite them, and question the belief in representation even as one must practice representation as a way to intervene critically in the constitutive constraints of discourses.

My guilty readings of the story of learning to teach began when I could admit my constructed categories and render them explicit, thus uncoupling my own voice from those of the participants in my study. Such guilty readings may well open my text to the charge of prescriptiveness, of judging the characters I constructed in ways that do not resonate with their own lived experience. There may be no escaping this charge because my own interested reading began with the belief that learning to teach is not simply about acquiring discrete and neutral skills, of reproducing the gestures of others, or even of developing a teaching style. Rather, the problem of learning to teach, like the problem of education itself, is a problem of which identities, which knowledge, and which practices might be offered and at what cost. The urgent question raised by Shoshana Felman (Felman & Laub, 1992) concerns the kind of people education can make. Felman asks, "In a post-traumatic century, a century that has survived unthinkable historical catastrophes, is there anything that we have learned or that we should learn about education, that we did not know before" (p. 1)?

Writing ethnography as a practice of narration is not about capturing the real already out there. It is about constructing particular versions of truth, questioning how regimes of truth become neutralized as knowledge, and thus pushing the sensibilities of readers in new directions. If ethnography is to provide a critical space to push thought against itself, then ethnographers must begin by identifying their own textual strategies and political commitments and pointing out the differences among the stories, the structures of telling, and the structures of belief. Put differently, educational ethnography and the writing of educational narratives might well begin to wander along what Samuel Delany (1991) terms as "the margins between claims of truth and the claims of textuality" (p. 28).

These critical practices require something more of readers. Readers of ethnography must also be willing to construct more complicated reading practices that move them beyond the myth of literal representations and the deceptive promise that "the real" is transparent, stable, and just like the representational. Poststructuralist theories of writing and reading may allow readers to challenge and rearrange what it is that structures the reader's own identity imperatives, the reader's own theory of reading that produces boundaries of the credible and the incredible. One's own structures of intelligibility might become open to readings not yet accounted for, not yet made. Perhaps the power of the writer and the reader can only reside in an awareness of the play of contradictions and the performances of power that both suture and unravel any ethnographic text. As a question of belief, reading and writing ethnography might provoke a different way of thinking, an ethic that refuses the grounds of subjectification and normalization and that worries about that which is not yet.

References

Atkinson, P. (1990). *The ethnographic imagination: Textual constructions of reality.* New York: Routledge.

Bakhtin, M. M. (1990). *Art and answerability: Early philosophical essays* (M. Holquist & V. Liapunov, Eds.). Austin: University of Texas Press.

Benjamin, W. (1969). The work of art in an age of mechanical reproduction. In H. Arendt (Ed.), *Illuminations* (pp. 217–52). New York: Schocken.

Britzman, D. (1991). *Practice makes practice: A critical study of learning to teach.* Albany: State University of New York Press.

Brodkey, L. (1987). *Academic writing as social practice.* Philadelphia: Temple University Press.

Butler, J. (1990). *Gender trouble: Feminism and the subversion of identity.* New York: Routledge, Chapman, & Hall.

Butler, J. (1993). *Bodies that matter: On the discursive limits of "sex."* New York: Routledge.

Clifford, J. (1986). Introduction: Partial truths. In J. Clifford & G. Marcus (Eds.), *Writing culture: The poetics and politics of ethnography* (pp. 1–27). Berkeley and Los Angeles: University of California Press.

Clifford, J., & Dhareshwar, V. (Eds.). (1989). *Traveling theories, traveling theorists.* Santa Cruz, CA: Center for Cultural Studies.

de Castell, S., & Haig-Brown, C. (1993). Book review [Review of *The ethnographic imagination: Textual constructions of reality*]. *Anthropology and Education Quarterly, 24,* 82–91.

Delany, S. (1991). Street talk/straight talk. *Differences: A Journal of Feminist Cultural Studies, 5*, 21–38.

de Lauretis, T. (1987). *Technologies of gender: Essays on theory, film, and fiction.* Bloomington: Indiana University Press.

Dippo, D. (1993). Tantalizing textuality. *The Review of Education, 15*, 29–40.

Feldman, A. (1991). *Formations of violence: The narrative of the body and political terror in Northern Ireland.* Chicago: University of Chicago Press.

Felman, S., & Laub, D. (1992). *Testimony: Crises of witnessing in literature, psychoanalysis, and history.* New York: Routledge.

Fine, M. (1991). *Framing dropouts: Notes on the politics of an urban public high school.* Albany: State University of New York Press.

Foucault, M. (1978). *The history of sexuality, Volume I: An introduction.* New York: Pantheon.

Fuss, D. (1989). *Essentially speaking: Feminism, nature, and difference.* New York: Routledge.

Kennedy, E. L., & David, M. D. (1993). *Boots of leather, slippers of gold: The history of a lesbian community.* New York: Routledge.

Lather, P. (1991). *Getting smart: Feminist research and pedagogy with/in the postmodern.* New York: Routledge.

Morrison, T. (1992). *Playing in the dark: Whiteness and the literary imagination.* Cambridge, MA: Harvard University Press.

Ong, A. (1988). Colonialism and modernity: Feminist re-presentations of women in non-western societies. *Inscriptions, 3/4*, 79–93.

Owens, C. (1992). *Beyond recognition: Representation, power and culture* (S. Bryson, B. Kruger, L. Tillman, & J. Weinstock, Eds.). Berkeley and Los Angeles: University of California Press.

Phelan, P. (1993). *Unmarked: The politics of performance.* New York: Routledge.

Pratt, M. L. (1992). *Imperial eyes: Travel writing and transculturation.* New York: Routledge.

Rooney, E. (1989). *Seductive reasoning: Pluralism as the problematic of contemporary literary theory.* Ithaca, NY: Cornell University Press.

Said, E. W. (1978). *Orientalism.* New York: Vintage.

Smith, P. (1988). *Discerning the subject.* Minneapolis: University of Minnesota Press.

Trinh, T. M-H. (1989). *Woman, native, other: Writing postcoloniality and feminism.* Bloomington: Indiana University Press.

Wolfe, M. (1992). *A thrice-told tale: Feminism, postmodernism, and ethnographic responsibility.* Stanford, CA: Stanford University Press.

Chapter 2

What's Going On? Black Feminist Thought and the Politics of Postmodernism

Patricia Hill Collins

Like other oppositional discourses, Black feminist thought can never remove itself totally from the ideas expressed by more powerful groups. Although it challenges social theories dominant to itself, in order to be both comprehensible and legitimated, it must use the constructs, paradigms, and epistemologies of those discourses. These tensions become apparent in the relationship of Black feminist thought to a loose constellation of academic discourses in the United States best known as postmodernism.[1] On the one hand, postmodernism opposes some of the core tenets of positivist science, structuralist literary criticism, and other discourses of modernity. Thus, postmodernism can foster a powerful critique of existing knowledges and the hierarchical power relations they defend. For example, postmodernism questions the taken-for-granted nature of categories such as race, gender, and heterosexuality and suggests that these seeming "biological truths" constitute social constructions. By focusing on marginalized, excluded, and silenced dimensions of social life, postmodernism destabilizes what has been deemed natural, normal, normative, and true. Overall, postmodernism rejects notions of epistemological and methodological certainty provided by the natural sciences, social sciences, and other discourses of modernity that have been used to justify Black women's oppression (Best and Kellner, 1991; McGowan, 1991; Rosenau, 1992).

On the other hand, postmodernism undercuts selected dimensions of African-American women's political activism. For example, postmodernism rejects ethical positions that emerge from absolutes such as faith. It also eschews social policy recommendations—to make such recommendations requires advancing truth claims and advocating specific political actions stemming from those claims. (McGowan, 1991; Rosenau, 1992). This absence of responsibility grounded in some sort of ethical stance is at odds with African-American women's long-standing contributions to Black civil society. Thus, although postmodernism provides a plausible response to dominant discourses and the politics they promote, it fails to provide directions for constructing alternatives.

This chapter has two main purposes. First, for readers who typically remain excluded, it highlights the "loose principles" permeating discourses of postmodernism (Appiah, 1992). Such a task necessarily flattens differences among postmodernists, leaving those who operate within postmodernism to ask, "Exactly which postmodernism does she mean?" Although these readers may be frustrated by the generalizations in this chapter, to me, the exclusionary language barring access to postmodernism is part of the problem. Second, the chapter provides a preliminary assessment of these ideas in light of their actual and potential utility for Black feminist thought. Toward this end, I emphasize postmodernism as a series of ideas and practices. I focus on the contradictory nature of postmodernism—the difference between what it says and what it does.

In approaching these goals, I build on Charles Lemert's (1992) thesis that postmodernism can be seen as a social theory of difference that follows from decentering the social world using a methodology of deconstruction. Recall that critical social theory encompasses bodies of knowledge and sets of institutional practices that actively grapple with the central questions facing groups of people differently placed in unjust political, social, and historical contexts. One might ask to what degree postmodernism is a critical social theory. Rather than examining the main ideas of postmodernism as concepts that can be proven correct or incorrect, I share David Wagner's (1992) view that it is more useful to view postmodernism as providing a series of orienting strategies that make theorizing possible.[2] As Wagner points out, "Strategies are directive; they tell us how to approach the sociological world, not what is true about the world" (p. 210). Thus, I treat the three main rubrics of decentering, deconstruction, and difference as orientating strategies for postmodern ideas and practices. Moreover, given the embeddedness of knowledges of all types in relations of ruling (Foucault, 1980), these orientating strategies are used differently by intellectuals differently placed in hierarchical power relations. Social theories of difference deployed by intellectuals who are privileged within hierarchical power relations of race, class, and gender may operate quite differently than comparable theories forwarded either by intellectuals emerging from the centers of oppressed groups or by those in outsider-within locations. My approach explores the political implications of the three rubrics of decentering, deconstruction, and difference for developing Black feminist thought as critical social theory.

The Rubric of Decentering: Claiming Marginality

One common popular assumption that permeates academic discussions of postmodernism identifies the origins of postmodernism exclusively with leftist intellectuals in Europe and the United States. Steven Seidman's (1992) otherwise excellent summary of the origins of postmodernism illustrates this approach. According to Seidman, postmodernism emerged from the break of the French left from both the Communist Party and Marxism in the 1970s, with leftist intellectuals in the United States, particularly feminists and gays, becoming leaders of the postmodern in the American academy. Seidman argues that by the 1970s, the left in the United States and in Europe became socially and ideologically less effective in challenging centers of power. Composed of a plurality of movements that each focused on its own local or particular struggle to build autonomous communities, these politics fostered a theoretical shift away from positivist science, Marxism, or other theories of this type in the academy. Seidman quite rightly points out, "The shift of leftist politics in the 1970's from the politics of labor to the new social movements and to a post-Marxist social criticism forms an important social matrix for the rise of a postmodern social discourse" (p. 50).

Noticeably missing from Seidman's (1992) analysis is any mention of race or Black women. It is not that Seidman is wrong—rather, his focus may be too narrow. Consider the difference between Seidman's account and that of Black feminist theorist Carole Boyce Davies (1994), who notes, "My contention is that postmodernist positions . . . are always already articulated by Black women because we experience, ahead of the general population, many of the multiple struggles that subsequently become popularly expressed" (p. 55). Or, as British scholars Michael Keith and Malcolm Cross (1993) observe, "The recently discovered postmodern condition of marginality and fragmentation, positively signified, has been lived and worked through for the last forty years, and more by racialized minorities in post-war metropolitan economies" (p. 22). From this perspective, Black women's experiences prefigured the themes of contemporary postmodernism.

One such theme is an emphasis on decentering, namely, unseating those who occupy centers of power as well as the knowledge that defends their power. Typically applied in relation to elite White male power, the concept of decentering can apply to any type of group-based power. A standard strategy of decentering is to claim the power of marginality. For example, when in the 1970s and 1980s Black women and other similarly situated groups broke long-standing silences about their oppression, they spoke from the margins of power. Moreover, by claiming historically marginalized experiences, they effectively challenged false universal knowledges that historically defended hierarchical power relations. Marginality operated as an important site of resistance for decentering unjust power relations. Thus, the center/margin metaphor has been an important precursor to decentering as one rubric of post-modernism.

Postmodern claims to decentering introduce one important question: Who might be most likely to care about decentering—those in the centers of power or those on the margins? By legitimating marginality as a potential source of strength for oppressed groups, the postmodern rubric of decentering seemingly supports Black women's long-standing efforts to challenge false universal knowledge that privileged Whiteness, maleness, and wealth. However, as with the changing interpretations associated with Black women's "coming to voice," current meanings attached to decentering as a construct illustrate how terms can continue to be used yet can be stripped of their initial oppositional intent (Winant, 1994).

Tracing the changing interpretations attached to the center/margin metaphor from its initial affiliation with global postcolonial struggles and social movements of the 1960s and 1970s in the United States reveals a dramatic shift in meaning. As a literary metaphor, the language of centers and margins emerged in tandem with similar social science emphases on core and periphery power relations. Designed to describe a range of unequal, exploitive political and economic relationships, these include the classical colonialism that characterized modern European nations' dominion over their Oriental and African colonies (Said, 1978, 1993); neocolonial relationships that juxtaposed the wealth of core industrial, developed nations of Europe and North America to that of the poverty of the largely colored Third World on the periphery (Said, 1990); the geographic reversal of internal colonial relationships that viewed the affluence of White suburban communities in the United States as intimately linked to the poverty of Black inner-city neighborhoods (Blauner, 1972); and the core and periphery industrial sectors that separated workers by race, class, and gender into segmented labor markets (Edwards, 1979; Gordon et al., 1982; Bonacich, 1989). In all of these cases, the construct of core/periphery relationships and its closely affiliated center/margin literary metaphor signaled unjust, hierarchical power relationships.

When embedded in an understanding of core/periphery relationships, this center/margin metaphor became a useful way of viewing Black women's experiences within hierarchical power relations in the United States (see, e.g., Glenn, 1985; Dill, 1988; Amott & Matthaei, 1991). Within power relations that constructed Whiteness, maleness, and wealth as centers of power, African-American women were relegated to positions of marginalized Others. One "decentered" hierarchical power relations by claiming the marginalized and devalued space of Black womanhood not as one of tragedy but as one of creativity and power. Marginality certainly proved to be a productive intellectual space for many African-American women thinkers. In her essay "Choosing the Margin as a Space of Radical Openness," Black feminist theorist bell hooks (1990) presents the potential danger and creativity of theorizing on the margins of power:

> Those of us who live, who "make it," passionately holding on as to aspects of that "downhome" life we do not intend to lose while simultaneously seeking new knowledge and experience, invent spaces of radical openness. Without such spaces we would not survive. Our living depends on our ability to conceptualize alternatives, often improvised. . . . For me this space of radical openness is a margin—a profound edge. Locating oneself there is difficult yet necessary. It is not a "safe" place. One is always at risk. (p. 129)

For African-American women as a collectivity, redefining marginality as a potential source of strength fostered a powerful oppositional knowledge (Collins, 1990). Moreover, the work of Black women and other similarly situated groups participated in a much larger project that used the margins as a source of intellectual freedom and strength (see, e.g., Anzaldúa, 1987; Awkward, 1995).

Despite these contributions, the continued efficacy of marginality as a space of radical openness remains questionable. Over time, the connections between the center/margin metaphor as a heuristic device and actual core/periphery relations became less clear. While continuing to reference power relations, talk of centers and margins became increasingly distanced from its initial grounding in structural, group-based power relations. Old centers of Whiteness, maleness, and wealth attached to core/periphery relationships in industrial sectors, labor markets, and among the colonial powers and their former colonies persisted. The center/margin metaphor, however, increasingly became recast as yet another ahistorical, "universal" construct applied to all sorts of power relations. Conceptions of power shifted—talk of tops and bottoms, long associated with hierarchy, was recast as flattened geographies of centers and margins.

Once decontextualized in this fashion, because all groups now occupied a flattened theoretical space of shifting centers and margins, decentering as a strategy could be more easily appropriated by groups situated anywhere within real-world hierarchical power relations. Decentering as a resistance strategy was no longer reserved for those actually oppressed within hierarchical power relations of race, class, and gender. Instead, decentering could now serve as a loose cannon/canon that could be aimed in any direction on this newly flattened center/margin power landscape. As Pauline Rosenau (1992) points out, part of the "magic" of postmodernism "is that its open-endedness, and lack of specific defini-tion is at once attractive to the affluent, the desperate, and the disillu-sioned of this world" (p. 11). Even though the language continued to refer to social relations of race, class, and gender, decentering lost its ini-tial analytical precision and assumed disparate meanings for groups dif-ferently positioned within hierarchical power arrangements. Decentering increasingly became recast as a literary term, a decontextu-alized, abstract construct immersed in representations, texts, and inter-textuality.

By attracting diverse intellectuals to an important collective enter-prise, on the surface, decentering the power exerted via representations and texts appears promising. However, since dissimilar groups construct different meanings out of the same system of signs, we might question what the term decentering means to diverse groups of intellectuals. Focusing on one group of academics who are privileged within the larger community of intellectuals sheds light on how groups' placement within hierarchical power relations might shape their intellectual productions. As political theorist Nancy Hartsock (1990) astutely points out, some academic intellectuals who espouse postmodernism bear a striking resemblance to Albert Memmi's (1965) portrayal of "colonizers who refuse" under conditions of classical colonialism.[3] Memmi's discussion of colonizers' reactions to the privileges that colonialism provided them offers a provocative metaphor for understanding why theorists occupy-ing positions of privilege might be attracted to postmodernism at this particular historical moment.[4] Although Memmi is clearly referring to a European male response to classical colonial situations, principally of the French in decolonization struggles in Algeria in the 1960s, his analysis clarifies why certain intellectuals might find postmodernism particularly attractive.[5]

Memmi (1965) notes that, whether they like it or not, all colonizers benefit from colonialism. But although privilege is built into social struc-tures, not all colonizers are comfortable with the power and privilege that their status in the colonial system confers upon them. Some refuse either by withdrawing physically from the conditions that privilege them or by remaining to fight and change those conditions. As the outsiders within the dominant group of colonizers, colonizers who refuse typically act as power brokers who represent the interests of the colonized natives to the colonizers who accept. By representing the interests of the colo-nized and claiming to understand their standpoint, members of this go-between group simultaneously challenge the colonial status quo and reproduce it. Although they understand how definitions of the colonized as "different" or as "Other" remain central to the way colonialism functions, they oppose colonialism in the abstract while continuing to enjoy its material benefits.

Despite their good intentions, when colonizers who refuse come into contact with actual colonized people who speak out, as compared to either ideas about the colonized people or natives who remain silenced, colonizers realize that their interests and those of the colonized are fundamentally opposed. If colonialism were abolished and colonized people were to gain power, little privilege would remain within new social relations for former colonizers, even those who refuse. A decolonized world would offer to colonizers who refuse no place comparable in power to that available under colonialism. As Memmi (1965) notes, "The left-wing colonizer refuses to become a part of his group of fellow citizens. At the same time it is impossible for him to identify his future with that of the colonized. Politically, who is he?" (p. 41). Although colonizers who refuse may reject relations of ruling that privilege them, removing those relations simultaneously eliminates their identity and purpose. Memmi continues: "One now understands a dangerously deceptive trait of the leftist colonizer, his political ineffectiveness. It results from the nature of his position in the colony" (p. 41).[6]

Memmi wrote in 1965 of members of classical colonial elites who could avoid the stark contrasts of privilege and penalty characterizing African and Asian colonies by returning home to the insulated homogeneity of France. A decolonized world linked via telecommunications into a global market offers no such escape. Postcolonial migrations of people from Africa, the Caribbean, and Asia to Europe demonstrate that self-contained, homogeneous European nation-states are largely relics of the past. Memmi's version of colonial relations also bears a strong resemblance to racial segregation in the United States prior to the 1970s. During that time, African-Americans were objects of knowledge, spoken about and for by sympathetic leftist intellectuals. As African-American women's experiences within sociology illustrate, the absence of Black people from higher education in any significant numbers, especially their absence from positions of authority, made this relationship palatable. In this regard, European decolonization and racial desegregation in the United States share important similarities. In both cases, the movement of people of color into formerly all-White spaces shattered the illusion of insider security maintained by keeping a safe distance from derogated outsiders. As Memmi observes, "It is not easy to escape mentally from a concrete situation, to refuse its ideology while continuing to live with its actual relationships" (p. 20). In a sense, since there is no place to hide, intellectuals privileged by systems of race, class, and gender oppression must find new ways to "refuse" in proximity to those whose interests they formerly championed and who now inconveniently aim to "come to voice" and speak for themselves.

Thus, the problem that confronted colonizers who refused foreshadowed that facing contemporary leftist academics. Under a system of colonialism in which the natives were safely tucked away at a distance, colonizers who refused could claim solidarity with the marginalized and be praised for their efforts. However, what happens when the natives gain entry to the center? Recently desegregated institutions of higher education where African Americans claimed legitimation as agents of knowledge created just such a new reality. Where do former allies of African Americans and other dispossessed groups now belong? Some identify the changing configuration of personnel within higher education since the early 1970s as a "crisis" and spend considerable time wondering what to do about it (see, e.g., Levine, 1995). Ann DuCille (1994) identifies the discomfort of many academics with the changing political climate in higher education when she observes that "a kind of color line and intellectual passing [exists] within and around the academy: black culture is more easily intellectualized (and canonized) when transferred from the danger of lived black experience to the safety of white metaphor, when you can have that 'signifying black difference' without the difference of significant blackness" (p. 600). How comfortable are colonizers who refuse when the formerly colonized refuse to be objectified as "texts" amenable to scholarly manipulation? How should they handle groups of natives who express self-defined standpoints?

Although this newly decolonized world creates new patterns of interaction for everyone, by themselves these patterns do not explain why postmodernism remains so appealing at this historical moment. British cultural critic Kobena Mercer (1994) alludes to the links between privileged intellectuals who have lost their former positions as representatives of the oppressed and the type of social theory that these intellectuals might find attractive. In his discussion of the disillusionment of many intellectuals with economic class analysis, Mercer observes that

> A whole generation of postwar intellectuals have experienced an identity crisis as philosophies of Marxism and modernism have begun to lose their oppositional or adversarial aura. . . . What results is a model of mourning and melancholia, or else an attitude of cynical indifference that seeks a disavowal of the past, as the predominant voices in postmodern criticism have emphasized an accent of narcissistic pathos by which the loss of authority and identity on the part of a tiny minority of privileged intellectuals is generalized and universalized as something that everybody is supposedly worried about. (p. 288)

Edward Said (1993) forwards a similar claim: "After years of support for anti-colonial struggles in Algeria, Cuba, Vietnam, Palestine, Iran, which came to represent for many Western intellectuals their deepest engagement in the politics and philosophy of anti-imperialist decolonization, a moment of exhaustion and disappointment was reached. One began to hear and read how futile it was to support revolutions" (p. 27). In her analysis of scholars engaged in Asian studies, cultural critic Rey Chow (1993) follows a similar logic. Chow's argument provides a suggestive link between Maoists, postmodernists, and colonizers who refuse:

> Typically, the Maoist is a cultural critic who lives in a capitalist society but who is fed up with capitalism—a cultural critic . . . who wants a social order imposed to the one that is supporting her own undertaking. The Maoist is thus a supreme example of the way desire works: What she wants is always located in the other, resulting in an identification with and valorization of that which she is not/does not have. Since what is valorized is often the other's deprivation—"having" poverty or "having" nothing—the Maoist's strategy becomes in the main a rhetorical renunciation of the material power that enables her rhetoric. (pp. 10–11)

If Hartsock, Mercer, Said, and Chow are correct, then postmodernism may be more grounded in the needs of contemporary colonizers who refuse than is typically realized. Antiracist Whites grappling with their position in institutionalized racism, antisexist males coming to terms with patriarchy, White women who treated their domestic workers like "one of the family," and highly educated, affluent individuals from diverse backgrounds who must justify their own privileges in the face of the stark realities of chronic global poverty—all experience a "crisis" of identity of the loss of authority vested in old centers. Consider, for example, how the following definition of postmodernism matches the concerns of intellectuals for whom the world no longer brings the certainty of authority and identity:

> Postmodernisms are responses across the disciplines to the contemporary crisis of representation, the profound uncertainty about what constitutes an adequate depiction of social "reality." . . . The essence of the postmodern argument is that the dualisms which continue to dominate Western thought are inadequate for understanding a world of multiple causes and effects interacting in complex and nonlinear ways, all of which are rooted in a limitless array of historical and cultural specialties. (Lather, 1991, p. 21)

One might ask which group might be most unnerved by a "crisis of representation" that criticized long-standing criteria for authority and identity and which might welcome such a crisis with open arms.

The changed meanings attached to the rubric of decentering emerge in this political and intellectual context. Despite the seemingly oppositional content of postmodernism—its often-stated commitment to the decentering of White male authority, subjectivity, and tradition—its use within the academy does very little to decenter actual power relations. In part, this situation reflects the identity of postmodernism as an academic theory. The placement of intellectuals almost exclusively within academia raises a valid question concerning how effectively academics can decenter power relations. African-American philosopher Cornel West (1993) points to the problems inherent in academic theories such as postmodernism:

> Even the critiques of dominant paradigms in the Academy are *academic* ones; that is, they reposition viewpoints and figures within the context of professional politics inside the Academy rather than create linkages between struggles inside and outside of the Academy. In this way, the Academy feeds on critiques of its own paradigms. These critiques simultaneously legitimate the Academy . . . and empty out the more political and worldly substance of radical critiques. This is especially so for critiques that focus on the way in which paradigms generated in the Academy help authorize the Academy. In this way, radical critiques, including those by black scholars, are usually disarmed. (p. 41)

The current academic pecking order privileges medicine, engineering, law, and the physical and natural sciences, all areas closely aligned with bureaucracies of power organized and administered through scientific principles. In this context, academic theories such as postmodernism seem unable to decenter the practices of their own institutions, let alone institutions of society overall.

In this academic context, postmodern treatment of power relations suggested by the rubric of decentering may provide some relief to intellectuals who wish to resist oppression in the abstract without decentering their own material privileges. Current preoccupations with hegemony and microlevel, local politics—two emphases within postmodern treatments of power—are revealing in this regard. As the resurgence of interest in Italian Marxist Antonio Gramsci's work illustrates (Forgacs, 1988), postmodern social theorists seem fascinated with the thesis of an all-powerful hegemony that swallows up all resistance except that which manages to survive within local interstices of power. The ways in which many postmodernist theorists use the heterogeneous work of French philosopher Michel Foucault illustrate these dual emphases. Foucault's sympathy for disempowered people can be seen in his sustained attention to themes of institutional power via historical treatment of social structural change in his earlier works (see., e.g., Foucault's [1979] analysis of domination in his work on prisons, and his efforts [1980] to write a genealogy linking sexuality to institutional power). Despite these emphases, some interpretations of his work present power as being everywhere, ultimately nowhere, and, strangely enough, growing. Historical context is minimized—the prison, the Church, France, and Rome all disappear—leaving in place a decontextualized Foucauldian "theory of power." All of social life comes to be portrayed as a network of power relations that become increasingly analyzed, not at the level of large-scale social structures, but rather at the local level of the individual (Hartsock, 1990). The increasing attention given to micropolitics as a response to this growing hegemony, namely, politics on the local level that are allegedly plural, multiple, and fragmented, stems in part from this reading of history that eschews grand narratives, including those of collective social movements. In part, this tendency to decontextualize social theory plagues academic social theories of all sorts, much as the richly textured nuances of Marx's historical work on class conflict (see, e.g., The Eighteenth Brumaire of Louis Bonaparte, 1963) become routinely recast into a mechanistic Marxist "theory of social class." This decontextualization also illustrates how academic theories "empty out the more political and worldly substance of radical critiques" (West, 1993, p. 41) and thus participate in relations of ruling.

In this sense, postmodern views of power that overemphasize hegemony and local politics provide a seductive mix of appearing to challenge oppression while secretly believing that such efforts are doomed. Hegemonic power appears as ever expanding and invading. It may even attempt to "annex" the counterdiscourses that have developed, oppositional discourses such as Afrocentrism, postmodernism, feminism, and Black feminist thought. This is a very important insight. However, there is a difference between being aware of the power of one's enemy and arguing that such power is so pervasive that resistance will, at best, provide a brief respite and, at worst, prove ultimately futile. This emphasis on power as being hegemonic and seemingly absolute, coupled with a belief in local resistance as the best that people can do, flies in the face of actual, historical successes. African Americans, women, poor people, and others have achieved results through social movements, revolts, revolutions, and other collective social action against government, corporate, and academic structures. As James Scott (1980) queries, "What remains to be explained . . . is why theories of hegemony . . . have . . . retained an enormous intellectual appeal to social scientists and historians" (p. 86). Perhaps for colonizers who refuse, individualized, local

resistance is the best that they can envision. Overemphasizing hegemony and stressing nihilism not only does not resist injustice but also
participates in its manufacture. Views of power grounded exclusively in
notions of hegemony and nihilism are not only pessimistic but also can
be dangerous for members of historically marginalized groups. Moreover, the emphasis on local versus structural institutions makes it difficult to examine major structures such as racism, sexism, and other
structural forms of oppression.[7]

Social theories that reduce hierarchical power relations to the level of
representation, performance, or constructed phenomena not only
emphasize the likelihood that resistance will fail in the face of a pervasive hegemonic presence but also reinforce perceptions that local, individualized micropolitics constitute the most effective terrain of struggle.
This emphasis on the local dovetails nicely with the increasing emphasis
on the "personal" as a source of power and with parallel attention to subjectivity. If politics becomes reduced to the "personal," decentering relations of ruling in academia and other bureaucratic structures seems
increasingly unlikely. As Rey Chow (1993) opines, "What these intellectuals are doing is robbing the terms of oppression of their critical and
oppositional import, and thus depriving the oppressed of even the vocabulary of protest and rightful demand" (p. 13). Viewing decentering as a
strategy situated within a larger process of resistance to oppression is dramatically different from perceiving decentering as an academic theory of
how scholars should view all truth. When weapons of resistance are theorized away in this fashion, one might ask, who really benefits?

Versions of decentering as presented by postmodernism in the American academy may have limited utility for African-American women and
other similarity situated groups. Decentering provides little legitimation
for centers of power for Black women other than those of preexisting
marginality in actual power relations. Thus, the way to be legitimate
within postmodernism is to claim marginality, yet this same marginality
renders Black women as a group powerless in the real world of academic
politics. Because the logic of decentering opposes constructing new centers of any kind, in effect, the stance of critique of decentering provides
yet another piece of the new politics of containment. A depoliticized
decentering disempowers Black women as a group while providing the
illusion of empowerment. Although individual African-American
women intellectuals may benefit from being able to broker the language
and experiences of marginality in a commodified American academic
marketplace, this in no way substitutes for sustained improvement of
Black women as a group in these same settings. In contrast, groups
already privileged under hierarchical power relations suffer little from
embracing the language of decentering denuded of any actions to decen-

ter actual hierarchical power relations in academia or elsewhere. Ironically, their privilege may actually increase.

Although many intellectuals live with this contradiction between the content of their theorizing and their actual material conditions, how they respond to this incongruity varies considerably. The version of decentering that I describe here represents but one option. There are others. As James Scott (1990) points out, "Those renegade members of the dominant elite who ignore the standard script . . . present a danger far greater than their minuscule numbers might imply. Their public . . . dissent breaks the naturalization of power made plausible by a united front" (p. 67). Those colonizers whose refusal is genuine represent more of a threat than is commonly imagined.

The Rubric of Deconstruction: Ironic Circles and Other Practices

In its most general sense, deconstruction encompasses a constellation of methodologies placed in the service of decentering. Although it has a specific meaning within literary criticism (see, e.g., Lather, 1991), it has taken on a more general meaning of dismantling truths. Deconstructionist methodologies aim to generate skepticism about beliefs that are often taken for granted within sociology, economics, psychology, and other social scientific discourses of modernity. Such beliefs include the following: philosophy grounded in reason provides an objective, reliable, and universal foundation for knowledge; "truth" resides in knowledge gained from the appropriate use of reason; knowledge grounded in universal reason, not in particular interests, can be both neutral and socially beneficial; and science, as the exemplar of the legitimate use of reason, constitutes the paradigm for all true knowledge (Flax, 1990). From a postmodern perspective, grand theories, or metanarratives, such as theories of institutionalized racism, Marxist theories of class exploitation, feminist theories of gender subordination, or Black feminist theories of intersectionality, are neither desirable nor possible. Any political action derived from such absolutes becomes similarly suspect. Since no theory of absolute truth is possible under postmodernism, postmodernist theorizing becomes reduced to producing a narrative that explores some socially constructed reality (Fraser & Nicholson, 1990). For this reason, postmodernist theorizing seems especially taken with textual analysis, seeing different texts or discourses as repositories for social constructions. Anything can be a "text" and thus is a possible candidate for deconstruction. By critiquing the texts of modernity, deconstructive methodologies also challenge the function of knowledge in legitimating power relations.

Thus, via deconstructive methodologies, postmodernism aims to reconfigure the relationship between scientific knowledge, power, and society. Any discourse or theory that claims to explain universals is rejected (Weedon, 1987; Fraser & Nicholson, 1990; Seidman & Wagner, 1992).

Deconstructive methodologies refute not just the context of scientific knowledge but also the very rules used to justify knowledge. In this regard, intellectuals from oppressed groups can put deconstructive tools to good use. For example, through a complex array of strategies, African-American women in sociology "deconstructed" scientific contexts of discovery and justification. Deconstructive efforts to dismantle notions of subjectivity, tradition, and authority offer clear benefits for Black feminist thought. For example, White male subjectivity has long stood as normative for "human." Deconstructing this narrow view by exposing its particularity creates space for Black women to be redefined as fully human and to accrue the "rights" associated with being human. Similarly, although the traditions taught in the academic canon masquerade as universal, they actually forward a narrow set of human experiences. Deconstructive methodologies applied to the canon have proved useful in allowing Black feminist traditions to be included in legitimated knowledge.

I have found such techniques especially useful in my own work. Specifically, my analysis of the emergence of Black women as agents of sociological knowledge relies on deconstructive techniques. I have identified how the absence of Black women from sociology participates in the self-definitions of sociology as a science (1988). Using insights from deconstructive methodologies, I treat sociology as text and challenge a series of sociological binaries—White male/Black female, objective/subjective, rational/emotional, scientist/nonscientist—as well as the effects of binary thinking on sociological subfields (e.g., race, class, and gender as separate areas of inquiry). Unpacking these binaries allows me to examine actual nonbinary social relations within sociology (specifically, the outsider-within location and its contributions to Black women's knowledge), as well as to sketch out a new conceptual space of intersectionality to replace the oppositions of race, class, and gender within sociology.

Despite these contributions, when it comes to the issue of the political implications of deconstructive methodologies for Black feminist thought, three issues merit special concern. The first involves the inability of deconstructive methodologies by themselves to construct alternative explanations for social phenomena. Deconstructive methodologies use three steps to "keep things in process, to disrupt, to keep the system in play, to set up procedures to continually demystify the realities we create, [and] to fight the tendency for our categories to congeal" (Lather, 1991, p. 13). The first step consists of identifying the binaries or oppositions that structure an argument—for example, the center and its double or Other. Reversing or displacing the dependent term from its negative position to a place that locates it as the very condition for the positive term constitutes the second step. The third step involves creating a more fluid and less coercive conceptual organization of terms. The goal is to transcend binary logic by simultaneously being both and neither of the binary terms (Lather, 1991). Thus, deconstructive methodologies aim to critique in order to evoke new ways of being outside the binary logic associated with science.

How often does this actually happen? Deconstructive methodologies yield impressive results when applied to ideas whose meanings emerge from binary categories such as Whites/Blacks, men/women, and other well-known dualities. In contrast to other approaches that fail to extract themselves from binary logic, deconstructive methodologies refute the very foundations of knowledge. However, when unanchored in power relations, the logic of deconstruction mandates that it apply deconstructive methodologies to its own practice. This can lead to multiple meanings, an endless string of interpretations, and the inability to construct alternative bodies of knowledge or truths (Bauman, 1992). Deconstructive methodology makes it difficult to develop alternative knowledge claims because to do so violates the fundamental premise of a deconstructive approach. Postmodernist theories refuse to have a list of the practices or principles of knowledge that are implied in their own methodology installed as new theoretical centers of process or content. As feminist theorist Linda Nicholson (1990) points out, "Postmodernism must reject a description of itself as embodying a set of timeless ideas contrary to those of modernism; it must insist on being recognized as a set of viewpoints of a time, justifiable only within its own time" (p. 11).

As the postmodern equivalent of the modernist dialectic, at best, deconstruction provides a corrective moment, a safeguard against dogmatism, a continual displacement. Unlike dialectical models that yield new constructions that are then challenged, deconstructive methodologies yield few new "truths." Because deconstructive methodologies must continually deconstruct their own practices, they cannot take themselves seriously. For example, the goal of Jacques Derrida's intertextuality is to generate an endless conversation among texts with no prospect of ever arriving at an agreed point (Bauman, 1992). Philosopher Richard Rorty's term *ironist* describes postmodernism's deconstruction of their own practices. Ironists hold radical and continuing doubts about vocabulary, realizing that arguments phrased in any vocabulary, including their own, remain questionable. "Irony creates confusion in order to say something that exceeds any logic," observes social theorist Charles Lemert (1992). In this sense, "irony is the discursive form of postmodernism" (p. 23).

Unfortunately, postmodern discourse that is overly dependent on this element of never taking itself too seriously lacks authority. As a result, deconstruction remains ineffective as a strategy either to produce new theories about oppression or to suggest new politics that might oppose it. For Black women grappling with a new politics of containment in the United States, deconstructive methodologies operate more effectively as a critique of power than as a theory of empowerment.[8]

Lacking an inherent authority to explain reality leads to a second important concern: How does deconstruction gain credibility, legitimation, and authority? If scientific standards of rationality, verifiability, empirical data, and objectivity are rejected, then what will take their place to make postmodernism convincing? Since deconstructive methodologies eschew internal mechanisms for legitimating themselves and, in fact, are dedicated to eradicating such absolutes, why does deconstruction have any credibility at all? I suspect that the answer lies in old ways of legitimating knowledge, that is, not so much in the logic of what is said but in the power of an interpretive community to legitimate what counts as knowledge (Mannheim, 1954). Although deconstruction appears to belong to no one, it actually constitutes the cultural capital or intellectual property of specific groups of intellectuals who claim deconstruction as their own (Bourdieu, 1990). In other words, for intellectuals who are skilled in deconstructing texts, the content of what is said remains less important than the ability of any given thinker to manipulate deconstructive methodologies. People become judged by their ability to create confusion in order to say something that exceeds any logic. In some situations, the more confusing, the more value attached to the knowledge.

Given this situation, the exclusionary language often associated with deconstruction, specifically, and postmodernism, in general, takes on added importance. On the surface, the tendency of some postmodern authors to write in nonlinear styles by presenting their work as a pastiche of many voices challenges long-standing practices of knowledge validation. Traditionally, less-established writers secure the validity of their own ideas by preparing a list of citations of important thinkers whom the author can use to legitimate his or her own work. Whether the less-established writer agrees or disagrees with the ideas of scholars with established reputations matters less than the placing of his or her arguments near theirs. Thus, under commodity relations, mixing a known commodity with a lesser-known one theoretically enhances the value of the lesser-known argument. Through its language practices, deconstruction claims to challenge this type of reputational hierarchy. In discussing her writing style, Patti Lather (1991) explains why she uses this method: "In my own writing, the accumulation of quotes, excerpts and repetitions is also an effort to be 'multivoiced,' to weave varied speaking voices together as opposed to putting forth a singular 'authoritative voice'" (p. 9). Despite Lather's good intentions, whom she actually cites matters greatly. Although presenting different voices as if they were equivalent appears to flatten existing power relations, in real-world academic politics, some voices garner much more credibility than others. Authors of all texts, even those claiming affiliation with postmodernism, must put forth "authoritative voices," or why would we read them? Unfortunately, in far too many texts, the author's "authority" hides behind an often confusing way of presenting material. As Lather points out, "Postmodernism is easily dismissed as the latest example of theoreticism, the divorce of theory and practice. This tendency is compounded by the desire of those who write in these areas to want to 'interrupt' academic norms by writing inside of another logic that displaces expectations of linearity, clear authorial voice, and closure" (p. 8). Unfortunately, writing within another logic necessarily excludes those who lack access to that new logic. It also damages those aiming to claim authorial voice within old logic.

Postmodern reliance on exclusionary language has tremendous implications for African-American women's struggle for self-definition. As a result of a continual critique carried out in exclusionary language, little room remains to construct an identity grounded in an authorial voice of Black women. Moreover, when coupled with the minimal decentering of actual power relations in higher education, commodifying and exchanging the new language of postmodernism has become a new form of cultural capital in the academic marketplace. By performing a powerful gatekeeping function for those who lack access to the exclusionary language of postmodernism, the rhetoric of deconstruction can be used to maintain the status quo. As is the case with any commodity, scarcity determines value. Despite postmodern lip service to decentering, the intellectuals writing articles, giving papers, populating the editorial boards of journals, and occupying positions of authority within academic disciplines seem remarkably similar to those of the past. To me, this is the ultimate postmodern irony. The ability to manipulate exclusionary language becomes yet another standard used to exclude Black women from legitimated intellectual work.

For those intellectuals currently privileged within hierarchical power relations, the issue of language appears to be a minor theme. As many speakers of Standard American English as a second language know, in the United States, language signifies access to or exclusion from communities of power. Not possessing the language, whether written or oral, remains a major device used to maintain boundaries between insiders and outsiders. Exclusionary language usually results in exclusionary outcomes. "I feel that the new emphasis on literary critical theory is as hege-monic as the world it attacks," argues Black feminist theorist Barbara Christian (1998). "I see the language it creates as one that mystifies rather than clarifies our condition, making it possible for few people who know that particular language to control the critical scene. That language surfaced, interestingly enough, just when the literature of peoples of color, black women, Latin Americans, and Africans began to move to 'the center'" (p. 71). How ironic—a major Black feminist literary critic sees the texts of Black women appropriated by and submerged within an exclusionary language of literary criticism that silences the creators of texts targeted for deconstruction.

Deconstruction raises a third issue especially germane to Black femi-nist thought. By challenging the notion of a self-defined Black women's standpoint, deconstructive methodologies undermine African-American women's group authority. Deconstructing identity, tradition, and author-ity simultaneously restricts Black women's appropriation of these marks of power in order to legitimate a Black women's standpoint. Black femi-nist literary critic Mae Henderson (cited in McKay et al., 1991) eloquently assesses the contradictory nature of deconstructive methodologies for African-American women:

> What is of value in the post-structuralist/deconstructionist school is that it aims at decentering what is essentially a white and male tra-dition and, in the process creating a space for the presentation of voices hitherto muted or marginalized. What is questionable is that it is a project that dismantles notions of authority . . . during a period when blacks, feminists and other marginalized groups are asserting authorship, tradition and subjectivity. (p. 23)

In essence, Black women cannot decenter Whiteness, maleness, and wealth as markets of power and at the same time claim the authority and power that these systems deliver. Contextualizing the rubric of decon-struction within hierarchical power sheds light on why the treatment of authority, subjectivity, and tradition within postmodernism presents spe-cial problems for Black women in the United States. Grounding their authority in their ability to speak self-defined voices as knowledge cre-ators, African-American women have carved out a modest authority emanating from a Black feminist standpoint (Collins, 1990). However, by rejecting the notion that "truths" such as Black feminist thought exist, deconstructive methodologies seem to be advocating the impossibility of objectivity or rationality for anyone, including Black women. From the relativist perspective implicit in extreme versions of postmodernism, no group can claim to have a better interpretation of any "truth," including its own experiences with oppression, than another. As a result, legitimation becomes plural, local, and embedded in practice (Fraser & Nicholson, 1990). Taken to its extreme, methodologically, there is no ownership over the intellectual product or thought produced. The shift becomes one of moving from conceptions of oppressed groups producing their own truths and politics to notions of the alienated subjects endlessly deconstructing all truths.

The postmodern critique of history and tradition is similarly troubling. If traditions are discredited as mere "stories" told by "different voices," oppression and other macro-social-structural variables not only recede into the background but also implode and are encapsulated with postmodern views of hyperreality. From this perspective, reality collapses and the hyperreal becomes a model of a "real without origin or reality" (Rosenau, 1992, xii). History and tradition are told not as linear narratives in which individual stories or voices are inserted, but as themes within individual narratives. Depending on which narrative is selected, this approach can lead to complete avoidance of specific political and social contexts. Because everything is contained within the narrative itself, no external, privileged position exists from which a critique of the absence of power dynamics may be launched. This move away from historical specificity that is associated with deconstruction resembles the long-standing apolitical ways of reading that are commonly associated with traditional literary criticism. "When historical specificity is denied or remains implicit," argues Valerie Smith (1989), "all the women are presumed white, all the blacks male" (p. 44).

Replacing group authority grounded in some notion of a shared standpoint emerging from a shared history with the notion of collectivities of alienated subjects linked by strings of discursive moments presents a fundamental difficulty for Black feminist thought. What good is a theory that aims to dismantle the authority that Black women in the United States have managed to gain via group solidarity and shared traditions? By removing altogether the notion of a "center," that is, a belief in some sort of verifiable, objective knowledge that one can deploy with authority, the rubric of deconstruction disempowers the very same historically marginalized groups that helped create the space for postmodernism to emerge. Moreover, one might ask who benefits from a methodology that appears unable to construct alternative explanations for social phenomena suitable for guiding political action; legitimates its own authority via exclusionary language; and dismantles notions of subjectivity, tradition, and authority just when Black women are gaining recognition for these attributes. It is one thing for African-American women and similarly situated groups to use deconstructive methodologies to dismantle hierarchical power relations. However, it is quite another for members of privileged elites to appropriate these same tools for different purposes.

The true irony is that elites can now undercut the bases of authority of those long excluded from centers of power while invoking their own fluency in the exclusionary language of postmodernism as the criterion used to keep the masses at the door.

The Rubric of Difference

The period from the 1880s through 1945 marked the high point of scientific interest in "racial difference" and "sexual differences." Thus, current scholarly fascination with the notion of difference within postmodernism represents less a new direction than a current manifestation of long-standing concerns of Western science. As Black feminist theorist Audrey Lorde (1982) contends, much of Western European history has conditioned us to see human differences in simplistic opposition to each other. "We have all been programmed to respond to the human differences between us with fear and loathing," argues Lorde, "and to handle that difference in one of three ways: ignore it, and if that is not possible, copy it if we think it is dominant, or destroy it if we think it is subordinate" (p. 115). Binary thinking legitimated by scientific authority proved central in generating this version of difference. Grounded in binaries such as White/Black, man/women, reason/emotion, heterosexual/homosexual, Eurocentric/Afrocentric, and self/other, science manufactured views of a world compartmentalized into either/or oppositional categories. Defining one side of the binary by the absence of qualities characteristic of the other side afforded one side normality and relegated the other to a deviant, oppositional Other. When linked to oppressions of race, gender, and sexuality, these ideas concerning oppositional difference helped construct the so-called essential group differences defined by biology and/or culture (Fuss, 1989).

Using deconstructive methods, oppressed groups have challenged these notions of oppositional difference. Rather than rejecting the lesser identities of being Black in White supremacist systems or of being women under patriarchal domination or of being gays, lesbians, and bisexuals confronting compulsory heterosexuality, these groups have claimed the identity of the Other in political organizing. Identity politics of this type usually reverse the negative connotation attached to oppositional difference by valorizing the formerly negative side of the term. For example, a "woman's way of knowing" associated with living in a female body characterized by cycles, flows, and change has been offered as part of the identity politics of feminism (Belenky et al., 1986). Similarly, Afrocentrism remains predicated upon notions of "soul" or the essence of "Blackness" (Gayle, 1971). Despite the limitations associated with these approaches, this type of identity politics fostered a group solidarity culminating in political resistance. Initially, its celebration of difference legitimated group challenges to the false universalism constructed from oppositional difference. However, in a context in which oppositional voices were routinely co-opted over time, politics organized around single axes of race, gender, or other badges of identity seemed increasingly doomed to failure.

Given the decreasing effectiveness of identity politics, what alternatives might a postmodern rubric of difference offer? Because postmodernism itself is a discourse of critique and not of construction, it hesitates to propose any alternative theories of difference other than those that emerge from within a critique. This stance of critique creates the illusion that postmodernism lacks a social theory of difference. However, the significance of the treatment of difference within postmodernism in the American academy may lie less in its critique of oppositional difference and more in insights about difference that are embedded and thereby constructed within its critique.

Two distinctive political implications of construction of difference within postmodernism merit review. The first deals with the important insight that the idea of difference is being increasingly commodified within relations of advanced capitalism (Jameson, 1984). In situations in which ideas and cultural capital are increasingly important in maintaining power relations, the idea of difference can be easily transformed into a commodity that can be sold in the global marketplace. Moreover, the difference to be commodified is an authentic, essential difference long associated with group differences of race, ethnicity, gender, economic class, and sexuality. "The Third World representative the modern sophisticate ideally sees is the unspoiled African, Asian, or Native American, who remains more preoccupied with her/his image of the real native— the truly different—than with issues of hegemony, racism, feminism, and social change," observes Trinh Minh-ha (1989, p. 88). Within this logic, essential differences become commodified, marketed, consumed, and eradicated. This commodification and marketing of difference not only strips it of political meaning but reformulates it as merely a matter of style. For example, consider the commodification of difference in practices such as using kente cloth as part of the uniforms of KFC employees in selected African-American neighborhoods. The emergence of Wiggers, a derogatory term applied to White youth who want to possess the trappings of Black hip-hop culture—rap music, baggy clothes, gang colors— but who shun the actual Black people who create that culture also illustrates this trend. The parallels abound, including a similarity between academics who invoke postmodernism to analyze the texts of Black women writers in academic departments that remain lily-White. As British cultural critic Stuart Hall (1992) points out, postmodernism has a "deep and ambivalent fascination with difference—sexual differ-ence, cultural difference, racial difference, and above all, ethnic differ-ence. . . . There's nothing that global postmodernism loves better than a kind of difference: a touch of ethnicity, a taste of the exotic, as we say in England, 'a bit of the other'" (p. 23).

Whether the object is Black women's texts or the latest hairstyles, cel-ebrating differences by commodifying and consuming them works to defuse the righteous anger of historically oppressed groups. After all, it's hard to remain angry if the "authentic" Afrocentric culture upholding one's Black identity politics becomes glorified in advertisements selling clothes, tanning products, lip collagen, and the like. Like the surveillance techniques applied to "welfare queens" and Black Lady Overachievers in the media, this focus on difference hides in plain sight new power rela-tions constructed from long-standing essential differences. Postmod-ernism seems to take a stand against this commodification. After all, much of the analysis of commodified difference is done by thinkers influ-enced by postmodernism. However, in its everyday practice, the way in which postmodernism has been inserted into the academy—for example, the appropriation of Black women's texts as voices—replicates practices associated with commodified differences.

A second implication of postmodern treatments of difference concerns the connections between difference and structural power. Up to this point, I have lumped all postmodernisms together, have treated them as one homogeneous discourse, and, some would say, have unfairly addressed my comments to one type of postmodernism. In actuality, the loose principles of postmodernism have been expressed along a contin-uum from extreme postmodern theories to reconstructive postmodern theories (Best and Keller, 1991).[9] One end engages in endless decon-structive activities, whereas the other tries to use postmodern ideas to reconstruct (but not construct) society. Conceptions of difference within postmodernism demonstrate similar patterns. However, arranging notions of difference along a continuum reveals a problematic analysis of structural power at both ends of the difference spectrum.

Because one end of the continuum—that occupied by extreme post-modern theories—takes deconstructivist reasoning to its logical extreme, it creates space for apolitical, often trivial differences. On this end, extreme constructionists argue that everything is constructed, all is in constant play, nothing is certain, and all social life consists of representa-tions. This end emphasizes individual differences as well as differences within individual identities. Group-based differences become devalued and erased within strict constructionist frameworks. Instead, virtually all experience is seen as being historically constructed. Thus far, I have framed much of my argument in opposition to this extreme constructionist posture, because I remain skeptical of any analysis that decouples difference from its moorings in hierarchical power relations. Doing so allows socially constructed differences emerging from historical patterns of oppression to be submerged within a host of more trivial "differences." Differences can then be discussed as a question of individual identity, leaving behind the troublesome politics associated with racism, sexism, and other oppressions. In describing this problematic use of difference, Black cultural critic Hazel Carby (1992) observes, "The theoretical paradigm of difference is obsessed with the construction of identities rather than relations of power and domination and, in practice, concentrates on the effect of this difference on a (white) norm" (p. 193). Or, as literary critic Chandra Mohanty (1989) states, such "difference seen as benign variation (diversity) . . . rather than conflict, struggle, or the threat of disruption, bypasses power as well as history to suggest a harmonious, empty pluralism" (p. 181). Under distributive paradigms of justice in which everyone is entitled to the same bundle of rights, for oppressed groups, diluting differences to the point of meaninglessness comes with real political danger.

The seeming fascination with identities of difference emerges in this practice of comparing stories of difference uprooted from ethical or political contexts. Such approaches minimize the significance of differences that are imposed from without—those resulting from oppression—and tacitly preserve the Enlightenment assumption of a freely choosing, rational human who is now free to be different. This is the liberal rational choice model applied to the issue of identity—one can emphasize or construct the different facets of one's subjectivity as differently as one chooses. Whereas views of individual identity that valorize difference can benefit those already positioned to enjoy them, such approaches remain less promising for oppressed groups with readily identifiable biological markers such as race, sex, and age. As cultural critic Coco Fusco (1992) points out:

> The complete transfer of identity essence to action, from innate property to consumable or reproducible activity, without any ethical referent or political grounding, is a form of cultural politics few blacks would benefit from, given the political and economic inequalities that continue to divide American society along racial lines. . . . This particular group of black cultural critics does not think of culture and identity without asking about politics—that is, about relations of power—and about ethics—that is, about responsibility. (p. 281)

Despite the surface validity of constructionist approaches to identity that emphasize not only individual differences but also differences within individuals, this approach erases structural power. Within systems structured along race, sex, gender, and sexual orientation, the fusion of these multiple identities determines one's overall place in a hierarchy. The fear is that once identity dissolves in a sea of meaningless differences, nothing stable and secure will remain upon which a politics of resistance can be built.

This emphasis on apolitical, often trivial differences that constitute individual subjectivity constrains Black women's collective political activism. As Black feminist theorist June Jordan (1992) points out, "The flipside of this delusional disease, this infantile and apparently implacable trust in mass individuality, is equally absurd, and destructive. Because every American one of us is different and special, it follows that every problem or crisis is exclusively our own, or, conversely, your problem—not mine" (p. 16). Jordan points out that difference taken to its deconstructed extreme meshes smoothly with notions of liberal bourgeois individualism so essential to contemporary forms of domination. We learn to think in terms of individual solutions to what are actually socially constituted problems. If everything becomes conceptualized as local, personalized, and constantly negotiated in relation to shifting constructions of difference, then it becomes difficult to conceive of collective action. As Hazel Carby (1992) notes, "Because the politics of difference work with concepts of individual identity, rather than structures of inequality and exploitation, processes of racialization are marginalized and given symbolic and political meaning only when the subjects are black" (p. 193).

Groups that have the most to lose appear least likely to replace both group-based notions of identity and any resulting identity politics with extreme constructionist understandings of difference. "Some of the most impassioned ramifications of the idea of an identity politics come from women of color," observes Diana Fuss (1989, p. 99). Both the critique of oppositional difference associated with identity politics and extreme constructionist treatments of difference that erase structural power ultimately undercut Black women's empowerment via self-definition. The development of Black feminist thought itself represents a hard-fought struggle to name oneself, to claim an identity that more accurately reflects Black women's lives and subjectivity. Individuals from groups that exercise real power run few risks in embracing identities organized around multiple differences, because they know that their power will remain intact. Consider Diana Fuss's (1989) comparison of lesbian and gay use of identity politics: "In general, current lesbian theory is less willing to question or to part with the idea of a 'lesbian essence' and an identity politics based on this shared essence. Gay male theorists, on the other hand . . . have been quick to endorse the social constructionist hypothesis and to develop more detailed analyses of the historical con-struction of sexualities" (p. 98). Since we must assume that Fuss's gay males are Whites, this group need not engage in identity politics because social institutions as currently constructed protect their interests.

The other end of the continuum on difference, occupied by recon-structive postmodern theories, appears unwilling to relinquish the possi-bility of a politically effective postmodernism organized around difference. Recognizing the implicit politics in any social theory, this end of the continuum aims to find a way to make postmodernism politically potent without supporting notions of oppositional difference. This end avoids extreme relativism by acknowledging the socially constructed nature of human differences of race, gender, and sexuality that emerge from "metanarratives," while simultaneously retaining a notion of some-thing that is "essentially" human. Claiming that human beings are all the same under the skin, this model of difference works well in a current color-blind and power-evasive era when to see racial differences is to be racist and to point out gender differences is to be sexist (Frankenberg, 1993). In this sense, this end of the continuum overlaps with, yet tries to distinguish itself from, liberal approaches to human difference.

Despite its contributions in maintaining a common ground for a poli-tics of resistance, this version of difference also has limitations. Although I sympathize with the spirit of this effort to balance universality (human essence) with specificity (human difference), the use of these terms may undercut the goals of this reconstructive project. Grounding theories of human difference on a bedrock of essential human qualities that typi-cally remains unexamined raises the troubling questions, who will con-stitute the essential human, and conversely, how will we know whether the list of "human essences" is, in fact, universal? Will White men remain, by default, the essential humans against which all others are now deemed equivalent? Moreover, this view of difference can suppress more radical political responses to domination of race, class, and gender. Attention to the racism, sexism, class exploitation, and heterosexism that constructed those differences can become diverted as an effort to toler-ate the differences that accompany an essentially human experience. Although humans can share commonalities, biology and culture can still be used to explain human differences. When differences are seen as benign, cosmetic variations on a common essence, tolerance becomes the strategy for constructing community. However, tolerance can be problematic. Historian Tessie Liu (1991) describes her puzzlement at the common reaction that her White students have when studying racism. Although they are highly sympathetic to the concerns of people of color, their tolerance is often coupled with the belief that racism does not affect them. Liu observes that tolerance "often encourages an ethnocentric understanding of differences because this form of comparison does not break down the divisions between us and them, between self/subject and other" (p. 266).

Unless they explicitly deal with structural power relations and wealth, expressions of the rubric of difference within postmodernism present a conflictual terrain for Black feminist thought. The belief that people are all the same under the skin and that difference is a matter of superficial commodified style meshes with long-standing beliefs that attribute differences of power and wealth among Blacks, women, and other historically oppressed groups as being their own fault. Hazel Carby (1992) queries, "At what point do theories of 'difference,' as they inform academic practices, become totally compatible with, rather than a threat to, the rigid frameworks of segregation and ghettoization at work throughout society?" (p. 193). To the end of this question, I might add, "and within academia itself."

Moving beyond Difference

Moving beyond difference (with its assumed question, difference from what?) to the conceptual terrain of intersectionality creates new conceptual space. By jettisoning the implicit assumption of a normative center needed for both oppositional difference and reconstructive postmodern tolerance for difference, intersectionality provides a conceptual framework for studying the complexities within historically constructed groups as well as those characterizing relationships among such groups. Drawing from the strengths of decentering and constructionist approaches to difference, the historical realities that created and maintain African-American women's particular history can be acknowledged, all the while recognizing the complexity that operates within the term *Black women.* Moreover, moving beyond difference to intersectionality may shed light on the mutually constructing nature of systems of oppression, as well as social locations created by such mutual constructions. In this sense, the postmodern legitimation of ongoing projects of oppressed groups to decenter power, deconstruct Western metanarratives, and rethink differences legitimates efforts to understand race, class, and gender intersectionality.

Despite these potential contributions, some might question whether postmodernism itself is a part of the new politics of containment dedicated to maintaining hierarchy in desegregated spaces. In his essay, "The New Politics of Difference," African-American philosopher Cornel West (1990) examines the oppositional nature not only of difference but of postmodernism overall:

The new cultural politics of difference are neither oppositional in contesting the mainstream . . . for inclusion, nor transgressive in the avant-guardist sense of shocking conventional bourgeois audiences. Rather, they are distinct articulations of talented (and usually privileged) contributors to culture who desire to align themselves with demoralized, demobilized, depoliticized and disorganized people in order to empower and enable social action and if possible, to enlist collective insurgency for the expansion of freedom, democracy and individuality. . . . For these critics of culture, theirs is a gesture that is simultaneously progressive and co-opted. (pp. 19–20)

Thus, the essential irony of the postmodern rubrics of decentering, deconstruction, and difference stems from the type of politics they suggest. Political struggles by people of color against racism, by women against patriarchy, and by gays, lesbians, and bisexuals against heterosexism fostered the decentering of Western beliefs about modernity. Yet the main ideas that grow from these struggles have been appropriated by a class of intellectuals who keep the language of resistance yet denude the theory of actual political effectiveness. This theory is then given back to people in a form that, because of the language used, becomes unusable for political struggle and virtually unrecognizable. The result is a discourse critical of hierarchical power relations that simultaneously fosters a politics of impotence.

Postmodernism neither gave African-American women license to decenter the authority of privileged White males nor planted the idea to do so. Rather, postmodernism provides powerful analytical tools and a much-needed legitimation function for those Black women and similarly situated intellectuals whose struggles take place in academic arenas. Thus, postmodernism can be a potentially powerful means for all of us who wish to challenge not just the results of dominant discourses but also the rules of the game itself.

Notes

1. Little agreement exists in classifying postmodern social theories. For example, whereas McGowan (1991) identifies poststructuralism, contemporary Marxism, neopragmatism, and feminism as four prominent variants of postmodern theory, Best and Kellner (1991) concentrate primarily on French poststructuralist theory as foundational for all postmodernist discourse. Despite clear differences among these areas, I discuss postmodernism as if it had a coherency that it neither seeks nor possesses. For discussions of poststructuralism, primarily as a

theory of literature, see Weedon (1987), Harding (1991), and McGowan (1991). For discussions of postmodernism that reflect its use as a more general theory of culture, see Lash (1990). For analyses of postmodernism and the social sciences, see Rabinow and Sullivan's (1987) edited volume on interpretive social science, Rosenau's (1992) analysis of postmodernism and the social sciences (1992), Bauman's (1990) approach to sociology and postmodernity, and Lash's sociology of postmodernity. Nicholson's (1990) introduction analyzing postmodernism and feminism raises concerns similar to those in this chapter, as does Best and Kellner's (1991) analysis of the politics of a range of postmodern social theories.

2. Sociologist Nicos Mouzelis (1995) makes a similar distinction. He notes that sociological theory can be divided into one of two types. Substantive theories constitute a set of interrelated statements trying to explain something that is new. Substantive theories can be proved true or false via empirical investigation. In contrast, a second approach defines theory as a conceptual framework—a paradigm, metatheory, or heuristic device—that provides guiding principles for exploring other social phenomena. In this chapter, my analysis of postmodernism evaluates its use under this second meaning. I have also presented it as a conceptual framework (see chapter 3 of *Fighting Words: Black Woman and the Search for Justice* [1998]).

3. Hartsock (1990) speculates that the social locations of two types of academics might influence the types of social theory they produce: "If, as a group, modernist theories represent the views of the colonizer who accepts, postmodernist ideas can be divided between those who, like [Richard] Rorty, ignore the power relations involved, and those, like [Michel] Foucault, who resist these relations" (p. 145).

4. In answering the question why such a relativist discourse exists now, Hartsock (1990) speculates, "I contend that these intellectual moves are no accident (but no conspiracy either). They represent the transcendental voice of the Enlightenment attempting to come to grips with the social and historical changes of the middle-to-late twentieth century" (p. 164). Henry Louis Gates Jr. (1992). also questions why the colonial paradigm seems to be returning as a metaphor when the field of studying colonialism has gotten more specific. Gates notes that "the sovereign-colony relation is simply another instance of the spatial topography of center and margin on which oppositional criticism subsists. And it is just this model that . . . has started to exhaust its usefulness in describing our own modernity" (p. 189). I suspect that the increasing attractiveness of colonial metaphors may stem from their attention to group-based, structural sources of power as compared to current emphases on individual sources of empowerment.

5. I find it fascinating that Michel Foucault, Jean Baudrillard, Jacques Derrida, Julia Kristeva, Roland Barthes, Jean-François Lyotard, and other French thinkers associated with the origins of postmodernism seem to have direct connections to the period of French decolonization, especially the Algerian Revolution. Despite these links, analyses of French poststructuralism and the emergence of postmod-

ernism in the 1960s routinely allude to the changing intellectual climate in France stimulated by student movements of 1968 and other social movements, leaving French colonial policy alone. Both Albert Memmi and Frantz Fanon write as colonial subjects dealing with the dismantling of old colonial centers that oppressed them. In contrast, the majority of thinkers viewed as important to postmodernism wrote from within the center of French colonial power, either as colonizers who accepted or as those who refused.

6. Pierre Bourdieu (1990) makes a similar point. He notes that the ambiguity of the positions adopted by the dominated among the dominant is linked to their "precariously balanced position. Despite their revolt against those they call the 'bourgeois,' they remain loyal to the bourgeois order, as can be seen in all periods of crisis in which their specific capital and their position in the social order are really threatened" (p. 145). My analysis emphasizes the structural conditions that frame the emergence of postmodernism at this time. It is not meant to be read as a discussion of the psychological makeup of individuals engaged in research from within postmodernist assumptions. This is where I part ways with Memmi, a theorist who wrote in a time when psychological models were more prominent in social theory and when the tendency to frame larger social conditions such as racism in the language of psychology (i.e., as prejudice and bias) was more prevalent.

7. In pointing out the problematic dimensions of postmodern views of power in the American academy, I am not arguing that local politics is irrelevant or is not growing. My argument addresses my concern with the absence of a structural analysis of power. I also recognize that many thinkers classified as postmodern, for example, Fredric Jameson, do write of large, global trends. One interesting issue is how thinkers are being reclassified. Jameson is more often identified with Marxism and linked to the Frankfurt school of critical theory, itself increasingly distinguished from the seemingly true postmodernists of France.

8. For a similar argument, see Dorothy Smith's (1987) recommendations concerning a sociology for women. Theories of power for women build on the "capacities, abilities, and strengths" of women and use these features as "guides for a potential transformation of power relationships" (Hartsock, 1990, p. 158). Postmodern theorists typically have no such agenda.

9. Many summaries of postmodernism allude to this continuum. Rosenau (1992) makes a distinction between skeptical and affirmative postmodernists. Best and Kellner's (1991) distinction between extreme postmodern theories (those of Baudrillard and parts of Lyotard, Foucault, Deleuze, and Guattari) and reconstructive postmodern theories (those of Jameson, Laclau and Mouffe, Flax, and postmodernist feminists) explores these relationships among variations of postmodernism most fully.

References

Amott, T. L., & Matthaei, J. (1991). *Race, gender, and work: A multicultural economic history of women in the United States.* Boston: South End Press.

Anzaldúa, G. (1987). *Borderlands: The new mestiza=La frontera.* San Francisco: Aunt Lute Books.

Appiah, K. A. (1992). *In my father's house: Africa in the philosophy of culture.* New York: Oxford University Press.

Awkward, M. (1995). *Negotiating difference: Race, gender, and the politics of positionality.* Chicago: University of Chicago Press.

Bauman, Z. (1992). *Intimations of postmodernity.* New York: Routledge.

Belenky, M. F., Clinchy, B. F., Goldberger, N. R., & Tarule, J. M. (1986). *Women's ways of knowing.* New York: Basic Books.

Best, S., & Kellner, D. (1991). *Postmodern theory: Critical interrogations.* New York: Guilford Press.

Blauner, B. (1972). *Racial oppression in America.* New York: Harper & Row.

Bonacich, E. (1989). Inequality in America: The failure of the American system for people of color. *Sociological Spectrum, 9*(II), 77–101.

Bordieu, P. (1990). I*n other words: Essays towards a reflexive sociology.* Stanford, CA: Stanford University Press.

Carby, H. (1987). *Reconstructing womanhood: The emergence of the Afro-American woman novelist.* New York: Oxford University Press.

Carby, H. (1992). The multicultural wars. In M. Wallace & G. Dent (Eds.), *Black popular culture* (pp. 187–99). Seattle, WA: Bay Press.

Chow, R. (1993). *Writing diaspora: Tactics of intervention in contemporary cultural studies.* Bloomington: Indiana University Press.

Christian, B. (1988). The race for theory. *Feminist Studies, 14*(I), 67–79.

Collins, P. H. (1990). *Black feminist thought: Knowledge, consciousness, and the politics of empowerment.* New York: Routledge.

Collins, P. H. (1998). *Fighting words: Black women and the search for justice.* Minneapolis: University of Minnesota Press.

Davies, C. B. (1994). *Black women, writing, and identity: Migrations of the subject.* New York: Routledge.

Dill, B. T. (1988). Our mothers' grief: Racial ethnic women and the maintenance of families. *Journal of Family History, 13*(4), 425–31.

DuCille, A. (1940). The occult of true Black womanhood: Critical demeanor and feminist studies. *Signs, 19*(3), 591–629.

Edwards, R. (1979). *Contested terrain: The transformation of the workplace in the twentieth century.* New York: Basic Books.

Flax, J. (1990). Postmodernism and gender relations in feminist theory. In L. J. Nicholson (Ed.), *Feminism/postmodernism* (pp. 39–62). New York: Routledge.

Forgacs, D. (Ed.). (1988). *An Antonio Gramsci reader: Selected writings, 1916–1935.* New York: Schocken.

Foucault, M. (1979). *Discipline and punish: The birth of the prison* (A. Sheridan, Trans.). New York: Schocken.

Foucault, M. (1980). *The history of sexuality, Volume I: An introduction* (R. Hurley, Trans.). New York: Vintage.

Frankenberg, R. (1993). *White women, race matters: The social construction of whiteness.* Minneapolis: University of Minnesota Press.

Fraser, N., & Nicholson, L. (1990). Social criticism without philosophy: An encounter between feminism and postmodernism. In L. J. Nicholson (Ed.), *Feminism/postmodernism* (pp. 19–38). New York: Routledge.

Fusco, C. (1992). Pan-American postnationalism: Another world order. In M. Wallace & G. Dent (Eds.), *Black popular culture* (pp. 279–84). Seattle, WA: Bay Press.

Fuss, D. (1989). *Essentially speaking: Feminism, nature, and difference.* New York: Routledge, Chapman, & Hall.

Gayle, A. (1971). *The Black aesthetic.* Garden City, NY: Doubleday.

Gates, H. L. (1992). *Loose canons: Notes on the culture wars.* New York: Oxford University Press.

Glenn, E. N. (1985). Racial ethnic women's labor: The intersection of race, gender, and class oppression. *Review of Radical Political Economics, 17*(3), 86–108.

Gordan, D., Edwards, R., & Reich, M. (1982). *Segmented work, divided workers: The historical transformation of labor in the United States.* New York: Cambridge University Press.

Hall, S. (1992). What is this "Black" in Black popular culture? In M. Wallace & G. Dent (Eds.), *Black popular culture* (pp. 21–35). Seattle, WA: Bay Press.

Harding, S. (1991). *Whose science? Whose knowledge? Thinking from women's lives.* Ithaca, NY: Cornell University Press.

Hartsock, N. (1983). The feminist standpoint: Developing the grounds for a specifically feminist historical materialism. In S. Harding & M. B. Hintikka (Eds.), *Discovering reality* (pp. 283–310). Boston: Reidel.

Hartsock, N. (1990). Foucault on power: A theory for women. In L. Nicholson (Ed.), *Feminism/postmodernism* (pp. 157–75). New York: Routledge.

hooks, b. (1990). *Yearning: Race, gender, and cultural politics.* Boston: South End Press.

Jameson, F. (1984). Postmodernism, or the cultural logic of late capitalism. *New Left Review, 146,* 53–92.

Jordan, J. (1992). *Technical difficulties: African-American notes on the state of the union.* New York: Pantheon.

Keith, M., & Cross, M. (1993). Racism and the postmodern city. In M. Cross & M. Keith (Eds.), *Racism, the city, and the state* (pp. 1–30). New York: Routledge.

Lash, S. (1990). *Sociology of postmodernism.* New York: Routledge.

Lather, P. (1991). *Getting smart: Feminist research and pedagogy with/in the postmodern.* New York: Routledge.

Lemert, C. (1992). General social theory, irony, postmodernism. In S. Seidman &

D. Wagner (Eds.), *Postmodernism and social theory* (pp. 17–46). Cambridge, MA: Blackwell.

Liu, T. (1991). Teaching the differences among women from a historical perspective. *Women's Studies International Forum, 14*(4), 265–76.

Lorde, A. (1984). *Sister outsider*. Trumansburg, NY: Crossing Press.

Mannheim, K. (1954). *Ideology and utopia: An introduction to the sociology of knowledge*. New York: Harcourt, Brace, & World.

Marx, K. (1963). *The eighteenth brumaire of Louis Bonaparte*. New York: International.

McGowan, J. (1991). *Postmodernism and its critics*. Ithaca, NY: Cornell University Press.

McKay, N., Collins, P. H., Henderson, M., & Jordan, J. (1991). The state of the art. *Women's Review of Books, 8*(5), 23–26.

Memmi, A. (1965). *The colonizer and the colonized*. Boston: Beacon Press.

Mercer, K. (1994). *Welcome to the jungle: New positions in Black cultural studies*. New York: Routledge.

Mohanty, C. T. (1989–90). On race and voice: Challenges for liberal education in the 1990's. *Cultural Critique*, Winter, 179–208.

Mouzelis, N. (1995). *Sociological theory: What went wrong? Diagnosis and remedies*. New York: Routledge.

Nicholson, L. J. (1990). Introduction. In L. Nicholson (Ed.), *Feminism/postmodernism* (pp. 1–18). New York: Routledge.

Rabinow, P., & Sullivan, W. M. (1987). The interpretive turn: A second look. In P. Rabinow & W. Sullivan (Eds.), *Interpretive social science: A second look*. Berkeley and Los Angeles: University of California Press.

Rosenau, P. M. (1992). *Post-modernism and the social sciences*. Princeton, NJ: Princeton University Press.

Said, E. W. (1978). *Orientalism*. New York: Vintage.

Said, E. W. (1990). Zionism from the standpoint of its victims. In D. Goldberg (Ed.), *Anatomy of racism* (pp. 210–46). Minneapolis: University of Minnesota Press.

Said, E. W. (1993). *Culture and imperialism*. New York: Alfred A. Knopf.

Scott, J. C. (1990). *Domination and the arts of resistance: The hidden transcripts*. New Haven, CT: Yale University Press.

Seidman, S. (1992). Postmodern social theory as narrative with a moral intent. In S. Seidman & D. Wagner (Eds.), *Postmodern and social theory* (pp. 47–81). Cambridge, MA: Blackwell.

Seidman, S., & Wagner, D. G. (1992). Introduction. In S. Seidman & D. Wagner (Eds.), *Postmodernism and social theory* (pp. 1–14). Cambridge, MA: Blackwell.

Smith, D. (1987). *The everyday world as problematic: A feminist sociology*. Boston: Northeastern University Press.

Smith, V. (1989). Black feminist theory and the representation of the "other." In

C. A. Wall (Ed.), *Changing our own words: Essays on criticism, theory and writing by Black women* (pp. 38–57). New Brunswick, NJ: Rutgers University Press.

Trinh, T. M-H. (1989). *Woman, native, other: Writing postcoloniality and feminism.* Bloomington: Indiana University Press.

Wagner, D. G. (1992). Daring modesty: On metatheory, observation, and theory growth. In S. Seidman & D. Wagner (Eds.), *Postmodernism and social theory* (pp. 199–220). Cambridge, MA: Blackwell.

Weedon, C. (1987). *Feminist practice and poststructuralist theory.* New York: Blackwell.

West, C. (1990). The new politics of difference. In R. Ferguson, M. Gever, T. M-H. Trinh, & C. West (Eds.), *Out there: Marginalization and contemporary cultures* (pp. 19–38). Cambridge, MA: MIT Press.

West, C. (1993). *Race matters.* Boston: Beacon Press.

Winant, H. (1993). Difference and inequality: Postmodern racial politics in the United States. In M. Cross & M. Keith (Eds.), *Racism, the city, and the state* (pp. 108–27). New York: Routledge.

Chapter 3

This Ethnography Called My Back:[1] Writings of the Exotic Gaze, "Othering" Latina, and Recuperating Xicanisma

Sofia Villenas

> We are Third World women writers. . . . In our common struggle and in our writing we reclaim our tongues. We wield a pen as a tool, a weapon, a means of survival, a magic wand that will attract power, that will draw self-love into our bodies.
>
> (Moraga & Anzaldúa, 1983, p. 164)

Introduction: *Mira!* The Anthro's Got *Chichis*

> We ask for revelations from others, but we reveal little or nothing of ourselves; we make others vulnerable, but we ourselves remain invulnerable. (Behar, 1993, p. 273)

Yolanda Fodora's drawing that dons the cover of *Women Writing Culture*, a collection edited by Ruth Behar and Deborah Gordon (1995), portrays a bare-breasted woman seated at a table, leaning into it, writing. She clutches a pencil in her hand, and her arm brushes gently against her nipples. The coloring of her body is purple, and her hair is multicolored in lavender, pinks, yellows, and greens. Different-shaped eyes look out from behind her where the sun has set in shades of bright orange and red, and a full blue moon is out. To Behar (1995), this drawing reminded her that most often in anthropology, bare breasts belong to the Other woman, "the native woman somewhere else, the woman who does not write, the *Kung!* woman, the Balinese woman, the *National Geographic* woman . . . breasts that can be seen, exposed, pictured, brought home, and put into books" (p. 1). Yet surely, the woman anthropologist, the writer of culture, also has breasts, "but she is given permission to conceal them behind her pencil and pad of paper" (p. 1). However, Behar continues, this concealment is perilous, as the woman anthropologist deceives herself into believing that her breasts are of no importance, "are invisible, cancer won't catch up with them, the male gaze does not take them into account" (pp. 1–2). While the woman writer, the woman anthropologist, may try to hide her breasts at the same time that she makes the Other woman into the object of her gaze, she too is observed and looked at, and she sees herself being seen. Somehow, her breasts are not invisible in the "discipline." She sees her writing scrutinized, "clutching her pencil, she wonders how 'the discipline' will view the writing she wants to do" (p. 2).

For Behar and Gordon (1995), this drawing captures the spirit of their edited collection, which is about centering women who write as anthropologists, always aware of how their identities are constructed as female within a patriarchal and Eurocentric discipline. It is about how women write culture and how culture writes women. For me, the drawing of the bare-breasted woman writer calls for an examination of precisely these interstices where, as women writers of culture, we often struggle against our own complicity in adopting and gazing through Western male eyes— eyes of objectivity, eyes of reason, eyes that are accustomed to taking pictures of the Other bare-breasted woman. Moreover, as we ask how women anthropologists are *written* by culture, we pay attention to the ways in which we are gazed upon with imperialist eyes and how that affects to whom we write and for what purpose. Indeed, an important question to ask is how we interpret and represent women's lives within the categories invented by anthropology and within the humanistic categories and narratives invented by the Enlightenment, modernity, and even postmodernity.[2] It is at this nexus (of writing culture and being written by culture) that we must become vulnerable and, figuratively speaking, expose our own breasts in contesting anthropology's perpetual project of inventing and redefining "culture" and "woman."

The questions of cultural representation and the ethnographer's complicity in reifying hierarchical power relations have been seemingly forever at issue. Gupta and Ferguson (1997a), in a somewhat mocking tone, reiterate the "guilt" questions anthropologists ask. They insist, "We have become used to a kind of anguished self-consciousness surrounding this issue. [For example, we ask:] How can 'we' anthropologists presume to speak for 'them' our informants?" (p. 24). But, as Gupta and Ferguson argue, these preoccupations assume an easy generalization of "an" anthropologist. Certainly, we are not all the same "we" anthropologists who occupy the same social/cultural/political locations of the Western, white, middle-class, heterosexual anthropologist (Gupta & Ferguson, 1997a; Villenas, 1996). As a Xicana and indigenous woman, I cannot escape my own experiences of marginalization and dislocation in this artificially bounded entity known as the United States of America. At the same time, I cannot escape the privilege afforded to me as a university professor. Yet precisely because we are not the same "we" anthropologists, our interrogations, revelations, and vulnerabilities in a feminist praxis generate intriguing insights and creations. For women-of-color feminist ethnographers, our uneasy predicament within the academic postmodern turn, which as Norma Alarcon (cited in Visweswaran, 1994) argues is "only a belated articulation of what the West's others have lived all along" (p. 90), requires that our voices become the conscious point of departure for intervention (Chow, cited in Visweswaran, 1994). An articulation of the ways in which women of color have *lived* the postmodern aesthetics of an oppositional consciousness (Sandoval, 1991), of border crossing and *mestizaje* (Anzaldúa, 1987) and of claiming space and place from the margins (hooks, 1984; Perez, 1991) can help us be reflexive and critical about how and why we take up the politics we do and why we evoke particular regimes of truth, such as spirituality and faith. In my case, a Xicanista *indigenista* interpretation emerges in the tensions of understanding resilience and survival in our own families and communities and of (re)creating Xicanisma as women who are the creatrix and visionaries of our worlds (Castillo, 1994). As a "native" ethnographer, how I make sense of my mother's life has everything to do with my own experiences, journeys, spiritualities, and struggles. Indeed, a Xicanista ethnography embedded within an articulation of the ways in which we are forced to experience the postmodern aesthetics in our everyday survival (Sandoval, cited in Visweswaran, 1994) can emerge from Behar's (1996) insistence that we practice an anthropology that breaks the heart—one that requires that our own revelations and vulnerabilities be exposed just as we expose those of the women we come to know in our field sites.

In this chapter, I narrate my own experiences as a Xicana, a mother, and an ethnographer of Latino communities who attempted to write about and represent Latina mothers in text. Indeed, like many women of color who reach the pinnacle of the academy, I find that being "officially" sanctioned to do critical ethnography is a bittersweet triumph. The "minority" researcher finds herself caught within and against the colonizing nature of ethnographic research. Racialized identities are often manipulated and commodified vis-à-vis majority culture in the research field and in the classroom, and the woman-of-color researcher herself remains embedded in and even reinforces the "colonizer/colonized" opposition structured by traditional ethnography (Villenas, 1996). I seek, then, to expose and interrupt the representation of the Other "bare-breasted woman" by addressing my own complicity in textually framing the lives of the Latina mothers I worked with so they would fit the anthropological tradition of the exotic. In analyzing my complicity, I am wary of my own claims about these women's lives, claims that cannot be divorced from hegemonic definitions and categories of culture, "woman," and education. Through an exploration of the ways in which the women "told" and "performed" their stories as well as my role as co-constructor and co-performer in these stories, I question the textual representations and interpretations emerging from traditional and postmodern ethnographic and feminist categories of seeing. Western ways of sense-making intersect with my Xicanista vision in tensions that make it difficult to get at the complexity and multiplicity of our "education" stories and "educated" identities.

Mr. Anthropology Meets Ms. Postpositivism Who's Going out with Mr. Feminisms but Re-Encounters Her Ex-otic Who Is Now Critically Married to a Xicana

Yes, this is my story, a Xicanista story, but one created within the interstices of critical ethnography, postmodern feminisms, and the persevering imperialist gaze of the Exotic. In order to situate my story, I find it imperative to discuss the ways in which the exotic has endured the continual reinventions of "culture," including my own Xicanista invention.

Anthropology invented the modern concept of culture. As Wagner (1981) argues, "The study of culture is in fact *our* culture; it operates through our forms, creates in our terms, borrows our words and concepts for its meanings, and re-creates us through our efforts" (p. 16). Moreover, anthropology itself was created within a centuries-old discourse of the Exotic,[3] a discourse historically rooted in conquest, expansionism, and colonialism. Indeed, "culture" and "exotic" were undetachable terms that went hand in hand to describe not only the subjects of the project of anthropology but also the relationship of anthropology, as a Eurocentric Western discipline, with the preservation of the logic of the world order. The discipline became embedded within the historical condition of colonialism and imperialism, and it developed a fascination with the exotic that was also a mirror of the ways in which West and East and North and South (First World versus Third World) were defined. In this context, anthropology was also complicit in defining the self/Other dichotomy. Self was the Western rational man, while East/Other was the "oriental," the primitive, the exotic, and most importantly, a category full of "colorful" culture. McLaren (1998), too, argues that, even today, culture remains invisible in the identities of the Western Self:

> Culture is seen as something very much linked to passion, something that is perhaps associated with irrationality or nonrationality

and those that don't have an ethnic attachment are more rational, they're more scientific, they're more objective. And it's those ethnic groups with all the culture, that's where you'll find the passion, the irrationality, people getting worked up about nothing. (interview)

Thus, the invention of the category of culture and its assignment to those exotic Others allows for, as McLaren points out, the ascription of the virtues of the Enlightenment (rationality, objectivity) to the Western white male self. In this way, American anthropology came into the world complicit in reifying the East/West, exotic/normal, self/Other dichotomies.

This complicity has remained a constant even through changing conceptions of culture. Enrique Trueba (1998, interview) summarizes how the concept of culture has experienced a crisis. In the nineteenth century, anthropologists viewed culture as traits that could be identified and considered in isolation. In this mode, as Stocking (1985) argues, the representation of cultures was comprised of "artifacts" arranged linearly from "primitive" to advanced, to "convey an ethnocentric message of conservative evolutionary gradualism" (p. 8). The early twentieth century brought a major shift in the concept of culture. With Boas and his protégés, such as Ruth Benedict and Edward Sapir, anthropology began to consider culture in more holistic terms. In other words, a consideration of the "artifact" could no longer be divorced from the language and multiple meanings attached to it. Moreover, Boas forwarded cultural relativism as a challenge to studies of racial superiority, though in a problematic way. Visweswaran (1998) suggests that Boas, in fact, fueled the "machine of scientific racism" (p. 70) by expunging race from the social sciences and assigning it to biology. Indeed, as Visweswaran argues, U.S. anthropology, or more precisely Boasian anthropology, failed miserably in its conception of culture and continues to do so, particularly in its failure to develop an understanding of race.

These crises of cultural racism and representation carried over into the 1950s when anthropology went home both literally and figuratively. Anthropologists came back from faraway places to study urban and rural communities in the United States, and they came home thinking of culture as "here" in the ways in which all people think about and configure their worlds in their everyday practices (Trueba, 1998). The concept of culture has been further developed in more recent work concerning new directions in anthropology (see Gupta & Ferguson, 1997a; Levinson, Foley, & Holland, 1996). Gupta and Ferguson (1997a) challenge anthropologists to move away from thinking of culture as the orderly, shared, and agreed upon and, instead, to link the local with "contemporary processes of cultural globalization and transnational culture flows" (p. 5).

They argue, "The emphasis is on the complex and sometimes ironic political processes through which cultural forms are imposed, invented, reworked, and transformed" (p. 5).

Yet with a more sophisticated understanding of anthropology's invention of "culture," the many crises in the modern concept of culture continue to emerge (albeit in varying forms) in the discipline as critical anthropologists struggle to create an anthropology that interrogates its complicity in domination. Almost 15 years ago, the crisis of representation, specifically textual representation, was acceptably interrogated in Clifford and Marcus's (1986) ground-breaking work, *Writing Culture: The Poetics and Politics of Ethnography*. This edited collection examined cultural representations and positioned anthropological writing within the poetic, the political, and partial truths. Ethnographers were no longer neutral and transparent observers and writers of culture, but rather were exposed in their own positionalities and worldviews. As Behar (1995) writes, "this 'new ethnography' was also expected to reflect a more profound self-consciousness of the workings of power and the partialness of all truth, both in the text and in the world" (p. 4).

However, the Writing Culture project itself reified the White male prerogative by failing to include and address women's anthropological writings that have long been a cross between anthropology and literature.[4] The use of personal voice has generally been dismissed as an undesirable trait of women's writing; however, men have co-opted it and recast it as "experimental" and "reflexive" (Behar, 1995). Indeed, feminist anthropology has challenged the ways in which anthropology writes women even as they have engaged the politics and poetics of how they write and represent other women. Women anthropologists confront and contest a Western male anthropology and, in turn, are challenged by working-class women and women of color who force a confrontation with cultural elitism, racism, white supremacy, and essentialist views of "woman." The intersections of critical ethnography with women-of-color womanisms/feminisms, critical race theory,[5] and poststructuralism lead us to embrace agendas of liberation that seek to uncover the multiple forms of oppression for women, while, at the same time, rejecting metanarratives and claims to truth. The postmodern imperative calls attention to the metanarrative character of "liberatory" and "emancipatory" agendas, while women of color call attention to the ways in which representations and interpretations of their lives are filtered through Western-based feminist lenses.

Moreover, in a continuation of the crisis of representation and adrift in postmodernism, the exotic continues to rear its head in feminist ethnography. Behar (1993) argues that "critiques of Western feminism by women of color make painfully obvious the ways in which even the most well-meaning first world women have unselfconsciously created a cultural other in their images of women of color upon whose backs they have built analyses that establish their authority and right to speak about what is a meaningful female life"[6] (p. 271). In other words, in naming and defining for other women what constitutes oppression and emancipation, there is no room for redefinitions of feminisms and womanisms that do not fit the experience of an almost grand narrative of "feminist" living. On the other hand, in an attempt to highlight women's agency and reverse the arrogance of Western-based feminisms, feminist anthropologists exoticize Third World women by defining their culture and lives in terms of "resistance." Yet, as Behar (1993) asserts, defining a female culture of resistance problematically extends "the Western feminist self-representation of what constitutes agency to their subjects" (p. 271). Certainly, resistance as interpretation may be a new wave of exoticism as it becomes chic and in vogue to frame people's actions as empowered "resistance."

Where, then, does the feminist anthropologist go to escape the grips of anthropology's complicity in neocolonialism and its reification of the exotic if she wishes, within the tensions of a postpositivist inquiry, to understand, emancipate, and deconstruct (Lather, 1991) and to expose the politics of authority and textual representation? How does the tenuous engagement of feminisms with poststructuralism serve a feminist anthropology? Certainly, an important contribution of feminist poststructural critiques to feminist ethnographic inquiry is the emphasis on the mutual co-constructedness and performance of identities. In this identity work, gender, sexual orientation, race, and class become verbs, rather than predetermined static categories within which to fit women (Mohanty, 1991). We need to understand how women are constituted and produced within relations and discourses of power embedded in kinship relations, religion, the economy, and so forth, while simultaneously looking at how women are implicated in forming these relations (Mohanty, 1991).

My own story of my work with Latina mothers in North Carolina is located within a performance analysis of our co-constructed identities in creating oral life histories. An emphasis on performance allowed for a passionate and nuanced look at the ways in which we created "educated" identities in relation to one another while, at the same time, negotiated and re-created practices and discourses of power (in the Foucauldian sense). Yet as I wrote about these women in my dissertation, I became complicit in othering Latina as I textually represented the mothers' performances with categories that reflected my unexamined embrace of a male Western anthropology. While I am not the same "we" anthropologist, I internalized the male Western gaze (albeit, not unproblematically) and became complicit in anthropology's reification of the exotic by privileging some life histories (those that showed resistance) over others. I found that postmodern analytics (such as a performance analysis) do not necessarily work against the ethnographic desire to find the exotic story of resistance, a Western colonial desire. Since postmodernism conceals its own power, it does not somehow "protect" the ethnographer from replicating dominant discourses. Rather, postmodern sensibilities derived from our own lives of struggle and resilience help us ask questions about our complicity and resistance in our methods and representations.[7] An examination of my textual representation of these Latina mothers reveals an ongoing journey to examine the very tensions of feminisms and critical ethnography, indeed, the interstices of women writing culture and of culture writing women (Behar, 1995).

Performing Theories of the Flesh

In thinking of and writing my research with Latina mothers, I move back and forth from the moments of performance and our friendships to my own connected world of motherhood and family, from an intimacy of community to ethnographer/researcher for the white world, from Hispana to Chicana, from "educated" to "uneducated," from colonizer to colonized and then back again.

I spent 2 years, from 1993 to 1995, as a participant observer in English as a Second Language (ESOL) classes and parenting classes for Latina mothers[8] who were recent immigrants and members of a newly forming Latino community in Hope City (a pseudonym), North Carolina. Latinos and Latinas in this town of about 6,000 residents now comprise 38 percent of the total population, with most of the growth having occurred only since 1992. Over the 2 years, I conducted in-depth, oral life history interviews with 10 Latinas of diverse backgrounds who came from Latin American countries such as Mexico, El Salvador, Guatemala, Honduras, and Colombia. In the interviews, the women performed very similar models of the "educated" person (Levinson, Foley, & Holland, 1996). Their/our models for raising "educated" and "knowledgeable" children are based on a foundation of morality and respect for family and kin (see Carger, 1996; Delgado-Gaitan & Trueba, 1991; Valdés, 1996). However, the ways in which they told about this moral education reflected their aims and role (against and alongside mine) in the interviews as well as the ways in which they experienced education in their public and private lives.

My passion in writing about Latina mothers is influenced by Moraga and Anzaldúa's (1982) edited collection, *This Bridge Called My Back: Writings by Radical Women of Color*, which foregrounds the self-theorizing of women of color through the stories and poetry of their lives. Soyini Madison (1994) asserts that, "theories of the flesh reflect the distinctive interpretations of the world carved out of the material realities of a group's life experiences" (p. 49). She argues that an analysis of performance guides one to the location of this self-theorizing or "theories of the flesh." Theories of the flesh are performed in the narration of oral life histories and framed by cultural motifs of collective memory.[9] They express "the harmony, the indifference, the ambiguity, the conflict, and so on, existing between self and society" (Chanfrault-Duchet, 1991, p. 81). It is precisely these theories of the flesh that I intended to reveal as I talked with and interviewed the Latina mothers in Hope City. It is also these theories of the flesh, or the performance of the fit between self and society (Chanfrault-Duchet, 1991), that I hoped to reveal in my textual representation of these women's lives. In my analysis and writing, I focused on the ways in which the women told their stories and made decisions about word choices and verb tenses as well as the gestures, movements, feelings, and emotions they expressed. By focusing on the interaction between the telling (the moment of acting and feeling in the interview) and the told (the content), I attempted to create a story that stressed the textual and the process, the worldview and the practice.

A performance analysis also called for implicating my own actions, feelings, and responses as well as my own "educated" identities co-created within a cultural collective memory of relationships among women and the distinct and diverse processes of teaching and learning rooted in our families and communities. Furthermore, these co-performances and co-constructions of "educated" identities also took place within a web of power relations that linked gendered, classed, and social hierarchies to the larger cultural processes of immigration and globalization as well as to larger discourses of the Other woman. In this manner, looking at the particular moments of performance in my interactions with the Latina mothers of Hope City is something akin to feminist ethnography, which is necessarily preoccupied with the contradictions of women talking to women. Behar (1993) suggests that "feminist *ethnography* has begun to emerge as distinct from feminist anthropology in its reflexiveness about the politics of practicing feminism and experimental cultural writing and in taking as its focus women's relationships" (p. 301).

Likewise, my relationships with the women were at the heart of looking at our co-performances and co-constructions of identities. The women challenged my feminist politics, my education, and my ways of teaching and learning as a mother and daughter. Within a feminist ethnography, I was challenged to *enfrentar el hogar* (face the challenge of the home) and theorize my own contradictions of being "educated" both in *el hogar* (the home) and in the university as an ethnographer of education. However, it is precisely through these tensions of "professional training," coupled with the contradictions of my own "home training," that I textually constructed the Latina mothers of my study as the exotic Other, the mundane Other, and the reflective self. In fact, I privileged those oral narrations of women who performed exotically both in the telling and the told, rather than those of women who co-performed with me the ordinary and the everyday.

I came to a performance analysis of my interviews with the women quite by accident. As I encountered, heard, and later reflected on each woman's life history of teaching and learning, what struck me most was not so much the content of their stories, but rather the ways in which the interviews had proceeded and the feelings and emotions of exhilaration, confusion, and sometimes anger I felt as I listened to them talk and, later, as I left their homes. What I witnessed in the moments of interview and then in reflecting back were the powerful ways in which these women narrated their educational lives and beliefs—some with a painful and powerful urgency, others with a matter-of-fact tone, and still others with the playfulness of camaraderie. I also remember what these interviews did to me—how I left some feeling like a very "uneducated" person and others, very "educated" in comparison. Still others I left feeling reflected and affirmed. The women's ways of telling touched the contradictory and complex cords of my own education as a Latina daughter and mother, as a Chicana/Indigena activist, and as a university-trained educator.

Performing a Different and "Special" Education— A.K.A. The Exotic

Nora, Marisela, and Carmen performed as teachers for me. They took control of the interview, not letting me get a word in edgewise, and taught me the "special" and "different" educations they had learned and had also taught their own children. Nora, a mother of three from Honduras, explains the different and special education she received from her father:

> No, well, my father, he, he was not an educated man of, how should I call it? University educated, no. He was a humble man . . . [In a serious and fast tone] he had a very different education, because well since he grew up that way [in a home with religious people], he was very different in raising us. He taught us that between brothers and sisters, we had to view each other as equals. He taught us that if one had something, then the other one would have it too, if not then there wasn't anything for anybody, *verdad*? (right?) That everything had to be fair. And he taught us that we shouldn't be selfish with our brothers and sisters. . . . He raised us, like I say, in

a humble home, but with HIS education that he BROUGHT from where he CAME from.

Moreover, these women were very experienced in the public sphere and in *batallando* (battling) with public institutions, including schools, and even against the government, as in the case of Marisela. In Guatemala, Marisela became involved in human rights campaigns and fled to avoid political persecution. She left behind four children, including a son who had barely turned 4 months old. Yet Marisela framed her story in terms of her strength and resilience, speaking proudly of her endurance in crossing through the hot deserts of northern Mexico. Indeed, all three of these women performed their interviews as stories of triumph over adversity. They triumphed because they were different from others. They possessed a "different" and "special" education, and they showed and performed this special education. Carmen from El Salvador, who was illiterate in her native language, explained that while her parents did not know how to read or write, she received a "good" education, which she has passed on to her 17 children.

> When they [her children] could work, it was to give them two, two educations, one of work from the morning until noon, and from noon on [to school]. . . . And now thanks to God, I don't have any that can't read or write. Yes, I gave them all *crianza* (an upbringing).

Carmen also talked about how she learned from common sense. According to her, raising a family just takes common sense, and learning is about watching or "assimilating the essence," as Marisela put it. Indeed, these were the lessons the women performed in their telling. They took on the role of teacher as if I were their daughter, younger sister, or pupil. They spoke about teaching their children indirectly through stories and *consejos* (advice or homilies in narrative form) with the goal of imparting to their children knowledge they will be able to adapt and make sense of in any context. These women performed their stories and *consejos* with full expression and role playing, as if reliving the moment in which they gave and received these lessons. In the process of performing their *consejos*, I was also *aconsejada* (given advice) and made to assimilate the essence of the storytelling. Their "educated" identities were thus performed as teachers and as intelligent, resourceful women. I performed as "uneducated," and, indeed, I was, since, for these women, I did not have the experiential knowledge of "educating" children properly. My formal training within our co-created definition of "education" did not count for much.

Although at first I did not like for the women who performed a "special" education literally to take over the interview, I did in fact thoroughly enjoy their stories and their narration of them. Further, *all* the women in the study spoke of the same kind of moral education. There would be no disagreement among them with respect to the moral education they subscribed to, one that should begin in the home. But why did I accept my place as pupil and daughter with the women who told of a special and different education, and why did I enjoy these stories and rave about them in my dissertation? This is about the "messiness" of feminist ethnography. Certainly, I was writing for myself with a Xicanista vision—inventing a Xicanista ethnography rooted in the knowledge of these women's ways of teaching and learning. I wrote with pride and celebration, for this education was also my own. But I also wrote with anger because these ways of knowing were discounted as "backward" and not equal to Western conceptions of child rearing. For example, local newspaper headlines such as "Program Enables Hispanics to Become Better Mothers" were meant to highlight community parenting classes, but at the same time, they announced to the English-speaking residents that Latinas were inadequate mothers. My aims were for a "liberatory" kind of research that could aid in changing oppressive responses to our ways of teaching and learning. The forcefulness of the mothers whom I interpreted as performing a special and different education served well both the critical and the feminist purposes of ethnography precisely because they explicitly stated how their education was special and good and even better than U.S. mainstream ways of teaching and learning.

Moreover, in trying to reverse the arrogance of a Western-based feminisms, I exoticized and romanticized these "Third World" women by defining them within the terms of a female culture of resistance. They were exotic with exotic histories and lives, women who faced the challenges of war and persecution. Their stories were stories of triumph over adversity—of war, political activism, and fighting back. I framed these women as empowered feminists. It is not only the women's struggles against social injustice that can be framed as resistance but also their practices of seizing the interviews for their own purposes, performances that resisted the desires of the ethnographer. Michelle Fine (1994) writes that critical and counterhegemonic ethnographers often practice subtle forms of ventriloquy. She defines ventriloquy as a condition of "truth" told with no name, no gender, no race, no class, no author. Referring to her own work, Fine says that it was easy to gather up the voices of dissent from youth in order to tell her story framed as political resistance. However, she had trouble with the nuanced narratives of adults who often repeated the scripts of dominant discourses. Likewise, I embraced the performances of a "special" education precisely because it was easy for me to talk about them and fit them into a resistance paradigm. In this way, I interpreted and represented the women's lives, othering them within the categories invented by anthropology and even within post-modern feminist interpretations of what constitutes agency (Behar, 1993). The women's "in your face" and take charge performances were easy to name in terms of "exercising agency." In contrast, the tables were turned when I was in charge and therefore felt more "educated" with the women who performed what I thought was the ordinary. The mundane was created for me by the lens of the exotic.

Un Buen Comportamiento: Performing Duty— A.K.A. The Mundane Other

Lydia, Alba, and Natalia answered my questions instead of telling their stories and thus seemingly performed "dutifully" and "responsibly" as interviewees. They seemed to accept the power of my university affiliation. Moreover, their answers about their own educations and the education of their children emphasized duties and behaviors, *los quehaceres, limpieza, comportamiento* (housework, cleanliness, good behavior). These answers were short and blunt and framed with *nomás* (just that, or that's all). *Nomás* emphasized the taken-for-granted, the mundane, and the ordinary teaching and learning that was rooted in the everydayness of their lives, and my life as well. To Alba, for example, these were necessary, obvious everyday lessons that she told in a matter-of-fact voice framed by the words, *pues nomás* (well just . . .). Alba explained what she had learned:

> *Pues nomás* (Well just) to work, in other words like in the house. Important things are the *limpieza* (cleaning) and then later it's like for each person to . . . try to *vivir bien* (live decently) in the state of marriage and then for the person who hadn't married yet, *pues* to *portarse bien* (behave properly) as a single woman . . . *portarse bien* and all that. Not to be running around.

Alba's education included learning to keep *un hogar* (a home) and to *portarse bien* (behave properly) morally in terms of virtuous female behavior. Framed as *nomás*, it was as if she were saying to me, "Of course, what else could there be?" *Nomás* emphasized what I thought to be the ordinary and everyday aspects of her education (and mine).

Indeed, these women did not talk about themselves performing in the public sphere or interacting with public institutions. They did not describe their lives as *batallando* (battling); neither did they describe their educational lives as special or different. Their lives and educations were rooted in the activities of *el hogar* (the home) and yet in collectivity with kin and friends. In their narratives, they emphasized duty to their children in all circumstances. Yet they wrestled with the experience of immigration and of trying to make sense of the changes it brought to their ways of raising children. The boundaries of freedom and licentiousness were compared and questioned many times in our conversations.

I felt very uncomfortable, not only with the short and blunt answers I received but also with their content—the ways in which these women defined education. In my way of thinking, the education they were telling me about was inadequate. I felt *more* educated when I was with Lydia, Alba, and Natalia, who spoke of an everyday kind of moral education, and *less* educated with Nora, Carmen, and Marisela, who forcefully performed a "different" and "special" education. At the same time, this moral education that seemed inadequate was quite familiar—*quehaceres* and *limpieza* were my own upbringing. I was very much in conflict with what I thought was their emphasis on the perpetuation of women's subordination in the home, including the sanctioned behaviors around being or not being married. While Nora, Carmen, and Marisela also emphasized women's duties and virtue, still, to me they represented the romantic rebels and idealists as well as the mother figures and *consejo* givers. In contrast, the women whom I categorized as performing dutifully were rooted very much in the "reality" of the everyday, doing and acting in a world they experienced on a day-to-day basis. Moreover, these women were confident and secure in their abilities to raise "educated" children.

What should I have done with the stories that stress the mundane and the everyday; stories that talk about *quehaceres, limpieza,* and *comportamiento* (house chores, cleanliness, and behavior)? Not only was the mundane too close to my own upbringing (one that I have rebelled against) but also, at the time, it was too conservative for my feminist perspective that defines a certain kind of feminist living—one that does not include definitions of virtuous womanhood, pride in always serving the husband, and an embrace of *el hogar* (the home space). There did not seem to be room in my feminist analysis to understand this kind of Latina womanism because it was too familiar, too full of tensions, and a kind of womanism I believed I had abandoned in my own life. Moreover, for the critical Xicana ethnographer, it was too "boring" for an ethnographic tradition that is rooted in the exotic. In the ethnographic tradition of the exotic, there is no room for the mundane and the ordinary; in critical feminism's anthropological schema, there is no room for the routine and the everyday.

While, historically, "ritual" has been the center of discussions of cultural Others, Rosaldo (1993) argues that everyday life processes are important and that rituals are merely points along the trajectory of everyday life. With the wave of exoticism expressed in cultures of resistance, what gets left behind is the self-theorizing that is rooted in the mundaneness of everyday practices. I found nothing glamorous about the mundaneness of *el hogar* (the home) as some Latina mothers performed it. I created the exotic Other with Nora, Marisela, and Carmen and the mundane Other with Lydia, Alba, and Natalia, thus making something less of their lives. My dilemma is whether, if I go beyond *nomás*, I will be creating another grand interpretation that is exclusively my own and therefore a violation of their theories of the flesh, their everyday lives created within ordinary routines and traditions. The "critical Western feminist" lens would have me focus on their oppression, yet the Xicanista space I/we am carving out is not only a political space but also one of faith, spirituality, and beauty. Why did I think I needed some grand theory to express lives that were performed as full and satisfying? I had to learn that these women, like the women I had constructed as resistant, are creators of dignified spaces, and they are also my own self.

Performing "Schooled" Identities: Performing as Peers—A.K.A. The Self

I identified a third group of Latina mothers, and I felt that, during our interviews, we performed as peers, sharing similar schooling and class experiences. In fact, Irene, Veronica, Rocio, and Eveline had in common higher levels of formal schooling than the other women in the study. Irene and Veronica had gone to the universities in Mexico and Colombia, respectively, while Rocio and Evelina had completed their high school degrees in their home countries of Mexico and Guatemala. In contrast, the other women in the study had between zero and seven years of schooling. These women, then, did not perform either to teach me or to describe their lives as ordinary and everyday. Instead, they performed as peers, as schooled women who understood something about research. They took on the role of cultural informers, and their interviews were characterized by a sharing of memories and conversation. Irene and Veronica established familiarity by using the informal *tu* along with my name to refer to me. This group also constructed their identities apart from the other women in the ESOL class. For example, Irene, a Mexican national from urban Ciudad Juarez, Mexico, cast herself as different from the women of central or southern Mexico. Irene described these women as holding *costumbres tradicionales* (traditional customs). Veronica, who is from Colombia, did the same, but by casting herself apart from the Mexican community of Hope City. Since my parents were born in Ecuador, we performed as peers, fellow South Americans. Rocio, a high school graduate, created a peer relationship with me as we shared

memories about schooling and family and as she became intensely interested and involved in my project. Evelina, who had written about her
journey of suffering to the United States, was also my peer, a writer of
history like me.

Moreover, unlike the other women, these more schooled women all
shared with me their vulnerabilities about raising children, stories that
resonated with my own doubts and concerns. In contrast, the less-
schooled women in this study performed with a confidence in their abilities to raise children "properly." The contradictions I faced along with
these schooled women concerned how to merge our schooled identities
with our "educated" identities that were rooted in the moral education
of *el hogar* (the home).

These women who performed schooled identities, then, were my
reflection. They were the formally educated women whose schooling
and middle-class experiences, and their vulnerabilities, resonated with
my own. As an ethnographer of education, I could justify describing
these Latina mothers as good educators despite their vulnerabilities and
insecurities about raising children precisely because they were like me.
They were neither the exotic Other nor the mundane Other. In fact, our
performances as peers were characterized by this separation from *costumbres tradicionales*, from those who seemed to be the particular objects
of my inquiry. Indeed, in my representation of them, I extended to these
schooled women (and we created together) the privilege of being beyond
othering because they were just like me. I could portray them as the
mainstream mother, the kind of mother I believe I am. What I learned is
that solidarity with any one of these women is difficult, because I am all
of them at once, mother and daughter, rooted in *el hogar*, yet faraway
from home in academia-land. How much heart can anthropology break?

Conclusion: A Xicana Files for Divorce from Her Ex-otic

That *muchachita* Dorotea and you know Toto, her mean-ass *perrito*, well
they're stuck in the land of Oz and they wanna go home. The good witch
from *el Norte* asks them if they have their *micas*, you know their green
cards, well they're pink now; but they ain't got none, *ni de las greens ni de
las* pinks, *nada*. So *la Bruja* asks *la Dorotea*, "What did you learn *mija*? Tell
me, *órale*, and you can go home." *Sabes*, Dorotea always wanted to go
home, *siempre, siempre, siempre . . .*

How do I go home in anthropology? How do I go home in feminist
ethnography? In academia? Indeed, what did I learn in my study? Certainly, I learned that the ways in which I performed with the Latina
mothers of Hope City and the ways in which I wrote about them are

embedded within my own struggles and contradictions of trying to find a space and place; of trying to reconcile Western education with the education of *el hogar*, of reconciling postmodern feminisms with Xicanisma and with Latina womanism/feminism, of reconciling my work as an anthropologist of education with its complicity in reifying neocolonial relations of power. Yet, *la Bruja* from *el Norte* tells Dorotea that she could always go home, she always had it in her. Is it possible that these crises of representation are of lesser consequence and meaning than I have thought? Is it possible that I am arrogant in assuming that I am disempowering women in my representation of them by privileging Western and, more so, "critical" definitions of power? Am I doing this while simultaneously ignoring the ways in which I/we can redefine power? Are anthropologists' anguished and guilty questions about the right to speak for the Other and about their projects' complicity in domination (Gupta & Ferguson, 1997a) assuming and exaggerating anthropology's importance and power in people's lives? American Indian activist/poet/writer John Trudell (1994) insists that we do not become deceived about power:

> There is no such thing as military power; there is only military terrorism. There is no such thing as economic power; there is only economic exploitation. . . . They try to program our minds and fool us with these illusions so that we still believe that they hold the power in their hands but they do not. . . . Power . . . we are a natural part of the earth. . . . The earth is a spirit and we are an extension of that spirit. **We are spirit. We are power.** (no page numbers)

No, anthropology cannot give this Xicanista her power back. It cannot give back power to *las mujeres*, the Latina mothers of Hope City, not even with understanding, emancipation, and deconstruction (Lather, 1991). When a Xicana files for divorce from her Ex-otic, an "anthropology that breaks your heart" (Behar, 1996) gives rise to the cry that says, "We can define ourselves!" Trudell (1994) writes:

> We're **not** conquered. We're not defeated. **Only we can conquer ourselves**. . . . There will be political and legal quarrels that go on where we use words like that and we should never ask them to give us our sovereignty because they can't do it. Only we can do it, as individuals and collective communities. (no page numbers)

In coming back to my own anguished questions about representing women's lives within categories invented by anthropology such as "exotic" and "domination," am I not giving my own power to anthropology—a Western-based male discipline? What role then does a feminist postmodern anthropology play in the world? How can it address hegemonic power redefined as military terrorism and economic exploitation (Trudell, 1994)? Gupta and Ferguson (1997b) argue that the power question should not enter into anthropology only at the moment of representation. They posit that "a politics of otherness exists that is not reducible to a politics of representation . . . the issue of otherness itself is not really addressed by the devices of polyphonic textual construction or collaboration with informant writers" (p. 46). Rather, Gupta and Ferguson (1997b) argue that we need to address the issue of the "'the West' and its 'others' in a way that acknowledges the extratextual roots of the problem" (p. 46). How can this be done? Gupta and Ferguson (1997b) ask why it is that anthropologists do not say much with respect to the contemporary political issue of immigration and immigration law in the United States. If, indeed, anthropology reinforces a concept of culture that is about defining distinct and separate cultures, then *la frontera* (the border) serves anthropology's constructions. Yet if anthropologists believe that "cultural difference is produced and maintained in a field of power relations in a world always already spatially interconnected" (Gupta & Ferguson, 1997b, pp. 46–47), then how does anthropology respond to this political spatial incarceration? How does it get involved in the politics of the border, of immigrant rights, or of the rights of transnational laborers (Gupta & Ferguson, 1997b)? If power relations are not reducible to resolution in text, then instead of anguished guilt about its complicity in maintaining Otherness, how can anthropology be a practice of solidarity with peoples of color, with gays and lesbians, and with working-class communities to struggle against material repression and for human rights? This is the stuff of anthropology and street politics.

Whoa, whoa, *híjole, que pasó*? Did I not come back full circle again? Did my divorce not go through? As I recall, it was my street politics combined with my education in the discipline of the exotic that got me into trouble in the first place by privileging those exotic performances of resistance. Where do I go from here? How do I keep myself grounded in collective struggle, mindful of the politics of representation, and critical of the concealment of power in the construction of the discourse of a crisis of representation? The answer is a processual journey, one that entails a constant accountability to our communities' and our own struggles for self-determination and self-representation, all the while remembering that sisterhood is fought for, rather than assumed (Visweswaran, 1994). The ways in which we carve out a space of faith, spirituality, and utopia (a Xicanisma) has no name in the language games of modernism and postmodernism. In a Xicanista vision, the mind and our spirituality is and has always been our power. This vision is expressed in Ana Castillo's (1994) words:

This undercurrent of spirituality which has been with women since pre-conquest times and which precedes Christianity in Europe—is the unspoken key to her strength and endurance as a female throughout the ages. (p. 95)

Fin . . . but to be continued every day.

P.S. I live with my two children on Dorothea Way.

Notes

1. This title is inspired from Moraga and Anzaldúa's (1983) edited collection, *This Bridge Called My Back: Writings by Radical Women of Color*.

2. Patricia Hill Collins (chapter 2 in this volume), among others, articulates a critique of postmodernism(s) as an academic construct that creates categories of race and ethnicity that are flattened on a map of shifting multiple "differences" and "hybridities" that are often divorced from arrangements of material and ideological oppression. In creating its own logic and narratives, the "postmodern turn" creates new categories of exclusion that undermine Black feminist authority based on what postmodernism rejects—mainly "ethical positions that emerge from absolutes such as faith."

3. See Said (1978, 1989) and Rosaldo (1993), among others, for a discussion of the topic.

4. Visweswaran (1994) discusses women anthropologists/novelists such as Zora Neale Hurston whose writings implicate ethnography as fiction.

5. See the work of law professor and critical race theorist Kimberlé Crenshaw (1995), who discusses the intersectionalities of race and other oppressions for women of color. I also have written about the Latina mothers of my study with an analysis of intersectionality. This manuscript, entitled "Small Town Racism and *Mujeres a la Lucha*: Latina Mothers Creating Counterstories of Dignity and Moral Education in Latino Communities," is in preparation; however, highlights of the analysis is included in a co-authored book chapter by S. Villenas, L. Parker, & D. Deyhle (in press).

6. Behar cites Cherie Moraga and Gloria Anzaldúa's (1983) edited volume, *This Bridge Called My Back: Writings by Radical Women of Color* and Chandra Mohanty's (1991) essay, "Under Western Eyes: Feminist Scholarship and Colonial Discourses" among others in her discussion.

7. I thank Wanda Pillow for helping me articulate this point.

8. I would like to thank *las mujeres* of Hope City, North Carolina, for their kindness and patience in teaching and reteaching me about my education. Many thanks to my friends and colleagues who offered me intriguing questions to ponder. They are Ed Buendia, Frank Margonis, Charise Nahm, Edwin Napia, Wanda Pillow, Octavio Pimentel, Troy Richardson, Audrey Thompson, and Ruth Trinidad.

These thoughts are collective ideas that have been shared and nurtured in dialogues with Shawn Colvin Montañez, Melissa Moreno, Troy Richardson, and Ruth Trinidad. The research in North Carolina was funded by the Frank Porter Graham Child Development Center and the North Carolina Humanities Council. The Spencer Foundation generously funded my year of dissertation writing.

9. Madison (1994) talks about the cultural motifs that reflect the collective memory of black people and that have reappeared throughout black oral traditions. Chanfrault-Duchet (1991) adds that in female life stories these myths incorporate "socio-symbolic images" (p. 81) of women, such as the whore, the good mother, the virgin, and so on.

References

Anzaldúa, A. (1987). *Borderlands: The new mestiza=La frontera.* San Francisco: Aunt Lute Books.

Behar, R. (1993). *Translated woman: Crossing the border with Esperanza's story.* Boston: Beacon Press.

Behar, R. (1995). Introduction: Out of exile. In R. Behar and D. Gordon (Eds.), *Women writing culture* (pp. 1–29). Berkeley and Los Angeles: University of California Press.

Behar, R. (1996). *The vulnerable observer: Anthropology that breaks your heart.* Boston: Beacon Press.

Behar, R., & Gordon, D. (Eds.) (1995). *Women writing culture.* Berkeley and Los Angeles: University of California Press.

Carger, C. L. (1996). *Of borders and dreams: A Mexican-American experience of urban education.* New York: Teachers College Press.

Castillo, A. (1994). *Massacre of the dreamers: Essays on Xicanisma.* New York: Plume/Penguin Books.

Chanfrault-Duchet, M. (1991). Narrative structures, social models, and symbolic representation in the life history. In S. Gluck & D. Patai (Eds.), *Women's words: The feminist practice of oral history* (pp. 77–92). New York: Routledge.

Clifford, J., & Marcus, G. (Eds.) (1986). *Writing culture: The poetics and politics of ethnography.* Berkeley and Los Angeles: University of California Press.

Collins, P. H. (1999). What's going on? Black feminist thought and the politics of postmodernism. In E. A. St.Pierre & W. S. Pillow (Eds.), *Feminist poststructural theory and methods in education* (pp. 41–73). New York: Routledge.

Crenshaw, K. W. (1995). Mapping the margins: Intersectionality, identity politics and violence against women of color. In K. Crenshaw, N. Gotanda, G. Peller, & K. Thomas (Eds.), *Critical race theory: Key writings that formed the movement* (pp. 357–83). New York: New Press.

Delgado-Gaitan, C., & Trueba, H. (1991). *Crossing cultural borders: Education for immigrant families in America.* London: Falmer Press.

Fine, M. (1994). Passion, politics, and power: Feminist research possibilities. In

Disruptive voices: The possibilities of feminist research (pp. 205–31). Ann Arbor: The University of Michigan Press.

Gupta, A., & Ferguson, J. (1997a). Culture, power, place: Ethnography at the end of an era. In A. Gupta & J. Ferguson (Eds.), *Culture, power, place: Explorations in critical anthropology* (pp. 1–29). Durham, NC: Duke University Press.

Gupta, A., & Ferguson, J. (1997b). Beyond "culture": Space, identity and the politics of difference. In A. Gupta & J. Ferguson (Eds.), *Culture, power, place: Explorations in critical anthropology* (pp. 33–51). Durham, NC: Duke University Press.

hooks, b. (1984). *Feminist theory: From margin to center.* Boston: South End Press.

Lather, P. (1991). *Getting smart: Feminist research and pedagogy with/in the postmodern.* New York: Routledge.

Levinson, B., Foley, D., & Holland, D. (Eds.). (1996). *The cultural production of the educated person.* Albany: State University of New York Press.

Madison, S. (1994). Story, history, and performance: Interpreting oral history through black performance traditions. *Black Sacred Music, 8*(2), 43–63.

McLaren, P. (1998). Interview in S. Villenas & Educational Management Group, Simon and Schuster Publishers (co-executive producers). *When differences become borders: Explaining differential school achievement.* Distance Education ESL Endorsement Program, University of Utah & the Utah Education Consortium.

Mohanty, C. T. (1991). Under western eyes: Feminist scholarship and colonial discourses. In C. T. Mohanty, A. Russo, & L. Torres (Eds.), *Third world women and the politics of feminism* (pp. 51–80). Bloomington: Indiana University Press.

Moraga, C., & Anzaldúa, G. (Eds.). (1983). *This bridge called my back: Writings by radical women of color.* New York: Kitchen Table, Women of Color Press.

Perez, E. (1991). Sexuality and discourse: Notes from a Chicana survivor. In C. Trujillo (Ed.), *Chicana lesbians: The girls our mothers warned us about* (pp. 158–84). Berkeley, CA: Third Woman Press.

Rosaldo, R. (1993). *Culture and truth: The remaking of social analysis.* Boston: Beacon Press.

Said, E. W. (1978). *Orientalism.* London: Routledge.

Said, E. W. (1989). Representing the colonized: Anthropology's interlocutors. *Critical Inquiry, 15,* 205–25.

Sandoval, C. (1991). U.S. Third World feminism: The theory and method of oppositional consciousness in the postmodern world. *Genders, 10,* 1–24.

Stocking, Jr., G. (1985). *Objects and others: Essays on museums and material culture.* Madison: The University of Wisconsin Press.

Trudell, J., with Paola Igliori. (1994). *Stickman.* New York: Inanout Press.

Trueba, E. (1998). Interview in S. Villenas & Educational Management Group, Simon and Schuster Publishers (co-executive producers). *What is multicultural education?* Distance Education ESL Endorsement Program, University of Utah & the Utah Education Consortium.

Valdés, G. (1996). *Con respeto: Bridging the distances between culturally diverse families and schools.* New York: Teachers College Press.

Villenas, S. (1996). The colonizer/colonized Chicana ethnographer: Identity, marginalization, and co-optation in the field. *Harvard Educational Review, 66*(4), 711–31.

Villenas S., Parker, L., & Deyhle, D. (in press). Critical race theory and praxis: Chicano(a)/Latina(o) and Navajo struggles for dignity, educational equity and social justice. In L. Parker, D. Deyhle, & S. Villenas (Eds.), *Race is . . . race isn't: Critical race theory and qualitative studies in education.* Boulder, CO: Westview Press.

Visweswaran, K. (1994). *Fictions of feminist ethnography.* Minneapolis: University of Minnesota Press.

Visweswaran, K. (1998). Race and the culture of anthropology. *American Anthropologist, 11*(1), 70–83.

Wagner, R. (1981). *The invention of culture.* Chicago: University of Chicago Press.

Chapter 4

Researching "My People," Researching Myself:[1] Fragments of a Reflexive[2] Tale

Lubna Nazir Chaudhry

> We have never acknowledged either the birth or the death of the subject. Ours has been an ongoing search for the unseparated subject. In other words, the metaphor for the West is the human cycle (birth, life, death); the metaphor for non-Western cultures is unity/oneness/totality, etc. The former lends itself well to narrative—it is a narrative; the latter isn't, except in fragments and anecdotes—a paradox! To us this search, perhaps for a partial totality, enforces and continues meaning, thereby allowing us to inhabit in the domain of memory.
>
> (Gabriel, 1989, p. 131)

> Though I tried I could not really write my story. Each time I tried to write, everything splintered into little bits. I could not figure out a line or theme for myself. . . . I had no clear picture of what unified it all, what our history might mean. We were all in it together, that's all I knew. And there was no way out.
>
> (Alexander, 1991, p. 28)

I

People have gotten killed
And I really don't want anyone to suffer or die
But despite my sorrow and guilt I can't help but think
"First World blood is so much more expensive than Third World
  blood."

My legs are trembling and so are my hands grasping the paper with the scribbled poems. I am very conscious of the fact that my jeans and shirt are not appropriate apparel for the evening. I surreptitiously try to display my *Allah*[3] medallion more prominently, but my fingers refuse to cooperate. I am not imagining the coldness from some of the other Muslim students, especially the two young women with *hijabs* sitting in the two chairs in front of the podium and the group of Muslim men sitting on one side on the floor. Since 1992, when I first started my dissertation research[4] with Pakistani Muslim women, I have interacted quite extensively with members of the Muslim community in various parts of northern California, including the Muslim Student Association at the university where I am working toward my doctorate as an international student from Pakistan. I know many of the Muslim students in the audience quite well.

I am also very conscious of the fact that my poem is bitter, and many people would find it offensive. Am I just reinforcing stereotypes about the intensity and hostility exhibited by Muslims? These days I am already struggling with my feelings of alienation from people I perceive as being affiliated with the dominant culture in the United States. So it is difficult for me to figure out whether I am projecting or whether I am actually the recipient of disturbed looks from some members of the audience.

Yet neither my voice nor my gaze waver. I enunciate each word firmly as I look directly into the eyes of the assorted group of students, faculty, and other university town residents. Out of the corner of my eye I see Aisha,[5] one of the chief participants in my critical feminist ethnography, smile at me encouragingly from her rather precarious position on one of the windowsills further away from the podium.

It is May 18, 1995. We are all gathered in a cafe bordering the campus to protest against the false arrest of a Jordanian-American after the Oklahoma City tragedy. Students of Arab origin from different religious backgrounds, the on-campus Muslim[6] Student association, and Muslim students like myself, who are not formal members of the association, have joined forces to organize this evening's program of poetry and prose readings, recitations from the various holy books, dramatic skits, and media clip presentations. The cafe's walls display artwork by Muslim and Arab students, and the doors and windows are adorned with enlarged posters of the Counterterrorist Act of 1995.[7]

> . . . a journalist on TV, "The Bangladeshis continue to multiply. The world is going to be over-run by Third-Worlders despite the cyclones, the floods, the riots, the droughts."
>
> I guess the blast would have been really useful in Asia or Africa, nature needs help in keeping the balance.

I continue with my rather angry recital. The participant-observer part of myself, which is never entirely shut off, mentally documents the exact moment when the cold and disturbed looks become warmer and less troubled. A few young men, active and vocal members of the association, start to clap. They give my words the stamp of their approval. Other people, especially my friends and people who know me, take the cue, and soon everyone is clapping. I have to shout out the last few lines,

> . . . all I wanted to ask was one thing,
> Where are the SAVE THE MUSLIMS T-shirts, guys?

I step off the podium, and my gang of graduate student friends, most of them non-Muslim and non-Arab, who are there for the specific purpose of taking care of my ego, and José, the man I am "kind of seeing" at that point, come forward to tell me what a wonderful job I have done. After many hugs and kisses, I am led to our table, and I sit down, high on the feeling that accompanies a successful performance, content to be an observer for a while. I am glad the poetry reading went well. After all, I have taken time away from my dissertation writing and my sick mother to be there. Aisha and the two chief organizers, Nargis and Sara, talked me into participating, although I have my own reservations about arranging an event designed to educate people about Muslims and Arabs.

My sensation of triumph does not last long, and neither does my status as supportive, but uninvolved, spectator. For one, there are too many glances, ranging from mildly curious to openly irritated, being directed toward our table. As the evening progresses, I become more and more uncomfortable with the fact that I am sitting quite close to an attractive man who is obviously neither Muslim nor Pakistani. José is part Native American, part Mexican.

Second, as the program unfolds, I realize that unscheduled routines and presentations are being allowed to interrupt and disrupt the sequence decided upon earlier by the planning committee. It annoys and upsets me at the same time that it is the Muslim students, particularly those of South Asian origin[8] born and raised in the United States, who are instigating these changes. They are continually pressuring Nargis and Sara, the two graduate students who have played the most active role in organizing the program and are now running it, to make space for more recitations by "real Muslims" and more preaching of Islam. When Sara, a Christian Arab, comes up to me to commiserate, I extend her my sympathies for dealing with a difficult situation but cannot help adding in a rather sharp tone that we need to understand why people who have hardly ever been heard want to make full use of the one opportunity they have been given. "It is perhaps the only time in their life that the Muslim students have a voice as Muslims," I declare emphatically.

"This was supposed to be an Arab and Muslim event. I have never before felt this urgent need to go run home and get my cross ever before in my life," Sara replies as she runs back to the podium to announce the break for the *Maghrib* prayers.

Many of the Muslim students, most of them formal members of the Muslim Students Association, stand together in two separate rows, one male, the other female, to offer their prayers. The non-Muslims and the non-praying Muslims just stand by and watch. "I feel so proud of them," mutters Sana, another Muslim graduate student who like myself does not join the *namaazis*. It is indeed an inspiring sight, these young people all facing Makkah, going through each step of the *namaaz* in near-perfect coordination. I am impressed by the unity and harmony I am witnessing. For a second, I am overwhelmed by a surge of emotion in my heart. These are my people, and it is a privilege to be part of the Muslim *Ummah*.

Then the critical feminist ethnographer with her post-colonial, post-structuralist[9] leanings rears her paradoxical head again. Why does the *namaaz* seem like such a staged performance to me? Why am I angry with them for making a spectacle of my religion, which happens to be theirs too? Why do we have to cater to the white gaze? Have I been contaminated too deeply by postmodernist discourses about presentations of selves and identities?

The program is resumed after the prayers. I am still plagued with contradictory emotions and conflicting loyalties. I am thrilled by the manner in which the Muslim students are enacting resistance to dominant modes of thought. I am threatened by their attempts to empower themselves, since their measures and intended outcomes could be oppressive in some ways. I suppose Salman Rushdie, in his reductive but effective style, would say the East and West are pulling me in different directions.[10]

"So this is what happens when margins generate their own centers," I manage to continue my analysis even as my various emotions ebb and flow. I burn with shame when many of the Muslim students pointedly refuse to applaud a poem read by a young Arab Jewish woman (I do remember her tendency to, on and off, categorize all Muslims as anti-Semitic, but I expect my Muslim friends to have more forgiving hearts). I want to go wipe the smirks off some non-Muslim Arabs' faces when Adil, the young man courting my research participant, Aisha, gets carried away as he pontificates about the five pillars of Islam in his desire to impress Aisha and us all with his knowledge (Adil does look very handsome, and his intensity is moving). I completely understand why Nargis, who is from a Muslim family but adheres to strict secular beliefs, blushes and almost cries when one of the young, strident women wearing the *hijab* reads her poem, chastising all women who do not cover themselves properly and looks directly at Nargis's bare arms and legs (I do wish momentarily that Nargis had had the sense not to show so much cleavage that evening).

Aisha, who wears the *hijab* herself, stands up and challenges the poem's logic. Soon we have a full-fledged contest brewing between the very strict believers and the strict, but liberal, believers. I am struck by how American the competitors are in their body language, their accents, and their demeanors. Most of us who were actually born and raised in Muslim or Third World countries huddle further into our seats. The thought is intriguing enough for me to dig out my notebook, and the tense Pakistani, not-so-good Muslim woman, takes refuge in the writing of field notes.

It is in the midst of all this that Nargis and Sara take charge and assertively announce the last few items of the evening. I have completely forgotten that I have to still read one more poem I wrote earlier in the day. The poem was hastily put together in response to an interchange with Sara and Nargis about their dealings with the association, a conversation that in retrospect appears to predict the evening's debacle. As I fumble through my papers, my first instinct is to just run. Nothing can be more timely than what I have to say. Nothing can be more likely to damage any relationship I have with the Muslim Student Association. Having always been more brave than circumspect, I take my visibly shaking body to the podium and begin with a voice that is definitely trembling this time.

> I am a Muslim, a Mussalman, an "Islamic person,"
> What do I mean when I say that . . .?

I doggedly read through the poem. Eyes are boring into me as I grapple with the complexity of claiming a Muslim identity in different contexts. The segments of the poem where I justify my Muslim identity to secular radicals and Western feminists go fairly well, although two Muslim students walk out looking bored, a young white woman laughs incredulously, and another mutters, "Too academic!" The air around me crackles with tension as I reach the climax of the piece.

> . . . my Muslim identity is both a site of rebellion and resistance,
> There is no such thing as a pure uncontaminated brand of unmediated Islam, Your Californian Islam is different than mine . . .

I stumble off the podium, trying to disregard the angry voices. I notice a few members of the Association, both men and women, heading in my direction. I ignore them and walk to my table, almost falling on the floor in the process. José tries to steady me by holding my arm, and although I know I should not, I cling to him. As I try to hastily leave the room, he pulls me back, "What's the hurry?"

I try to explain that everything—the atmosphere, the gazes, the words—are too much like the University of Punjab, Lahore, Pakistan, where thugs and hoodlums used Islam to intimidate me and my fellow students. These troublemakers were backed by the military regime that was, in its turn, backed by the United States.[11] I also try to tell him that I do not want to be perceived like Salman Rushdie.[12] The main impetus for my dissertation research comes from my desire to reclaim and reinscribe knowledge about Muslim women as a Pakistani Muslim woman researcher. I do not want to attack the beliefs and faith of my fellow Muslims, but that is how my plea for understanding was being perceived.

I give up when I see his blank face and just pull him through the door. That night I decide it will not work with José.

II

It is around eleven o'clock at night on February 11, 1993. I am getting ready to go to bed after a protracted struggle with Paul Ricoeur's notion of the text. The telephone rings, and I pick up the receiver.

"Did I wake you up?" It is Fariha, one of the research participants in my study with Pakistani Muslim immigrant young women, sounding apologetic. "I am sorry, but I really need to talk to you. And you have to promise you won't tell my mother anything. If it is all right with you . . . ," she says hesitantly.

I assure her that it is, expecting her to share news of another bad grade on a test. Last week I helped Fariha with two makeup papers over the phone.[13] She did not want her mother to know about her poor performance, so we pretended to talk about world politics and its impact on Muslim lives, an issue dear to *Appa*'s heart. Fariha made it a point to mention Bosnia and Kashmir intermittently in order to alleviate my guilt.

School and grades, however, are not on Fariha's mind this evening. She launches into a rather complicated narrative about a quarrel with her mother, a recent letter from her estranged father, and her decision to marry the young man she loves. I ask her a few clarifying questions here and there. After she talks for a while, she suddenly asks me what she should do, adding that she counts on me to help her since I know so much about the real world.

I am rather taken aback by her question. I am not prepared for the switch from the role of confidant to that of an adviser, at least in this instance. I was flattered when, a few weeks ago in early January, Fariha trusted me enough to tell me about her secret love affair with this 19-year-old young man who has recently moved to California from Pakistan. She accidentally ran into him outside her school sometime in November 1992, and they fell in love quite dramatically at first sight. I was extremely flattered when Fariha sent Razzaq to meet me at my department in the first week of February in order to elicit my opinion. I was also thrilled when she told me that she did not mind my writing down her confidences as part of my fieldwork. Somehow her insistence that my age and varied experiences bestow on me a wisdom that makes me an expert is neither flattering nor thrilling. I silently chide myself for being open to her about my divorce and my love life. I have been very selective in what I revealed to her, but I probably should have just abstained from the topic.

"So what should I do? What would you do if you were in my place?" Fariha repeats her query.

"Well," I begin cautiously, "I wouldn't want to be married when I was 16 or 17, even 18, because I would want to finish my education."

"Well, I can do whatever I want when I am married to him," she responds. "In fact, I will do it better, because I won't feel so alone. I will be with someone who understands me and will help me fulfill my ambitions."

And so begins an intense 4-hour session in which I struggle to strike a balance between displaying consideration for Fariha's feelings toward this man, painting a bleak picture of a runaway marriage and its consequences, and ignoring my stress about the paper that I am supposed to start writing early next morning. We talk in Urdu, English, and Punjabi, and both of us draw from our multiple cultural bases to substantiate our reasoning. I, however, gradually become aware that my predominant persona is that of an older sister wanting to protect the little one from the clutches of an unsuitable man. Much to my horror, this older sister also wants to run to the mother to get her help, even as she keeps on promising Fariha that she will never disclose her secret. I respect and admire Fariha's mother. In the few months that I have known her, I have become quite close to her. I address her as "*Appa*," which means older sister.

What I can gather from Fariha's outpouring is that *Appa* has found out about this young man in Fariha's life and has forbidden her to ever see him again. She has behaved, in my opinion, somewhat unreasonably. I can see why she does not want Fariha to be involved with the man. But she has really made Fariha angry by comparing her to her father and threatening to send her off either to stay with him or live with his parents in Pakistan. After her outburst, *Appa* has locked herself up in her room.

I delicately suggest to Fariha that she try to talk to her mother. I offer to come over and be the mediator. After all, that seems to be my predominant role in their lives. Fariha resolutely turns down the proposal.

Finally, we reach a point in the conversation where I feel that I have convinced Fariha to put off her plan for at least a week. She is still adamant about wanting to get married as soon as possible but decides to give me a chance to come up with a plan that is likely to have less disastrous consequences. Restating my promise not to tell her mother about our conversation, I hang up and drift off into a restless sleep.

I spend a lot of time in the next two days trying to figuring out my course of action. I attempt to thrash out the issue with my colleagues and friends. Mostly, these attempts are a waste of time, because people seem to be more interested in critiquing Muslims for not allowing their daughters to date than offering me advice. A few friends, however, do present me their points of view succinctly.

Away from Fariha and her mother, back in my academic world, the simplicity of the logic employed by these friends appeals to my distraught mind. I decide my guilt at breaching *Appa*'s trust is misplaced. My first commitment is toward Fariha and her desires. Fariha is 17 and, by Islamic standards, an adult. She can marry anyone she wants. I would neither divulge her secret nor force my ideas on her. I would respect her choice and be supportive no matter what she does.

When I get home from the library on February 14, there are six frantic messages from *Appa* on my answering machine. I immediately call her back. Fariha has run away. She left a letter for her mother. *Appa* has decided to tell people that she is staying with me. Only her youngest brother, one of Fariha's *mamoons*, knows the truth. *Appa* tells me that the least I can do for her and Fariha is to back up her lie, since my negative influence on Fariha is, to a large extent, responsible for her elopement.

Fariha has told me where she would go if she ran away. *Appa*'s pain is hard for me to bear, but I force myself not to say anything. I know I would find it very difficult to maintain my confidentiality in *Appa*'s presence, so I try to stay away from her as much as possible.

Nonetheless, both *Appa* and Fariha's *mamoon* realize I know more than I admit. When *Appa* contacts Fariha's father in desperation and he almost takes the other children away, her uncle practically begs me to help look for her. I eventually give in and, using the information I give him, he traces her whereabouts. He cannot meet her physically but sends her a message telling her to at least let them know where she is.

Fariha comes back to her mother's place after a week all by herself in very bad shape. She looks haggard and seems to have bruises on her face. She tells her mother that she received her uncle's message. She has gone through the *nikah*, the Muslim legal marriage contract, with Razzaq, but she wants help in getting it annulled. Her mother brings Fariha over to my place, and she stays with me for about 2 weeks while her mother and uncle arrange for the *nikah* to be declared void. During the time she spends at my apartment, Fariha is very quiet and lost in a world of her own. We barely communicate. I see her crying on and off.

The sequence of happenings, Fariha's running away, her coming back, and my involvement in these, assume a nightmarish quality in my memory. My reflective journal and fieldnote entries constantly remark on the "unreal nature of the experience." The most authentic part of the whole episode for me is the rhetorical question *Appa* poses to me at one point when I am still mired in issues of confidentiality, choice, and agency: "What if this had happened to your own sister?"

Yes, what if it was my own sister instead of Fariha? Would I have not thought of words other than confidentiality, choice, and agency instead, words that I cannot translate into English? In my initial interactions with Fariha, in my attempt to have access to data, I dexterously mobilized my multiple identities. For instance, I got into the older sister mode with Fariha quite smoothly because of our shared Punjabi ethnicity. When it came to defining empowerment for Fariha, however, I set myself apart from the cultural bridge that connects me to her family. Choosing to ally myself with my Western modes of thought, I became the so-called objective "feminist," detaching myself from my subjectivity as a Pakistani Muslim woman and from my familial relationship with Fariha.

III

I get off the telephone feeling amused, exasperated, worried, relieved, all at the same time. My mother is up to her old tricks again. My father just told me how she hides the fruit from him, follows him to the kitchen to see he does not eat the food cooked by her or her children, and this morning even snatched his plate of toast and butter from in front of him, saying she has saved the bread for her daughter. If *Abbu* tries to cook, Mamma complains incessantly about the mess he makes and now has told him to acquire a stove of his own. These are all signs that Mamma is feeling better after her surgery, but my poor father is suffering, and it is getting difficult to eat again, knowing *Abbu* is probably hungry. My mother does have a rationale for her treatment of her husband. Her logic is something like this: after his retirement and move to the United States my father is not fulfilling his role as a provider, so she too deserves to retire as his wife and homemaker. They are living with their children, but again Mamma has more rights over them because she helped them with their early schooling and made sure they were trained into civilized, sensible human beings.

I turn on my computer. Instead of diligently working on my dissertation, I load the "paintbrush" program and play with colors. This is an old habit of mine. Even when I was a child, *Abbu* and Mamma used to confide their troubles in me. After listening to them, I would lock myself up in the bathroom—I shared a bedroom with my three siblings—and proceed to destroy any paintbox I could lay my hands on. I could not draw realistic sketches, and I always got Cs in art (they never failed me, because I was their star student). But I liked mixing colors. I still do.

I cannot remember Mamma ever being happy with *Abbu*. I could not understand why my sweet-tempered, sensitive father irritated her so much. I myself got impatient with *Abbu* for putting up with so much abuse. I used to pray for him to get more strength. I still do not understand everything about my parents' relationship. But now I do perceive the irony of my mother feeling cheated out of a real man because my father is not enough of a patriarch in a very patriarchal society. She resents his reaping any of the benefits of being born a male and tries to ensure he does not have any privileges on the domestic front. She said once that she was more of a man than my father could ever be.

I am still playing with colors but now starting to feel guilty. I have not had my fill of orange and green, my favorite colors, but I know in order to be on schedule I should at least try to compile all the data illustrating the nature of hybridity[14] today. The year 1994 is coming to an end, and I need to embark officially on to the dissertation writing stage. So far, it has been very difficult to analyze the material about hybridity. It is so hard to be focused, concise, and clear about an obsession. The orange and green web on the screen in front me is invaded by splashes of purple spray paint as I let myself slide into my compulsive questioning mode.

How far back in time and space should I go when talking about the hybridization of meaning systems and identities? How do I date the rupturing of my own ethnic identity? Could I just trace that rupturing to when my village-born father became the first person in his family to attend the school set up by the British government, or did it all begin more recently just before I was born when my father received the award for a Ph.D. in the United States? Or did my hybrid state come into being when my paternal great-grandfather, who was born a Sikh, converted to Islam because a voice in the fields told him to go to Makkah? Or was it more significant that my maternal Hindu great-grandfather chose to migrate to the Punjab from Persia and became a Muslim to avoid going to trial after being accused of murder? What about my great-grandmothers and their stories? Why does no one talk about them?

The ringing of the phone interrupts my questioning and my computerized spraypainting. I wait for the answering machine to go on. I decide to screen the call. My mother's voice, a strident and incisive, "Luby, if you are there, pick up at once," and my own cheery, rather phony sounding recorded message reverberate in my tiny studio simultaneously.

Mamma will definitely ask how much I have accomplished today. I am in no mood to be scolded, nor do I feel up to lying. I do not pick up. Instead I think about Mamma's multiple migrations and her relationship to formal education, particularly higher education. The last time she was visiting my apartment my mother's glasses got misplaced. "Books! Cursed books!" She exclaimed angrily and knocked a few of them onto the floor as she searched the shelf where she thought she had earlier kept her glasses (I later found them in the kitchen). I was deeply hurt; Mamma was cursing my entire life. I grew up hearing Mamma instruct her daughters to stay away from men who have Ph.D.s, and so I knew I was already engaging in inappropriate behavior by studying for a Ph.D. myself. Still, Mamma has always been pushing me to do well in school, and I know from my older cousins how she broke her jewelry to protest her marriage to my father because she wanted to go to college instead. What does Mamma's frustration with books really mean?

Mamma first came to a small university town in the United States with her baby daughter in the mid-1960s to join her husband who was then pursuing a doctorate. She cooked and cleaned for him, had two more children, and sewed herself *shalwar kameezes* out of material bought during her midday explorations of the downtown before she went back to Pakistan in the early 1970s. During this time period, before she had her son, she tried killing herself and her two small daughters because the letters from my father's family indicated their unhappiness with her inability to provide a heir to the family's mystic legacy.

Mamma returned to the United States, to another small university town in the mid-1990s, this time to join her daughter, who is now working toward a doctorate. Unlike my father, she is very understanding of my need to live by myself in my own little studio apartment. She cooks and cleans (although not for her husband), takes care of her grandchild (my sister's baby), and keeps a watchful eye on her older daughter's progress with her dissertation in between sessions of debilitating chemotherapy and bouts of intensive crying. She was diagnosed with breast cancer 3 months after she moved to the United States, and her younger son was killed in a car accident 4 months before she left Pakistan.

Tears well up in my eyes. I ignore them and get busy retrieving the file titled "Analysis." I scroll through the document after it is loaded. I am pleased to realize that although I am still technically working on hybridity, I have a lot of work already done on resistance and empowerment.[15] I know what I want to say. I just do not know how to say it. The data are supporting what I have known for a long time and have never learned how to articulate very clearly. There is no one right path to empowerment; there is no one right way to enact resistance against oppressive power relations. The terms of resistance and bids for empowerment emerge out of the specific circumstances of a particular life, and who is to say what terms and which bids are more efficacious? What matters is the challenging of power relations.

I am stifled by my own abstractions and realize I need to either listen to tapes from my data set or go through transcripts and fieldnotes to regain a sense of how the lives of the four research participants anchor the theoretical observations. I flip through my transcripts, and the scribbled notes in the margins somehow transport me to the era when discourse analysis was the focus of my graduate work. I mull over my interactions with the other Pakistani female graduate students during my 2¹/₂-year stay in Hawai'i. It was those interactions that paved the way for the writing of this dissertation on resistance and empowerment.

Of the five women from Pakistan at the East-West Center going to graduate school at the University of Hawai'i, I was the only one whose mother was not a professional or whose paternal and maternal grandfathers did not have illustrious records of either serving or fighting the British rule in India. Moreover, although I was the youngest, I was the only one whose family was "backward" enough to make sure I was married before I was allowed to study outside my country. Yet I never accepted I was not enough of a feminist because my family or myself were not liberated. The continual insistence by some of these women that my family was more oppressive than theirs because my mother did not finish high school or because I did not even know what feminism was before I came to the United States did not detract from my realization of the value of the resistance enacted by myself or my mother. I just needed to figure out a way to talk about the contextual nature of resistance and oppression.

I have been conscious of my marginality[16] for a long time now. Mamma wanted to leave my father when I was 8. My aunt, her oldest sister, begged her to stay for the sake of Salman and Noman, her sons. I was surprised my aunt had not mentioned my name. I was the oldest child, my mother's favorite, and the one who always stood first in class. Then the woman who sometimes helped my mother out with her seasonal cleaning emphatically told my 4-year-old little brother when I was 10 that I could not be the prime minister to Abbu King and Mamma Queen because I was *paraya dhan*, an outsider, and my brother Noman, who was the third child, was the one qualified for the position.

At 13, I was considered the most intelligent child on both sides of my extended family, yet I began to realize I was not going to be seen as a good enough match for any of my cousins by their parents unless I paid some attention to the domestic sphere I had started to see as my mother's prison. I decided to forfeit the claims to beautiful clothes and ostentatious displays of affection that accompanies a marriage proposal from a cousin because I could not force myself to do what Mamma did even as she lamented her *kismet*. I had to get a higher degree, be like my father, in order not to be as angry as Mamma. Despite being proud of my accomplishments, my mother at times has expressed her resentment of my path over the years. Does she feel betrayed? I wish I could explain to Mamma how my resistance took a different form than hers, but it is her resistance that has made mine possible.

I give up looking at the transcripts. I am not into the women enough today. Maybe I should go for a walk. It might take my mind off my life and my mother's life. Why did I not write a dissertation about my mother? Why did I go out and seek other Pakistani Muslim women and investigate their marginality, hybridity, resistance, and empowerment, when I keep on going back to the history of my own consciousness? And then why do I choose to situate myself in the field of education? I used to wonder if I was obtaining a degree in education almost by default, but now I am aware that I am fascinated by the role of formal education in women's lives. Perhaps it all goes back to the historical gold bracelet, the one my mother denies flatly she ever broke. "Only people with no practical sense want to go to college," she says as she looks at me squarely in the eye.

Acknowledgment

This paper and the research on which it is based would not have been possible without the support of the following people, each one of them a friend and a teacher, each of one them either a formal or an informal member of my dissertation research committee: Jane Adan, Concha Delgado-Gaitan, Patricia Gandara, Kate Elder, Michele Foster, Suad Joseph, Jeffrey Lewis, Clare Norelle, Jeanne Russell, and Karen Watson-Gegeo.

Notes

1. Spivak (1993) points out how the nature of her "Third-Worldness" as an intellectual from an elite background in a developing country teaching in the West differed from the "Third-Worldness" of a peasant woman in India. In a similar vein, and more specifically concerned with the complex positioning of an ethnographer researching his or her so-called cultural group, Narayan (1993) asks, "How native is a 'native' anthropologist?" Arguing for anthropologists to engage in the "enactment of hybridity" (p. 681) whereby the constant reconstitution of the researcher's identities in different contexts is acknowledged, she writes, "Whether we are disempowered or empowered by prevailing power relations, we must all take responsibility for how our personal locations feed not just into our fieldwork interactions but also our scholarly texts. When professional personas efface situated and experiencing selves, this makes for misleading scholarship even as it does violence to the range of hybrid personal and professional identities that we negotiate in our daily lives" (p. 681).

Visweswaran (1994) makes a similar argument for anthropologists to move from a politics of identity to a politics of identification and to study the shifting, multiple subject positionings of the researcher in order to take responsibility for the knowledge being produced as well as to study the so-called postcolonial self itself as a site where multiple centers of power inscribe their meanings. Lavie (1990), Kondo (1990), Abu-Lughod (1992), and Behar (1993) are examples of anthropologists who have enacted hybridity in their writing in order to highlight the complexity of their positioning vis-à-vis their research participants and to illustrate how the self is transformed by the ethnographic process.

This present chapter is my attempt to problematize my positionality as a Pakistani Muslim woman "studying" other Pakistani Muslims as well as my bid to contextualize the research project within those aspects of my self that are, for the most part, denied voice in mainstream academic discourse. Here I strive to represent, in the words of Abu-Lughod (1990), "that moving back and forth between the many worlds [I] inhabit is a movement within one complex and historically and politically determined world" (p. 27).

2. The term *reflexive* has been used by several people writing about ethnography and other forms of qualitative research. Whereas Lather's (1991) notion of self-reflexivity as an attempted deconstruction of one's work and the desire behind the work has influenced my own particular conception, Trinh's (1989) usage best reflects my understanding of the term, "There is no such thing as a 'coming face to face once and for all with objects'; the real remains foreclosed from the analytic experience, which is an experience of speech. In writing close to the other of the other, I can only choose to maintain a self-reflexively critical relationship toward the material, a relationship that defines both the subject written and the writing subject, undoing the I, while asking, 'what do I want wanting to *know* you or me?'" (p. 76).

3. I have italicized Arabic, Punjabi, and Urdu words. A glossary (Appendix I) lists translation equivalents in English.

4. My dissertation research was a critical feminist ethnographic analysis of the processes whereby young Pakistani Muslim immigrant women in northern California forge hybrid cultural identities in response to their experiences and interaction with changing contextual realities within formal educational as well as community contexts. Using the margins as a site of resistance, these women deployed their hybrid identities and worldviews to enact resistance against oppressive power relations in various contexts resulting in either their empowerment or further disempowerment in those contexts. I drew from feminist anthropological theories (e.g., Trinh, 1989, 1991; Abu-Lughod, 1990; Lather, 1991; Behar, 1993; Visweswaran, 1994), the body of literature on critical ethnography (e.g., Carspecken & Apple, 1992; Thomas, 1993), and poststructuralist critiques of anthropology (e.g., Clifford, 1988) to devise my particular conception of critical feminist ethnography. Using participant observation and various interview-interactional data collection techniques, I was officially in the "field" for 2 years, from April 1992 until April 1994. My involvement with the women, their families, and the

larger community circles within which they participated has continued to the present and was particularly intense when I was analyzing and writing up the data in the period between May 1994 and August 1995 before I moved from California.

5. All people with the exception of me, the researcher and the writer, have been given pseudonyms.

6. The on-campus Muslim Student Association comprised American Muslims as well as international students who identified themselves as Muslims. Not all of the Muslim students were of Arab origin.

7. The Omnibus Counterterrorism Act of 1995 was introduced on February 10, 1995, as H.R. 896 in the House and as S. 390 in the Senate. It was subsequently signed by President Clinton in April 1996. This Contract on the Constitution allows the U.S. government to deport aliens, convicted of no crime at all, based on secret information. It violates notions of equal protection by making aliens, but not U.S. citizens who engage in the same conduct, responsible for a wide range of federal crimes unrelated to immigration status. Under this act, aliens who contribute to the legal, nonviolent, even charitable activities of organizations or governments unpopular with the U.S. government are deportable. The act was ostensibly introduced to make it easier for authorities to evict immigrants suspected of terrorism.

8. South Asia includes the countries of the Indian subcontinent: Pakistan, India, Nepal, and Bangladesh, the island of Sri Lanka, and sometimes Afghanistan.

9. Theories that fall under the rubric of poststructuralism as well as postcolonialism generally stress the fluid nature of identity and are built around the notion of self as multiple and contingent on the working of power relations informing a particular context. Ultimately, there is no authentic self; each manifestation of what we perceive as the self is a response to the demands of a context, a specific performance, and representation. See Sarup (1993) for a delineation of this dimension of poststructuralist thought and Bhabha (1996) for a treatment of the subject from a postcolonial perspective.

10. "I, too, have ropes around my neck, I have them to this day, pulling me this way and that, East and West, the nooses tightening, commanding, *choose, choose*" (Rushdie, 1994, p. 211).

11. Grewal and Kaplan (1994) write, "When the United States gave billions to General Zia of Pakistan to fight the Soviets in Afghanistan, the United States propped up a regime that was inimical to women" (p. 19). For a succinct analysis of the U.S. involvement in Pakistan's affairs during the Soviet Union occupation of Afghanistan, see Bajpai and Cohen (1993).

12. The publication of Salman Rushdie's *Satanic Verses* in 1988 generated a controversy that led to rioting and violence in different parts of the world. Muslim communities were offended by what they perceived as Rushdie's defamation of the Prophet Mohammad and his life.

13. Reciprocity in a research design has been put forth by feminist researchers as a way to mitigate the exploitative potential of the researcher-researched hierarchy (Skeggs, 1994). Following Golde (1986/1970), I wanted to give back something concrete to the participants for allowing me to collect the data. Given my relative familiarity with both so-called home and school cultures, I assumed the role of a counselor and broker for the research participants in institutional and community contexts.

14. Hybridity results through the yoking together of unlikely traditions of thought. Hybrids, those in a state of hybridity, exhibit hybrid identities as well as hybrid worldviews deriving from different systems of meaning. According to Bhabha (1990), "All forms of culture are continually in a process of hybridity . . . hybridity is the third space which enables other positions to emerge, . . . sets up new structures of authority, new political initiatives, . . . a new area of negotiation of meaning and representation" (p. 207).

15. Resistance refers to the opposition of structures of domination. Resistance is essentially contextual and can be deployed in spaces that open up because of the fluid, constantly shifting, nonhomogeneous nature of power relations. This notion of resistance is based primarily on a reading of Foucault (1978, 1982) and Sandoval (1991).

Empowerment implies a change in power relations in a certain context. These power relations are multilayered and dynamic (Foucault, 1978). My conception of empowerment is based in an explicit transnational perspective (as in, for example, Basch, Schiller, & Blane, 1994), whereby the sphere for political power goes beyond the nation-state and incorporates an understanding of global relations of power.

16. Marginality refers to the fluid, complex, and disputatious condition of existing in peripheral relations to the centers of power (Tucker, 1990).

Appendix I. Glossary of Italicized Words and Phrases

Abbu   father
Allah   Arabic word for God used by Muslims
Appa   a term of respect for an older sister or someone you want to give that status
hijab   the Muslim veil; a head scarf worn by certain Muslim women covering their hair
kismet   fate; destiny
Maghrib   the Muslim evening prayer; after sunset
mamoon   mother's brother, maternal uncle
nikah   the Muslim marriage contract
paraya dhan   literally meaning wealth belonging to someone else; refers to status of daughters in a family

shalwar kameez   the Pakistani national dress, although worn in other
South Asian countries, and by South Asians elsewhere; an outfit consisting of a tunic and baggy trousers worn by both women and men
Ummah   the Muslim community of believers that transcends ethnic,
national boundaries; the followers of the Prophet Mohammed

References

Abu-Lughod, L. (1990). Can there be a feminist ethnography? *Women and Performance: A Journal of Feminist Theory, 5*(1), 7–27.

Abu-Lughod, L. (1992). *Writing women's worlds: Bedouin stories.* Berkeley and Los
Angeles: University of California Press.

Alexander, M. (1991). *Nampally Road.* San Francisco: Mercury House, Incorporated.

Bajpai, K. P., & Cohen, S. P. (Eds.). (1993). *South Asia after the Cold War: International perspectives.* Boulder, CO: Westview Press.

Basch, L., Schiller, N. G., & Blanc, C. S. (1994). *Nations unbound.* Langhorne, PA
& Reading, UK: Gordon and Beach Publishers.

Behar, R. (1993). *Translated woman: Crossing the border with Esperanza's story.*
Boston: Beacon Press.

Bhabha, H. (1990). The third space: Interview with Homi Bhabha. In J. Ruther-
ford (Ed.), *Identity* (pp. 206–21). London: Lawrence Wishart.

Bhabha, H. (1996). Unpacking my library . . . again. In I. Chambers & L. Curti
(Eds.), *The post-colonial question: Common skies, divided horizons.* London and
New York: Routledge.

Carspecken, P. F., & Apple, M. (1992). Critical qualitative research: Theory,
methodology, and practice. In M. LeCompte et al. (Eds.), *The handbook of qualitative research in education* (pp. 507–51). San Diego, CA: Academic Press.

Clifford, J. (1988). *The predicament of culture.* Cambridge, MA: Harvard University
Press.

Foucault, M. (1978). Method. In *History of sexuality, Volume I. An introduction* (pp.
92–102). New York: Vintage Books.

Foucault, M. (1982). Afterword: The subject and power. In H. Dreyfus & P. Rabinow (Eds.), *Beyond structuralism and hermeneutics* (pp. 208–26). Chicago: University of Chicago Press.

Gabriel, T. (1989). Theses on memory and identity: The search for the origins of
the River Nile. *Emergences, 1,* 131–38.

Golde, P. (1970, 1986). *Women in the field: Anthropological experiences.* Berkeley and
Los Angeles: University of California Press.

Grewal, I., & Kaplan, C. (Eds.). (1994). *Scattered hegemonies: Postmodernity and
transnational feminist practices.* Minneapolis and London: University of Minnesota Press.

Kondo, D. (1990). *Crafting selves: Power, gender, and discourses of identity in a Japanese workplace.* Chicago: University of Chicago Press.

Lather, P. (1991). *Getting smart: Feminist research and pedagogy with/in the postmodern.* New York: Routledge.

Lavie, S. (1990). *The poetics of military occupation: Mzeina allegories of Bedouin identity under Israeli and Egyptian rule.* Berkeley and Los Angeles: University of California Press.

Narayan, K. (1993). How native is a "native" anthropologist? *American Anthropologist, 95,* 671–86.

Rushdie, S. (1994). *East, West: Stories.* New York: Pantheon Books.

Sandoval, C. (1991). U.S. Third World feminism: The theory and method of oppositional consciousness in the postmodern world. *Gender, 10,* 1–24.

Sarup, M. (1993). *An introductory guide to post-structuralism and postmodernism.* Athens: University of Georgia Press.

Skeggs, B. (1994). Situating the production of feminist ethnography. In M. Maynard & J. Purvis (Eds.), *Researching women's lives from a feminist perspective* (pp. 72–92). London and New York: Taylor & Francis.

Spivak, G. C. (1993). *Outside in the teaching machine.* London and New York: Routledge.

Thomas, J. (1993). *Doing critical ethnography.* Newbury Park, London, and New Delhi: Sage Publications.

Trinh, M-H T. (1989). *Woman, native, other.* London and New York: Routledge.

Trinh, M-H T. (1991). *When the moon waxes red.* London and New York: Routledge.

Tucker, M. (1990). Director's foreword. *Out there.* London and Cambridge, MA: MIT Press.

Visweswaran, K. (1994). *Fictions of feminist ethnography.* Minneapolis and London: University of Minnesota Press.

Chapter 5

Researching
Libraries, Literacies,
and Lives:
A Rhizoanalysis

Donna E. Alvermann

Introduction

About the same time that I was introduced to Deleuze and Guattari's
(1980/1987) notion of the rhizome (and rhizoanalysis) in *A Thousand
Plateaus: Capitalism and Schizophrenia*, I had just finished writing up the
last in a series of 3-year-long qualitative studies begun while I was co-
directing the National Reading Research Center. Although since published or in press, these studies (Alvermann et al., 1996; Alvermann,
Commeyras, Young, Randall, & Hinson, 1997; Alvermann, Young,
Green, & Wisenbaker, in press) continued to interest me, largely, I suppose, as a consequence of my having read *A Thousand Plateaus*. In part, I
remained fascinated with Deleuze and Guattari's notion of rhizoanalysis
and the possibilities it might (or might not) hold for looking once again
at the data that informed the three earlier studies. This fascination ultimately led me to use it as an analytic method for re-examining the findings from one of those studies—the one we (Alvermann et al., in press)
referred to as the "Read and Talk Club" study—in preparation for writing the present chapter.

A Brief History of the Study

The purpose of this 15-week study of 20 adolescents' after-school talk
about a variety of texts in a public library setting (Alvermann et al., in
press) was to trace how their perceptions and negotiations of Read and
Talk Club[1] discussions were shaped by (and helped to shape) the larger
institutional and societal contexts that regularly influence young people's actions and interactions with peers and adults. In framing the study,
we had drawn from a theoretical perspective that views discourse and

literacy as critical social practices (Freebody, Luke, Gee, & Street, in press; Lankshear, Gee, Knobel, & Searle, 1997; Street, 1995) and locates such practices within and across three contexts: the local, the institutional, and the societal. Working within that perspective, we had used Fairclough's (1989, 1995) critical discourse analysis to trace patterns in the Read and Talk Club members' locally mediated talk about texts to the larger institutional and societal structures that constituted such talk and through which it was interpreted.

Briefly, what we found was this: as a study site, the public library afforded a relatively safe niche in which both adolescents and adults felt free to experiment with alternative ways of doing school-like discussions. For example, the adolescents in the Read and Talk Clubs negotiated a discussion genre that differed appreciably from the one reported in a school-based study of Book Club (McMahon & Raphael, 1997), where small groups of students met to discuss a common reading and later shared their interpretations of that reading with the whole class. In the Read and Talk Clubs, participants opted to discuss something other than a common reading; they negotiated the right to read different materials of their own choosing, with the proviso being that club discussions would focus on discovering common themes across those materials. Free to question existing arrangements about *what* they would read, the adolescents engaged in a form of communal activity that challenged the status quo of small-group discussions. In doing so, they also made visible the dynamic and permeable boundaries within and across adolescents' and adults' life worlds.

A second conclusion we reached was that the public library provided a climate of acceptance—a liminal space of openings and closings (Foucault, 1986/1984) in which adolescents who liked to read could enjoy the company of other readers like themselves, isolated from the taunts of peers who viewed them as nerds because they were avid readers. Within this welcoming climate, the discourse of the Read and Talk Clubs closely resembled that of adult book clubs (Flood et al., 1994; Marshall, Smagorinsky, & Smith, 1995). As was true for adults, socializing was central to maintaining adolescent members' interest in participating in the clubs. The opportunity to talk about what they read was repeatedly mentioned by both adolescents and adults as helping them make new acquaintances and deepen existing friendships.

A final conclusion was that the adolescents in the Read and Talk Club study were particularly adept at fashioning new subjectivities as they engaged in positioning themselves and each other in ways that drew attention to existing ambiguities and dissenting voices within the context of club discussions. Figuratively speaking, the clubs were stages on which the adolescents could try out ways of speaking and acting within rela-

tively safe confines.² That such performances sometimes led to more permanent ways of interacting during club discussions is not surprising,
given Marilyn Frye's observation (cited in West & Zimmerman, 1987)
that "we do become what we practice being" (p. 146). In rehearsing their
new personas, they often engaged in talk that brought to the surface
varying contradictions traceable to the larger institutional and societal
contexts that regularly shape (and are shaped by) such talk. This was
particularly the case when talk turned to gender-related literacy practices, such as those that involved the adolescents in making choices
about what would be read and discussed at their club meetings. Recur-
rent patterns of "doing gender" (West & Zimmerman, 1987) in ways that
fit the occasion left little or no doubt as to the distinctions the adolescents
were drawing between what they considered appropriate male and
female tastes in reading materials. That such practices were merely social
arrangements whereby socially constituted differences took on appearances of being "normal and natural" seemed not to matter.

Tracings and Maps

As mentioned earlier, the motivation behind this present chapter was my
reading of Deleuze and Guattari's (1987/1980) introduction to *A Thousand Plateaus* in which they describe a rhizome network capable of
"strangling the roots of the infamous tree" (p. xiii)—the allusion here
being to the tree of Western thought that supports a binary logic and
symbolizes linear and ordered systems of thinking. Rhizomatous³ cartography, in contrast, involves experimenting with how to move between
things in ways that nullify beginnings and endings. From Deleuze and
Guattari's perspective, researchers interested in theory building would
do well to make maps, not tracings. In their metaphoric use of the term,
"a map is a part of the rhizome . . . open and connectable in all its dimensions . . . [with] multiple entryways, as opposed to the tracing, which
always comes back 'to the same'" (p. 12). This rhizomatous image of a
map, in contrast to the rooted knowledge one obtains from the tree (a
symbol of received knowledge passed down from the humanism of
Enlightenment time), is what distinguishes it from a tracing.

Maps, unlike tracings, are always becoming; they have no beginnings
and endings, just middles. It is by looking at middles that we begin to see
how, in perspective, everything else changes. Dimitriadis and Kamberelis
(1997) explain the process this way:

> In drawing maps, the theorist works at the surface, "creating" pos-
> sible realities by producing new articulations of disparate phenom-
> ena and connecting the exteriority of objects to whatever forces or

directions seem potentially related to them. As such, maps exceed both individual and collective experiences of what seems "naturally" real. (p. 150)

To avoid the kind of dualistic thinking that rhizomatous images are meant to counter—that is, good maps, bad tracings—Deleuze and Guattari recommend that once we have drawn a map, it is important to put the tracing back on the map. By inspecting the breaks and ruptures that become visible when the more stable tracing is laid upon the always becoming map, we are in a position to construct new knowledge, rather than merely propagate the old.

Rhizoanalysis and Texts

Texts, whether those used as the basis for discussion in the Read and Talk Clubs or the texts associated with the present analysis (i.e., field notes, interview transcripts, and conversations transcribed from videotaped club discussions), are typically thought to signify meaning, albeit meaning that is contingent upon the interaction of subject (reader) and context. Less typical is Deleuze and Guattari's (1987/1980) concept of a text, which is predicated on their particular decentering project—the avoidance of any orientation toward a culmination or ending point. In their sense of the term, a text is neither signifier nor the signified; therefore, it is inappropriate to think of interpreting or understanding texts in the conventional way. As Grosz (1994) explains:

> It is . . . no longer appropriate to ask what a text means, what it says, what is the structure of its interiority, how to interpret or decipher it. Instead, one must ask what it does, how it connects with other things (including its reader, its author, its literary and nonliterary context). (p. 199)

The conventional modes of interpretation and analysis espoused by linguists, literary theorists, and semioticians do not hold in a rhizo-textual analysis. In analyzing texts from Deleuze and Guattari's (1987/1980) perspective, it is how texts function outside themselves that is of interest. This interest stems from the belief that texts, like rhizomes, connect with other things (e.g., readers, other texts, contexts). This analogy between texts and rhizomes can be extended, as suggested by the following:

> Any point of a rhizome can be connected to anything other, and must be. . . . A rhizome ceaselessly establishes connections between semiotic chains, organizations of power, and circumstances relative to the arts, sciences, and social struggles. A semiotic chain is like a

tuber agglomerating very diverse acts, not only linguistic, but also perceptive, mimetic, gestural, and cognitive. (Deleuze & Guattari, 1987/1980, p. 7)

In sum, rhizoanalysis is a method of examining texts that allows us to see things in the middle. Looking for middles, rather than beginnings and endings, makes it possible to decenter key linkages and find new ones, not by combining old ones in new ways, but by remaining open to the proliferation of ruptures and discontinuities that in turn create other linkages. In this chapter, I use the figuration of rhizomatous map making to explore what had been invisible to me when Josephine Young, Colin Green, and I first analyzed the data from the Read and Talk Club study. In reanalyzing the texts of that study—the field notes, the transcripts of interviews with the adolescents, their parents, the librarian, and the videotapes of club discussions—I attempted to connect diverse fragments of data in ways that produced new linkages and revealed discontinuities that had gone unmarked in the original analysis. A description of what this map making entailed is presented next. Following that is a discussion of what I learned from putting the tracing back on the map.

Map Making

In an effort to map disparate phenomena at the surface level of the data texts from the Read and Talk Club study (Alvermann et al., in press), I passed through several phases of experimenting with different ways of thinking about those texts. Initially, I played with drawing actual maps (of the webbing or graphic organizer type) in which I juxtaposed key linkages from the study's findings with forms of popular culture (e.g., MTV, films, comics, and CD-ROMs) that were seeping into my work as part of another study that a new group of doctoral students and I were doing. Although helpful to my growing awareness of what rhizoanalysis entailed, these one-page maps were too concrete and seemed grossly lacking in terms of Deleuze and Guattari's (1987/1980) "acentered, non-hierarchical, non-signifying system" (p. 21) of map making. Gradually, I improved upon my earlier attempts at map making by drawing rhizomes whose tubers linked the study's findings to popular culture forms in less hierarchical ways. In true rhizome fashion, offshoots of these tubers began to spread to other pages, sometimes fragmenting into unregulated networks that took off on their own. And so it went.

Still dissatisfied with the two-dimensional and literal nature of my maps, I began to read books on cultural studies (e.g., Grosz, 1995; Storey, 1998) and youth cultures (Amit-Talai & Wulff, 1995; Skelton & Valentine, 1998). At the same time, I engaged in a series of rereadings of the adolescent Read and Talk Club texts (Alvermann et al., in press) for the express purpose of asking questions of those texts. For example, what did the Read and Talk Club texts do in relation to the other texts that I was reading on youth cultures? What did they do to my textual "others" (in the Bakhtinian sense of the *dialogic other*[4])? Did the texts connect to me in any personal way? Was the connection an emotional one, and if so, what was it? Questions such as these stemmed from works already mentioned (Deleuze & Guattari, 1987/1980; Dimitriadis & Kamberelis, 1997; Grosz, 1994) and from the work of Lynne Pearce (1997) at Lancaster University. Pearce developed the method of implicated reading to theorize her own processes and practices of reading novels, paintings, photographs, and films within their gendered contexts.

In this chapter, I adapt Pearce's (1997) implicated reading method and use it in conjunction with Deleuze and Guattari's rhizoanalysis to look for discontinuities and ruptures in the smooth tracings from my earlier analysis of the Read and Talk Club texts. Because implicated readings engage us in intimate relationships with texts and evoke a full range of readerly emotions—including enchantment, devotion, envy, frustration, disappointment, and so on—they are, like Deleuze and Guattari's rhizome, open and connectable, always becoming. In applying Pearce's method to the data texts of the Read and Talk Club study, I interweave excerpts from my rememories and rereadings of those texts with retrospective commentaries on those rereadings. To distinguish one from the other, I use italicized print for the rememories and boldface for the rereadings. The commentaries appear as regular print.

Mapping Connections to Popular Culture

Mapping disparate phenomena found in popular culture enabled me to think differently about the social networks in which the adolescents in the Read and Talk Clubs were anchored. In the following excerpts from several rememories and rereadings that I constructed as part of my approach to rhizoanalysis, I work at the surface of five texts to ask what each does to the other, what they do to my textual others, and how they connect to me, personally. The five texts include: a draft of a manuscript that became part of a book on teaching critical media literacy (Alvermann, Moon, & Hagood, 1999); a clip from Lorri Neilsen's interview with her son (Neilsen, 1998); a popabilly hip-hop recording; a *Newsweek* article featuring TV's comedy hit *South Park* (Marin, 1998); and a critique of an advertisement for cyberculture software (Luke & Luke, 1997).

■ ■ ■

*I remember wondering what a rhizomatous book-talk practice would look like.
To find out, I began mapping disparate phenomena from several print and non-
print popular culture texts that I was using in writing a book on critical media literacy. My purpose in mapping media phenomena in the image of the rhizome,
with its proliferating shoots that have no central axis, no point of origin, and no
endpoint, was to think differently about the social networks in which the adolescents in the Read and Talk Club study appeared to locate themselves. Whether or
not any of the map's exterior and nonhierarchical meanderings would connect
with elements from the study's original analysis became less and less a concern as
I worked at the surface level to associate phenomena from disparate media forms,
including Tarantino's* Pulp Fiction.

*I recall noting when I first read a transcript of Lorri Neilsen's (1998) interview
with David, her teenage son, that Tarantino was David's favorite director, and*
Pulp Fiction *was his all-time favorite movie. I also recall that while* Pulp Fiction *had won the Cannes Film Festival's highest prize and an Academy Award
for best original screenplay, it was routinely criticized for its "blaxploitation" and
graphic violence—factors that seemed not to figure into David's assessment of this
film.*

■ ■ ■

A rereading of David's description of the appeal that *Pulp Fiction* **and Tarantino held for him reveals something quite different
from the critics' evaluation of the film. In David's words:**

> **I liked the way the story was told—the story line all jum-
> bled. I liked the cinematography and the dialogue. It was
> both vulgar and smart. . . . I thought it was hilarious. And I
> really liked the way Tarantino messed with linear structure
> and chopped up the film. . . . Plus the writing was really
> good. You know, the dialogue about nothing . . .**
>
> **My close friends and I got the sound track which was a
> kick-ass soundtrack which also added to my love for the
> film because there were excerpts from the movie on the
> soundtrack, which I memorized. . . . We even went so far as
> to do our own** *Pulp Fiction* **movie, Simon and I. We went
> downtown to an apartment building and did the scene
> about the foot massage. We took the video camera from
> Simon's house, decided to look for an old building that
> looked kind of '70s, carpeted and all that. We found a place
> on Queen Street, went up to one of the floors and asked
> Simon's sister to film us. We walked around, we were
> dressed up, and then we went downstairs and did the scene
> about Royale with cheese.**
>
> **Tarantino seems like us. Hanging around making films.**

Hanging out with friends. Our conversations are like that kind of dialogue. Or like *Seinfeld* . . . We argue about nothing and are funny. Like Ross will go, hey, I like your shoes, let's just say. And I go, yeah, man, they *are* the shoes. And Ross will say, Oh, they are the shoes. And then we just go off talking about shoes. Just think of a situation and we'd try to one up each other, playing, not like competition. (Neilsen, 1998, pp. 15–18)

■ ■ ■

David's perception that he and his friends have conversations about nothing in particular, yet they find such dialogue funny, reminded me of another form of popular culture that I had recently encountered. In the popabilly hip-hop hit, "Are You Jimmy Ray?" the songwriter Jimmy Ray also celebrates a studied lack of regard for meaningful lyrics: "It's fun . . . You can sing along. You know, don't bore us, get to the chorus" (Hammer, 1998, p. 47). Pitched as popabilly hip-hop's perfect song, "Are You Jimmy Ray?" was set to move into Billboard's top 10 list according to *Newsweek*'s newsmaker department for the week of March 23, 1998. This recording, with its empty lyrics, left me wondering if the language of Stan, Kyle, Cartman, and Kenny—the four foul-mouthed third graders from Comedy Central's animated cartoon show *South Park*—wasn't preferable to Jimmy Ray's brand of communication.

South Park, described by Marin (1998) as "a paranormal Colorado town inhabited by flatulent third-graders" (p. 56), is an adult underground pop-cult obsession with irresistible kid appeal. It is fast turning Wednesday and Saturday nights into family nights. Despite a recent ruling by the Federal Communications Commission that will enable parents to block the show by buying TV sets that have FCC approved built-in V-chips, Marin explains why this option may not be necessary. Already, he notes, 23 percent of the viewing audience is under 18, and with 5.2 million cable viewers, *South Park* recently beat ABC's *Prime Time* in the ratings game.

In true rhizomatous fashion, then, I have gone from *Pulp Fiction* to popabilly hip-hop to *South Park*, and all by way of a book on teaching critical media literacy (Alvermann et al., 1999). Only one connection remains to be made, and that is to an article by Carmen and Haida Luke (1997) on the gendered politics of naming. I recall writing in my journal the following reaction to that article.

■ ■ ■

Although the pointless banter found in Pulp Fiction *may appeal to my textual other, David Neilsen, I am neither motivated to respond to his assessment of it, nor prone to give this form of dialogue much thought. Such is not the case, however, when it comes to the language used in Prodigy's* Amber, *a cyberculture software advertisement.*

■ ■ ■

In rereading the Luke and Luke (1997) article, I was reminded once again of the gendered relations of power and naming in the ingratiating pose of Amber, the young adolescent girl in the Prodigy advertisement. Featured in the March 1996 issue of *Wired,* a magazine for the cyberculture crowd, the ad shows Amber with this message typed in quotation marks next to her: "It all started when I typed hello." As Luke and Luke have pointed out, the sexual innuendo in this statement is hard to miss:

> "It all started when I typed hello." We can read this to be a take on the way we talk about the start of an intimate relationship which, taking a cue from Amber's winsome smile, might just suggest that "the on-line experience" really did start something more than a chat-group experience. The sexual innuendo here is hard to miss. We note that Amber is in quotation marks which tells us that Amber is her sigfile, her on-line persona. . . .
>
> She leans her hand into her neck which catches some hair strands pushed against her lips. Her smile betrays nothing: can we assume she's just come off-line after a particularly satisfying on-line encounter, or is she waiting to plug in to get into "whatever you're into," or is she just taking a reflective moment to ruminate over the Prodigy experience? (p. 56)

■ ■ ■

Although the stereotyping in the Prodigy advertisement is no less blatant than that found in "the hot-buttered voice" (Marin, 1998, p. 60) of the black chef in *South Park*, or in Samuel Jackson's portrayal of Jules in *Pulp Fiction*, I have to wonder if Amber's allusion to a chat-group experience isn't but one more lynch pin in the inscription of female sexuality in relations of power. I also have to wonder how my own positioning relative to this ad has affected my interpretation. As map maker, I am historically constituted in certain Discourses (Gee, 1996)[5] that can never be, or at least are not yet, part of the Discourses taken up by the adolescents in the Read and Talk Club study. Thus, the degree to which the popular culture phenomena that I chose to map here can contribute to thinking differently about the social networks in which the adolescents were situated is limited by the choices I made and the Discourses in which I am constituted.

Putting the Tracing Back on the Map

Foucault (1985/1984) observed, "There are times in life when the question of knowing if one can think differently than one thinks, and perceive differently than one sees, is absolutely necessary if one is to go on looking and reflecting at all" (p. 8). This observation has taken on special meaning for me as a consequence of having used Deleuze and Guattari's (1987/1980) rhizoanalysis to help me think differently about the data from the Read and Talk Club study. By mapping that data in ways that looked for "middles," rather than beginnings and endings, I was able to make connections that would otherwise have gone unnoticed, or more likely, unthought. But such was the focus of this chapter's previous section. Here, I concentrate on what happened when I put the tracing back on the map in order to locate potential ruptures and discontinuities in the different interpretations of the data.

One discontinuity that became evident when the tracing was compared to the map had to do with relations of power and adolescent sexuality. In retrospect, it seems dangerous to have missed this domain of power relations, especially since Foucault (1985/1984) demonstrated how one's sexuality is a prime site for the exercise of social power over the body. Studies of young children's and adolescents' literacy-related talk have also documented the increasingly complex ways in which sexuality is a Discourse (Davies, 1993; Gee, 1996) that figures into everyday social interactions both in and out of school (Buckingham & Sefton-Green, 1994; McRobbie, 1994; Muspratt, Luke, & Freebody, 1997). Why we failed to make a connection between sexuality and relations of power in adolescent literacy practices in the original analysis is not clear, although I would suspect such an oversight can be explained at least partially by Freebody et al.'s (in press) contention that every statement we make about texts we read, write, or speak raises "a bristling array of silences—things we could have said instead, aspects of a topic we could have highlighted but chose not to" (p. 1). Reasons behind the choices that we make when speaking out or remaining silent are inherently tied to how we perceive ourselves in relation to others, to what we are willing to reveal about our own interests and desires, and to whether or not we believe we can make a difference by adding our voices to the mix.

A second area of silence revealed by the rhizoanalysis was the veritable lack of student discussion around issues of race and social class in the Read and Talk Club study, though these two issues were at the forefront of the popular culture forms that I read and wrote about. While Josephine, Colin, and I (Alvermann et al., in press) noted several manifestations of privilege, both as a racial and class construct, during student interactions in the weekly Read and Talk Club meetings, we found no evidence that the adolescents themselves were explicitly aware of such privilege. And, our field notes and interview transcripts indicate we did not press the issue with them. In retrospect, allowing this disjuncture between what we noticed and what the adolescents chose to address to go unmarked was a limitation of the study. Our lack of action in instigating such discussion also inhibited what we could say about how relations of power may have simultaneously reproduced and rendered legitimate particular views of privilege.

A third way that putting the tracing back on the map made it possible to see the original study's findings in a new light had to do with choice of reading materials. As a consequence of the rhizoanalysis and the attention given to different communication styles, it became clear that numerous breaks in communication had occurred between the adolescents and the adult facilitators of the Read and Talk Clubs over issues related to who would read what and when. Although the adolescents had established early on that they wanted to be free to choose the materials over which they would hold a "common" discussion, it was not always the case that they followed through on their end of the bargain. Nor was it the case that the only adults who involved themselves in issues of book choice were the Read and Talk Club facilitators. Parents, too, sometimes got into the act. For example, Jane's mother did not approve of her daughter's sudden liking for such low-status books as those found in the *Sweet Valley High* series. In an interview with Colin, she shared some doubts she had about the Read and Talk Club's influence on Jane:

> MOTHER: [*Initially*] Jane did say that some of the kids [in her group] read some awful books. And then the next minute she turned around and checked out *Sweet Valley High,* so I don't know if you all have helped her or if you have led her astray. But she has gone from reading fairly classical work to *Sweet Valley High.*
>
> COLIN: It's interesting because there are two girls [in Jane's group] who have read everything in the series. I think they have read everything published by . . .
>
> MOTHER: [*interrupting Colin*] I notice that she [Jane] has one, and she even apologized when she checked it out of the library last week because she felt that it was awful. She said, "I'm getting that book there because I think it will put me to sleep at night." And I said, "It probably will."

Finally, putting the tracing back on the map revealed that the adolescents in the Read and Talk Club study had been engaging in a rhizomatous literacy practice of their own making all along; it simply took the rhizoanalysis to draw attention to this fact.[6] For surely their practice of reading different books, rather than the same book, for a "common" group discussion is analogous to Deleuze and Guattari's (1987/1980) notion of map making, where one works at the surface to connect disparate phenomena in ways that exceed what is typically regarded as "naturally" real (Dimitriadis & Kamberelis, 1997). Breaking with the "natural" or the norm in a highly institutionalized practice such as book club discussion is noteworthy in its own right. That a group of adolescents initiated such a break, albeit in a nonschool setting, is especially significant.

Some Closing Thoughts on Rhizoanalysis

Experimenting with any new form of analysis presents certain challenges, and while exploring the potential of rhizoanalysis proved no exception to this rule, it was at least an informative exploration—one in which I learned about my own tolerance for ambiguity. But before listing some of the difficulties I experienced along the way, I begin with this observation: the irony did not escape me that in my attempt to use rhizoanalysis as a method for thinking differently about a previously analyzed set of data, I came close to concretizing a process that prides itself on being "open and connectable in all its dimensions" (Deleuze & Guattari, 1987/1980, p. 12). It is also a process that looks for ways to move between things in ways that nullify beginnings and endings. Although I consciously worked to overcome my closure-seeking proclivities, in the end I suspect it was these tendencies (at least in part) that kept me from exploring many of the other multiple entryways that rhizoanalysis promised. Educated in the early 1960s as a history teacher, I also suspect that my earlier understanding of knowledge as being rooted in the tree—a symbol of received knowledge passed down from the humanism of Enlightenment time—was struggling throughout the process to resist the knowledge produced from my rhizomatous meanderings.

On a less philosophic note, I attribute my difficulties in using rhizoanalysis to the fact that I had no examples to follow. At times I wondered (and still do) whether or not this was an analysis meant for application. Would it have been better to consider rhizoanalysis in the abstract only? More to the point, does it even make sense to contemplate thinking differently about previously interpreted texts when individuals writing about rhizoanalysis suggest that "it is no longer appropriate to ask what a text means" (Grosz, 1994, p. 199)? By choosing to use Pearce's (1997) method of implicated readings, I had hoped to address Grosz's point. That is, I had hoped to avoid asking the meanings of texts per se and to concentrate instead on engaging with those texts through my textual "others" and through becoming aware of how I personally connected with the texts. In retrospect, while the implicated readings seemed to serve me well, I am not certain that I was ever fully able to leave behind the notion that meaning, at least partially, does reside in the text. Years spent as a reading specialist steeped in the schema-theoretic view of text comprehension threatened to do me in at every turn of the rhizoanalytic process.

But self-doubts aside, I can say with all sincerity that attempting to think differently through rhizoanalysis was an exercise I am glad I undertook. Free to move about in texts only tangentially related to researching libraries, literacies, and adolescents' lives, I felt energized by the serendipitous nature of the process. Just as importantly, I found it intellectually fulfilling to engage in a process where, by looking for the "middles," rather than the beginnings and endings, I was able to see how, in perspective, everything else changes.

Finally, at the risk of sounding too accepting, I would venture to say that this one experience in using rhizoanalysis will not be my last one. Whether it is through further exploration and experimentation with "real" data, or simply through additional readings on the topic, I can imagine the image of the rhizome remaining with me for quite a spell. Because rhizoanalysis provides a different and "freeing" way of looking at data, I find it appealing. For unlike some of the feminist and race-based theories of analysis that I have used in the past, rhizoanalysis has made it possible for me to "see" in the data something other than what I went looking for in the first place.

Acknowledgments

The study discussed in this chapter was funded in part by the National Reading Research Center of the Universities of Georgia and Maryland. It was supported under the Educational and Development Centers Program (PR/Award No. 117A20007) as administered by the Office of Educational Research and Improvement, U.S. Department of Education. The findings and opinions expressed here do not necessarily reflect the position or policies of the National Reading Research Center, the Office of Educational Research and Improvement, or the U.S. Department of Education.

Notes

1. Although the Read and Talk Clubs (so named by one of the adolescents in the study) bear a resemblance to Book Club (McMahon, Raphael, & Goatley, 1995; McMahon & Raphael, 1997), they differ in two important ways. Unlike Book Club, the Read and Talk Clubs were not conceived for instructional purposes, nor were they restricted to discussions of one kind of print literacy (books). These differences set them apart from the type of book clubs literacy researchers typically study.

2. I am indebted to Mark Dressman of the University of Houston for suggesting this interpretation.

3. *The Compact Edition of the Oxford English Dictionary* (1971) defines rhizomatous as having rhizomata, the plural form of rhizome, which is the botanical term for a "subterranean root-like stem emitting roots and usually producing leaves at its apex" (p. 2536).

4. According to Holquist (1990) in his introductory book on Bakhtin, *dialogism* is a term coined by Anglo-Americana to refer to the notion of reciprocity between speaker and addressee that undergirds so much of Bakhtin's work. Bakhtin, himself, did not use the term. Relatedly, Pearce (1997) uses the term *textual other* to refer to the idea that "no utterance (either written or spoken) is made in isolation, but is always dependent upon the anticipated response of another (actual or implicit) addressee" (p. 29).

5. The sociolinguist James Gee (1996) uses Discourse with a capital *D* to delineate it from discourse (e.g., conversations, arguments) with a lowercase *d*. From his perspective, Discourses are ways individuals have of speaking, thinking, and behaving in the world so as to take on a particular role that others will recognize as being like themselves. Gee refers to Discourse with a capital *D* as one's identity kit. In his words:

> Each Discourse incorporates a usually taken for granted and tacit "theory" of what counts as a "normal" person and the "right" ways to think, feel, and behave. These theories crucially involve viewpoints on the distribution of social goods like status, worth, and material goods in society (who should and who should not have them). (p. ix)

6. For bringing this to my attention, I thank Linda Brodkey, who was the discussant for an earlier version of this chapter, which was presented at the 1998 meeting of the American Educational Research Association, San Diego, California.

References

Alvermann, D. E., Commeyras, M., Young, J. P., Randall, S., & Hinson, D. (1997). Interrupting gendered discursive practices in classroom talk about texts: Easy to think about, difficult to do. *Journal of Literacy Research, 29*, 73–104.

Alvermann, D. E., Moon, J. S., & Hagood, M. C. (1999). *Popular culture in the classroom: Teaching and researching critical media literacy* (IRA/NRC Literacy Studies Series). Newark, DE: International Reading Association.

Alvermann, D. E., Young, J. P., Green, C., & Wisenbaker, J. (in press). Adolescents' perceptions and negotiations of literacy practices in after-school Read and Talk Clubs. *American Educational Research Journal.*

Alvermann, D. E., Young, J. P., Weaver, D., Hinchman, K., Moore, D. W., Phelps, S. F., Thrash, E., & Zalewski, P. (1996). Middle and high school students' perceptions of how they experience text-based discussions: A multicase study. *Reading Research Quarterly, 31,* 240–67.

Amit-Talai, V., & Wulff, H. (Eds.). (1995). *Youth cultures: A cross-cultural perspective.* London: Routledge.

Buckingham, D., & Sefton-Green, J. (1994). *Cultural studies goes to school: Reading and teaching popular media.* London: Taylor & Francis.

The compact edition of the Oxford English dictionary (1st ed.). (1971). Oxford: Oxford University Press.

Davies, B. (1993). *Shards of glass: Children reading and writing beyond gendered identities.* Cresskill, NJ: Hampton Press.

Deleuze, G., & Guattari, F. (1987). *A thousand plateaus: Capitalism & schizophrenia.* (B. Massumi, Trans.) Minneapolis: University of Minnesota Press. (Original work published 1980)

Dimitriadis, G., & Kamberelis, G. (1997). Shifting terrains: Mapping education within a global landscape. *The Annals of the Academy of Political and Social Science, 551,* 137–50.

Fairclough, N. (1989). *Language and power.* London: Longman.

Fairclough, N. (1995). *Critical discourse analysis: The critical study of language.* London: Longman.

Flood, J., Lapp, D., Alvarez, D., Romero, A., Ranck-Buhr, W., Moore, J., Jones, M. A., Kabildis, C., & Lungren, L. (1994). *Teacher book clubs: A study of teachers' and student teachers' participating in contemporary multicultural fiction literature discussion groups.* (Reading Research Report No. 22). Athens: National Reading Research Center, Universities of Georgia and Maryland.

Foucault, M. (1985). *The history of sexuality, Volume 2: The use of pleasure.* (R. Hurley, Trans.). New York: Vintage Books. (Original work published 1984)

Foucault, M. (1986). Of other spaces. (J. Miskowiec, Trans.). *Diacritics, 16,* 22–27. (Original work published 1984)

Freebody, P., Luke, A., Gee, J., & Street, B. V. (in press). *Literacy as critical social practice.* London: Falmer Press.

Gee, J. P. (1996). *Social linguistics and literacies: Ideology in discourses* (2d ed.). London: Taylor & Francis.

Grosz, E. (1994). A thousand tiny sexes: Feminism and rhizomatics. In C. V. Boundas & D. Olkowski (Eds.), *Gilles Deleuze and the theater of philosophy* (pp. 187–210). New York: Routledge.

Grosz, E. (1995). *Space, time, and perversion: Essays on the politics of bodies.* New York: Routledge.

Hammer, J. (1998, March 23). Catchy kitsch. *Newsweek,* 47.

Holquist, M. (1990). *Dialogism: Bakhtin and his world.* London: Routledge.

Lankshear, C. (with Gee, J. P., Knobel, M., & Searle, S). (1997). *Changing literacies.* Buckingham, UK: Open University Press.

Luke, C., & Luke, H. (May, 1997). Techno-textuality: Representation of femininity and sexuality. *Media International Australia, 84,* 46–58.

Marin, R. (1998, March 23). South Park: The rude tube. *Newsweek,* 56–62.

Marshall, J. D., Smagorinsky, P., & Smith, M. W. (1995). *The language of interpretation: Patterns of discourse in discussion of literature.* Urbana, IL: National Council of Teachers of English.

McMahon, S. I., & Raphael, T. E. (1997). *The book club connection: Literacy learning and classroom talk.* New York: Teachers College Press.

McMahon, S., Raphael, T., & Goatley, V. (1995). Changing the context for classroom reading instruction: The book club project. In J. Brophy (Ed.), *Advances in research on teaching* (pp. 123–66). Greenwich, CT: JAI Press.

McRobbie, A. (1994). *Postmodernism and popular culture.* London: Routledge.

Muspratt, S., Luke, A., & Freebody, P. (Eds.). (1997). *Constructing critical literacies.* Cresskill, NJ: Hampton Press.

Neilsen, L. (1998). Playing for real: Performative texts and adolescent literacies. In D. E. Alvermann, K. A. Hinchman, D. W. Moore, S. F. Phelps, & D. R. Waff (Eds.), *Reconceptualizing the literacies in adolescents' lives* (pp. 3–26). Mahwah, NJ: Lawrence Erlbaum.

Pearce, L. (1997). *Feminism and the politics of reading.* London: Arnold.

Skelton, T., & Valentine, G. (Eds.). (1998). *Cool places: Geographies of youth cultures.* London: Routledge.

Storey, J. (Ed.). (1998). *Cultural theory and popular culture: A reader.* Athens: University of Georgia Press.

Street, B. (1995). *Social literacies: Critical approaches to literacy in development, ethnography, and education.* New York: Longman.

West, C., & Zimmerman, D. H. (1987). Doing gender. *Gender & Society, 1,* 125–51.

Chapter 6

Electronic Tools for Dismantling the Master's House: Poststructuralist Feminist Research and Hypertext Poetics

Wendy Morgan

> Will the collage/montage revolution in representation be admitted into the academic essay, into the discourse of knowledge, replacing the "realist" criticism based on the notions of "truth" as correspondence to or correct reproduction of a referent object of study?
>
> (Ulmer, 1983, p. 86)

An Experiment on an Experiment

The previous pages of this volume bear ample witness to the diverse ways in which feminists working in the social sciences have taken up poststructuralist theories as tools to "dismantle the master's house" (Lorde, 1984). In research, this has led us to question how we do our "head work," "field work," and "text work." My interest here is in that third form of work—although, of course, it does not follow only after the other two: language, in the form of discourses, is always involved in our thinking and practice. One of the most radical examples of such text work is the book *Troubling the Angels: Women Living with HIV/AIDS* (Lather & Smithies, 1995, 1997),[1] which will be discussed in this chapter.

Poststructuralist theorizing and practice have also been of interest to those (still few) feminists exploring experimental hypertext (e.g., Greco, 1996, 1997; Jackson, 1995; Page, 1996). This is hardly surprising, since the birth of hypertext was attended by poststructuralist theorists (e.g., Bolter, 1992; Johnson-Eilola, 1997; Joyce, 1995; Landow, 1992, 1997; Lanham, 1989; Tuman, 1992). For hypertext enthusiasts generally agree that if poststructuralist theory can give a theoretical account of hypertext, then hypertext tests that theory and even realizes it in ways not previously possible (Landow, 1997, p. 2).

The salient characteristic of hypertext lies in its electronic linkages between parts of a work and between works. It is sometimes said that hypertext is "nonlinear"; rather, it is "multisequential" in offering any of an almost infinite number of lines through the text's constituent portions or nodes. On any occasion, the ordering depends on the reader's decisions in choosing which links to follow from which phrase or node to which other. She can trace (and in some hypertexts create) many pathways, following various lines of desire and argument and thereby crossing various borders—whether between texts, genres, disciplines of knowledge, or viewpoints. Such ordering creates an order only for the time of the textual "performance" choreographed by the reader. In a word, the difference between print and hypertext is between place and space. It is between, on the one hand, the apparent stability, in print, of contexts and hence meanings created by the fixed sequence of parts (words, sentences, paragraphs, sections, chapters, parts, front and end matter and sequences of chronology, syllogism, proposition-and-substantiation, or rhetorical buildup) and, on the other, the indeterminacy of a hypertext with its nodes like so many shards of colored glass that fall into ever new patterns as the viewer turns the device. It is between a hierarchical and logical fixity of text parts, and a rhizomatic growth ("all adventitious middle," to quote Moulthrop, 1991a, p. 254). The one is fixed in place; the other a space intersected by mobile elements (this useful distinction of de Certeau, 1984, is taken up for its hypertextual application by Johnson-Eilola, 1997). As Joyce (1995) puts it, "Hypertext, at least when it is seen as constructive rather than exploratory, is serial thought. Its 'mode of spatialization,' Deleuze and Guattari's term, is being *for* space, what I call the constructive, a form for what does not yet exist, rather than being *in* space, or the exploratory and colonizing" (p. 189). Print is presented as a product; hypertext is necessarily a reader's performance, an event.

Foremost, therefore, among the claims made for hypertext's poststructuralist credentials is that it blurs the boundaries between authors and readers, giving to the latter more power to construct the text in the reading by choosing pathways through the material and thereby juxtaposing textual segments in a once-off assemblage. It demonstrates intertextuality through the display on-screen of texts visibly associated with one another. It promotes multivocality with the dynamic launching of one screen after another. No single voice or viewpoint can have a stable, privileged claim to authority or centrality when it can be replaced (juxtaposed or overlaid) by another, maybe dissenting, point of view. Hypertext can similarly transgress the boundaries between genres as readers move from one form of text to another and back in the same, almost seamless electronic environment. These are some of the ways in which hypertext exhibits its own textual deconstruction, subverting the conventions of coherence in structure and viewpoint through a network of contingencies. So, too, it reassembles the textual hierarchies of print (whether of "main text" vis-à-vis footnote or of core argument vis-à-vis elaboration and exemplification), and so it resituates the marginal. Its multisequentiality invites divergence from the singular, onward-driving linearity of conventional narrative and argument. And hypertext thereby deconstructs closure, since a hypertext is finished when the reader is, on any occasion. In such ways then—at least in the hands of experimental practitioners—it exemplifies the "open" text of Eco (1978) or the "writerly" text of Barthes (1970).

While there are certainly correspondences between hypertext and poststructuralist theory, this may not mean that the former in all its manifestations inevitably realizes the latter, since radical potential can always be recuperated for conservative ends (Johnson-Eilola, 1997; Aarseth, 1997). Nevertheless, the very characteristics of hypertext encourage its exploitation for poststructuralist work.

It is all the more surprising then that, despite such convergences between feminism and poststructuralism on the one hand (hereafter called "postfeminism") and between hypertext theory and poststructuralism on the other, there have been no examples to date, in theory or practice, of convergence between postfeminist research in the social sciences and a poststructuralist hypertextuality. (There are instances of hypertext being used as an organizational and presentational tool for research data, but it has not been exploited as a reflexively re-presentational medium.) This chapter describes such a project. With Lather's permission, I have reinscribed parts of *Troubling the Angels* in hypertextual form, adding links and pathways and nodes containing additional materials. My unpublished hypertext document, "Monstrous Angels,"[2] as a tissue of quotations, could therefore be seen as an instance of postmodern plagiarism. The politics and ethics entailed by this experiment are discussed below.

The experiment had several aims: to inquire into the conditions of such writing and reading, to begin to describe a poetics of postfeminist research hypertextuality, and to evaluate the im/possibilities of so perverse a form(lessness) of writing. Through examining such hypertextual elements as associative linking for nomadic thinking, intertextual and intratextual juxtapositions in a multigeneric collage, the unfixing of textual hierarchies in a rhizomatic text, and a nonsequential polylogic, I shall attempt to show how poststructuralist theories of language and knowledge are enacted in this electronic environment.

My choice of *Troubling the Angels* was no accident. The text is situated at the far reaches of the postfeminist push to inquire into the conditions of knowledge and their effects on researchers and research. This is visible also in its experimental form. Any of the pages presents a horizontally split text, the upper offering the women's tales and their conversations; the lower, the researchers' conversations, journal entries, and meditations on the context of the tale telling, the processes of researching and the construction of the text; side bars of anecdotes and "footnotes"; and boxes with quotations or factual information. And between each of the five story series are "intertexts," chapters in which materials from sociology, philosophy, poetry, history, and other fields are woven into or juxtaposed with Lather's meditations on the nature of the angelic. Indeed, as soon as I read Lather's description of the work as

> organized as layers of various kinds of information, shifts of register, turns of different faces towards the reader . . . a book that puts things in motion rather than captures them in some still-life . . . moving from inside to outside, across different levels and a multiplicity and complexity of layers . . . a format that folds both backward and forward . . . a weaving of method, the politics of interpretation, data, analysis. (Lather & Smithies, 1997, p. xvi)

I knew that here was a book that aspired to the condition of hypertext. For hypertext is always an event—a text just in the process of becoming as we read and ceasing to exist in that sequence when we quit the program. I believed that a "constructive" hypertext (described by Joyce, 1995, p. 420, as those that "require a capability to act: to create, change, and recover particular encounters within the developing body of knowledge") could push further than even a codex book like Lather's toward the limits of the textual representation of social science research knowledge. Hence my hypertextual assay.

The congruence between Lather's textual project and the capacities of hypertext is striking. Her print text reaches toward a form that will be homologous with the ex-centric, marginal, borderline narratives and subaltern knowledges both of women with HIV/AIDS and of postfeminists, a form that will foreground the disorderly and heterogeneous and keep in play some of the possible meanings of the lives of those women—meanings that must remain "fragments and traces of what is impossible to think whole and clear" (Lather & Smithies, 1997, p. 196). Such a text attempts to represent the condition of social science knowledge as unstable (not cumulative and coherent in its "advance"), contextual and relational (rather than appearing as a distinct opus that stores up the authoritative meanings of an original author), and provisional (awaiting the supplementation that does not complete but always renders partial and inadequate).

It might seem that the form of Lather's text is a demonstration of what can be achieved *without* the benefit of hypertext. Yet I do not believe that my experiment is superfluous. For despite its heterogeneity, Lather's troubling new textwork grasps at what is beyond the linear mode of the book with its historical will to closure and resolution. It yearns for its own undoing, "Within such a book, reading both becomes a brooding over that which is beyond the word and the rational, and gestures toward the limits as well as the possibilities of knowing" (Lather & Smithies, 1997, p. xvi).

The hypertext form, as demonstrated and discussed below, is, I believe, among the best ways currently available for acknowledging those very conditions of social science research knowledge foregrounded in poststructuralist theorizing: that shifting contexts (for texts and reading) lead to shifting meanings; that discourses and genres are constitutive of objects of knowledge (research "facts") and human subjects; that there is no possibility of attaining a single, complete truth in a coherent account; and that reading and writing are interested, desirous acts.

This is not to suggest that writing in the hypertextual mode can simply escape out of all the regularities of previous text forms into some still uncontaminated space of sheer possibility—since language brings its own constraints and subversions (whether of authorial authority, discourse, or genre) that depend on an expectation of norms. And therefore, poststructuralist feminist research cannot totally evade complicity with the mainstream traditions. Nonetheless, if my experiment demonstrates some potential, other postfeminist researchers might also utilize hypertext to rock the boat on that smooth-flowing mainstream.

Toward a Poetics of Postfeminist Research Hypertext Writing

Neither this chapter nor "Monstrous Angels," my hypertext document, represents a finished argument; rather, it is a more open-ended process of investigation and speculation concerning the conditions of such hypertextual writing/reading. What follows here are some first items in that poetics with illustrations from my exemplar.

Associative Links

Hypertext, say Moulthrop and Kaplan (1994), is "promiscuous (in the root sense of 'seeking relations')" (p. 227). Another metaphor occurs to me: in the rapid transitions between one node and another, in the intertextual interstices, an electric arcing of meaning occurs, like light leaping between electrodes. This is very different from what Slatin (1990) calls "linear thinking" (p. 874), which spells out its steps. By contrast, "asso-

ciative thinking is discontinuous—a series of jumps like . . . the movements of the mind in creating metaphor." Such thinking, and the hypertextual form that represents it, might seem fragmented, but it is also
therefore accretive: it works on a logic of "and/and/and" and will not
accept the objective-seeming paradigm of reality as "either/or" (Douglas,
1996). "I want to learn how to write and think electronically," wrote
Ulmer (1989) "in a way that supplements without replacing analytical
reason" (p. x). But, as any supplementation alters the original (Derrida,
1981), such associative leaping and linking calls into question the suffi-
ciency of analytical argumentation.

   This point is developed below. Here let us follow the link to post-feminist skepticism about the impossibility of giving a coherent and completely reasoned account of "the" truth in social science research. For a
hypertext to include at least other, maybe incoherent, data, interpretations, voices, and viewpoints and to permit the superfluities of an associative imagination (consider Lather's angelic interchapters) is to
demonstrate how any account is made by excluding other possible
accounts as marginal, even inexpressible. In the hands of a postfeminist,
then, a hypertext may give the lie to her account of the truth—even subverting her own dearest desire to tell it her way. (And, of course, the
unforeseeable textual conjunctions a reader creates will undo willy-nilly
even her attempts to determine the nature of her ironies.) Moreover,
links preestablished by the writer may encourage the reader's further
associative leaps: a text that displays the patterns of its weaving promotes
the mind's tendency to play over and through its web to produce other
readings. And, where a hypertext is available in "write-enabled" mode,
such associations may form an ongoing supplementation in both links
and further nodes. For example, I have created links between aspects of
the women's narratives that deal with issues of categorization (in moral,
medical, and insurance discourses) and Lather's information boxes, comments, and quotations about the social consequences of such status
assignment that appear elsewhere in her print text. I have added a range
of linked materials relating to the monstrous as that which challenges
specific categorizations and hence the social and moral order of things.
Thus my associative work is both literal (at the level of the given text)
and metaphorical, in its extensions. And/and/and: there is always more
that can be said.

Intertextual, Intratextual Juxtaposition

After Derrida (1976), textual theorists can no longer accept the notion of
a self-contained text distinct from others. Instead, we recognize that texts
mean in relation to other texts, which they may quote or allude to
explicitly, parody, or reject—or which they may implicitly engage with as

part of a larger conversation whose discourses and genres mingle together in the spaces of a culture. Scholarly texts in the social sciences make overt intertextual references in citations, quotations, and bibliographies; however, these are not only necessarily limited in size and scope, they are also placed in a fixed position at the end or set off within brackets and indentations from which position they can only set up a subvocalizing murmur. In this way, paradoxically, a print text can still promote the pretence that there is an "intellectual separation of one text from others" (Landow, 1992, p. 53). By contrast, in a hypertext, such materials can more easily be explicitly, fully present. Not only are they center stage on the space of the screen when the node containing intertextual material is opened, but links can be made to other corpora included in the hypertextual space or (perhaps) accessible online. Thus hypertext can "weaken and perhaps destroy any sense of textual uniqueness" (Landow, 1992, p. 53); indeed, it can call to account the egotistical sublime of an author who claims to have sprung fully armed from his own head. It does so by promoting an "intertextual conceptual space" (Johnson-Eilola, 1992, p. 112). Thus, what is inherent in any text is foregrounded in hypertext, as "links within and without a text—intratextual and intertextual connections between points of text (including images)—become equivalent, thus bringing texts closer together and blurring the boundaries between them" (Landow, 1992, p. 61).

Since such inter/intratextuality becomes an ordering principle in hypertext, it offers postfeminist writers a species of "deterritorialised" writing (Moulthrop, 1991b, p. 154). Hypertext may therefore open up a more collegial space in which voices may speak to and with one another across what had been static boundaries. It may be used to create an intricate network of a text whose intertextual complications bear witness to the impossibility of claiming single authority for a single account. It may become a space in which text is juxtaposed with dissenting text to create sparks out of their friction. And, even where there are such disagreements, a hypertext may choose not to privilege one over another by placing the latter as a subordinate "paratext." (More of this below.) Postfeminists may thus deconstruct the singularity of their own position and so perform their understanding of how we are each multiple subjectivities, constituted intertextually out of diverse discourses:

> The self, like the work you produce, is not so much a core as a process; one finds oneself, in the context of cultural hybridity, always pushing one's questioning of oneself to the limit of what one is and what one is not. . . . Fragmentation is therefore a way of living at the borders. (Trinh, 1992, pp. 156–157)

The dynamic melange of a hypertext goes well beyond what the static juxtapositions of a printed page allow. Consider the following possi-

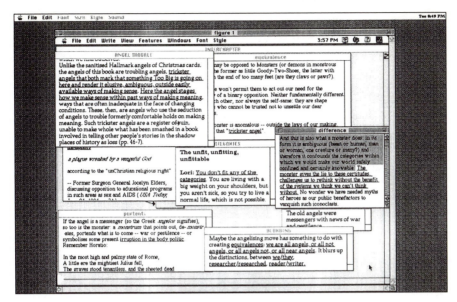

FIGURE 6.1

ble screen from my hypertext document, "Monstrous Angels" (See Figure 6.1). Here, each emerging node, which displays various sections of *Troubling the Angels* or my irruptive additions (the two sources being distinguished by different fonts and colors for the text boxes in the hypertext program), meditates associatively and intertextually on the nature of the monstrous, in relation not only to questions of categorization and portentous difference but also to Lather's angelic. (More will be said below about the monstrous.) The intertextual engagements are thus both the writer's and the reader's, and the geometry of those collocations increases exponentially in the hypertext.

The Unfixing of Textual Hierarchies:
Rhizomatic Text, Nomadic Thinking

Even in so subversive a book as *Troubling the Angels,* there are fixed textual hierarchies: the women's narratives come at the top of the page; prefatory material precedes; epilogue, appendix, and references follow the "main" text; and endnotes follow in the wake of the intertexts. In traditional scholarly texts, the conventions of such paratexts certify the credibility of the "central" text even when they ostensibly allow for the—sub-vocal—presentation of an opposing case. But their conventional subordination is realigned in a hypertext. For an electronic network, when it is read, has no primary axis of orientation, no given top or bottom, center or periphery. In a word, "there is no central executive authority that oversees the system" (Pagels, 1989, p. 50). When any node—even material that would be marginal in a print text—is opened up on the screen, it does not have a fixed subtextual dependency on any other. Instead, it has a kind of impermanent preeminence in time and also in place, as the "top" level, selected node—whether or not other nodes are open and visible. (This is so even when a node has been positioned by the writer in an "inferior" position at the bottom of the screen. And, of course, if the hypertext is available in a read-write mode, the reader can alter the position of the node on screen.)

Thus, we can foreground for interrogation the conventionality of what is usually presented as "core business" and of what is relegated to the periphery. The implications and applications of this will not be lost on postfeminists. Certainly *Troubling the Angels* questions the usual orders of authority of research that "drown the poem of the other with the sound of our own voices, as the ones who know, the 'experts' about how people make sense of their lives and what those searchings for meaning mean" (Lather & Smithies, 1997, p. xvi). But even while it offers as an answer, "various kinds of information, shifts of register, turns of different faces toward the reader," the printed text nonetheless establishes a counterorder in the fixity of relations of its various components. My "Monstrous Angels" is the more troubling, therefore, in repositioning on center stage whatever node or chain of nodes the reader chooses. Ironically, therefore, the very potentiality of the hypertextual medium could permit a reader's revalorizing of the feminist researcher's commentary and a marginalizing of the "voices" to which the researchers would bear witness by dismantling that residual hierarchy of participants' testimony over the researchers' "underwriting." So, too, any research hypertext might more easily permit supporting data to be detached from "findings" and filed away from all but the assiduous reader, thus undermining those warrants of the research that are under our noses in a print text.

Conventionally ordered scholarly texts are defined as "striated" by Deleuze and Guattari (1987) and differentiated from "rhizomatic" writing, "an organic growth that is all adventitious middle, not a deterministic chain of beginnings and ends" (Moulthrop, 1994, p. 300). As a nonhierarchical network, hypertext is effectively rhizomatic. And in its filamented space, the nomadic reader's camp shifts endlessly with her desire to traverse the landscape. Any occasional resting points are of course a very long way from the urban(e) architecture, gridded roads, and trivialized pedestrian precincts of normative social science research. Postfeminist researchers will be more interested in the kind of text (See Figure 6.2) whose very spaces work against such "standing orders," whose openness permits crossings that would elsewhere be impermissible, and whose directions in motion transform the striated texts it absorbs.

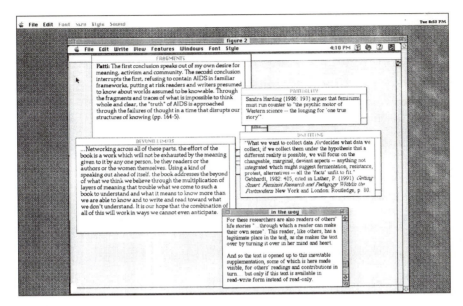

FIGURE 6.2

A Nonsequential Polylogic

Conventional positivist research writing moves in a decorous and coherent sequence from exposition of the research puzzle, to the search, and so to discovery, which has all the force of an epiphany. But the form of hypertext permits no such relentless triumph of narrative coherence toward closure. As we have seen, it allows more space for apparently extraneous matter and for an associative logic. A postfeminist research hypertext, then, will be characterized by its polylogic (Douglas, 1996), a term that encompasses voice, discourse, and argumentation.

Such hypertext may enable us to think otherwise about the explicit propositional form of chained argument, which seeks to close down positions and to subsume the voices of others in order to effect singularity and closure. (Feminists see here the delusions of patriarchal grandiosity.) For the multifariousness of any hypertext extends also to the argumentation carried out across its nodes, "Hypertexts are, in more than a manner of speaking, three dimensional. Fuguelike, they can carry on an argument at several levels simultaneously. And if we cannot read them exactly simultaneously, we can switch back and forth with great rapidity" (Lanham, 1989, p. 283). We may also assemble lines of argument different from those set up in any default path. This may lead to the reframing of an argument. For example, what may be a claim in one sequence of nodes could become a proof or justification when read in another sequence. (For an extended discussion of scholarly argumentation in a hypertextual environment, see Kolb, 1997.)

The risks of so dynamic an interplay of polylogic are likely to be accepted by postfeminists who wish to work with, not against, the instability of knowledge. We readers may still desire coherence and closure, but postfeminists also recognize the terrorism of this imperative and may choose to subvert it through hypertext. Indeed, as Moulthrop (1997) puts it, "cybertextual works are structures for breakdown in semantic space" (p. 661). And a breakdown in human understanding, as Winograd (cited in Haraway, 1991) reminds us, "is not a negative situation to be avoided, but a situation of non-obviousness, in which some aspect of the network of tools that we are engaged in using is brought forth to visibility" (p. 214). Thus, questions of validation or reliability, perennially debated among researchers in the social sciences, become an even more contentious issue in a dynamic and fragmented text form in which reasoning and evidence can be separated from their propositions. This makes clearer the fragility of our structures of argument—which is no bad thing, say postfeminists. And instead of attempting to conceal this, we should frankly acknowledge the rhetorical stratagems by which an argument seeks to present its structures as a permanent monument to reason.

It could be argued that this will make readers more open to the persuasions of rhetoric, when a hypertext can only be judged by its effectiveness as it is performed by the reader. Certainly, the hypertextual medium makes clearer the reader's contribution to the building of an argument. We read any link as a particular kind of transition in sequence or argument. And we may deliberately assemble a different pattern of argument out of the nodes we choose. Thus, we engage in the processes of argumentation instead of merely following another's. And so our attention will be drawn to the conventional means through which we construct order through argument and to a world in which any event has multiple causes, effects, and explanations.

This contingent and participatory polylogic sits more comfortably with postfeminists than with those committed to a (phal)logocentrism. It allows us to explore a different, less singly focalized view of coherence as patterns of always emergent meanings, patterns that arise out of and in distinction from other possible meanings. (A hypertext is thus overflowing with significance, not empty of it.) And it marks a shift from an emphasis on argument, as the more static structure supporting a claim, to one of argumentation, as a more dynamic process of interaction within which arguments may be co-constructed as well as deconstructed and reconstructed.

Figure 6.3 exemplifies something of this polylogic. Here the already fragmented segments of the original text (drawn from widely separated

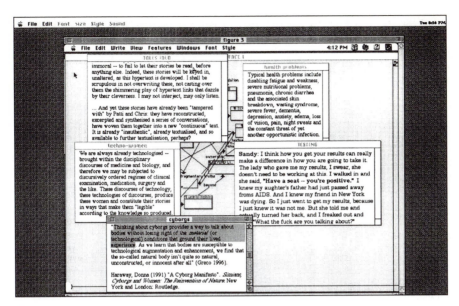

FIGURE 6.3

pages of print) jostle one another on the screen. Their mobile display and displacement in time resembles the interchanges of conversation: associative, additive, interruptive.

Multigeneric Collage

Associative or disjunctive juxtapositioning, intertextual concatenations, the transgression of genre boundaries, multivocality, and polylogic—such features contribute to the collage effects of hypertext. Collage is a familiar form in painting and sculpture; in verbal text it is a postmodern mode whose patterning, according to Ulmer (1992), supplements and supplants narrative and exposition, those other previously dominant modes of representation. In a collage, the bricolage that comes to hand is appropriated and assembled into a composition reminiscent of a Baudrillardian simulacrum, a copy without an original. Something of this is already visible in *Troubling the Angels,* which presents a miscellany of research disciplines, discourses, genres, and registers (academic and popular). But "Monstrous Angels," the hypertext document, goes beyond this in the electronic dynamism of its collage making. With the click of a mouse, it presents a series of surprises as one fragment is abruptly juxtaposed with another, and then another and another, on the same screen, in a collocation that need never be repeated. Despite the rather coarse granularity of this hypertext program and the clunkiness of its mechanized linking, as one reads across the component texts on screen, one may glimpse something of the oscillation between always unstable meanings.

Such boundary transgression or "fringe interference" (Hutcheon, 1989, p. 118) does not necessarily create new, monstrously hybrid genres. Nor does it mean that feminists can claim hypertextual collage as reflecting an essentially womanly quality (Greco, 1996). Nevertheless, the interplay of heterogeneous genres, discourses, and declaratory and stylistic registers in a collage may be exploited by postfeminist social science writers. For example, the constructed authority of a research text may be simultaneously displayed and subverted in a hypertext; after all, it can have no fixed place in the universe of discourse when it is a restless item in a collage. In postfeminist research work, any irony can be taken as playfully serious, integral to its poetics and politics. It could be said that "Monstrous Angels" itself, with its partial quotations and subversive repetitions, is a kind of parody (a not-quite, not-right parallel text). Certainly, its dynamic juxtapositions may bring about tremors of irony in the reader. Consider for example Figure 6.4, which raises an eyebrow, so to speak, about Lather's attachment to a stable text, even as she invites the participation of readers.

In an electronic writing space, such ironies can be enhanced, given fresh piquancy. They may even become transformative of writers and readers and not just texts through the new modes of agentic and interrogative reading they call into play.

The Reader as Textual Agent

Writers of conventional scholarly research texts would have no patience with the insights of poststructuralist theorists about the significance of the reader as the site where the text is negotiated, let alone the contention that the implied author—the researcher in his or her text—is an effect of a particular textual practice. (On hypertext and the poststructuralist blurring of the boundaries between writer and reader, see Johnson-Eilola, 1997, and for cautions, see Aarseth, 1997.) In such conventional academic writing, author-producers and their defining texts are privileged over receptive reader-consumers. To such a writer, my laying claim in "Monstrous Angels" to terrain explored by another is little short of plagiarism—all the more so, since Lather recognizes her role as a witness to others' words, "Thus the writing debt is not so much a debt of words as it is a debt of silence, a moving softly and obliquely, a not knowing too quickly" (Lather & Smithies, 1995, p. 133). In contrast to her tactful reticence, the desire that drives me to intrude my links and words into these accounts of women with HIV/AIDS is scandalously self-interested: to create a web for my own writing satisfactions and so to

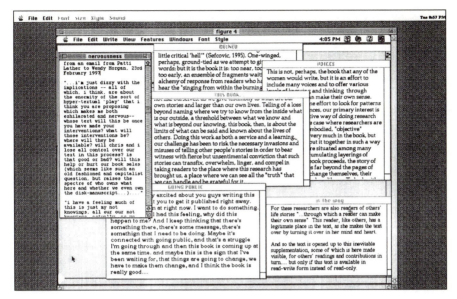

FIGURE 6.4

learn about the potential of hypertext for postfeminist research. (The ethical dilemmas entailed by this desire for appropriation, and by the consequent desire for self-censorship, are canvassed in several nodes.)

However scrupulous the collegiality may be in the processes of research between women as researchers and as informants, in a printed report the research is likely to be presented as having occurred before the acts of writing and subsequent reading. In hypertext, however, something more of the research process can continue even in the reading, for here the reader comes to know as she sifts through the text materials and reassembles them. Thus, as noted above, she contributes actively to making the argument her own. And here, too, it could be argued, theory coincides with practice. Postfeminism has maintained a theory of agency (Hutcheon, 1989) while recognizing that any agent is also subject to the discourses, structures, and practices of the field of its operation. So, too, it could be claimed that such hypertextual reading is a practice of agency—not, of course, to be conflated with political praxis, but nonetheless a performance of active intervention—and sometimes a tussle with the structuring already set up in the authored links.

In "constructive" hypertexts (Joyce, 1995), it is possible to go further: readers can literally become writers, adding materials, commentary, and links that can be saved for other readers in turn. Such supplementary texts may ferment like yeast in dough. Or rankle like a splinter in flesh.

As an example of a little sliver from reading against the grain—while I sided with the *Angels* and understood how vital it was that the book should speak to readers in its local context, as an Australian I noted a bias toward things American in statistics, references to welfare agencies, and the like. Therefore, alongside such statistics, I inserted a hypertextual "splinter," a series of empty writing spaces awaiting information about women in African, South American, and Asian nations. In postcolonial times, while the center may not hold, it can still exercise power through our texts. A hypertext, however, may contribute to the work of decolonization (Odin, 1997).

Or, in another example alluded to above ("Associative Links"), my hypertext plays with/off/around Lather's various references to the angelic. In a cluster of nodes, I muse on the monstrous via fictional texts and references to the ancient and more recent writings of biologists, medical men, theologians, theorists, and others. For if angels are to Lather "outside easily available ways of making sense," to Montaigne "those we call monsters are not so with God." In one node ("Equivalence") I reflect:

> Angels may be opposed to monsters, or to demons in monstrous shape. The former are little Goody Two Shoes, the latter have talons on the end of too many feet (are they claws, or paws?). But I refuse to line them up in this way, to act out my need for the certainty of a binary opposition. Neither fundamentally different from each other, nor always the self-same, they are shape changers who cannot be trusted not to unsettle our dear delusions. If the monster is anomalous—outside the laws of our making—so too is that "trickster angel."

However, it is not just the angelic or monstrous in the text that I draw attention to; it is also the angelic or monstrous nature of the hypertext itself. For, like a hypertext, the monstrous is a practice of the interstices, as I note in another node ("Wreader"):

> If the distinction between reader and writer is blurred, then most certainly a hypertext is a hybrid, a monster that permits boundaries of being and knowing to be crossed. In our turn it makes us monstrous in our capacity to be simultaneously one thing and another.

These and other such metaphorical associative links are my peripheral investment in the text, a reader's imaging that answers to the writer's.

It is clear that there are advantages for hypertext readers in this irruptive power. And for writers? To give more scope to readers they have to yield up some control over their text. The gains for a postfeminist writer, then, must lie in performing theory, in admitting that her text is open to other ideas contributed by interested readers. This can be pretty troubling, even to a writer like Lather (see Figure 6.4). In a poststructuralist, postprint universe, the author is no longer God enthroned before his creation; he becomes the creature of writing, rather than its creator (so Barthes, 1974). In this electronic medium a different kind of (textualized) author may be evolving, one who is formally and discursively decentered, disunified, fragmented, desirous, always in process, already a cyborgian hybrid (Haraway, 1991; Sophia, 1993). The shifting multiplicity of texts in hypertext, each with the subject position it proffers, enacts the multiplicity of our writerly and readerly desires and satisfactions, which are also the making of us as text makers.

Some Opening Remarks

In learning how "to write and think electronically" (Ulmer, 1989, p. x), I have created a hypertext that is an ill-formed, monstrous mutation of a text. It is also deliberately unfinished. I wanted, in this way, to represent the always incomplete nature of hypertext, which is productive of diverse readings and open to supplementary texts. I wanted to demonstrate thereby its unruliness—its breaking the bounds of perfection (as finite) and of finiteness (as perfection) (Greco, 1996). Nonetheless, my textual experiment on an experimental text does not seek—impossibly— to raze the disciplines of research but to raise questions about its (hyper)textual conditions of possibility. Just as postfeminist research offers no tidy set of answers to its questions, only a set of problematics, so hypertext can lay no claim to be "the" definitive form of research text. Rather, it demonstrates the dynamic nature of both postfeminist research and (hyper)text in process.

This is not to say that hypertext is of itself liberatory. Like any technology it can be recuperated for conservative ends—or it may be enlisted for reconstructive purposes, "to appropriate, reinvent, and criticise structures of meaning and power" (Johnson-Eilola, 1997, p. 48). In this way, my hypertextual palimpsest is also a demonstration of the practice of "subversive repetition," which Lather (1996), following Butler (1993), argues is "a way to keep moving within the recognition of the non-innocence of any practice of knowledge production. Within/against, then, is about both 'doing it' and 'troubling it' simultaneously" (p. 3).[3] If the codex book of *Troubling the Angels* is already doing it (research with women living with HIV/AIDS) and troubling it, the hypertext version is also both doing it (reading/writing a text which is already multigeneric, interrogative, and reflexive) and troubling it (hypertextually). And in this lies a further demonstration of the argument that "agency exists within the possibility of a variation within a repetition" (Lather, 1996, p. 3). "Variation within a repetition" describes my hypertextual practice here; agency lies in my ready movement between reader and (contributory, supplementary) writer, which the medium facilitates. The subversive quality of such repetition lies in both the dependent status of the hypertext and its further destabilizing of an already interrogative text.

It is appropriate, then, to conclude provisionally by listing just a couple of questions for further investigation that my practice has raised for me: first, if the new cannot be measured by the old rules for (traditional) research writing, by what standards of logic, rhetoric, and poetics can postfeminist research hypertext writing in the social sciences be assessed; and second, if critical, logical thought as we know it has been tied to print technology and if hypertext promotes different modes of thinking, how can postfeminist researchers best use this hypertextual space for rethinking without either self-indulgence or overdiscipline?

This leads me to a caution:

> To the extent that hypertext challenges traditional intellectual structures, it may be that this cardinal technology, like others before it, will threaten too much to unhinge us. We may perhaps, in the short term at least, lack the vision to appropriate these tools to the new tasks they suggest. (Joyce, 1995, p. 49)

Doors have hinges. When postresearchers step over the threshold into this new electronic space, we will have provisional answers to my questions. And further questions.

Notes

1. First called *Troubling Angels*, the book was desktop published in 1995 because of the women's justified impatience to see their work in print without delay. It was subsequently published by Westview Press in 1997 as *Troubling the Angels*.

2. The hypertext has been developed using the Storyspace program (Eastgate Systems, 1990). This form of hypertext is like the World Wide Web in being a nonlinear or nonsequential form that offers multiple pathways between text segments in a dynamic network of alternate routes, any of which are determined by the reader's decision. However, this stand-alone form of text is hypertextually and visually much richer than the Web. Among other features, it allows for map views of writing spaces and their links, one-to-many and many-to-one links, and several windows to be open on the same screen in a tiled presentation.

3. A revised version of this paper is included in McWilliam, Lather, & Morgan's (1997) *Headwork, Fieldwork, Textwork: A Textshop for New Feminist Research.*

References

Aarseth, E. (1997). *Cybertext: Perspectives on ergodic literature.* Baltimore: Johns Hopkins University Press.

Barthes, R. (1970). *S/Z.* Paris: Editions de Seuil.

Barthes, R. (1974). The death of the author. In *Image, music, text* (S. Heath, Ed. & Trans.) (pp. 142–48). New York: Hill and Wang.

Bolter, J. D. (1992). Literature in the electronic writing space. In M. Tuman (Ed.), *Literacy online: The promise (and peril) of reading and writing with computers* (pp. 19–42). Pittsburgh, PA: Pittsburgh University Press.

Butler, J. (1993). *Bodies that matter.* New York: Routledge.

De Certeau, M. (1984). *The practice of everyday life* (S. Randall, Trans.). Berkeley and Los Angeles: University of California Press.

Deleuze, G., & Guattari, F. (1987). *A thousand plateaus: Capitalism and schizophrenia* (B. Massumi, Trans.). Minneapolis: University of Minnesota Press.

Derrida, J. (1976). *Of grammatology* (G. Chakravorty Spivak, Trans.). Baltimore: Johns Hopkins University Press.

Derrida, J. (1981). *Dissemination* (B. Johnson, Trans.). Chicago: University of Chicago Press.

Douglas, J. Y. (1996). Abandoning the either/or for the and/and/and: Hypertext and the art of argumentative writing. *The Australian Journal of Language and Literacy, 19*(4), 305–16.

Eco, U. (1978). *The role of the reader: Explorations in the semiotics of the text.* Bloomington: Indiana University Press.

Greco, D. (1996). Hypertext with consequences: Recovering a politics of hypertext. *Hypertext '96 Proceedings* (pp. 85–92). New York: Association for Computing Machinery.

Greco, D.(1997). *Cyborg: Engineering the body electric.* Boston: Eastgate Systems [computer program].

Haraway, D. (1991). *Simians, cyborgs and women: The reinvention of nature.* New York: Routledge.

Hutcheon, L. (1989). *The politics of postmodernism.* London: Routledge.

Jackson, S. (1995). *Patchwork girl.* Boston: Eastgate Systems [computer program].

Johnson-Eilola, J. (1992). Structure and text: Writing space and storyspace. *Computers and Composition, 9*(2), 95–129.

Johnson-Eilola, J. (1997). *Nostalgic angels: Rearticulating hypertext writing.* Norwood, NJ: Ablex Publishing Corporation.

Joyce, M. (1995). Siren shapes: Exploratory and constructive hypertexts. In *Of two minds: Hypertext pedagogy and poetics* (pp. 39–60). Ann Arbor: The University of Michigan Press.

Kolb, D. (1997). Scholarly hypertext: Self-represented complexity. *Hypertext '97 Proceedings* (pp. 29–37). Southampton: Association for Computing Machinery.

Landow, G. (1992). *Hypertext: The convergence of contemporary critical theory and technology*. Baltimore: Johns Hopkins University Press.

Landow, G. (Ed.). (1994). *Hyper/text/theory*. Baltimore: Johns Hopkins University Press.

Landow, G. (1997). *Hypertext: 2.0: The convergence of contemporary critical theory and technology*. Baltimore: Johns Hopkins University Press.

Lanham, R. (1989). The electronic word: Literary study and the digital revolution. *New Literary History, 20*(2), 265–90.

Lather, P. (1996, April). Methodology as subversive repetition: Practices toward a feminist double science. Paper presented at the annual meeting of the American Educational Research Association, New York City, NY.

Lather, P., & Smithies, C. (1995). *Troubling angels: Women living with HIV/AIDS*. Columbus, OH: Greyden Press.

Lather, P., & Smithies, C. (1997). *Troubling the angels: Women living with HIV/AIDS*. Boulder, CO: Westview Press.

Lorde, A. (1984). *Sister outsider*. Trumansburg, NY: Crossing Press.

McWilliam, E., Lather, P., & Morgan, W. (1997). *Headwork, fieldwork, textwork: A textshop for new feminist research*. Brisbane, Australia: Queensland University of Technology.

Moulthrop, S. (1991a). The politics of hypertext. In G. Hawisher & C. Selfe (Eds.), *Evolving perspectives on computers and composition studies: Questions for the 1990s* (pp. 253–71). Urbana, IL: National Council of Teachers of English.

Moulthrop, S. (1991b). Polymers, paranoia, and the rhetoric of hypertext. *Writing on the Edge, 2*(2), 150–59.

Moulthrop, S. (1994). Rhizome and resistance: Hypertext and the dream of a new culture. In G. Landow (Ed.), *Hyper/text/theory* (pp. 299–319). Baltimore: Johns Hopkins University Press.

Moulthrop, S. (1997). Pushing back: Living and writing in broken space. *Modern Fiction Studies, 43*(3), 651–74.

Moulthrop, S., & Kaplan, N. (1994). They became what they beheld: The futility of resistance in the space of electronic writing. In C. Selfe & R. Hilligloss (Eds.), *Literacy and computers: The complications of teaching and learning with technology* (pp. 220–37). New York: Modern Language Association of America.

Odin, J. (1997). The edge of difference: Negotiations between the hypertextual and the postcolonial. *Modern Fiction Studies, 43*(3), 598–630.

Page, B. (1996). Women writers and the restive text: Feminism, experimental writing and hypertext. *Postmodern Culture, 6*(2) [E-journal].

Pagels, H. R. (1989). *The dreams of reason: The computer and the rise of the sciences of complexity*. New York: Bantam.

Slatin, J. (1990). Reading hypertext: Order and coherence in a new medium. *College English, 52*(8), 870–83.

Sophia, Z. (1993). *Whose second self? Gender and (ir)rationality in computer culture*. Geelong, Australia: Deakin University Press.

Trinh, T. M-H. (1992). *Framer framed*. London: Routledge.

Tuman, M. (1992). *Word perfect: Literacy in the computer age*. Pittsburgh, PA: University of Pittsburgh Press.

Ulmer, G. (1983). The object of post-criticism. In H. Foster (Ed.), *The anti-aesthetic: Essays on postmodern culture* (pp. 83–110). Seattle, WA: Bay Press.

Ulmer, G. (1989). *Teletheory: Grammatology in the age of video*. London: Routledge.

Ulmer, G. (1992). Grammatology (in the stacks) of hypermedia: A simulation. In M. Tuman (Ed.), *Literacy online: The promise (and peril) of reading and writing with computers* (pp. 139–58). Pittsburgh, PA: Pittsburgh University Press.

PART II

DISCIPLINES
AND PLEASURES

Chapter 7

Skirting a Pleated Text: De-Disciplining an Academic Life

Laurel Richardson

Fields of Play: Constructing an Academic Life (Richardson, 1997) is the story of a woman's struggles in academia in the context of contemporary intellectual debates about entrenched authority, disciplinary boundaries, writing genres, and the ethics and politics of social scientific inquiry and presentation. The woman is myself; the story, an embodiment of these issues. I hope the story resonates with those who are struggling to make sense of their lives in academia.

I believe that writing is a both a theoretical and practical process through which we can (a) reveal epistemological assumptions, (b) discover grounds for questioning received scripts and hegemonic ideals—both those within the academy and those incorporated within ourselves, (c) find ways to change those scripts, (d) connect to others and form community, and (e) nurture our emergent selves.

Applying my theoretical understandings to sociological writing, I asked: How do the specific circumstances in which we write affect what we write? How does what we write affect who we become? In answering these questions, I found that if I were to write the Self into being that I wanted to be I would have to "de-discipline" my academic life.

What practices support our writing and develop a care for the self despite conflict and marginalization? What is (are) the ethical subject's relation(s) to research practices? And, what about the integration of academic interests, social concerns, emotional needs, and spiritual connectedness?

Fields of Play explores these issues through what I call a pleated-text, traditional and experimental papers written over a period of 10 years folded between what I call "writing-stories"—about the contexts in which I wrote those papers. The pleats can be spread open at any point, folded back, unfurled.

Framing academic essays in writing-stories displaced the boundaries between the genres of selected writings and autobiography, "repositioning them as convergent genres that, when intertwined, create new ways of reading/writing." These ways are more congruent with poststructural understandings of how knowledge is contextually situated, local, and partial. At the beginning the book, the writing-story is a personal story, framing the academic work. As the book progresses, distinctions between the "personal" and the "academic" become less clear. The last essay, "Vespers," stands in a section by itself, simultaneously a writing-story and a sociology-story, though I do not name a single sociological concept. In the genre of convergence, neither "work" nor "Self" is denied.

The present chapter is a (very) partial-story about the construction of *Fields of Play* and how writing it has changed me. I skirt around the text but enter one of its pleats: departmental politics as one context for writing and as a site of discipline. I provide three examples of departmental politics: (a) an excerpt from a writing-story about my own department; (b) the first act of a surrealist drama about a surreal, yet real, sociology department; and (c) an excerpt from a multivoiced text, which builds community across departments and academic status. The three examples span a decade. They are not a narrative of progress.

We are restrained and limited by the kinds of cultural stories available to us. Carolyn Heilbrun (1998) suggests that we do not imitate lives, we live "story lines." To the extent that our lives are tied to our disciplines, our ability to construct ourselves in other stories will depend upon how the discipline can be deconstructed. Social scientific disciplines' story line includes telling writers to suppress their own voices, adopt the all-knowing, all-powerful voice of the academy, and keep their mouths shut about academic in-house politics. But contemporary philosophical thought raises problems that exceed and undermine that academic story line. We are always present in our texts, no matter how we try to suppress ourselves. We are always writing in particular contexts—contexts that affect what and how we write and who we become. Power relationships are always present.

"Authority"

I began *Fields of Play* with a writing-story called "Authority." Here is an excerpt:

> I begin this collection, and my reflections on it, at the time when I found a different way of "playing the field," of exploring its boundaries and possibilities, and my life within it. This was the mid-1980s. No more children living at home; no major medical or

family crises; a husband who liked to cook; friends; completion of a major research project and book tour; academic sinecure; and severe marginalization within my sociology department, which relieved me of committee work and of caring about outcomes. For the first time in my adult life, I had free time, playtime, time I could ethically and practically call "mine."

Like a medieval warlord who executes or banishes all who might pose a threat to his absolute authority, my newly appointed department chair deposed the three other contenders for the position, all men, from their "fiefdoms," their committee chairships. He stonewalled written complaints or queries. He prohibited public disagreement by eliminating discussion at faculty meetings. He abolished one of the two committees I chaired, the "Planning Committee," a site of open dialogue. He restricted the departmental Affirmative Action Committee's province, which I also chaired, to undergraduate enrollments. I publicly disagreed with him on his new affirmative action policy. Then, at the first university Affirmative Action Awards dinner, where I was being honored, surrounded by top university administration, my face making a face, repulsed, I shrugged his arm off from around my shoulder.

The chair hired a consultant, a well-known functionalist, to review faculty vitae. The consultant declared me "promising"—the chair told me as one might tell a student, not the full professor I was—but the consultant had also declared "gender research" a "fad." The chair advised me to return to medical sociology, a field I was "in" during a one-year postdoctorate, ten years earlier. Research it, teach it, he advised, teach it now, at the graduate level. He may have already had me down to do it. He discarded ten years of my research, teaching, and service, it seemed. I told him I strongly disagreed with his plans for my academic future. Perhaps it was only coincidental that sometime later that same year at the annual departmental banquet, hitherto a lighthearted gathering of colleagues and friends, the visiting consultant, now hired as an after-dinner speaker, lectured for an hour about why people, in the interests of smooth institutional functioning, should yield to authority.

I was on quarter break, out of town, when the department chair's secretary called to tell me that the chair had added an extra undergraduate course to my teaching schedule for the next quarter, a week away. My stomach cramped in severe pain. No, I said, I absolutely will not accept this assignment. I was adamant, unyielding. I telephoned the new dean, a sociologist and putative feminist, who would soon be elevated to provost. Her "best advice" to me—

on this and subsequent matters—was to "roll over." I refused. She then taught the course herself, in my place. Rather than pull rank on the chair, a man, she modeled "rolling over." It was a course on the sociology of women.

I felt no gratitude to her. I had wanted protection, for my colleagues as well as for myself, from a chair's punitive and arbitrary actions. Instead, she presented herself in my place, as the sacrificial lamb. The clear message, it seemed to me, was that if she, the dean of the college, was willing to sacrifice herself, so should we all. Her action legitimated the chair's right to do anything he wanted.

My new chair was empowered to micromanage all aspects of "his" department's life, even to the point of dictating a senior colleague's intellectual life. Any refusal to "roll over" precipitated punitive action in salary, in what one could teach and when, in virtual exile to Coventry. Thus in the mid-1980s, I experienced what has, by the mid-1990s, become an experience common to faculty members of American colleges and universities: "Total Quality Management" in pursuit of "Excellence."

Many departmental colleagues understood that, like the chair's previously conquered opponents, I had become dangerous to associate with, dangerous to even know. In their minds I had brought it upon myself, which of course I had.

As I write these paragraphs, my stomach swells and hurts just as it did then. (Richardson, 1997, pp. 9–11)

In the mid-1980s not only did departmental life surprise me; so too did the theoretical concepts of feminist poststructuralism—reflexivity, authority, authorship, subjectivity, power, language, ethics, representation. Soon, I was challenging the grounds of my own and others' authority and raising ethical questions about my own practices as a sociologist.

Experimenting with textual form, I wrote sociology as drama, responsive readings, narrative poetry, pagan ritual, lyrical poetry, prose poems, humor, and autobiography. Experimenting with content, I wrote about narrative, science writing, literary devices, fact/fiction, ethics. Experimenting with voice, I co-authored with a fiction writer, played second theorist to a junior scholar, turned colleagues' words into dramas. Experimenting with frame, I invited others into my texts, eliding the oral and the written, constructing performance pieces, creating theater. Troubled with the ethical issues of doing research "on" others, I wrote about my own life. I did unto myself as I had done onto others. And, troubled by academic institutions, I began to discover more agreeable pedagogical and writing practices and alternative community-building sites.

I experimented around three interrelated questions: (a) how does the way we are supposed to write-up our findings become an unexamined trope in our claims to authoritative knowledge, (b) what might we learn about our "data" if we stage it in different writing formats, and (c) what other audiences might we be able to reach if we step outside the conventions of social scientific writing?

My intentions then—and now—have never been to dismiss social scientific writing, but rather to examine it. My intentions then—and now—have never been to reject social scientific writing, but rather to enlarge the field through other representational forms.

By the mid-1980s, I could no longer write in science's omniscient Voice from Nowhere. Responding to the long-suppressed poet within, I wrote up an in-depth interview with an unwed mother, "Louisa May," as a five-page poem, adhering to both social scientific and literary protocols. A poem as "findings" was not well received at my sociology meetings; I was accused of fabricating Louisa May and/or of being her, among other things. To deal with the assault, I wrote a realist drama about it from my (very accurate, nonfabricated, easily checked for reliability) "field notes" taken at the meeting. In 1993, with the assault warming up in my home department, I decided to write a surreal drama—"Educational Birds"—about my life in academia. Surreal seemed appropriately isomorphic to the real.

ACT I FROM THE ETHNODRAMA, "EDUCATIONAL BIRDS"

(Scene One: It is a chilly September afternoon in a sociology department chair's office. The walls are catacomb drab; there are no mementos, pictures, or plants in the room. Seated at one end of a large conference table are two women: a department chair with her back to the windows, and full professor Z. looking out to the silent gray day.)

CHAIR: I've been reading your work, because of salary reviews—
PROFESSOR Z.: —
CHAIR: —You write very well.
PROFESSOR Z.: —
CHAIR: But is it Sociology?
PROFESSOR Z.: —

(Scene Two: On leaving the department office, Professor Z. sees Visiting Professor M. at the drinking fountain. The pipes are lead. The university says it's not a problem if you let the water run. Professor M. is letting the water run into his coffee maker. His hair is flat, plastering his head; he's heavy-looking, somber, wearing worn blue pants and a stretched-out dun cardigan, hanging loosely to his mid-thighs. Not the eager Harvard man hired a year ago.)

PROFESSOR Z.: —Looks like you've acclimated.

(Scene Three: It is an overcast November noon at the Faculty Club. Pictures of deceased faculty, men in drab suits, line the room; wrought-iron bars secure the windows. Professor Z. and assistant professor Q., whose five-author paper "Longitudinal Effects of East to Midwest Migration on Employment Outcomes: A Log-Linear Analysis" has made her a member of the salary committee, are having lunch.)

ASSISTANT PROFESSOR Q.: Everyone says, "You write very well."
PROFESSOR Z.: Is that a compliment?
ASSISTANT PROFESSOR Q.: "But is it Sociology?"

(Scene Four: A cold and dismal January afternoon in the sociology seminar room. During one of the department's "reconstruction" phases, the oak conference table was disassembled and the legs lost. Without a leg to stand on, it lies, in pieces, at the far end of the room next to discarded computer equipment. The wallpaper is flaking away like mummy wrappings. Assembled are the new graduate students, the graduate chair, and the department chair. The new students are being taught how to teach.)

NEW GRADUATE STUDENT: *(Addressing the department chair)* Can you tell us about the worst undergraduate sociology class you ever took?
DEPARTMENT CHAIR: Yes. The worst course was one where the professor read a poem.
GRADUATE STUDENTS: —
DEPARTMENT CHAIR: What a waste of time! (Richardson, 1997, p. 197)

The story of a life is less than the actual life, because the story told is selective, partial, contextually constructed and because the life is not yet over. But the story of a life is also more than the life, the contours and meanings allegorically extending to others, others seeing themselves, knowing themselves through another's life story, re-visioning their own, arriving where they started, and knowing "the place for the first time."

My fears for this "place"—academia—had grown over the course of writing the book. Over the decade, academia had become increasingly inhospitable to those who would change it and to those who are most vulnerable—graduate students. In the penultimate paper in *Fields*, I wanted to link the embodiedness of scholarship across generations, disciplines, and theoretical positions. I wanted the book to include the voices of graduate students in different sociology departments, to link my story with their stories, to write a new collective story. I wrote "Are You My Alma Mater?" as the vehicle.

"Are You My Alma Mater?"

New mines have been set. As in real war fields, the young, inexperienced, and adventurous are the most vulnerable to detonations. Graduate students. Four examples have passed over my desk in the past two weeks. On a feminist e-mail list came this request from a first-year graduate student:

> My department has been having a series of "feminist epistemology" debates. . . . The anger/hostility/backlash/defensiveness in some of the faculty and the increasing alienation and marginalization of feminist (and students pursuing critical race theory) students is troublesome to me (one of the disenchanted grad students). When I raised my concern, it was suggested that I organize the next seminar. While I am not altogether sure this is a responsibility I want, I am wondering if any of you have had successful . . . forums which address hostilities within the discipline/departments yet does not increase those hostilities or place less powerful people (untenured faculty or graduate students) at greater risk. . . . Please reply to me privately.

When I asked the student for permission to quote her e-mail, she asked for anonymity:

> It drives me crazy that I have to be afraid to even speak, but it is realistic. Actually, even posting to [the listserve] made me nervous, but I can't think of other ways of accessing resources beyond my pathetic institution.

Another graduate student, Eric Mykhalovsky (1996), writes about what happened to him when he used an autobiographical perspective in the practice of sociology. Changing his "I" to "you," he writes in *Qualitative Sociology*:

> During a phone call "home" you hear that your application for doctoral studies has been rejected. Your stomach drops. You are in shock, disbelief. When doing your M.A. you were talked about as a "top" student. . . . Later you receive a fax giving an "official account" of your rejection. Your disapproval, it seems, was based on reviewers' reservations with the writing samples submitted as part of your application. One evaluator, in particular, considered your article, "Table Talk," to be a "self-indulgent, informal biography—lacking in accountability to its subject matter." You feel a sense of self-

betrayal. You suspected "Table Talk" might have had something to do with the rejection. It was an experimental piece,
not like other sociological writing—YOU SHOULD HAVE
KNOWN BETTER!

Slowly self-indulgence as assessment slips over the text to
name you. You begin to doubt yourself—are you really self-
indulgent? The committee's rejection of your autobiographical text soon feels, in a very painful way, a rejection of you.
All the while you buy into the admission committee's implicit
assessment of your work as not properly sociological
(133–134).

Third, in a personal letter requesting advice on whether to apply
to my university, a lesbian graduate student from another university recounts:

I cannot do the research I want to and stay here. The department wants to monitor how many lesbians they let in because
they're afraid that gender will be taken over by lesbians. I'll be
allowed to do gender here if I do it as part of the "social strat-
ification" concentration, but not if I want to write about lesbian identity construction or work from a queer studies
perspective.

And fourth, there are documents on my desk pertaining to a
required graduate seminar, in a famous department, on how to
teach sociology. In that seminar, according to the documents, a
non-American student of color questioned the white male professor's Eurocentrism. Following a heated dispute, the professor provided a statistical count of the racial distribution of students in
undergraduate classes—80 percent are white. The professor, then,
putatively said that instructors cannot afford to alienate students by
teaching multiculturalism; that professors are uncomfortable teaching multiculturalism "crap"; that the student raising these issues
could "go to hell"; and that white heterosexual males were being
discriminated against. When the student of color complained to the
department administrators, they proposed he "voluntarily" with-
draw from the class. The department administrators (including
another new chair) later attended the seminar, supported the syl-
labus, and sidestepped discussion of the race-based issues. The professor apologized to the seminar for breaking his own code of
proper behavior in the classroom, but he apparently had not
grasped the import of postcolonialism. He was modeling his teaching model.

As a result, at least one graduate student has chosen to go else-where for the Ph.D. The student sent an e-mail to all faculty, staff, and graduate students to avert "idle speculation" regarding the reasons for departure:

> It has disgusted, saddened and enraged me that this depart-ment has chosen to ignore and avoid the serious occurrences of racism going on within it. Instead of admitting to these problems and dealing with them, the department has used its institutional power to scapegoat, marginalize and penalize individuals who dare to challenge its racist structure. Then those in power go back to their computer screens to study race as a dummy variable, not even realizing that a sociologi-cal process called *racism* is happening in their midst. . . . Stu-dents are advised to study social movements, not participate in them. . . . [H]ere racism is not considered real sociology, as evidenced by students having to start "extracurricular" groups to do reading on postmodernist or Afrocentric thought.
>
> I am leaving because, while I respect, learn and appreciate the importance of things like demography and statistics, the same appreciation and respect is not offered here to other areas of sociology which are very influential in the field, and institutional power is used to prevent students from learning about them.
>
> I sincerely hope that the prospect of losing more talented students, especially those who are students of color (who are not leaving because they "can't handle it [statistics courses]," will compel this department to reevaluate its capacity to serve its students of diverse backgrounds and interests more effec-tively. My career just didn't have time to wait for all that to happen.

Feminist epistemology, autobiographical sociology, queer stud-ies, and Afrocentric and postcolonial perspectives are apparently so dangerous that the graduate students who have been exposed to these plagues must be quarantined, invalidated, or expelled from the university nest. Graduate students are "terminated" lest they reproduce themselves. (Richardson, 1997, pp. 208–213)

As I pause in the writing of this paper, wondering what to write next, the UPS man delivers an advance shipment copy of *Fields of Play*. The production editor's note says, "Congratulations" and "Thanks for all your cooperation along the way; I hope you're as pleased as we are with the final result."

The final result for the production editor is the book, I think. But what is it for me? What have been the consequences of the book's feminist-poststructuralist practices? How have I changed?

For starters, I have taken early retirement from my "home" sociology department. I have left it physically and emotionally. As a shaman might say, I have called my spirit back; the place no longer has power over me. I go into the building and do not feel alienated. Sometimes, I sing while I am there.

Leaving my department, however, has not meant leaving the socio-logical perspective, the academy, or professional associations. I teach qualitative methods to Ph.D. students in the Cultural Studies program in Educational Policy and Leadership at Ohio State University. There, I find a positive commitment to qualitative research among the faculty and the graduate students. I visit universities and colleges, teach, lecture, present at conferences, write handbook chapters and sociology articles, edit a feminist reader, and serve on editorial boards. My professional life is full and nurturing, having let go of that which I did not value.

Indeed, I have let many things go.

In 1985, while working on a book that I was tired of working on, I cross-stitched into a sampler the aphorism: "I finish what I start." I put the sampler over my computer so I could read the affirmation over and over again, and I finished the book, as I have most things I start. My per-sistence has been a point of pride.

But, now, as I apply poststructural understandings of temporality to my life and work, my ideas of "start" and "finish" have changed. When does a project start? When is it finished? Says who? Now, I find I can put projects aside, perhaps never to return to them purposively, but never to be away from them either; they remain as traces in that which I do.

The sampler I have moved to the living room; metaphorically, that seems apt. In its place on the wall, I have a picture of my flapper mother wearing a kid leather cloche and fox coat, holding my sister—then 7 months; now 70 years. When does a project start? When is it finished?

And my writing. Oh, how I value my writing time. I understand auto-biographical writing as a feminist practice. It is how I both center myself and connect to others. The last essay in *Fields of Play*, "Vespers," is an account of how an experience at a vespers service when I was 8 shaped my relationships to my parents and to my academic work; it is a forgive-ness story. Others have told me it resonates with their lives. A new essay, "Paradigms Lost" (in press), recounts a car accident and a coma. It is a recovery story. Only now—25 years after the accident—am I able to tell that story, and only, I think, because I have accepted writing as a process of discovery, and writing autobiographically as a feminist-sociological praxis. "Jeopardy" and "Meta-Jeopardy" (in press) narrativize some of my experiences with parenting and grandparenting. In the next few years, I plan to write more of these essays, structured rhizomatically, the way my life is experienced—lines of flight, whirling whirling skirts of pleated-texts. A surprisingly surprising de-disciplined life . . .

Acknowledgments

An earlier version of this paper was presented to the American Educational Research Association (AERA), Chicago, Illinois, March 24, 1997, and was published in *Qualitative Inquiry, 3,* 1997, 295–303. I thank Ernest Lockridge for his careful reading of this paper and Sage Press for permission to reprint it here.

References

Heilbrun, C. (1988). *Writing a woman's life.* New York: W. W. Norton.

Mykhalovsky, E. (1996). Reconsidering table talk: Critical thoughts on the relationship between sociology, autobiography, and self-indulgence. *Qualitative Sociology,* 19(1), 131–51.

Richardson, L. (1997). *Fields of play: Constructing an academic life.* New Brunswick, NJ: Rutgers University Press.

Richardson, L. (in press). Meta-jeopardy. *Qualitative Inquiry.*

Richardson, L. (in press). Paradigms lost. *Symbolic Interaction.*

Chapter 8

Laughing within Reason: On Pleasure, Women, and Academic Performance

Erica McWilliam

At a feminist seminar I attended recently, one woman described an incident she witnessed at a committee meeting in the university. A female colleague of hers was laughing heartily just as the meeting was about to start, when one of the male committee members interrupted her by saying, "I don't know whether you are aware of this, but you have a really irritating laugh! You should tone it down a bit." "I don't know of any university rule that says I am not supposed to laugh," came the hurt and angry reply. "Sure you can laugh," retorted her critic, "but *within reason!*"

There are a number of points that could be made about this story. The one I want to pursue here is how the story was interpreted by the women at the research forum. Typical, they said, of male attempts to dominate women. This was a very comfortable positioning for the group, who laughed at the stupidity of the male accuser as well as expressing their exasperation and anger at his presumptuousness. Then the storyteller added in a somewhat apologetic tone, "Well, actually, she does have a pretty . . . er . . . *distinctive* laugh!" There was unanimous agreement that this was not the point.

In the context of the collective reaction of outrage, the only available reading of the male committee member's action was negative. It was impossible to think—and certainly to speak—the thought that the male critic could be providing useful training in proper professional behavior in the modern university. It was patently clear that the woman in question was entitled to laugh as she pleased—no one had the right to tell her how or when to laugh! I am inviting the reader nevertheless to consider that the notion that we all need and receive training in how to laugh within reason—to laugh "properly"—may not be as bizarre or need not be as infuriating as the reaction of this group suggests. The way we come to laugh in the academy is part of a broader set of performative practices that mark our ability to read what is proper in a particular time and place and to self-shape accordingly.

In the formal settings of universities, all academics regulate themselves constantly, including how and when they laugh. There are times we may stifle a laugh because we are good academics, and we know that laughing at an unintentional classroom clanger might impact negatively on student learning. However, it is more likely that we will not even *feel* like laughing when students are producing "bloopers" in their struggle to learn, and furthermore, we will feel and express strong disapproval of those who attempt to do so. Likewise, there are also times when we laugh delightedly in order to perform pedagogical work correctly. I am not arguing that we are so oppressed by the university context that we have no choice about such things; merely, that as people working within a particular setting named as "academic," we moderate ourselves or suffer certain penalties. We do not just learn to do particular things but we learn *to feel like doing them*. My point is not that we should all learn to welcome unsolicited criticism from male colleagues. However, I am suggesting that there may be other ways of reading such remarks beyond simple impertinence. They may also be read as one form of training in how individuals *ought to behave and feel like behaving* as professionals and academics.

In this chapter I want to consider the matter of pleasure and women's scholastic and pedagogical work and how we have come to understand it. In order to do so, I begin by exploring the idea that we take our pleasures *within reason*, drawing on Michel Foucault's (1985) work to examine the relationship between feelings such as pleasure and modes of rationality. I then move on to situate pleasure within a Western historical tradition, noting how pleasure-as-fun has been framed outside bourgeois traditions of conduct, including subversive traditions. Carnival is then examined more precisely as a site of fun whose remembering could be productive for women in the academy, and I use Mary Russo's *The Female Grotesque: Risk, Excess and Modernity* (1994) to elaborate this point. The fact that fun so often eludes feminism as an academic performance I then explore more fully, using two exemplars from feminist writing, and also commenting on Camille Paglia's (1995) dangerous idea that "all roads from Rousseau lead to Sade" (p. 20). By means of this rhizomatic journey, I seek to bring the reader to consider the value of playful irony for academic women, arguing for a reconsideration of its legitimacy alongside, not instead of, advocacy.

The F Word Again

In what sense might our feelings, and their outward expression, be reasoned rather than spontaneously occurring? In *The Use of Pleasure: The*

History of Sexuality, Volume 2 (1985), Foucault examines the feeling we call sexual desire as a discursively organized phenomenon, rather than a natural expression of an inner world. His examination of the ways that human beings in the West have come to recognize themselves as individual "subject[s] of desire" (p. 6) is an analysis of the ways that individuals "[have been] led to focus their attention on themselves, to decipher, recognize, and acknowledge themselves" as sexually desiring persons (p. 5). It is to ancient Greece that Foucault turns to recover notions of sexuality and desire that preceded a Christian tradition of thinking about sexuality and "the flesh."

In describing his project as a genealogy, rather than a history, Foucault (1985) indicates that this is an analysis of "games of truth," rather than truth itself (p. 6). This means that he does not understand human experience as naturally occurring or as occurring through rational or true fields of learning. Instead, experience is historically constituted out of games of truth and error. This is how we come to believe that "something . . . can and must be thought"(p. 7). His interest in Greek and Greco-Roman culture is in "how, why and in what form sexuality was constituted as a moral domain," and why such a particular ethical concern "was so persistent despite its varying forms and intensity" (p. 10).

The method by which Foucault (1985) undertakes his project is to inquire into the discursive organization of what he terms "techniques of the self" (p. 11). This does not mean an analysis of behavior or ideas or sociology or ideology, but rather of what he terms problematizations (the ways "being offers itself to be, necessarily, thought") and the practices on the basis of which such "problematizations" are formed (p. 11). So Foucault takes as the object of his analysis the manner in which sexual activity is problematized in texts written by philosophers and doctors, focusing on what he terms "prescriptive texts," i.e., "texts which elaborate rules, opinions and advice as to how to behave as one should" (p. 12). His understanding is that such texts serve as devices that enable individuals to "question their own conduct, to watch over and give shape to it, and to shape themselves as ethical subjects" (p. 13).

To analyze pleasure this way is clearly a departure from either the idea that pleasure occurs as a sudden outpouring of feeling or the idea that individuals, when left to their own devices, will sacrifice everything else to maximize their own gratification. Instead, Foucault (1985) demonstrates that texts written by Plato, Aristotle, and others serve as important ways of training a population in knowledge about the limits beyond which certain attitudes or acts may be considered excessive. This knowledge can be applied by individuals to themselves. It is not, therefore, a process of top-down coercion but one of training the individual in the sort of relationship with the self that is necessary to the achievement of proper pleasure. Proper pleasure is not achievable by "going for broke," i.e., through excessive or immoderate behavior, but in the very exercise of moderation (p. 65). The ethical individual, as a subject of certain discourses of training about how pleasure ought to be taken properly, "deliberately chooses reasonable principles of action that he is capable of following and applying them" (p. 64). To deliberately choose bad principles and surrender to the weakest desires, thus taking pleasure in "bad conduct," is to produce oneself as a "shameless and incorrigible" individual (p. 65). What Foucault makes clear is that an ethic was being laid down by Plato, Socrates, and others that continues to be important to Western thought—"the superiority of *reason over desire*" (p. 87, emphasis added). Pleasure is, therefore, not to be taken "without knowledge . . . and at the wrong time"(p. 87). One takes one's pleasure within reason. To do otherwise is to risk much, because it risks failure within prevailing social and cultural norms.

To return to the advice to "laugh within reason" in the light of this sort of thinking is to give the anecdote a new twist. Other interpretations become possible beyond the idea that such advice from a man to a woman is patriarchal oppression at work, including the possibility that the woman may irritate others less and indeed stand a better chance of promotion—if she accepts the advice and learns how to laugh properly. I am not advocating that she should, merely, that it is another way of interpreting the event. Of course, this does not negate the point that what is proper utterance is invariably gendered with all that this means in terms of how loud and commanding women can *reasonably* be!

Pleasure as Fun

To speak of laughing within reason is to acknowledge that pleasure is always inevitably caught by modes of thinking and ways of being—by conventional ways of thinking. Given that conventional thinking is neither static nor all of a piece, our pleasures, though always framed, are never entirely fixed. This means, among other things, that certain ways of taking pleasure can and do offer up subversive possibilities within a lived condition of being always unfree. While "fun" never escapes rationality, it can and does trouble it.

Harvey Ferguson's work *The Science of Pleasure* (1990) is useful here, in particular, his analysis of the *carnivalesque*, and it might be applied to understanding how female academics might come to take their pleasures. I understand this analysis as particularly relevant because carnival was never an alternative to officialdom and orthodoxy, never finally outside orthodoxy, just as pleasure is never finally outside reason, nor can academic women be outside the academy. Carnival in the feudal order of things was a temporal space in which it became possible to indulge the appetites and at the same time parody the practices of officialdom. It was not an alternative to officialdom. Individuals are thus never freed from orthodoxy by carnival but are permitted to indulge themselves, to experience that "unrestrained sensuousness" (p. 109) that in all other times and places is *verboten*.

Carnival is productive of fun, and fun, as Ferguson (1990) argues it, is perverse, which makes it different from the other heterodox modes of thought he calls "happiness," "pleasure," and "excitement" (p. 109). The fun of the carnival has a "degrading significance" (p. 109), because it is pitted against enlightened aspirations to transcend the material world. It drags us down from spirituality and intellect into a Rabelaisian world of mockery, ribaldry, foolishness, and excess. It substitutes fart for faith *and* fact. This sort of fun is hinted at in the graffiti which appears on the canteen wall, the staffroom joke made *sotto voce* at the Vice-Chancellor's expense, crude language and behavior at the "Thank-God-It's-Friday" club. As with carnival, none of these activities are necessary to, or inspirational in, the work of the university, and none of them threaten the continuation of such work. There is no revolution being born in such moments, notwithstanding the Dean's Monday morning reaction to the graffiti or the bourbon-assisted bravado of the academic in the pub. No liberation is intended or likely. There is merely a momentary glimpse of perverse pleasure.

Carnivalesque, Grot(to)esque

Carnival, however, was more than a fleeting moment involving a few individuals. As Ferguson (1990) describes it, carnival in early modern Europe could occupy up to a quarter of the calendar year and involved not just the downtrodden but also the privileged (p. 109). The "ceremonials, feasts, theatrical shows and public spectacles" that marked it included more than one "feast of fools," and similar "grotesque degradations of church various rituals and symbols" (p. 109). Moreover, as Ferguson notes, it was strongly sanctioned by the very officials and hierarchies it parodied. For example, the Paris School of Theology published a justification of such practices in 1444, arguing that the "foolishness, which is our second nature and seems to be so inherent in man, [ought to] freely spend itself at least once a year"(cited in Ferguson, 1990, pp. 109–110).

Mikhail Bakhtin's work *Rabelais and his World* (1984) documents the practices of carnival more closely. Bakhtin speaks of three forms of carnival folk culture, including ritual spectacles (feasts, pageants, festivals), comic verbal compositions (oral and written parodies), and various genres of coarse utterance (curses, oaths, profanations, and low speech) (pp. 37–38). He argues that the sort of laughter such spectacles and speech making evoked was irrepressible and unrestrained, but that we have seen a gradual containment of laughter ever since.

The feminist writer Mary Russo (1994) makes much of Bakhtin's work in claiming the political importance of the carnivalesque to contemporary feminism. In *The Female Grotesque: Risk, Excess and Modernity* (1994), Russo explains its value as rising from the fact that the carnivalesque is "set . . . apart from the merely oppositional and reactive" (p. 62), allowing "a redeployment or counterproduction of culture, knowledge, and pleasure"(p. 62). For Russo, the imperative that arises for feminists is not to reconfigure the classical body politic "as the basis of a new universalism" but as "an uncanny connection characteristic of the discourses of the grotesque" (p. 14).

I want to stay with Russo's thesis a little longer because it has relevance for a feminist imagining a freakish performative pedagogy—one that refuses to become normal—notwithstanding the diminished possibilities for laughter of the carnivalesque type in modernist institutions such as universities. Like Ferguson and Bakhtin, Russo (1994) argues that it is the materiality of the body that is the site of the carnivalesque. This material body is not, however, the "classical body" of modernity, "transcendent and monumental, closed, static, self-contained, symmetrical and sleek" (p. 8), but the "grotesque body" of carnival—"open, protruding, irregular, secreting, multiple, and changing" (p. 8).

Grotesque bodies, according to Russo (1994), are "only recognizable in relation to a norm," which they exceed in a way that involves "serious risk" (p. 10). Russo acknowledges the importance of Foucault's *Discipline and Punish: The Birth of the Prison* (1979) in demonstrating the power of normalization as an instrument of modernity. The body of the academic, like that of any other modern citizen, has been normalized—measured, catalogued, segmented, and examined—through disciplinary discourses. Such practices work to eliminate risk inasmuch as risk means the real possibility of mistake, error, and failure. This is not simply failure to complete a particular task to an acceptable standard, but, as I indicated earlier, failure to produce oneself as a reasoning, reasonable citizen; and it is this possibility that makes risk taking so serious.

Drawing on Foucault, Russo (1994) argues the importance of a discourse of risk in working against the normalizing process:

> Unlike the models of progress, rationality and liberation which disassociate themselves from their "mistakes"—noise, disso-

nance or monstrosity—this "room for chance" emerges within the very constrained spaces of normalization. It is not, in other words, that limitless, incommensurable, and transcendent space associated with the Kantian sublime. (p. 12)

One of the hallmarks of normalizing texts about universities is that, as modernist appeals to rationality and order, they characteristically leave a particular sort of material body behind. This excluded body is characterized by problematic processes such as "illness, aging, reproduction, non-reproduction, secretions, lumps, bloating, wigs, scars, make-up, and prostheses" (Russo, 1994, p. 14), and this is particularly pertinent to women in an aging academy. A discourse of risk, on the other hand, does not seek to reassure us about how "normal" and "inclusive" a project is, whether it is feminist or minoritarian or otherwise. Nor is it to be found in the "thriving on chaos" rhetoric that is the hallmark of new business management texts. Discourses of risk do not arise from appeals to pluralism of the "let-all-voices-speak" kind, nor from any other appeal to authenticity—or, indeed, to popular fiction. They protrude to unsettle and disorder, "telling flesh" (Kirby, 1997)[1] as asymmetrical, vulgar, and disruptive.

Disorderly Women

According to Russo (1994), it has been the figure of woman—as hysteric, hag, witch, and whore—whose body has been marked as deviant by way of its historical subjection to pathological attention, and thus it is the figure of woman that has more to offer the production of a discourse of risk. Russo cites Natalie Davis's argument that "disorderly women" have always "undermined as well as reinforced" power hierarchies and social order (p. 58). Disorderly women may incite and embody deviance as well as being the means for bringing it under control.

I want to explore this logic further, particularly in terms of how disorderly feminisms impact on the academy. To do so, I move to examine two accounts, given in academic feminist pedagogical texts, of women enacting pedagogical work in an unruly way, to consider how they function as discourses of risk working *within*, and thus *limited by*, the feminist project itself. The first object of my scrutiny is Vicky Kirby's (1994) account of a pedagogical debate[2] between two feminist academic teachers—Jane Gallop[3] and Helene Keyssar—that appears to be a scholarly example of the redeployment of pedagogical knowledge made possible by foregrounding the disorderly, irregular, female body.

As Kirby (1994) describes it, Jane Gallop had written a paper, "The Teacher's Breasts," as a critical analysis of Helene Keyssar's published essay "Staging the Feminist Classroom" (in Culley & Portuges, 1985). Kirby writes:

> The drama began well before Jane Gallop's arrival, when I received the gossip that she had "attacked" [Keyssar] in the form of a paper . . . and that she was coming to deliver the blow personally. Gallop's indecency was indeed grotesque because Helene Keyssar, the target of critique in "The Teacher's Breasts," has recently suffered a double mastectomy. Gallop would consequently appear in the role of bitch in this coming event, the wicked witch whose symptomatic reading had magically conjured forth a pathology in the unsuspecting Keyssar. (p. 17)

Kirby (1994) understands how Gallop "offended feminist protocol" (p.17) inasmuch as her "incisive intellect and theoretical sophistication" were pitted against a woman with "impeccable" feminist credentials who was, moreover, "a victim whose vulnerable and wounded body guaranteed her privileged status"(p. 17). She describes the debate as an "ordeal" involving some belated back-pedaling on Gallop's part and a display of maternal benevolence on the part of Keyssar (p. 18). Kirby's account works as a counterreading of the event, given her particular view of the outcomes:

> The ordeal . . . saw Keyssar speaking interminably about Gallop's misrepresentation of her position. If only it had been true. Ironically, and this is my point, any serious engagement with Gallop's subject matter was now effectively gagged by the problem's staging; the tyranny of the maternal, performed for all it was worth before our very eyes. There was something sufficiently compelling about this piece of theatre that left most of the audience speechless. (p. 18)

Kirby's (1994) reflections on the audience response—the demonization of Gallop, the canonization of Keyssar—lead her to pose the question, "Why is the maternal guise of benign innocence, purity of purpose and desire, natural devotion and selflessness not openly recognized as fraudulent, and a burden of prescriptions that are ultimately paralyzing for women?" (pp. 18–19). For Kirby, the fact that Keyssar won so much audience allegiance, and Gallop so little, speaks more powerfully about conditions in which a feminist pedagogy is rendered *im*possible, rather than possible (p. 19). "The perceived need that Gallop make reparation to Keyssar was an example of [reversing masculinism's privileging of reason] as if intellectual scholarship, especially when its criticisms successfully engage the work of other women, wounds the body of feminism itself" (p. 20).

Kirby (1994) does not let anyone off the hook in this analysis. Her "double take" underlines feminism's intimacy with power, rather than any need to name patriarchal oppression. It is an awkward and uncomfortable moment for her and for feminist readers, not because it points to debates *within* feminism but because she documents what it meant to perform feminism *properly* on that day in that pedagogical event.

Unlike Kirby's paper, Alison Bartlett's paper "A Passionate Subject: Representations of Desire in Feminist Pedagogy" (1998), does not interrogate one particular pedagogical moment. However, Bartlett does draw attention to the body of the female teacher as an unruly and subversive material object in the classroom. Bartlett cites bell hooks's (1994) account of her days as a beginning teacher when "she was perturbed by her body signaling a need to go to the toilet in the middle of class" (p. 86). hooks "had no clue as to what [her] elders did in such situations" because "no one talked about the body in relation to teaching" (p. 86). Bartlett continues:

> I have had similar fears, not of going to the toilet, but of beginning to menstruate before a lecture. I double up in cramps, dizziness and nausea at the onset of bleeding: how does a woman teach in such a position? A friend of mine tells me that when she was teaching and suddenly thought of her nine month old baby, her breast milk would sometimes leak visibly onto her professional lecturer's blouse. Can this be possible? Do teachers' breasts leak and their wombs menstruate? What else might (teaching) women's bodies entail, and how does this affect their pedagogical positions? (pp. 86–87)

In "doubting the likelihood" that certain teachers' bodies leak milk and blood, Bartlett (1998) uses irony to unsettle orderly accounts of teaching. She indicates that the means through which we have come to think and write the proper teaching body renders certain "normal" bodily processes unspeakable. We might *know* that all premenopausal women must spend approximately one quarter of their teaching time menstruating, but this is not a body likely to be spoken of in discussions of teacher quality and professional development. Nevertheless, its absence from these texts speaks loudly about how troublesome this leaky materiality is. The female teacher who has menstrual blood on her clothing is a very differently disordered figure from the male teacher who has his fly undone. While the latter is a momentary figure of fun, the former mobilizes disgust, shame, and ridicule in a way that does not allow order (as teacher authority) to be quickly and harmlessly restored. To insist on speaking the former, as Bartlett does, is to engage in a discourse of risk but from within the safe terrain of feminist pedagogy's challenge to orthodox notions of professionalism.

No Safety in Sade

Both of the above stories, when taken together, support the case that feminist documentations of disorderly, leaky, and malformed pedagogical bodies can work as a redeployment or counterproduction of culture and knowledge about teaching. There is, however, little evidence here of the pleasure—or, indeed, the fundamental subversion of modernity— that Russo (1994) hopes will be forthcoming from such a deployment. Pleasure seems so often to be the casualty of academic productivity. Exploring the carnivalesque as a site of the grotesque seems to take academics away from fun at the very time that we seek to deploy it for the purposes of subversion. Must academic women give up on fun to be properly academic?

In performing her own risky challenge to a number of academic traditions, Camille Paglia (1995) argues that this serious state of affairs is the present outcome of a more general tendency in Western modes of thought to privilege tragedy over comedy. The seductive call to seriousness prevents us from attributing value to the obscene, the comic, or the burlesque. In *Sex and Violence, or Nature and Art* (1995), Paglia argues:

> Modern criticism has projected a Victorian and, I feel, Protestant high seriousness upon pagan culture that still blankets teaching. . . . Paradoxically, assent to savage chthonian realities leads not to gloom but to humor. Hence Sade's strange laughter, his wit amid the most fantastic cruelties. For life is not a tragedy but a comedy. . . . Nature is always pulling the rug out from under our pompous ideals. (p. 9)

Paglia's (1995) insistence that "[e]very road from Rousseau leads to Sade" (p. 20) is risky indeed! It refuses, perversely, the modernist logic of an upward and forward movement of identity, demanding that "we go full circle" as libidinal beings (p. 20), that "intellectual control over nature" is no more than a "comforting illusion" (p. 25). In evoking "Sade's strange laughter," Paglia calls forth a murky and subversive tradition of un-reasonableness that cuts across the classical renderings of the body, the stuff of which modernist accounts are made.

Whether the un-reason Paglia insists on invoking is really a product of the work of Sade or of modernist texts *about* Sade may well be the subject of further debate outside the parameters of this chapter. My interest is in the ways academic women as reason-able citizens (enlightened and ethical thinkers) have distanced themselves from such perversity. Reading about how to do research and pedagogy properly allows us to achieve such a distancing effect. Just as each repetition of a comic performance distances the actors a little more from what had once been funny, so good academics continue to move away from the risk of perversion and excess by repeated rehearsals of proper academic work and, thus, proper self-pleasuring. We have learnt to feel *appropriate disgust* at the mere mention of Sade.

Irony Deficiency

While many of us women in the academy might be well versed in when and how to be disgusted, the matter of taking our pleasure within reason can continue to elude many of us, just as fun has eluded bourgeois modes of rationality. As Bakhtin (1984) understands the fate of the carnivalesque in modernity, each era has already distanced us more from the possibility of having (carnivalesque) fun. According to Bakhtin, the romantic period saw carnivalesque laughter "cut down to cold humor, irony and sarcasm" (p. 38). So if the fun of the carnivalesque is out—if its expulsion from normal and deviational prescriptions of academic work is more or less complete—then it is time to consider the possible pleasures available to academic women in the "cutdown" space that is the modern academy. This invites us to explore the more restrained space called *play*.

I am aware of Jean-François Lyotard's (1979) assertion that the age of the professor is ending because it is incapacitated in relation to play: "[A] professor is no more competent than memory bank networks in *transmitting* established knowledge, no more competent than interdisciplinary teams in imagining new moves or new games" (p. 53). In such a "postprofessor" era, that form of play called irony can serve the double function of allowing the pleasure of a particular sort of language game and the opportunity to create a sub/version of reality-as-common sense. Where sarcasm is ruled out of proper language deployment in education on the grounds of its intention to wound, where cold humor may be cold comfort, and where overt opposition is anticipated as the first step to unemployment, irony is a bright and shiny bauble among modernity's store of tarnished playthings.

What is so useful about irony is its capacity to keep ideas *in play*, constantly moving, jumping about, making trouble. It is a way of refusing to settle finally on *the* account, *the* formula, *the* set of principles for good moral, political, economic, or pedagogical order. Of course, this means that irony is not the medium of the literalist or the evangelist, given that the performative stress is on the importance of *not* being earnest. Moreover, as with all humor, irony depends on knowing how something works. Many successful comedians make people laugh by setting up an absurd proposition and then piling on proof in support of it. This means using reason for the very purpose of unfixing reason. So, too, irony unfixes words, meanings, accounts by using them against themselves. An ironist is sincere about her insincerity, serious about her pleasure.

Clearly, irony is not for those who seek to overcome oppression in all its forms. Richard Rorty (1989) makes mention of the "special resentment" (p. 90) that ironists arouse in others, particularly those others whose common sense is "redescribed" in ways that apparently render it "futile, obsolete, powerless" (p. 90). For those who know that "there is a connection between redescription and power" (p. 90), the ironist's refusal to assure others that any one redescription is more liberating than any other comes as both a desire to humiliate (p. 90) but, more crucially, "an inability to empower" (p. 91). The ironist then must wear the tag of the dilettante, the socially useless, the antithesis of the problem solver, the advocate, the social worker, because her concern "to intensify the irony of the nominalist and the historicist" is "ill-suited to public purposes" and thus "of no use to liberals *qua* liberals" (p. 95).

Rorty (1989) goes on to argue that one should not discount the social usefulness of certain literary enactments of irony (pp. 95–96). Moreover, his work also allows me to understand that the pleasure I take in performing ironic texts in my writing and teaching will be different from the pleasure of the transformative intellectual. This is because I am not committed to getting my message across by speaking a language that "all of us recognize when we hear it" (Rorty, 1990, p. 94). Unfortunately for me and my ironic sisterhood, such recognition translates into publication royalties, among other things. The ironist is much less likely to benefit materially from her work than authors of metaexplanatory, "blockbuster" texts like *Men Are from Mars, Women Are from Venus: A Practical Guide for Improving Communication and Getting What You Want in Your Relationships* (Gray, 1992). Moreover, the fact that ironic texts do not lend themselves to being easily reduced to a list of dot points or an executive summary diminishes the likelihood of corporate influence and/or career promotion. And there is no guarantee that ironic female academics will use humor any more successfully than their emancipationist and/or entrepreneurial colleagues. One of the hallmarks of active, enterprising educational consultants, as I currently see them operating, is that they outpace conservative and radical pedagogues alike, in combining the skills of the slapstick comedian with the slickness, sincerity, and missionary zeal of the tele-evangelist. They are certainly more likely to be influential than those of us who have learned to be properly disgusted by the combination of gloss and fast capitalism.

The pleasures irony affords are the more private pleasures of self-creation in keeping with the ironist's location as a "private philosopher" (Rorty, 1990, p. 95). Thus, the laughter of the carnival is reduced to an individual snigger, but it is not silenced altogether. However, tension certainly remains between self-creation as a vocabulary "necessarily private, unshared and unsuited to argument" and the vocabulary of justice that is "necessarily public and shared" (p. xiv). As Donna Haraway (1991) understands it, working as an ironist is "perhaps more faithful as blasphemy is faithful" (p. 149). I concur with Haraway that irony-as-blasphemy is important in the business of "keeping the faith," whether it is the faith of feminism, socialism, materialism, liberalism, or any other common purpose. Haraway writes:

> Blasphemy protects one from the moral majority within, while still insisting on the need for community. Blasphemy is not apostasy. Irony is about contradictions that do not resolve into larger wholes, even dialectically, about the tension of holding incompatible things together because both or all are necessary and true. (p. 149)

For those whose pleasure is taken within a certain domain of "unreasonableness," there may be little pleasure in struggling with a text that blasphemes by refusing to resolve tensions and by troubling the texts of those who seek to do so. Irony may look too much like caprice, whimsicality, as well as lack of commitment, even cowardice. For me, irony is a seductive means to *underline and undermine* those ways of speaking and thinking and being that have come to characterize woman and academic, and this includes ways of thinking that have been generated by feminist scholarship and research. Examples of the latter may include the familiar research finding that has become something of a mantra for women in the academy—that women academics are more collaborative while men are (naturally) more competitive or that women are more "balanced" in relation to home and family commitments while men are more work-obsessed. The fact that this high moral ground turns to swampland come the promotional round might well invite us to turn our attention to the work our research stories do as part of the social production of identity in the academy. This means acknowledging women's complicity in the games of truth and error out of which our selves and our pleasures are constituted—all those formulae and visions and truths and knowledge objects that we use to make ourselves into "the quality professional" or "the nurturing caregiver" or the "collaborative researcher" or "the reflective practitioner" or the "critical feminist" or the "participative manager." Put simply, the end is to constantly unsettle what it means for women to behave properly in the academy—and to take pleasure in so doing.

Notes

1. *Telling Flesh: The Substance of the Corporeal* is the title of Vicki Kirby's (1997) recent book in which she interrogates critical theoretical developments in the study of corporeality.

2. The debate was held during a conference at the University of California at San Diego in April 1993.

3. Jane Gallop is committed to the Freudian idea that teaching is better understood as an emotional and erotic experience than as a cognitive, informative one (Gallop, 1997). This Lacanian view of the nature of pedagogical work is disturbing to many academics, and many feminists.

4. For more on this debate, see Peter Cryle's (1997) essay, "Sade as a Figure of Radical Modernity: Making-and-Breaking the History of Sexuality" in Clare O'Farrell's edited volume, *Foucault: The Legacy*.

References

Bakhtin, M. (1984). *Rabelais and his world* (H. Iswolksy, Trans.). Bloomington: Indiana University Press.

Bartlett, A. (1998). A passionate subject: Representations of desire in feminist pedagogy. *Gender and Education, 10*(1), 85–92.

Cryle, P. (1997). Sade as a figure of radical modernity: Making-and-breaking the history of sexuality. In C. O'Farrell (Ed.), *Foucault: The legacy* (pp. 12–16). Brisbane, Australia: School of Cultural and Policy Studies, Queensland University of Technology.

Culley, M., & Portuges, C. (Eds.). (1985). *Gendered subjects: The dynamics of feminist teaching*. New York: Routledge.

Ferguson, H. (1990). *The science of pleasure*. London: Routledge.

Foucault, M. (1979). *Discipline and punish: The birth of the prison*. New York: Vintage Books.

Foucault, M. (1985). *The use of pleasure: The history of sexuality, Volume 2* (R. Hurley, Trans.). London: Penguin.

Gallop, J. (1997). *Feminist accused of sexual harassment*. Durham, NC: Duke University Press.

Gray, J. (1992). *Men are from Mars, Women are from Venus: A practical guide for improving communication and getting what you want in relationships*. New York: HarperCollins.

Haraway, D. (1991). *Simians, cyborgs and women: The reinvention of nature*. London: Free Association Books.

hooks, b. (1994). *Teaching to transgress: Education as the practice of freedom*. New York: Routledge.

Kirby, V. (1994). Response to Jane Gallop's "The Teacher's Breasts." In J. J. Matthews (Ed.), *Jane Gallop Seminar Papers, Proceedings of the Jane Gallop Semi-*

nar and Public Lecture "The Teacher's Breasts," June 1993 (pp. 17–22). Canberra, Australia: The Humanities Research Center.

Kirby, V. (1997). *Telling flesh: The substance of the corporeal.* New York: Routledge.

Lyotard, J-F. (1979). *The postmodern condition: A report on knowledge.* Manchester, UK: Manchester University Press.

Paglia, C. (1995). *Sex and violence or nature and art.* London: Penguin.

Rorty, R. (1989). *Contingency, irony, and solidarity.* New York: Cambridge University Press.

Russo, M. (1994). *The female grotesque: Risk, excess and modernity.* New York: Routledge.

Chapter 9

Eclipsing the Constitutive Power of Discourse: The Writing of Janette Turner Hospital

Bronwyn Davies

Postmodernity brings with it a multiplicity of competing discourses. That multiplicity affords human subjects the possibility of undermining the (previously unquestioned or unquestionable) power of those discourses that have had a monopoly on consciousness. Inevitably, that possibility also brings with it increased surveillance as populations appear to become less governable, less eager to take up dominant discourses as their own. Poststructuralist theory analyses the dynamics of postmodernity, and the possibilities (and restrictions) it affords, in terms of the relations among discourse, subjection, and desire. Feminist poststructuralist theorizing, in particular, has focused on the possibilities opened up when dominant language practices are made visible and revisable.

Understanding the twofold nature of subjection in which we are subjected and, in that same process, become speaking subjects has been central to searching out the ways in which we might make sense of the extent of the constitutive force of discourse and of our capacity to use the power that subjection gives us to move against and beyond the very forces that shape us. As Butler (1997) says:

> Power acts on the subject in at least two ways: first, as what makes the subject possible, the condition of its possibility and its formative occasion, and second, as what is taken up and reiterated in the subject's own acting. As a subject of power (where "of" connotes both "belonging to" and "wielding"), the subject eclipses the conditions of its own emergence; it eclipses power with power . . . the subject emerges both as the *effect* of a prior power and as the *condition of possibility* for a radically conditioned form of agency. (p. 14)

Much of my writing has been aimed at finding ways to open up feminist poststructuralist theory to teachers and to students (for example, Davies, 1993, 1994, 1995, 1996, 1997b). More recently, I have been paying particular attention to the ways in which fiction writers create imaginary possibilities that make visible and also eclipse the certainties of dominant discourses (Watson and Davies, 1998). In doing so, I am searching out particular instances of what it might mean for the writing/reading subject to "eclipse the conditions of its own emergence" (Butler, 1997, p. 14).

"To eclipse" means to cast a shadow, to overshadow or surpass in importance. The subjected being, in its trajectory, overshadows, surpasses in importance the discourse through which it takes up its being. This is a possibility of crucial importance to feminist poststructuralist writers and activists who do not gainsay the constitutive power of the originary luminary bodies of discourse but who insist on refusing its permanent and inevitable supremacy.

Some poststructuralist theorists, however, declare such an eclipse impossible; for them the constitutive force of discourse rules out the possibility of agency, of a subject who *wields power*, while simultaneously being constituted by it (Jones, 1997). My understanding, in contrast, is that such a reading is a structuralist one and that the power feminists have found in poststructuralist theorizing is precisely in its opening up of possibilities for undermining the inevitability of particular oppressive forms of subjection. They have done this by making the constitutive force of discourse visible and thus revisable. By making visible the ways in which power shifts dramatically, depending on how subjects are positioned by and within the multiple and competing discourses they encounter, they can begin to imagine how to reposition themselves, realign themselves, and use the power of discourse they have to disrupt those of its effects they wish to resist (Davies, 1997a; Davies and Harré, 1990).

Fiction Writing

Fiction writers have played an important part in the process of imagining alternatives and in generating new ways of speaking/writing. The creative deconstruction of and play with language that writers such as Cixous and Derrida and Deleuze engage in is not unlike the imaginative work some novelists engage in using language to break open old certainties and generate new ways of speaking/writing, new forms, new images that give a life to previously unimagined possibilities. Indeed, Cixous (in Cixous and Calle-Gruber, 1997) comments that her real work is achieved through her fictional writing and that she can achieve far less with her theoretical texts.

The play and opening up of possibilities in fictional texts does not entail "escape" from being constituted through discourse. To think of it as escape would be to place it in some binary relation to subjection. Rather, we are subjected, we become human, and, in that becoming, can search out, in writing, the possibilities for creative movement beyond the terms of our subjection. As Cixous (in Cixous and Calle-Gruber, 1997) says:

> We live, but why do we live? I think: to become more human: more capable of reading the world, more capable of playing it in all ways. This does not mean nicer or more humanistic. I would say: more faithful to what we are made from and to what we can create. (p. 30)

Within poststructuralist theory, language is understood as the most powerful constitutive force shaping what we understand as possible and what we desire within those possibilities. We can be overwhelmed by the constitutive force of language, or we can, like Cixous (in Cixous and Calle-Gruber, 1997), embrace the intoxicating power of language and use it to move into the not-yet-known:

> To think that we have at our disposal the biggest thing in the universe, and that it is language. What one can do with language is . . . infinite. What one can do with the smallest sign! . . . This may be why so many people do not write: because it's terrifying. And conversely, it is what makes certain people write: because it's intoxicating. Language is all powerful. You can say everything, do everything, that has not yet been said, not yet been done. (p. 12)

It is the act of imaginative writing that is the central interest of this chapter. I want to look more closely at the ways in which writers make new discursive and interactive practices possible and, in particular, new practices that hold the possibility of eclipsing the power of established discourses. How is it that fiction writers and poets are able to produce writing that invites the possibility of an imaginative takeup beyond what is already known? And how is it that (some) readers move with them into the not-already-known? In asking such questions I am moving into unmapped territory, or rather territory for which I find the existing maps of literary criticism of little use, with their authoritative declarations about what is to be found in the texts they read and write about. Cixous (in Cixous and Calle-Gruber, 1997) says of these existing maps, "All that advances is aerial, detached, uncatchable. So I am worried when I see certain tendencies in reading: they take the spare wheel for the bird" (p. 4).

Deleuze's understanding of what reading is, like Cixous's, lays emphasis not on the inevitability of particular forms of subjection from which there is no escape but on the shifting, ephemeral nature of being a subject. He envisages a subject in transition, a "nomad," rather than an overcoded and fixed subject. It is the nomadic subject who brings texts to life or lets them die.[1] Grosz (1995) elaborates Deleuze's position thus:

> Instead of a Derridean model of the text as textile, as interweaving—which produces a close, striated space of intense overcodings, a fully semiotized model of textuality . . . texts could, more in keeping with Deleuze, be read, used, as modes of effectivity and action which, at their best, scatter thoughts and images into different linkages or new alignments without necessarily destroying their materiality. . . . Instead of the eternal status of truth, or the more provisional status of knowledge, texts have short term effects, though they may continue to be read for generations. They only remain effective and alive if they have effects, produce realignments, shake things up. In Deleuzian terms, such a text, such thought, could be described as fundamentally moving, "nomadological" or "rhizomatic." (p. 126–27)

In entering into the writing or reading of a novel, we are, to a large extent, entering the "already known" and experiencing it afresh, perhaps finding how the already known can be spoken for the first time. We do not enter the fictional text as if it were a philosophical, analytic, or logical piece of writing to be grasped and possibly dissected for its flaws in reasoning. We enter into the novel as another form of living in the world through imagining the lives of others as we bring them to life on the page. In doing so, we live the emotions of the characters, experience life from their point of view, and expand our consciousness to include the possibility we lived there in the writing/reading. We find certainty there in the already known. But we may also find the unexpected, the thrilling, the element that unsettles, that makes undecidable the controlled, the rational, and the already decided. The openness to undecidability is what many have an ambivalent relation to. The power that subjection brings with it often resists the questioning of the terms of subjection, since such questioning might undermine the power already grasped. Yet taking risks, going beyond, also seems to be what being human leads us to. Cixous (in Cixous and Calle-Gruber, 1997) sees that openness to risk, to movement, as *indissociable* from human life:

> [O]rdinary human beings do not like mystery since you cannot put a bridle on it, and therefore, in general they exclude it, they repress it, they eliminate it—and it's *settled*. But if on the contrary one remains open and susceptible to all the phenomena of overflowing, beginning with natural phenomena, one discovers the immense

landscape of the *trans-*, of the passage. Which does not mean that everything will be adrift: our thinking, our choices etc. But it means that the factor of instability, the factor of uncertainty, or what Derrida calls the undecidable, is indissociable from human life. (p. 52)

Janette Turner Hospital

I met with Janette Turner Hospital while she was visiting Australia to launch her book *Oyster*. I wanted to talk to her about her writing because her writing of body/landscape relations invites the possibility of an imaginative takeup beyond dominant and established discourses. Although much of her writing is located in Australia, she spends most of her life in other countries, and so I felt myself very lucky that she was here and that she agreed to meet me. Over lunch she expressed a sense of vulnerability about the interview, telling me she was not very articulate when it came to spoken words and that what she had to say was already in her books. But when the tape recorder was turned on, her words were like perfectly formed jewels. She spoke with insight and emotion about the embodied nature of her writing. I was, during our hour over lunch, panic-stricken that we did not have enough time for all my questions, in a state of rapture at the careful and profound answers she made to my questions, and delighted to find that so many moments of her life echoed in my own memories. We were both born in the 1940s in Australia and so had grown up through the same historical and discursive shifts through which we had become "girls," "people," and "Australians." For her part, Janette Turner Hospital expressed surprise and pleasure at the careful, detailed reading I had made of her texts and at the fact that I treated her with such respect. Given my social science background, I accorded her the same respect I would any interviewee. The discourse of literary criticism, it would seem, does not tend to accord authors such respect; rather, they are treated as imagined extensions of the texts about which anything that comes to the mind of the critic can be said. Through our talk about her life and her writing, in working through the transcripts later, and in our subsequent communication about aspects of the interview and my interpretations of it, I developed a deep sense of affinity with and respect for her.

Janette Turner Hospital's life was, as a child, and is, as an adult, one in which she often feels deeply precarious. Her subjection within the various discourses through which family and Australian colleagues are constituted is not something she takes for granted for herself. The difference between family and school and family and work makes the terms of subjection in each, for her, highly visible. She described to me the effect of this while on her current lecture tour and, at the same time, visiting her family:

> I felt exhausted—psychically exhausted at the immensity of the difference and the fact that I've learnt to pass as a native in both worlds and in fact I feel profoundly alien and deeply precarious in both because I just—there are days when I simply feel fraudulent, there are days when I just feel I can't manage it. (Turner Hospital, 1996a)

Janette Turner Hospital describes herself as a child who did not accept the terms of her subjection without question. She wanted to interrogate the discourses that her family insisted must be taken on trust. Her childhood home, she says, was a place where you did not ask questions, particularly about the apparent irrationality of stories in the Bible. School, too, was a place where you did not ask questions. In her novel *Charades*, she has created a character, Kay, who attempts to pass as one who is acceptably subjected in school terms but finds that her fraudulence is visible to teachers and the other students who "know" without question the terms of their subjection. In the following excerpt from *Charades*, Kay's lack of knowledge about a famous horse race held each year in Australia leads to her being positioned by teacher and students as outsider, as one who has no right to know as they know, to be as they are:

> Kay felt she would run out of storage room for all the puzzling things she knew. Most of her knowledge was of the wrong kind. She could, for example, rattle through the names of the books of the Bible, from Genesis to Revelation, but could not produce the name of a single horse in the Melbourne Cup. She had never even heard of Phar Lap—"the *legendary* Phar Lap," Miss Kennedy said, incredulous.
>
> On the other hand she knew that the blue bodypaint of Boadicea's warriors was called *woad*, and that King Harold had been felled by an arrow in the eye at the Battle of Hastings.
>
> Miss Kennedy, surprised but grudgingly pleased, asked: "Now just *where* do you pick up these things?"
>
> "In the library," Kay said guiltily. In the library, while the rest of the class engaged in Maypole dancing and sundry other forbidden licentious acts. "In the picture-book encyclopedia."
>
> Not acceptable, she knew it instantly. She could feel the disapproval like a sudden tropical fog. They would *do* things again, the boys would, if Patrick wasn't with them and they caught her alone after school. Don't tell, don't tell, they would taunt. If you tell we will get you tonight . . .
>
> . . . she had gone and *memorized* the page on Phar Lap in the pic-

ture-book encyclopedia. She waited and waited and when at last he was mentioned again by Miss Kennedy, her hand shot up. "His greatest win was the 1930 Cup," she said, breathless. "He had thirty-seven wins, the last one in America. And then," she rattled on, "he was murdered by the Americans, but his heart was one and a half times the normal size for a thoroughbred."

There was an eerie silence.

They all looked at her very strangely, she could feel the stares like pins and needles on her skin.

"What would *youuuuu* know?" someone taunted.

Wowser, wowser, wowser! voices said.

"Youuu've never been to the races in yer life."

What would you know you know you know? voices chanted later in the playground. And the circle formed a kind of dance, a skip, a game. (Turner Hospital, 1988, p. 132)

Novelists such as Janette Turner Hospital, invite openness and susceptibility to the "immense landscape of the *trans-*, of the passage." They do not write with the clichés, the obviousnesses, that forms the *settled* certainties of existence. They write out of their own existence as (subjected) human beings, but the flow of their writing comes from the *in(terre)conscious* zones, with an emphasis here, not on the individualized consciousness, but on all the subterranean possibilities earthed in the human body as a result of experiencing life—*in(terre)conscious: between earth and consciousness.*[2]

Janette Turner Hospital troubles the separation of consciousness from the earth *(terre)*: she writes from the space between *(terre)* earth and consciousness. She invites us into an imaginary space in which we encounter (and in part become) embodied beings not separated from the earth but of it. She writes into the space between landscapes and bodies and finds them, on occasion, inseparable:

In the green pool the two heads floated with their dark hair fanned about them: waterlilies on lily pads. (Turner Hospital, 1995a, p. 200)

Uncle Seaborn's hair is soft as water, crinkly (one thinks of wavelets rippling back over sand), the colour of seaweed. . . . A gleaming creature, barebacked and slick with sweat . . . Behind him . . . the Great Divide falls away to the coastal plain, and the wet tendrils of hair drip down ravines of muscle and bone, of eucalypt scrub, of Fitzroy River silt, making their way to the Pacific. It sucked at him ceaselessly, the ocean. (Turner Hospital, 1995b, p. 203)

The cane pushes through the rotting window blinds and grows into the cracks and corners of the mind. It ripens in the heart at night, and its crushed sweetness drips into dreams. I have woken brushing from my eyelids the silky plumes that burst up at harvest time. (Turner Hospital, 1995c, p. 15)

Janette Turner Hospital describes how, in the face of such silencing as a child at home and at school, she sought unpeopled spaces in which to think, to ask the questions she wanted to ask. When she climbed trees or swam in the sea, she could explore the concepts that seemed weighty to her and discover a language of the *in(terre)conscious* zone, a language in which her openness to the flows of the earth and her consciousness opened new possibilities. From as young as 6 years old, she describes herself as experiencing a "fusion of landscape and body and thought":

> And I was told, you know: you don't ask these questions, we don't understand what God's thinking. So I wasn't allowed to ask questions at home, and for quite other reasons at school the questions I would have asked would be deemed stupid or the class would laugh at them. So my first experience of where I could think my own criminal and puzzling and unanswerable thoughts was a fusion of landscape and body and thought. I would climb and hide up our mango tree, you know, or I would go off alone to the beach or I would actually be in the surf or—so actually for me freedom, intellectual freedom and critical thinking and language and bodily pleasure and the eroticized highly speaking landscape all seemed to fuse extremely early for me, you know, and I had these thoughts about it, not so highly articulated and verbalized, I'm sure, by the time I was 6 years old. (Turner Hospital, 1996a)

She describes her first visit to North Queensland, as a schoolgirl, as one of ecstatic fusion with the landscape. She could not join in the chatter of the other girls—their talk of boys and sex was "totally unknown territory." Instead, she went walking alone: "[I] walked around on Green Island by myself and just was ecstatic. And I found the North Queensland rainforest" (Turner Hospital, 1996a). The "eroticized, highly speaking landscape" she experienced then as a schoolgirl and later as a teacher in North Queensland has become a resource she can write out of, not just as a memory of events and places, but as an embodied experience of knowing beyond the already available words that shape her. Her writing opens the possibility for others to enter that space. That which is beyond words is made knowable through sound and imagery, through an invitation to imaginatively enter the bodily and emotional space inhabited by her characters.

In Turner Hospital's short story "The Last of the Hapsburgs," the teacher, Miss Davenport, newly arrived in North Queensland, stands on the Port Douglas beach and hears the landscape speak to her, bidding her to find words to *"Sing me North Queensland"*:

The young woman leaves no footprints at all. She stands with her feet and ankles in the erratic line of froth, at the point where ocean and shore eat each other, and reads the Port Douglas beach. Cabrisi's horse [the wild brumby], nostrils flaring with the smell of her, rears: a salute of sorts.

"Caedmon," she says—here, the naming of creatures is all her—"you beautiful show-off!" Of course he knows it. So bloody beautiful that a cry catches in her throat. Caedmon whinnies again, a high jubilant note, and brushes the air with his delicate forelegs. Another sign. The beach is thick with them, but who has time enough for the decoding, the translating, the recording?

Surf rises from her ankles to her knees. *Sing me North Queensland,* it lisps with its slickering tongues.

I can't, she laments, hoisting up her skirt. *I can't.*

She would need a different kind of alphabet, a chlorophyll one, a solar one. The place will not fit into words.

Surf rushes between her thighs. *Sing me North Queensland,* it commands.

The young woman lifts her arms high above her head and faces the ocean. She begins to dance. She sings. When the sun slides behind Double Point, she climbs the hill at the end of the beach still singing. (Turner Hospital, 1995a, p. 190)

The sea, in which she is partially immersed, "lisps with its slickering tongues," commanding her to "sing me creation." Her silence holds her mute, but the sea commands again, rushing through her thighs, in an erotic salty embrace. This place will not fit the words already available to her, but the sea does not cease in its command. She needs a "a different kind of alphabet, a chlorophyll one, a solar one." Existing words fail her, and yet "She begins to dance. She sings." A song without end. And in that singing lies the possibility of a new relation between body, language, and landscape. Although as readers we cannot hear that song, it exists as an imaginary possibility, a voice that responds to the voice of the sea. Janette Turner Hospital says of such writing:

I suppose, in a way, I know I'm always writing about silent women, mute women who nevertheless are highly in tune with their own bodies and the landscape, and an attempt to speak of a language that is sensually eroticized, quite profoundly communicative, but has to exist outside established language forms because they've just not served the purpose of communicating. So I guess I'm always—that's what my writing is actually looking for. Metaphors that speak of the fusion of body, landscape, and the will to communicate. Will is altogether too analytical, patriarchal a word. The eroticized *desire* to communicate might be a better way to put it. And seeking to do that in a language that sneaks below the water table perhaps of the existing language forms. I feel as though I will write my way, that I've been writing my way out of silence, but that in fact I'll write my way back into it somehow. (Turner Hospital, 1996a)

The experience of being embodied as silent, unable to speak—an experience fundamental to growing up female (Davies et al., 1997)—is disrupted, and yet it is always there as a possibility to return to. The return to silence she talks of is not necessarily a return in the original terms of exclusion but a return made possible by the discovery of another way of being beyond words that is experienced as more powerful than words. However, in what follows, it becomes clear that these two kinds of silence cannot so clearly be separated out, one from the other.

Later in the story of the young woman on the beach, she seeks out two of her students who are loners in the school, one an Aboriginal girl from a poverty-stricken background and one a Jewish girl with an eccentric family escaped from Europe to a place where they hope they will be safe. The three young women walk together to the Mossman Gorge. When they arrive at the Gorge, Hazel, the Aboriginal student, slips off her tunic and dives in. Rebecca, more cautious in taking off her clothes, hesitates, then follows Hazel. Miss Davenport has longed all day for the coolness of the pool but has not thought about the problem of clothes. She has brought the young women with her as a spontaneous afterthought. She is uncertain of the situation but finds the repeated phrase from the fourteenth century mystic Julian of Norwich, *"all manner of thing shall be well,"* and thus finds the desire and the freedom to follow the young women into the water:

Miss Davenport, with a careless rapture, took off all her clothes and walked into the water.

The pool, from dark subterranean places, was chilly, a shock to the body for whole minutes. Time must have passed, though the three women were not conscious of it. They did not speak, but they were aware of each other. Birds piped and flashed their colours, the falls kept up their subdued chatter.

This is where we have escaped to, Miss Davenport thought. One is safe in water.

One is helpless in water.

Afterwards, she could never understand how there was no warning, no transition. Just peace and then chaos, the jarring laughter and catcalls, the five boys standing on boulders.

Joanna Goanna's tits? they whooped. *Cop those black tits! Plain-jane hasn't got any tits, she's flat as a bat. Oh struth, cop that! You can see old dried up Davenport's pussy!*

The boys, Miss Davenport noted, were in an intense and spiritual state, a kind of sacrilegious ecstasy, leaping from boulder to boulder around the pool. Like kings of the wild, they stood high on the great black rock and pissed into the water. Then one of them, Ross O'Hagan, eldest son of the local policeman, an ordinary boy who sat at an ordinary desk in Miss Davenport's English class, that boy turned his back and pulled down his shorts and squatted. A turd emerged slowly and hung suspended from his hairy anus. It was long, amazingly long, making its celebrity appearance to a chanted count. One! the boys chanted. Two, three, four, five . . .

Miss Davenport, Rebecca, and Hazel watched, mesmerised. The turd had attained the count of ten, a plumbline reaching for water. Eleven, twelve, thirteen . . . It detached itself at last and fell into the pool with a soft splash. Cheers went up, and more whoops of laughter, and then the boys were off like possums, flying from rock to rock. They scooped up the bundle of female clothing, and ran off . . .

Water lapped at their shoulders. Polluted water. Hazel, inured to indignity perhaps, was the first to move. She clambered onto the boulder below the falls and let the water hammer her . . .

But what comfort could Miss Davenport give to Rebecca whose face had put on its whitewax look-alike mask? How could she unsay the sentence that had been spoken, become an anti-Circe? In her teacherly mind, she rehearsed possible spells: *This says more about the boys than it does about us.*

But it would not serve, she knew it. It might be true, but it would not serve. That steaming fact, dropping stolidly into the pool, spoke a thick and dirty language. The acts of men, even when they are boys, Miss Davenport thought, are shouts that rip open the signs that try to contain them. We have no access to a language of such noisiness. Our voices are micemutter, silly whispers.

We will have to stay here in the pool forever, she thought. We are dead ends, the last of a line, masters of the genre of silence. We will have to invent a new alphabet of moss and water. (Turner Hospital, 1995a, p. 201–02)

In such writing and reading from the body, from the vulnerable body, Janette Turner Hospital produces a shock of knowledge of what it is to be embodied as woman—not only woman with all the power of the earth speaking a new language but woman vulnerable to the words of boys, boys like possums who constitute them as other, as objects to be desired or rejected, playthings who can be left stranded naked in the forest, their words reduced to "micemutter, silly whispers." But the finding of a new alphabet of moss and water does momentarily eclipse the dominant patriarchal discourses through which these women and these boys are shaped. Janette Turner Hospital says of that moment:

> [T]he kind of language exchanged in the Mossman Gorge say, in the rock pool at the Mossman Gorge with students, that didn't have words at all and it was sort of shared bodily epiphanies, and I don't mean sexual and I don't mean eroticized exactly, although I do think of language and the body as eroticized—instruments, perhaps, is the word. (Turner Hospital, 1996a)

In creating such a powerful image of the body as instrument for speaking the landscape without words, Janette Turner Hospital does not essentialize such power and so allow us to fall into the naive assumption that such eclipsing of other language forms might be permanent or capable of rendering powerless those more usually positioned as powerful. The energy that led Miss Davenport to seek something new and different, that enabled her to run against the grain of dominant discourses, is generated afresh in the anger erupting from the fact of the steaming stolid turd speaking the boys' contempt. That anger does not rest with Janette Turner Hospital as author, nor Miss Davenport as character, but is potentially lived again by each reader, in each reading of it. At the same time, Janette Turner Hospital leaves many of her readers with a deep unease, since the new alphabet that makes it possible to go beyond known discourses makes the young women's vulnerability all the more vivid. Old discourses that render women and landscape the same, as passive objects to be used and abused, are textually present in their reading of this episode at the Mossman Gorge. The new is always partially generated out of the old and thus partially contained by it. The seeking of ecstatic fusion, the sensual awareness of embodiment in landscape, the discovery of one's body as an instrument that speaks a language beyond words, is partially generated by a desire for escape from oppressive discourses. The oppressive discourse cannot be ignored, therefore, as a generative force.

It is fascinating to compare this with Cixous's description of what writing is for her. She describes how she searches, not in the possibilities afforded by rational thought, but for what she can find on her own body's deep surfaces, in the *in(terre)conscious* zones. She finds on the deep surfaces of her body jewels and corals, matter of the earth and of the sea, matter earthed in the lived human body.

At the same time, she sees that embodied searching as a searching for language, for deeply embodied words that, she finds, spark off the same resonances in her readers as they do in her:

> As for this weaving you [Mireille Calle-Gruber] spoke of a minute ago, here to there is nothing voluntary for me; I do not take an ele-

ment *a* and an element *b* to connect them. This happens in my deepest depths. The signified and the signifier work together without my being able to say which one leads, because the one calls for the other. And vice versa. How? A kind of work takes place in this space that we do not know, that precedes writing, and that must be a sort of enormous region or territory where a memory has been collected, a memory composed of all sorts of signifying elements that have been kept or noted—or of events that time has transformed into signifiers, pearls and corals of the "language" of the soul. . . . . There must be a sort of magnetic "force" in me that collects, without my knowing it, jewels, materials of the earth, that are propitious for a future book. It is my memory of writing that does this. I say "my memory of writing" because it is not the memory of life, or the memory of thought. It happens with sound elements, aesthetic elements, etc. Perhaps there is also a recording surface deep in me receiving micro-signs—it must guess that these signs are not solitary and lost, but emitters; in communication with other signs. An example: I had been struck, without realizing it, by the red geranium that lights up in *The Possessed* of Dostoevsky. It was as if, quite by chance, I had picked from the ground a key that opened a magic world. In the end, the geranium was absolutely not accidental, it was overdetermined. And it was not only my own mania or my own memory, but in effect a clue that functioned in more than one unconscious. Not only my own. Many others. (Cixous, in Cixous and Calle-Gruber, 1997, p. 29)

Janette Turner Hospital's writing also reveals such deeply resonating words—such as *"all manner of thing shall be well"*—from Julian of Norwich. Her most recent novel, *Oyster*, is itself a profound exploration of words in relation to embodied being. It tells the story of a teacher who defied the power of men who would control her words and managed to pass some of those words on to one of her pupils, who used them to escape the extreme domination and control of her particular community. It is also a story about young new-age people seduced into their own destruction through the words of a prophet named Oyster.

The novel is set in Outer Maroo, somewhere in North Queensland. Outer Maroo is in an unmapped zone, free of the surveillance of government bodies and captive to the surveillance of the local graziers, miners, and religious leaders who have cut their local population off from the outside world in order to take all power to themselves, to make their own fortunes, and to wage their own wars. They have removed all traces of Outer Maroo from the map and have closed the lines both out and in. By controlling what can be written and spoken and what can be read, they hope to take total control. One of the characters, Jess, makes her own freedom from control through refusing to speak. Her silence cannot be read, and her thoughts are therefore not subject to control. Miss Rover, the teacher, brings into Outer Maroo books full of dangerous ideas and a will to speak that is so forceful that she chooses the dangerous path of opposing the men, of naming what they are doing, and of pointing out to them that their control can never be absolute.

A "rover" is a nomad, a subject in transition, not overcoded and fixed. "To rove" is to "wander about (a place) with no fixed direction" (*Collins English Dictionary*). Miss Rover takes up her existence as the ideal post-structuralist subject: a subject in process, a subject who exists as verb, rather than as noun, a subject who cannot be fixed by the controlling gaze of powerful others (cf. Davies, 1997a). Miss Rover sees what is there, she sees the dangerous power of the men in control, and she speaks despite their threats of brutally silencing her. In this, she reveals the kind of agency written about in poststructuralist theorizing in which the subject is aware of being subjected through multiple discourses, and she looks for ways to make that subjection visible and to subvert its power when it works in ways that run counter to other preferred forms of subjection (Davies, 1991).

Unlike Miss Davenport, who could find no words to pass to her students, Miss Rover not only speaks against the will of the men, she passes words in spoken and written form to Mercy, her student, another central character in the novel. Mercy, too, has been raised in a fundamentalist Christian household and community, but her father has lost his faith, and Mercy listens carefully to what Miss Rover has told her. In the following scene, Miss Rover confronts the men in the pub about the fact that no mail comes in or out of Outer Maroo, and she tells them she has found a way to get letters out from their closed community:

> "I think," Bernie said, "that you should apply for a transfer, Miss Rover. I don't think we got that much need for a school after all." *Miss Rover, come over,* the children sang.
>
> "And I think," Miss Rover said, "that you won't shut me up so easily. I think that you don't realize just how many messages are getting out. For example, a letter or two of mine went to Bourke with the Murris, which may be the long way round to Brisbane, but then again, it might be more expeditious than Australia Post."
>
> "Jesus," one of the men said, seemingly casual. "What big fucking foreign words she keeps in that slutty little mouth."
>
> "I think maybe she should wash her filthy tongue," someone said.
>
> "Maybe a few other private places, eh? She admits she's a *Boong-*

lover. How many of those black bastards do you reckon she's fucked?" (Turner Hospital, 1996b, p. 62–63)

The men's strategies for silencing her are primitive. They differ little from the silencing strategies of primary school boys who sexualize the powerful girls whom they wish to silence (Davies, 1993). Their collective sexual talk nonetheless excites them, excites their sense of power over the woman who will not be silent. The children watch and chant their chorus; the people in the chapel across the road watch; and Miss Rover's one ally, Pete, tries helplessly to take the focus away from her:

> "Listen, mates," and there was a sharper edge of anxiety in Pete Burnett's voice, "just ignore her. Teachers come and go. They come and go and change nothing . . . "
>
> "Words are like bushfires," Miss Rover warned. She was high on something. She was high on having crossed the line. "You can't stop them. And you can't tell where they'll end up."
>
> She turned and saw Mercy through the window and waved the remnants of her torn letter, and before Mercy had time to think, she had raised a hand in salute, and Miss Rover put a word there and it burned.
>
> "Thank you Mercy," Mr. Prophet said tightly. "You may sit down. And may the Lord inscribe His Word upon our hearts." The congregation, as one, was transfixed, its gaze on the scene across the street. "We will bow our heads in prayer," Mr. Prophet said, "that the peace which passeth understanding may settle like a dove in every heart."
>
> Something brushed Mercy's heart and her wrist. It was the dove of Miss Rover's word and she closed her fingers round it and kept it in her fist where it fluttered violently and bucked about like a trapped thing. (Turner Hospital, 1996b, pp. 64–65)

The words that pass from Miss Rover to Mercy are words from the *in(terre)conscious* zone. They are words that lodge themselves in the deep surface, in the grain of Mercy's heart and her wrist; they are embodied words that flutter and buck but that she holds tight. The words of Mr. Prophet provide her with the image of a dove, an image that, like the geranium in Dostoevsky for Cixous, provides a key that opens up a magic world.

Once again Janette Turner Hospital has written about a woman positioned by men as vulnerable, as sexually vulnerable, and as one who can and will be removed from the situation. But this time they do not manage to silence her; she continues to speak despite their overwhelming power. And, for the moment, her words change nothing except perhaps the shifting grain of Mercy's hand and heart. And the effect of words is unpredictable. Text, as Grosz (1995) points out, is labile, explosive:

> A text is not the repository of knowledges or truths, the site for storage of information (and thus in danger of imminent obsolescence from the "revolution" in storage and retrieval that information technology has provided as its provocation to the late twentieth century) so much as a process of scattering thought, scrambling terms, concepts and practices, forging linkages, becoming a form of action. A text is not simply a tool or an instrument; this makes it too utilitarian, too amenable to intention, too much designed for a subject. Rather, it is explosive, dangerously labile, with unpredictable consequences. Like concepts, texts are complex products, effects of history, the intermingling of old and new, a complex of internal coherences or consistencies and external referents, of intension and extension, of thresholds and becomings. Texts, like concepts, do things, make things, perform actions, create connections, bring about new alignments. They are events—situated in social, institutional, and conceptual space. (p. 126)

Mr. Prophet knows the power of his words; he utters words to contain the power of his congregation, but one of the words slips out of his control. The familiar words whose intention is to subject and contain Mercy do not do so. "The peace which passeth understanding" that Mr. Prophet wishes to "settle like a dove in every heart" and put an end to questioning instead provides Mercy with an image, alive and fluttering wildly in her hands, opening up new questions, disrupting the promised peace of unquestioning subjection to that which is settled. The conflict for Mercy is agonizing, like warfare in her head between opposing discourses, each vying for dominance:

> Since her departure, Miss Rover has taken up permanent residence as a sniper inside Mercy's head. There are other snipers. There are the irreverent and earthy voices of Ma Beresford and Ma's Bill. And the voices of the elders. And others, and others. Mercy is trapped in the crossfire. Also, there are the clamouring voices of books, Miss Rover's books and her father's library, what used to be her father's library, two different worlds. Is all this listening so exhausting for everyone, or only for Mercy? She feels like the conductor of an orchestra full of musicians who have run amok; they play discordant instruments; they have set up permanent and competitive rehearsal within her mind. (Turner Hospital 1996b, p. 116)

At the end of this novel Mercy escapes to Brisbane—she gets back on the map, out of the danger zone of a patriarchal attempt at total subjection and the exclusion of all other knowledges. Miss Rover, the teacher who gives her the words that enable her to escape, is lost—the men's will to control and exclude is violent, dangerous. Other young women and men in this novel also lose their lives in a brutal fashion as they are drawn into the discursive web of the prophet Oyster. Only Mercy grasps the possibility handed her by Miss Rover, opens herself to the flow of conflicting words, and, although she almost drowns in the contradictions, finds her way to life. She makes a choice—she has agency, agency that comes from the power of words, from the agency that arises from subjection. She enables the reader to live what Butler theorizes; she is made a possible subject through conflicting discourses; and she eclipses the conditions of her own emergence.

This, for me, is a harrowing text about language and desire and about resistance to others' will to control and to maintain power. It shows how submitting to domination may seem easier than resistance but constitutes such submission as deadly. Janette Turner Hospital makes the power of words visible, and the struggle with them and against them is also made visible. She makes them more than visible. In reading this text, I, and others, find ourselves living and breathing the oppressive force of discourse and the explosive desire for freedom which other discourses make possible.[3] Janette Turner Hospital does not set up a binary in which discourse is oppressive, while freedom lies outside discourse, although that is one reading of what she does in "The Last of the Hapsburgs." Rather, she invites the reader, as nomad, to move freely in dangerous places they have not been before, to live out the enormous differences experienced by her characters, and to know life as volatile, labile, and capable of movement in multiple directions. She shows the weight and power of language as it is lived by the embodied beings that she (and the reader) bring to life on the page. She shows the force of will and of desire, the potential danger of dominant and dominating discourses, and that the eclipsing of that power is possible.

That eclipsing is brought about through three related strategies and lived out through different subjects. The first is the development of an awareness beyond words of embodiment in landscape, an awareness that invites the stretching of words to accomplish what is, until that point, unknown, mysterious. This awareness opens the possibility of writing/speaking from the surface/depths of one's own body. Such speaking/writing displaces empty language that exists only as well-practiced clichés or accepted ways of speaking. The second is the power to recognize and name oppressive and controlling forces and to refuse the power of those who use silencing others as a major strategy for maintaining power. The third, lived out through Mercy, is the combination of the first two, and involves a movement "into different linkages or new alignments" (Grosz, 1995, p. 126). It brings together an awareness of language and its force in/on the surfaces of the body. Mercy lives and breathes words and is able to examine their effects in/on her and on those around her. She moves beyond the modes of being available to the rational humanist self and develops what Turner Hospital calls "the eroticized desire to communicate." She is not limited to and controlled by one discourse, by the limitations of rational forms of thought, or by the will of others. She is able to read her own embodiment and its inscription through language, to recognize the multiplicity of it, and to act in ways that enable her to move beyond the existing patterns of power and powerlessness.

Postscript

Several readers of this chapter have found themselves deeply shaken by it without being quite sure why. I suspect this is because although Janette Turner Hospital's writing opens up the possibility of eclipsing patriarchal discourses, it also takes us, bodily, into landscapes where we are deeply vulnerable. Turner Hospital says of this aspect of her writing (personal communication):

> [In Australia, though nowhere else] I've frequently been charged with writing too eloquently, too "beautifully," too "disturbingly" about violence. I was completely mystified and shell-shocked when these charges first began cropping up. To me it's like accusing a war vet of having nightmares that are too vivid, too colorful, too dramatic. As though he has any control over that! For god's sake, what else is violence and trauma if not disturbing?
>
> . . . The process of writing is, to use Clément's terms, a long syncope for me. I climb down into the bat cave of sensory, moral and philosophical and interrogative data, and I grope around down there, and things happen, things both euphoric and terrifying, and I set them down during this long syncope when I lose track of everything else (of time, of my body, of my normal functions in the world; I am seriously dysfunctional when I am writing), and when I climb out again with written pages, they are as mysterious and alarming and beautiful to me as an opal pulled out of the dark.

Notes

1. Brian Massumi (1992) says of nomad thought: "'Nomad thought' does not lodge itself in the edifice of an ordered interiority; it moves freely in an element

of exteriority. It does not repose on identity; it rides difference. It does not respect the artificial division between the three domains of representation, subject, concept and being; it replaces restrictive analogy with a conductivity that knows no bounds. . . . Rather than reflecting the world [the concepts it creates] are immersed in a changing state of things. A concept is a brick. It can be used to build the courthouse of reason. Or it can be thrown through the window" (p. 5).

2. Cixous uses the term *"in(terre)conscious"* zone when she talks of the writing of Derrida. She says, "I see in him this brilliant explorational cast, which brings him to discover structures or logics that have never before been thought, to sketch the course of rivers that flow in the *'in(terre)conscious'* zones" (Cixous, cited in Cixous & Calle-Gruber, 1997, p. 88).

3. Paula Smith (1998) in her dissertation, *Syncopations in the Life of a Woman Religious,* writes a deeply moving account of her bodily experience of reading this novel.

References

Butler, J. (1997). *The psychic life of power.* Stanford, CA: Stanford University Press.

Cixous, H., & Calle-Gruber, M. (1997). *Hélène Cixous' Rootprints: Memory and life writing* (E. Prenowitz, Trans.). London: Routledge.

Davies, B. (1991). The concept of agency: A feminist poststructuralist analysis. *Social Analysis, 30*(December), 42–53.

Davies, B. (1993). *Shards of glass: Children reading and writing beyond gendered identities.* Creskill, NJ: Hampton Press, Inc.

Davies, B. (1994). *Poststructuralist theory and classroom practice.* Geelong, Australia: Deakin University Press.

Davies, B. (1995). What about the boys? The parable of the bear and the rabbit. *Interpretations, 28*(2), 1–17.

Davies, B. (1996). *Power/knowledge/desire: Changing school organisation and management practices.* Canberra, Australia: Department of Employment, Education and Youth Affairs.

Davies, B. (1997a). The subject of poststructuralism: A reply to Alison Jones. *Gender and Education, 9*(1), 271–83.

Davies, B. (1997b). Critical literacy in practice: Language lessons for and about boys. *Interpretations. Special Edition: Critical Literacies Vol. 2, 30*(2), 36–57.

Davies, B., & Harré, R. (1990). Positioning: Conversation and the production of selves. *Journal for the Theory of Social Behaviour, 20*(1), 43–63.

Davies, B., Dormer, S., Honan, E., McAllister, N., O'Reilly, R., Rocco, S., & Walker, A. (1997). Ruptures in the skin of silence: A collective biography. *Hecate: A Women's Studies Interdisciplinary Journal, 23*(1), 62–79.

Grosz, Elizabeth (1995). *Space, time and perversion.* Sydney, Australia: Allen and Unwin.

Jones, A. (1997). Teaching post structuralist feminist theory in education: student resistances. *Gender and Education, 9*(1), 261–69.

Massumi, B. (1992). *A user's guide to* Capitalism and Schizophrenia. *Deviations from Deleuze and Guattari.* Cambridge, MA: MIT Press.

Smith, P. (1998). *Syncopations in the life of a woman religious.* Unpublished doctoral dissertation. James Cook University, Townsville, Australia.

Turner Hospital, J. (1988). *Charades.* Brisbane, Australia: University of Queensland Press.

Turner Hospital, J. (1995a). The last of the Hapsburgs. In J. Turner Hospital, *Collected Stories.* Brisbane, Australia: University of Queensland Press.

Turner Hospital, J. (1995b). Uncle Seaborn. In J. Turner Hospital, *Collected Stories.* Brisbane, Australia: University of Queensland Press.

Turner Hospital, J. (1995c). You gave me hyacinths. In J. Turner Hospital, *Collected Stories.* Brisbane, Australia: University of Queensland Press.

Turner Hospital, J. (1996a). *Conversation with Bronwyn Davies.* Brisbane, Australia.

Turner Hospital, J. (1996b). *Oyster.* Milson's Point, Australia: Alfred A. Knopf.

Watson, S., & Davies, B. (1998). Reading and writing the Kadaitcha Sung: A novel by Sam Watson. *Interpretations, 31*(1), 35–49.

Chapter 10

Exposed Methodology: The Body as a Deconstructive Practice

Wanda S. Pillow

> She had the two courages: that of going to the sources, to the foreign parts of the self. That of torturing, to herself, almost without self, without denying the going. She slipped out of the self, she had that severity, that violent patience, she went out . . . by laying bare the senses, it requires unclothing sight all the way down to naked sight.
>
> (Cixous, 1994, p. 91)

> Bodies are essential to accounts of power and critiques of knowledge.
>
> (Grosz, 1995, p. 32)

The body has gained both attention and importance, not only in feminist and postmodern theories but also more broadly in social theory as a place from which to theorize, analyze, practice, and critically reconsider the construction and reproduction of knowledge, power, class, and culture. Michel Foucault's reformulation of the social body and feminist accounts of the gendered body have proliferated discussions concerning the absent (Moore, 1994); regulated, inscribed, and docile (Foucault, 1974); gendered (Butler, 1990, 1993; Diprose, 1994; Gaskell, 1992; Moore, 1994); classed (Allison, 1994; Davis, 1981); raced (hooks, 1990; Trinh, 1989; Walker, 1995); and sexed (Diprose, 1994; Grosz & Probyn, 1995) body. Recent works in ethnography have explored and critiqued the use and representation of the body in methodological practices and analyses (Moore, 1994; Visweswaran, 1994).

This chapter draws upon these previous works to consider how paying attention to the body, literally and figuratively, can inform and disrupt methodological practices. How does paying attention to bodies change what we look at, how we look, what we ask, and what we choose to represent? I found myself immersed in these questions and their problematics 3 years ago when I began a research project on teenage pregnancy programs. I entered field settings filled with critical, postmodern, feminist, and qualitative research theories and practices yet found myself unprepared for the utter *physicality* of my research experiences.

During my research, I spent almost every day in classrooms with young women whose bodies were continually changing and changed—pre- and postpregnancy swelling, stretching, widening, lactating. Our bodies provided a place and space from which we talked, shared experiences, and gained confidences. As I attempted to write stories and representations of the girls,[1] I repeatedly turned and returned to the body—to our bodies. Henrietta Moore (1994) states that feminist scholars have been "struggling with the question of how or to what degree women might be the same or similar without being identical. What is it, if anything, that we share" (p. 1)? What seemed shared, common with difference, across the girls and myself, were our bodies, their reproductive capacities, and the interests in such by the state.

However, the stories I heard from the girls, the observations I had made, were varied and complex, and I did not wish to simplify them by claiming some essentialized identity related to our female bodies. Yet I did not want to, and indeed could not, ignore the body in this research. I began to question what it would mean to pay attention to bodies, in this case, in an arena where teenage girls' bodies are simultaneously stereotyped, proliferated, ignored, and silenced. How could I, as a woman studying young women who were pregnant, use the flux of our own bodies as a site of deconstruction[2] toward an understanding of the paradox of how social structures and modes of representation simultaneously "form and *deform*" women (de Lauretis, 1984)? What kinds of strategies and commitments might a move toward the body make possible or hinder?

Elizabeth Grosz (1995) delineates what she terms "two broad kinds of approaches to theorizing the body"—one, "inscriptive," a Nietzchian, Foucauldian notion of the social body upon which "social law, morality, and values are inscribed" (p. 33). The second is the "lived body," which references the "lived experience of the body, the body's internal or psychic inscription" (p. 33). Grosz suggests that, while we are becoming adept at naming the inscriptive details of the body, we tend to shy away from the messiness of the corporal body—the lived experiences. Grosz (1995) states, "If the notion of a radical and irreducible *difference* is to be understood with respect to subjectivity, the specific modes of corporeality of bodies in their variety must be acknowledged" (p. 32).

There is, however, little research on the lived experiences—the specific physicality of the teen pregnant body (Burdell, 1993, 1995; Lesko, 1990, 1991, in press; Pillow, 1994; Tolman, 1992, 1994). Thus, in this chapter, I explore what is exposed when I pay attention to the *messiness* of bodies that exceed the boundaries of what we think we know about young women who are pregnant. After an overview of the specific corporeality of the pregnant body, I present two stories (in)formed by a specific attention to bodies. The first story considers what gets exposed when we pay attention to how teen girls experience and use their pregnant bodies as sites of resistance, specifically around issues of sex, pleasure, and power. The second story exposes the literal impact of space and architecture on teen girls' bodies and how this affects issues of self-representation, teacher pedagogy, and program implementation. I conclude by reflecting upon what these stories tell us and how the body worked in the telling of these stories.

Exposing the Pregnant Body

Bodies are not new to feminist theory. Feminist theory has utilized the specificity of the woman's body to challenge the separation of theory from experience under what has become to be known as the caveat "the personal is political." The *personal is political* highlights how the practices, representations, and knowledge of the female body are not simply innate, natural occurrences, but rather are *political*—that is, contrived, monitored, controlled, and moralized by a social system in which the female body as a collective has not had much say. The body, particularly the female body, is at best a curious and conflicting site to "go from"—a site of paradoxical social attention and avoidance. Our bodies are sites of humanist prescription, places from which binaries are structured forming polemical categories that define them: "inside/outside, subject/object, surface/depth" (Grosz, 1995, p. 33). Grosz (1995) states that "bodies speak, without necessarily talking, because they become coded with and as signs. They speak social codes. They become intextuated, narrativized; simultaneously, social codes, laws, norms, and ideals become incarnated" (p. 35). These social codes we live by are complex and conditional and are further coded, often without acknowledgment, by issues of gender, race, class, physical characteristics, and sexual identity.

The pregnant female body further confounds and conflates our social codes and norms. "The significance of the maternal body differs from the public body in that it is *the site of the reproduction of the social body*" (Diprose, 1994, p. 25). Tamsin Wilton (1995) states that it is "precisely because of their ability to mother that women's bodies (and their political and social selves) have been so rigidly controlled within all patriarchal political systems" (p. 182). Even in a "normal" pregnancy, what the mother does with her body—what she eats, where she goes, how and when—is open to public scrutiny. She, the mother, is a "legitimate target for moral concern" (Diprose, 1994, p. 26) and thus "subject to very direct state control" (Wilton, 1995, p. 183).

Pregnancy further interrupts accepted and assumed demarcations of the body and self. Questions of what is woman and fetus, woman and society, and where the locus of decision making and control lies during pregnancy have resulted in moral, ethical, and legal debates surrounding issues of birth control, abortion, and surrogacy (Diprose, 1994). Pregnancy confounds our notions of where one body ends and another begins and interrupts assumptions of a single self (Young, 1990, p. 163). Because pregnancy exists and exhibits itself in a fluctuating, changing state, it is unclear where the pregnant body ends and the world begins (Young, 1990, p. 116).

Teen pregnancy offers further complications and excessiveness to the already complicated issue of the state and reproduction. Teen pregnancy operates outside the norm of legitimate reproduction, marking it as a site of moral concern and state control. Teen pregnancy presents itself as a paradox to the state. While giving birth is the obligation of the female citizen, the state also has controlling interests in who gives birth. Articles promoting fear of a "browning of America" (Bane, 1986; Center for Population, 1990) feed into the concerns of the public over who gives birth, proliferating the idea that "reproduction is most certainly the obligation (and hence the right) of white, middle-class, able-bodied women" (Wilton, 1995, p. 183). Teen pregnancy presents the paradox of young women fulfilling their reproductive responsibilities, but not in the way the state wishes them to (Cusick, 1989).

The paradoxical issues surrounding teen pregnancy make it difficult even to define what teen pregnancy is. Is teen pregnancy primarily a problem of "morality, fertility or poverty" (Lawson & Rhode, 1993, p. 1)? At what age is a woman a teen parent? Are you a teen parent when you are 18 or 19 years of age or only if you are in public school? Is teen pregnancy as a social problem defined as only pregnancies that are carried to full term, or does it include all teen pregnancies, including those that are terminated by a miscarriage or an abortion? Are you a teen parent if you are married and/or middle class?

Correspondingly, teen pregnancy intervention and prevention programs present conflicting messages to the girls they target. On the one hand, a major purpose of teen pregnancy programs seems aimed at helping pregnant teens be good mothers, and such programs include topics related to child development, health care, enrichment, household management, and responsibility (Pillow, 1994). At the same time, these programs have the goal of preparing young mothers[3] to be independent (i.e., not on welfare) and thus concentrate upon job skills and enforce many "tough love" requirements in the interests of teaching the girls to take responsibility[4] (Lesko, 1990, 1991; Pillow, 1994). These goals—good mother and fiscal provider—and the actions they require are often conflicting and even polemical.[5]

Consistent across teen pregnancy programs, however, is an avoidance of engagement with the specific physicality of the pregnant female body. Teen pregnancy programs ignore the body outside of linear, taxonomic lists of expected changes and corresponding, acceptable, required actions (Burdell, 1995). Teen pregnancy programs thus promote and assume a clear separation of teen girls' pregnant bodies and their selves as woman, mother, student, and provider. Teen pregnancy research avidly avoids mentioning teen girls' bodies—ignoring and silencing what Nancy Lesko (in press) terms "the leaky needs" of pregnant teen girls. Research and policy aim at controlling the behavior of the teen girl's body while remaining silent about the changes and needs of the female body.

Yet, even as pregnant teen girls' bodies are silenced or even removed from some settings,[6] our society maintains a voyeuristic fascination with the sexualization of the female body as evidenced in our media, advertising, fashion, cultural practices, and myths. Research and popular media articles on teen pregnancy replicate this phenomenon, displaying visuals depicting the contrast of the young teen girl's face with her swollen belly. Such images feed our fascination and incite a moralistic response without ever acknowledging the sexual physicality of teen pregnancy (Burdell, 1995; Lesko, 1988). Ironically, teen pregnancy research and policy simultaneously ignore and proliferate the teen pregnant body (Pillow, 1977). What is made possible, then, by paying attention to the coded bodies of teen girls who are pregnant? How do the girls themselves enact, resist, and live with the increased interest and control their pregnant bodies incite in others?

Exposure I: Sex, Pleasure, and Power

While the state, policy, and research arenas may avoid the pregnant body, the teen girls I talked with, in a study conducted during 1992–1994 (Pillow, 1994), certainly could not ignore their bodies. To the contrary, I found girls who talked openly and loudly about their bodies, sex, pleasure, and their feelings on being pregnant "schoolgirls." I was drawn to these *unruly* (Rowe, 1995) girls with their strong voices and display of confidence in their bodies; however, I did not want to simply script the vocal girls' voices as victory narratives and ignore or script the "silent" girls as suffering from low self-esteem as most teen pregnancy research does.

By paying attention to bodies, I began to observe how the girls used their bodies—their changing bodies—as sites of resistance. The girls were working toward and resisting the terms of their lives as well as the requirements of the teen pregnancy program in which they participated. Whether verbally or nonverbally, I observed the girls gain an awareness of the power their bodies had over the behavior and attitude of the adults with whom they worked. For example, many girls found that adults were "uncomfortable" with their pregnant teen bodies and would use that fact to their advantage. One girl stated, "I could always get out of that teacher's class. He could not look at me without staring at my stomach. He could not get over it, y'know, he just couldn't handle me being pregnant."

One way to have power over adults, to resist, was to talk about what was forbidden or to make obvious what adults did not want to acknowledge. This was clear around issues of sex and sexuality. The program guide for the teen pregnancy program I observed had defined units to discuss sexual activity and assumed the teen girls would be silent in this process, reinforcing the gendered stereotypes of women, particularly young women, that to voice and take control of their sexual lives is not appropriate. However, during a discussion of birth control options, one girl interrupted:

> Well it not like I don't know what I'm doing, I do, and I get tired of people acting like I don't. So I had sex—I got pregnant. I'm dealing with it. Y'know at some point you've gotta have sex—this isn't like the 60's—you can't wait anymore, or maybe you don't want to. But it's hard for girls to get birth control and most of the boys won't. At least while I'm pregnant I won't have to worry about getting pregnant!

This young woman's comments—that a teen girl was aware of the choices and consequences of being sexually active, that she spoke pleasure, and that she may remain sexually active during her pregnancy—exceeded the boundaries of what the teen pregnancy program (and, in this case, the teacher) was designed or prepared to address.[7] Often such comments would later be described to me as "immature" or "flippant" by the teachers—they were not to be taken seriously, except to the extent these comments spoke to how deep the girl's problem was. The girls' "silences" were coded as acquiescent and appropriate, responsible behavior, while their verbal participation was often coded as irresponsibility. In this way, presentations on birth control options that ignored factors that many women find objectionable about birth control and contribute to their nonuse—limited access, limited choice, changes in body, the idea that you are "bad" if you plan ahead for sexual activity, interruption of pleasure, and the ways to handle birth control with a guy who may not go along with it—can legitimately be continued with minimal involvement from the girls.

Fine (1988) states that, precisely because young females' discourses of desire usually occur only in marginalized settings, young teens are learning that what they, as females, feel, think, or desire is not pertinent or important enough to be discussed in a "legitimized" setting. In this way, a female discourse of desire becomes an object of regulation. However, in classrooms during discussions of sex and birth control, I observed silence both as repression and resistance. It was easy to characterize girls' silences—their lack of discussion about their own sexuality—as repression. In this way, "silence is pathologized as absence" (Walkerdine, 1990, p. 35). But I also came to identify girls' silences as resistance,[8] resistance to a teacher's regulatory discourse, resistance to what was being left unsaid in the presentation of the lesson.

For example, after observing a teacher-presented lesson on the girls' taking responsibility for their sexual activity, during which the class had remained mostly silent and noncommittal, a girl remarked to me and her friends:

> What is that teacher talking about when she says just say "no" to sex? What if I don't wanna say no! But they'll never talk about that with us—they look down their noses at you, like you're bad. Whatta she know anyway—she's wound so tight she looks like she hasn't had any in over a year!

Nowhere were the girls' voices stronger, more independent, and resistant than when they were talking about their school experiences. Repeatedly, I heard the girls talk about how they felt they had been treated unfairly in their schools. They voiced a strong desire to learn, but because they did not "fit," they felt they were often ignored or put aside. They felt they had not been given opportunities or chances, and they were not afraid to state this fact to teachers, principals, and administrators. One girl stated:

> I made him nervous. . . . I stuck my pregnant stomach out at him and said if I'm gonna be in someone's class I expect to learn something. They were harassing me for about five weeks telling me I wasn't smart enough to go to day and night school and creating problems for me. I say you're here to help me to understand—that's what you're paid for. If you can't help me then I'm getten out.

Another girl, a middle-class, white, attractive, honor roll student was a tuition-paying student at a high school out of her district when she became pregnant.

> He called me into his office and he said I hear you are pregnant. And I say "yeah," so what. He says we don't have pregnant girls in

this school—how it was bad for the school's reputation and would give other girls ideas. I said give me that slip right now; I'm signing and getting out of here.

"Kelley" transferred from her high school with its good reputation to "Parkside," an alternative school for students experiencing learning or behavior problems because "no other high school would let me in." She said she never felt like she fit in at Parkside—"it's not challenging; it's boring." Kelley had been on a college preparation track and felt Parkside was ill-suited to her academic needs as it focused on minimal graduation requirements and passing proficiency tests. She and her mother and the teen pregnancy teacher spent 2 months petitioning and moving through paperwork so that she could receive a variety of advanced placement courses either through home tutoring, night courses, or additional courses after her baby was born.

After the birth of her baby girl, Kelley thus shuttled across counties to attend her "old" school for academics and Parkside for her family life courses. For Kelley, this was a hard-won battle. While she felt she had lost her fight to attend her school while she was pregnant because "he [the principal] couldn't handle seeing my pregnant body in his school,"[9] she remained determined to attend her school after the birth of her baby, to show the school in her words "that having a baby didn't take away your brains." She had to repeatedly petition the administration at her home school to attend classes and functions at her school, and the decision about whether she could attend graduation and receive her diploma was not finalized until one week before graduation.[10]

Kelley was very proud of graduating "on time" and "with my class," even after the birth of her baby. She brought her graduating class sweatshirt into Parkside and showed her name on it to everyone in the school. Kelley found herself making friendships and alliances with girls at Parkside who "I never would even have talked to before," stating, "we're going through the same things, with our bodies, with our schools." These friendships were also reciprocated. Kelley had received the respect of fellow students at Parkside across marked differences of race and class because "she," as one girl said, "wore 'em down. She know now what it's like to have to fight for everything you want for your life. We all have a lot of feelings for Kelley—she deserved to graduate with her old school." Kelley commented on and summarized the events in her life over the past year by stating simply, "I never thought anyone would ever treat me this way."

Exposure II: Physically Exceeding Boundaries

What happens when pregnant schoolgirls can no longer fit into the traditional student desk? Where do school administrators decide to place the teen pregnancy classroom in their schools? How visible is the teen pregnancy classroom in the school setting? While these questions may appear simplistic and pragmatic, I believe they are questions that are vital to understanding and analyzing the lives of teen pregnant girls in schools. How do the bodies of teen girls fit into their schools? How is it that teen pregnancy and thus the teen girl's body come to be an issue to be regulated and contained?

I did not visit teen pregnancy classroom sites with these issues in mind. It was only after several visits to suburban classroom settings when I felt myself continually being led "downstairs," "around the corner," or "down and back to the left" that I began to question a classroom's physical and embodied positioning in the school as speaking and impacting on a larger discourse about teen girls who are pregnant within schools. Scheurich (1995) describes Foucault's notion of governmentality, of regulatory practices, as "a kind of governmental rationality" that is concerned with "an insatiable management of social spaces, social practices and forms" (p. 20). I began to view teen pregnancy classrooms as spaces that were the recipients of this "insatiable management."

Architecture operates as a form of disciplinary power that is exercised in its invisibility. We tend not to turn our gaze on spatial and structural practices—except, for example, the "natural" character and design of a school building. Weedon (1987) defines "space as the site for a range of possible forms of subjectivity" (p. 34) through which we define "our sense of ourselves" (p. 21). Thus, the following analysis also seeks to undo the traditional mind/body split that is prevalent in modernist discourse and stories of education. Ann Game (1991) writes that she is interested in "practices of space" in terms of the "practices a place makes possible, or closes off" (p. 83). Particularly, I am interested in how practices of surveillance, self-surveillance, and regulatory practices are reinforced through architectural discourses and how these spatial practices are written onto the bodies of students and teachers. How, then, did teen pregnancy classrooms produce their own "insatiable management" of teachers' and girls' bodies?

As I visited classroom sites, I began to notice differences in classroom location, size, accessibility, and physical set-up of the rooms. I identified two main classroom styles: first, traditional classrooms and, second, home economics classrooms. The seven teen pregnancy classrooms situated in traditional classroom settings shared several features, including their location and (in)visibility in their schools. These classrooms were all located down- or upstairs off the beaten path of main hallways. Five of the classrooms were approximately half the size of normal classrooms, and none of the seven classrooms were identified as teen pregnancy classrooms. In other words, a visitor to the school would not to be able to identify the presence of a teen pregnancy classroom in the building without help. Indeed, in six of the schools I visited, I was led to the teen pregnancy classrooms because I was told, "you will not be able to find it on your own." In two of the buildings, students working in the office who were asked to take me to the teen pregnancy classroom did not know where it was, and, in one building, a student and I wandered a corridor as the student said "I know it [the classroom] is here somewhere."

A teacher described the invisibility and obscurity of the teen pregnancy classroom in this way:

> We have to keep it very quiet that we are here. I am not allowed to hang a banner or flier up saying this is a GOALS[11] classroom. Some of the teachers do not even know I am here. I cannot go into other classes and talk about GOALS, so the girls really have to find me.

Another teacher stated:

> The fear is that if we are too visible that the community will get upset—kids will go home talking to their parents about the pregnant girls in their school and the parents will call the principal. This hasn't occurred yet, but the principal is very clear that he does not want this to happen. So I keep it pretty quiet. That makes it hard because I don't feel like I really belong to this building.

When asked how this invisibility affects the implementation of the teen pregnancy program, the teachers responded in a similar manner:

> Well, you just do what you have to do. I still feel like what I'm doing is important, and I make the agency contacts and help the girls as much as I can. But, yeah, I think I am probably missing some girls because they do not know that help is available to them in the school.

Another teacher states:

> You have to start out with a low profile, then when your principal, other teachers and school board sees results, you'll get support. It is difficult though because there is always the idea that GOALS is endorsing teen pregnancy by making it too easy for them [the girls].

While the teachers discussed the placement and invisibility of their classrooms as impacting on implementation in terms of numbers of students they served (a fact supported by other research; see Burdell, 1995), they did not mention the placement and invisibility of their classrooms as affecting program and curriculum implementation. However, the second similarity found in these seven sites, in addition to issues of location and visibility in the school at large, concerns issues of implementation, situating the physical classroom environments as important to the kinds of discourses occurring in the classrooms. Traditional classroom environments evoked similar pedagogy and also similar body discourses.

The seven traditional classroom sites operated in very traditional teacher-student relationships. The students sat in desks in rows, while the teachers stood at the front of the room and taught. The teachers in these classrooms tended to be the teachers who "followed the APRG [the program guide] closely" and developed their discourse and relations with the girls based upon the suggestions in the program guide. For example, the teachers in these classrooms, although situated in middle-class suburban communities, were more likely to describe teen parents (girls) as[12]

> hard luck kids. They are just hard luck kids. They haven't had very much go right in their life, and they've made a mistake which is now going to affect another innocent life. You have to try to help them deal with their mistakes in a mature and responsible way.

The pregnant girls at these sites were "good" girls who had make a mistake. When adults—teachers, administrators, parents—in these communities face the need to develop programs for teen girls who are pregnant, they do so with a sense of alarm. Comments such as "we have good girls here" and "this has never been a problem here before" incite cause for alarm and practices of containment. Lesko (in press) finds that school districts, limited by the political rhetoric of the New Right and its focus on "family values," respond to the "specific needs" of school-aged mothers with neglect and invisibility. The needs of teen mothers are excessive, "leaky," overflowing the current boundaries that attempt to contain them in the realm of "just economic" or "just family" issues (Burdell, 1995, p. 190).

The pregnant girls in these settings also *seemed* to embody a similar contained view on teen pregnancy. They spoke more often of their own pregnancies as "mistakes" and were quick to classify other girls' pregnancies as "definitely a mistake." Lesko (1988) found that girls in teen pregnancy programs speak a type of reformation talk—what Lesko calls "rites of redemption" (p. 125). This discourse of redemption was also typified by the girls in the traditional classroom settings:

> I made a mistake and did some things I should not have done. I know that now. And now I need to learn how to take care of my baby and be a responsible parent and get a job . . . and yeah . . . this program will help me do that.

These discourses were embodied through the teachers' interactions with the students and the students' regulation of their own bodies in school.

Seldom did the girls at these sites interact actively together in the class-room—exchanging stories or friendly gossip. In fact, I observed only one instance of this behavior during 60 visits to these classrooms. While the teachers showed warmth and jocularity with their students, there was little physical interaction. The girls also regulated their own bodies in these classrooms. While girls' bodies became relaxed in the home economics classrooms, the girls in traditional classroom settings remained proper and stiff, even as they tried to fit into traditional desks, which, by their second trimester, often became difficult to sit in and were certainly uncomfortable. By their last trimester, many of the girls had to sit on the edge of the desk seat and turn sideways to fit within the confines of the desk space.

The contrast of the girls' emerging pregnancies and the confines of the traditional classroom were not discussed in these classrooms. Sometimes, as a girl attempted to fit into a desk and made a grunt or a comment, wry smiles would pass around the room, and others stared until she was "comfortable," but there were no verbal complaints. The teachers and girls seemed to expect that the girls should adapt to their environment even if it did not suit their changing bodies. A couple of girls explained this adaptation in the following ways:

> You're just not supposed to complain in this school or act like you should be treated different because you are pregnant.

> But they treat us like we're different and you get watched twice as closely. Mrs. _____ [their teacher] says we have to set a good example, that some people think we should not even be in school.

> Yeah, it's like we shouldn't be here so you just get watched a lot, and you can't make any mistakes or let anyone know you feel sick—not when you're pregnant.

> I can't wait to get home at the end of the day and relax on my couch. I think I will do home schooling for my last month—it's just too hard to be here.

While in school, these girls knew they were being watched, regulated, and expected to perform in ways that show their gratitude to be at school and demonstrate redemption for their mistakes. These girls realized they had engaged in a contract, albeit an unwritten one, with their schools that allowed them to stay in school and stay on track with their classes only if they behaved in certain ways.[13] As one girl stated:

> It's like when you're pregnant and in school you have to be quiet or people think you're bad. They act like something is wrong with

you anyway, and you can forget about being in clubs or anything—
they won't let you. It's like you have to pay for your mistake and
you better do it quietly or only say the things he [the principal]
wants you to say.

In contrast, the three teen pregnancy classrooms that were housed in
home economics rooms provided stories of bodies and practices different
from the stories described above. The home economic rooms, although
they varied in size, were situated in the main floors of their schools on a
main hallway. Two of the rooms had doors opening onto two main hallways. Thus, the rooms were visible and often served as "stop-in" spots or
"resting" places. These rooms had banners hanging on windows or doors
acknowledging the presence of the teen pregnancy program in the building, and inside the rooms hung announcements and pictures of recent
births.

The rooms were certainly more comfortable than traditional classrooms with chairs separate from large tables. Two of the rooms had
couches. One room had playpens, although it did not provide on-site
child care.[14] The addition of stoves, refrigerators, sinks, end tables, lamps,
and rugs provided a more homey, if often crowded, feeling to the rooms.
The teachers in these classrooms were more likely to "do my own thing"
in implementing the teen pregnancy program and were less likely to say
that the girls in their classes had made "mistakes." Rather, these teachers
described the girls they worked with in the following way: "They got in
trouble and society tells them [the girls] that they're the ones who have
to deal with it. They just don't get a break, so I try to help them make it
against everything else."

Well, I don't think they are necessarily bad. I don't think they have
thought very clearly—and part of it is they get so wrapped up in
boys. But now they have to stop and think of themselves and their
babies, and they need help to do that.

The teachers in these settings engaged in differing pedagogical strategies
to increase student participation, and the formal line between teacher
and student was much less rigidly drawn. Group discussions, popular
culture (for example, rap, pop music, or videos), and games were used
to introduce topics of relationships, gender roles, sex, and birth control.
Every time I observed in these settings, I witnessed student/student and
student/teacher interactions that were friendly and informal. It was in
these settings, often during "informal" times, that I heard stories of independence and "discourses of desire" (Fine, 1988, p. 48). The girls in these
rooms looked forward to their times together and shared information
with each other about pregnancy, boyfriends, sex, birth control, and
their own sexuality. Often the teachers would let these conversations

continue, interjecting only to correct misinformation or provide further information.

The most emphatic difference noted in these classroom settings, however, was the differences in bodies in the rooms. As described previously, the girls in the traditional classrooms remained "proper" in their classrooms and had to work to adapt their changing bodies to the limits of the classroom environment. The girls in the home economics classrooms claimed this space as their own—they spewed textbooks and notebooks on the tables, draped sweaters and coats on the chairs, drew on the chalkboards, admired baby pictures on the walls, and relaxed their bodies onto sofas or into chairs, putting their feet up or heads down.

Here was a space where the pregnant teen could be pregnant. Here she could put her feet up, complain about nausea or swollen ankles and get sympathy, a soda cracker, or a foot rub. Here girls loosened pants that were too tight, massaged abdomens and backs, and compared "stomachs" to "see who's biggest." Here girls shared stories and secrets. Here girls stayed in school until their ninth month and after, often sharing frank and explicit ideas on sex, sexuality, labor, and childbirth:

> You all are laughing at me, and I know this sounds gross but the nurse was telling me to do it, and I wanted to have my baby—so I'm in the room rubbing my nipples, like not to get off or something, but it can help you have your baby 'cause it makes you have, what is it?

Here the teacher intervened and answered "contractions" and confirmed to the other girls who were looking skeptical that the girl was right. And the girl continued: "You wait—you'll be so ready to have your baby you'll do anything. 'Tanya' be twisting her nipples off by 8 months."

This discussion exceeded the boundaries of what the program guide suggests should be included in the curriculum, and I never observed such a conversation in the traditional classroom settings.[15] This teacher allowed many conversations like this to occur and felt that "the girls know what they need to know about and this way gives the girls important information on pleasure and childbirth in a way they can hear it." This ease and relaxation of bodies did not mean that there were not "lessons" presented and regulatory practices in place. The teachers in these classrooms still monitored their students' diets and home lives and still had clear goals of helping the students in their programs. As described, however, these lessons took place through alternative formats and discussions and often followed the lead of the girls themselves.

"Relaxed" bodies also did not mean more easily regulated bodies. The girls in these classrooms spoke the strongest stories of independence and evoked the strongest messages of self-esteem. The girls acknowledged the importance of the classrooms in their lives in the following ways: "I can't wait to get in here and see everyone and just relax." "It's about the only place in the school where I feel comfortable—where you can just let it all hang out." "It's [the teen pregnancy room] where I come if I'm feeling depressed or sick or something—just to get away and feel okay about myself or get a hug." "I'm glad we don't have guys in our class. It's the only time you can get away from them teasing us and pulling on you and stuff. Sometimes we have to close our doors to keep 'em out too."

Thus, the teen pregnancy classes housed in home economics rooms demonstrated that space regulates practices and bodies in very different ways than in the traditional classroom setting. In the home economics classrooms, the girls reacted in more relaxed bodies and coveted their space to do so. A combination of teacher attitude and school setting provided a space where teen pregnant girls' bodies were allowed to be excessive, proliferative, leaky, and openly pregnant. These settings also provided more space for countervoices of independence and "discourses of desire" not heard in other teen pregnancy classrooms.

Concluding with Bodies and Exposures

For this research, paying attention to bodies methodologically highlights the fact that there is a physicality obvious in teen pregnancy that has for the most part been avoided. Working in a research arena that is already overexposed, such as teen pregnancy, the body as site of deconstructive practice can work to make explicit what is both overexposed and obscured elsewhere. Both of the exposures presented point to the inability of our theories, practices, and programs to deal with certain bodies, in this case, the pregnant teen body.

While school-based teen pregnancy programs assume that a separation of school and the body can be regulated and sustained (Burdell, 1995), the girls in this research demonstrated that the body is not so easily separable, nor do they desire it to be. The first exposure points to how teen girls use the tension and the discomfort that their changing, pregnant bodies invoke in others as a site of resistance. Paying attention to the bodies of teen girls who are pregnant and how they negotiate their bodies interrupts a simplistic telling of representation and resistance. Can teen girls' silence in their teen pregnancy classrooms be written simply as acquiescence or repressive practice? This research suggests it cannot. McNay (1994) points out that such a "(re)formulation of power does not deny the phenomenon of repression, but it does deny it theoretical primacy" (p. 91).

In this case, paying attention to the body methodologically seeks to acknowledge how teen girls who are pregnant take on the repressive discourse of the teen pregnancy program and speak it back, tracing how they use their bodies to this end. This move toward the body is not about celebrating what is marginalized, but an engagement in a move that interrupts a simplistic telling or a goddess worshiping of the body, moving instead toward what Elizabeth Grosz (1995) describes as

> more an enjoyment of the unsettling effects that rethinking bodies implies for those knowledges that have devoted so much conscious and unconscious effort to sweeping away all traces of the specificity, the corporeality, of their own processes of production and representation. (p. 2)

Turning the gaze upon the teen pregnancy program itself, holding a teen pregnancy program accountable for its corporeality raises many questions and exposes alternative interpretations. A view from the body sees teen pregnant girls' interruptions, silences, and/or unruliness as not simply irresponsible behavior, but as interruptive, *embodied* forms of resistance. The second exposure further explores how the *invisibility and locatedness* of teen pregnancy programs may affect the implementation of these programs. How does spatial management of teen pregnancy classrooms regulate and/or contain the bodies of teachers and girls?

Paying attention to the body and embodied practices necessitates specific and particular attention to the body as a site of information and practice, of regulation, power, and resistance. Tracing the body, its practices and exposures, is particularly important in regards to the study of gendered social issues like teen pregnancy. Brian Fay (1987) points out that "oppression leaves its traces not just in people's minds, but in their muscles and skeletons as well" (p. 146). In other words, bodies bear the marks of our culture, practices, and policies.

I have proposed a deconstructive reading of the body that calls for attention to the body deconstructively, not to build new formulations but to open possibilities for further strategies. Donna Haraway (1988) describes the view from the body as "always complex, contradictory, structuring" (p. 585). While my own research experiences have demonstrated that attention to bodies in practice and theory is complex and at times uncomfortable (Pillow, 1996b), I view this complexity as desirable in working toward social justice. Working with the complexity of our bodies—their messiness and "leakiness"—allows a thinking beyond our current boundaries, exposes what we may be too uncomfortable to portray, and works to makes what is obscured explicit.

Notes

1. I use the term *girls* here and throughout this paper to refer to the females ages 13–17 who were a part of a study I conducted during 1992–1994 (Pillow,

1994). "Girls" was the preferred term they used among themselves, and I have come to consider how the term captures the tension between their lives as girls and lives as women.

2. I am alluding here to what I see as a critical difference between reflective and deconstructive practices in ethnography. Visweswaran (1994) differentiates the two by stating that while reflexivity "says that we must confront our own processes of interpretation," deconstruction "says we must confront the plays of power in our processes of interpretation" (p. 79). See Pillow (1996b) for a discussion of the body as site of reflective and deconstructive practice.

3. While public interest has lately been focused on the fathers of teen pregnancies, intervention programs remain focused on the teen mother. Although the traditional married, two-parent family may be presented as a model, it is expected that teen mothers, in most cases, will bear full physical, developmental, and fiscal responsibility for their children.

4. Many teen pregnancy intervention programs begin with the assumption that the girls have made a mistake and must learn to make better, rational decisions in their lives. Girls who are teen parents are already viewed as having made irresponsible decisions and thus must demonstrate and prove their ability to engage in responsible decision making. Thus, programs that require girls to return to school one month after childbirth, make their own child care arrangements, excuse only three absences a year for sick children, expect girls to schedule doctor appointments for their children after school hours, and require girls to demonstrate that they are actively searching for employment justify these requirements as in the best interests of the girls (Burdell, 1995; Pillow, 1994). However, many of these practices seem aimed at the best interests of the state. Nancy Lesko (1990) in fact, refers to these practices as "rites of redemption" (p. 125).

5. Combining mothering and work is something that is difficult for any mother, regardless of age, and is certainly compounded by single-parent status and socioeconomic class. In essence, we are asking teen parents to overcome society's own conflicting and stereotypical messages about single mothers and to do so in a responsible fashion. I have often wondered how I and the other single parents I know would hold up under the scrutiny, standards, and judgment of the teen parent programs I have studied.

6. Most programs for teen girls who are pregnant operate in separate classrooms, buildings, or campuses away from the rest of the public school setting.

7. Ironically, most teen pregnancy programs enforce and promote an asexual, neutral approach toward young women's sexuality, ignoring the fact that they have obviously already been and may continue to be sexually active (Pillow, 1994).

8. I do not want to encourage a simplistic definition of resistance (see Haney, 1996, for a discussion of the complexities of resistance between girls and the state), but rather I want to focus on how I observed girls in the teen pregnancy program become aware of the way in which their pregnant bodies were both

assumed resistant and how the girls came to use this phenomenon to incite further resistance. Additionally, with the stories presented here, I am not attempting to situate a case of girls versus the program, where the girls are "right," but rather to provide a forum for a discussion of girls' bodies and resistance. I have explored and discussed elsewhere the complexities of telling teen girls' stories of resistance, where the forms of resistance may occur in ways that resist a critical or feminist telling and are stories which are uncomfortable to tell (Pillow, 1994, 1996a, 1996b).

9. Kelly also discussed how, while her mother, the teen pregnancy teacher, and she were working to arrange a continuation of her advanced placement classes, she "took pleasure" in going to every meeting "myself, with my pregnant body so that they (the school administration) would have to deal with the fact that yes, I was pregnant and that I was still a student at their school."

10. Kelley received support from the students at her old school. Against administrative wishes, the senior class included Kelley's name on a sweatshirt with signatures of the "Class of '92." The administration threatened not to let the seniors sell the sweatshirt and then later said the sweatshirt could not be worn on the school grounds—a decision that was later revoked.

11. Pseudonym for the teen pregnancy program I studied.

12. It is important to note here that the goal is not to critique these discourses or say they are "wrong"—the teachers I talked with are dedicated, caring professionals for whom I developed much respect—but to situate and attempt to understand what impact the regulatory function of architecture may have on the discourse spoken and embodied in these classrooms.

13. Similar to Fine's (1988) work on school dropouts, this research raises questions about who teen pregnancy programs do serve and perhaps, more importantly, who do they want and not want to serve? Several girls at these sites told me that they had friends who had opted not to enroll in the teen pregnancy program "because of the way you're treated in school." While the teen pregnancy program I researched claimed a high graduation rate of its students, by my closest estimations, the program served less than 35 percent of the teen pregnancies in the state. Burdell (1995), in a review of related literature, found similar findings: programs tend to target "specific segments of students and ignore the rest" (p. 185).

14. Child care was not provided at any of the settings I observed and not condoned by the state teen pregnancy program. Girls in the suburban schools were particularly discouraged from bringing their babies to school for any reason as it was, in one teacher's view, "an inappropriate thing to do—this is a high school—a place to learn with your mind not to show off what you made with your body."

15. As discussed above, this is not to say that this type of conversation did not occur in the traditional school settings, only that these conversations were regulated out of the official space of the teen pregnancy classrooms I observed.

References

Allison, D. (1994). *Skin: Talking about sex, class and literature.* Ithaca, NY: Firebrand Books.

Bane, M. (1986). Household composition and poverty. In S. H. Danziger & D. H. Weinberg (Eds.), *Fighting poverty: What works and what doesn't* (pp. 209–31). Cambridge, MA: Harvard University Press.

Burdell, P. A. (1993). *Becoming a mother in high school: The life histories of five young women.* Unpublished doctoral dissertation. University of Wisconsin-Madison, Madison, WI.

Burdell, P. A. (1995). Teen mothers in high school: Tracking their curriculum. *Review of Research in Education, 21*(3), 163–208.

Butler, J. (1990). *Gender trouble: Feminism and the subversion of identity.* New York: Routledge.

Butler, J. (1993). *Bodies that matter: On the discursive limits of "sex."* New York: Routledge.

Center for Population Options. (1990). *Teenage pregnancy and too early childbearing: Public costs, personal consequences* (6th ed.). Washington, D.C.: The Center for Populations Options.

Cixous, H. (1994). In S. Sellers (Ed.), *The Helene Cixous reader.* London: Routledge.

Cusick, T. (1989). Sexism and early parenting: Cause and effect? *Peabody Journal of Education, 8*(4), 113–131.

Davis, A. Y. (1981). *Women, race, and class.* New York: Vintage Books.

de Lauretis, T. (1984). *Alice doesn't: Feminism, semiotics, cinema.* London: Macmillan.

Diprose, R. (1994). *The bodies of women: Ethics, embodiment and sexual difference.* London: Routledge.

Fay, B. (1987). *Critical social science.* Ithaca, NY: Cornell University Press.

Fine, M. (1988) Sexuality, schooling and adolescent females: The missing discourse of desire. *Harvard Educational Review, 58,* 29–53.

Fine, M. (1991). *Framing dropouts: Notes on the politics of an urban high school.* Albany: State University of New York Press.

Foucault, M. (1974). *The history of sexuality: An introduction, Volume I.* New York: Vintage Books.

Game, A. (1991). *Undoing the social: Towards a deconstructive sociology.* Toronto, Canada: University of Toronto Press.

Gaskell, J. (1992). *Gender matters from school to work.* Philadelphia: Open University Press.

Grosz, E. (1995). *Space, time, and perversion.* London: Routledge.

Grosz, E., & Probyn, E. (Eds.). (1995). *Sexy bodies: The strange carnalities of feminism.* London: Routledge.

Haney, L. (1996). Homeboys, babies, men in suits: The state and the reproduction of male dominance. *American Sociological Review, 61,* 759–78.

Haraway, D. J. (1988). Situated knowledges: The science question in feminism and the privilege of the partial perspective. *Feminist Studies, 14*(3), 575–99.

hooks, bell (1990). *Yearning: Race, gender, and cultural politics.* Boston: South End Press.

Lawson, A., & Rhode, D. L. (Eds.). (1993). *The politics of pregnancy: Adolescent sexuality and public policy.* New Haven, CT: Yale University Press.

Lesko, N. (1990). Curriculum differentiation as social redemption: The case of school-aged mothers. In R. Page & L. Valli (Eds.), *Curriculum differentiation: Interpretive studies in U.S. secondary schools* (pp. 113–36). Albany: State University of New York Press.

Lesko, N. (1991). Implausible endings: Teenage mothers and fictions of school success. In N. B. Wyner (Ed.), *Current perspectives on the culture of schools* (pp. 45–64). Brookline, MA: Brookline Books.

Lesko, N. (in press). The 'leaky needs' of school-aged mothers: An examination of U.S. programs and policies. *Curriculum Inquiry.*

McNay, L. (1992). *Foucault: A critical introduction.* Cambridge, MA: Polity Press.

Moore, H. L. (1994). *A passion for difference.* Bloomington: Indiana University Press.

Pillow, W. S. (1994) *Policy discourse and teenage pregnancy: The making of mothers.* Unpublished dissertation. The Ohio State University, Columbus.

Pillow, W. S. (April, 1996a). *Embodied analysis: Unthinking teen pregnancy.* Paper presented at the annual meeting of the American Educational Research Association, New York, NY.

Pillow, W. S. (April, 1996b). *Reflexivity as discomfort.* Paper presented at the annual meeting of the American Educational Research Association, New York, NY.

Pillow, W. S. (1997). Decentering silences/troubling irony: Teen pregnancy's challenge to policy analysis. In C. Marshall (Ed.), *Feminist critical policy analysis I: A primary and secondary schooling perspective.* London: Falmer Press.

Rowe, K. (1995). *The unruly woman: Gender and the genres of laughter.* Austin, TX: University of Texas Press.

Scheurich, J. J. (1995) Policy archaeology: A new policy studies methodology. *Journal of Policy Studies, 9*(4), 297–316.

Tolman, D. L. (1992). *Voicing the body: A psychological study of adolescent girls' sexual desire.* Unpublished doctoral dissertation. Harvard University, Cambridge, MA.

Tolman, D. L. (1994). Doing desire: Adolescent girls' struggles for/with sexuality. *Gender & Society, 8,* 324–42.

Trinh, T. M-H. (1989). *Woman, native, other: Writing post-coloniality and feminism.* Bloomington, IN: Indiana University Press.

Visweswaran, K. (1994). *Fictions of feminist ethnography.* Minneapolis: University of Minnesota Press.

Walker, R. (Ed.). (1995). *To be real.* New York: Anchor Books.

Walkerdine, V. (1990). *Schoolgirl fictions.* London: Verso.

Weatherly, R. A., Perlman, S. B., Levine, M., & Klerman, L. V. (1985). *Patchwork programs: Comprehensive services for pregnant and parenting adolescents*. Seattle: Center for Social Welfare Research, School of Social Work, University of Washington.

Weedon, C. (1987). *Feminist practice and poststructuralist theory*. Cambridge, UK: Basil Blackwell.

Wilton, T. (1995). *Lesbian studies: Setting an agenda*. London: Routledge.

Young, I. M. (1990). *Throwing like a girl and other essays in feminist philosophy and social theory*. Bloomington: Indiana University Press.

PART III

FIGURATIONS

Chapter 11

Feminist Figurations: Gossip as a Counterdiscourse

Mary Leach

A Preface

My project stems from a number of questions that trouble my research. As a feminist working within a state institution, I want to use the reconceptualization of academic work to ask what becomes possible when our work is intentionally positioned as both within and against normalized disciplinary conventions, what it would mean to rehearse other practices in some effort to change the social imaginary about discourses of research, pedagogy, and philosophical frameworks. What happens when normatively fixed categories and identities are disrupted?

I ask in this work what it would mean to create a different space in which to undertake other performances, other thinking, power, and pleasures. What would it mean to create new lines of flight, fragments of other possibilities, to experiment differently with meanings, practices, and our own confoundings? Such questions owe much to Foucault (1972, 1979, 1980, 1988), Deleuze (1986, 1987, 1988), and Irigaray (1985a, 1985b, 1993) and their suggestions of routes of escape, moments and practices to refuse what we are, to contest the dominate in order to move toward some place that might be called a counterdiscourse of feminist imaginaries.

This particular effort was given birth by the literatures of critical pedagogy, much of which situates the activity of "dialogue" as the answer to feminist concerns about dealing with difference in the classroom. My argument in this chapter is that such a move has not escaped the desire of a "Habermasian" ideal speech community in which, if we just listen hard enough to each other in the most respectful way, we can under-

stand and accommodate differences of power and meaning in our classroom communicative interactions.

In my own urge to escape, to think differently about our historical
condition, I share the concern expressed in the work in this volume to
invent new images of thought to replace the classical system of representation in order to figure an activity of thinking differently about discourse, dialogue, and our practices of talking to one another.

Rumor Has It . . . Scattered Thoughts on An/Other Discourse

Feminist discourses have focused on various debates such as the problem
of gendered knowledge and gendered language, cultural constraints on
the representation of sexuality, the oppressive nature of the concepts of
race and class, the characteristics of a feminist aesthetic, and women's
strategies for cultural and political change. Recently, efforts have con-
verged on the questions of how women might locate their own subjectivity. This work is grounded in the (problematized) notion that
difference exists between "you" and "I" and between "man" and
"woman." French feminists, particularly, argue that these binaries are
not simply mirror equivalents but are instead fundamentally different.
Their deliberate resistance to conventional, masculine conceptual patterns of analysis reflects in part their conviction that social change beneficial to all depends not least upon changes in women's thinking and
language (Alcoff & Potter, 1993; Irigaray, 1993).

This feminist epistemology that proposes a radically different vision of
subjectivity as embodied, sexually differentiated, multiple and relational,
remains very much within a politics of everyday life. Central, then, to
the starting point for new conceptual and political schemes of thought
remains the simultaneous use and problematization of women's experience and activities. In this, much feminist theorizing diverges from that
of contemporary poststructuralist thought. While both theoretical
streams move toward the seemingly common goal of redefining the subject, feminists have added a specific gender inflection resulting in the
political and epistemological project of asserting difference in a nonhierarchical manner, refusing to disembody and therefore to desexualize a
vision of the subject. By defending *female* feminist specificity in terms of
a new, relational mode of thought, this brand of feminism is seeking
reconnection while accepting noncomplementarity and multiplicity. In
revalorizing the lived experience and the embodied nature of the subject,
this view works to give a positive value to the embodied self as a mater-
ial-symbolic agent of change. This is not some lyrical celebration of

female positivity, however. There is the recognition that this positivity needs to be constructed through action.

Luce Irigaray, particularly, works upon opening out conditions of possibility for such a difference to be enacted. Without falling into biological reductivism, she sees the body as a libidinal surface that allows for the construction of subjectivity through the complex interplay of identifications and, consequently, language and alterity (Irigaray, 1985b). Her texts display a quest for an analysis of some characteristics of what might be women's language. As such, her work gives a privileged relation to play and laughter (rather than seriousness or meaning), to what is near, to that which is both shifting and connected, and to notions of intimacy in order to discover new forms of communication among women. Her aim is to articulate and embody a new kind of relation that, in turn, would help promote a new subjectivity (Irigaray, 1985a). It is in the spirit of her project that I take up my own reflections.

My "American" reading of these feminists' attempts to redefine the knowing subject finds its connections in classical American pragmatism. Indeed, American feminist Charlotte Perkins Gilman wrote this passage in 1914:

> Humanity, thus considered, is not a thing made at once of unchangeable, but a stage of development; and is still . . . in the making. Our humanness is seen to lie not so much in what we are individually as in our relations to one another; and even that individuality is but the result of our relations to one another. It is in what we do and how we do it, rather than in what we are. Some, philosophically inclined, exalt "being" over "doing." To them this question may be put: can you mention any form of life that merely "is" without doing anything? (pp. 16–17)

In no way am I arguing that feminist thought can be systematized or represented as a continuous sequence of clearly elaborated theoretical points. As you will see, I am adopting a philosophical style that can be considered nomadism: thus the reference in my heading to "scattered thoughts." The first part repeats the words of a country-and-western song that refers to the actual subject I want to address here—"serious gossip," a discursive practice familiar to us all.

In what follows I would like to take a good look at an activity in which we all engage, an activity where women have been historically and particularly implicated. My purpose, like the project mentioned earlier, is to explore this activity in light of the themes outlined above—those of process, movement, identity, the self defined in relation to others, and praxis as determinative of the self. My idea here is to focus on what happens when we (particularly women) talk to each other in our everyday lives, what we are *practicing* when we gossip with one another, which, to date, seems to elude description in our liberal stipulations constitutive of discourse. What we can ferret out about the kinds of relations constructed when we engage in some serious gossiping may well be worth noting in our efforts to connect meaningfully with each other so that all participants can be said to benefit.

My approach recalls Irigaray's (1985a, 1985b, 1993) primacy of place for play, laughter, and intimacy and stands as a way to disrupt the vision of subjectivity that posits rationality as the dominant mode of praxis. Also, this approach, I believe, fits with feminists' active seeking of a redefinition of the community bond and, consequently, of the heterosexual social contract and is in direct opposition to the molarization and the exacerbated individualism of traditional philosophical thought.

Conceptions of Gossip

I am not going to begin with a definition of gossip. Not unlike poetry, gossip means many things to many people and, even at different times and in different contexts, to a single person. At its extreme, however, it is easy to think of all gossip as petty, ill-willed, too often unfounded; as either trivial and thus demeaning to those whose lives it rakes over; or outright malicious. Indeed, dictionary definitions reinforce the view of gossip at its worst as destructive or, at best, trivial. The *American Heritage Dictionary* (1969) defines it as "trifling, often groundless rumor, usually of a personal, sensational, or intimate nature; idle talk."

Three kinds of gossip that have been judged reprehensible are easily distinguishable: gossip as a breach of confidence; gossip the speaker knows to be false; and unduly invasive gossip (Bok, 1989). In other words, breaking a promise of secrecy, intentionally misleading others about people's lives, purposefully deceiving listeners, and passing along matters that can unquestionably injure the person talked about are all activities we can generally agree, at least in the abstract, may be judged as indefensible. Morally questionable, at least, is talk that gains prestige, power, affection, or income for the speaker who passes on gossip best left untold. The stuff of scandal that serves to damage competitors or enemies, to gratify envy or rage by diminishing another, or to generate disparaging or discreditable representations in hopes of benefiting one's own position obviously invites our condemnations.

There is no doubt that gossip enjoys a terrible reputation. In religious and secular contexts, by prevailing standards of morality and of decorum, loose talk about people and events has been deplored. No nearly universal activity has been the object of such sustained and passionate attack.

A short rundown of distinguished thinkers who adopt a normative point of view against gossip will give some sense of its traditional, overwhelmingly negative, evaluation. Aristotle's (1962) vision of the great-souled man declares he is no gossip "for he will not talk either about himself or about another, as he neither wants to receive compliments nor to hear other people run down" (p. 94). Thomas Aquinas (see Baldewyn, 1556) distinguished between "talebearers" and "backbiters" (p. 105) but both, he said, bespeak evil of their neighbors. Modern philosophers rearticulated the long-standing attack. Kierkegaard abhorred gossip. Gossip and chatter, he wrote, "obliterate the vital distinction between what is private and what is public" and thereby trivialize all that is inward and inexpressible. He negatively compares frivolous, trivial talk to "real" talk that he believes concerns the inner life—specifically the inner religious life. In *The Present Age* he rails against his own time in which he sees the expanding press offering snide and leveling gossip to a news-hungry public (Kierkegaard, 1962, p. 212).

Heidegger (see Krell, 1977), too, opposes gossip to "authentic" discourse, authenticity of course, meaning that which is elicited from profound sources. Our "average understanding" in Heidegger's view merits contempt because of its inability to discriminate between the trivial and the profound. Like Kierkegaard, his focus concerns itself with the avowed content, the subject matter of this talk that refers to nothing beneath the apparent, "circulating the new of the most private concerns to large audiences" (p. 125). They both condemn a mode of chatter that deviates from the "ideal point of view," "trivial facts," that "meaningless talk" largely based on personal, rather than public, values. Talk in the kind of detail that interests gossips concerns itself with events in "language that having no original taking-place, occurs on unauthorized epistemological grounds." Gossip or rumor blurs the distinction between the public nature of the important, the "true" grounds of "being," and that talk that communicates the "ordinary." In their view this deters knowing the *true* "nature of the entity talked about" (p. 213).

The moralistic castigation of private gossip over the centuries suggests continuing vivid perception of it as a *social* threat. While criticism does not abandon the language of Christian reference, the establishment of a political context for moral doctrine called attention to the increasing value of social reputation. The authority of linguistic control suggests the proliferation of slanderous rumor and perceived social danger for public figures, religious, political, and professional. Gossip as a public instrument is fully recognized as having power and as such takes its place as a real force in the events of the world.

It is clear that the abundant moral literature about gossip constitutes one site of domestic politics. The traditional and historical linkage of loose talk with women is made not only by moralists but also by novelists, dramatists, educationists, and anthropologists as well. By the eighteenth century, moral commentary aimed specifically at women reached new proportions. Male authors' prescriptions for community rules became increasingly complex and well defined, often addressing the most minute aspects of women's behavior. All forms of public intercourse, such as the fact of social visiting, letter writing, and conventional conversing among women, came under increasing scrutiny. Women's right to belong to "society" depends here not only upon her marriage but also upon social knowledge of matters such as singing, dancing, and, especially, discretion in talking in secular, social contexts. The implicit standard of conduct for aspiring young women in much of the writing was that of silence and solitude. From Rousseau's Sophie to Lord Halifax's daughter, a good name was a woman's halo (Ronell, 1988, pp. 146–99).

The special fragility of women's sexual reputation deserves more discussion here. Let us just say that women's delight in scandal mongering is not only attributed to her "weak and degenerate mind" but other perversions of primary modes of human connectedness as well. Verbal, like sexual, expression may rise from passion, and women's minds may not be their only weakness.

None of this is new, but that is not to say it has vanished from present common perception. Patricia Spacks relates in her 1985 book about gossip a joke that shows women's supposed promiscuity as well as men's denial of engaging in promiscuous talk. It is worth telling:

> In the first frame, a man leans against a woman's desk. The balloon over his smugly smiling face reads, "Say, did you hear about Shirley? They say she's got something going with that guy from. . . . " The woman responds, "I've got to run, Ralph. . . . I'm afraid I don't have time to gossip." The second frame shows the man saying: "*Gossip?* Men don't gossip! I was merely analyzing her shortcomings." (p. 38)

Analogies in literature and life between sins of sex and speech abound. The picture one is left with is that women make up for lack of intelligence by being nosy, and their verbal indiscretion just may be symptomatic of indiscretions in other modes of intimate communication—read SEX. What is seemingly frighteningly posited in both cases is a secret female life, the possibility of activity outside the socially sanctioned and polite.

With this much stigmatization, often savage denigrations, diatribes, and denunciations by so many, it would seem reasonable perhaps to give up on suggesting there is any value either from the subject matter or the practice of gossip. The activity seems inherently questionable from a

moral point of view and surely a waste of time, if not outright superficial. Given all its problems, one would think it dangerous to promote it
as a counterdiscourse, one that would replace ideal conceptions of communicative discursive practices. Still, I think there are a number of things
to look at here that can generate interest, not least a feminist one.
Indeed, gossip as an activity has been recognized in a less dismissive way
by at least two current authors, both women, interestingly. Even after
her careful consideration of the moral problems some forms of gossip
clearly raise, Sissela Bok (1989), in her book *Secrets*, takes pains to
address some of its uses in a more positive light. Her careful delineations
show gossip in its subject matter as well as its practice to be at least
ambiguous across a number of important issues of concern. Patricia
Spacks (1985), in her book on gossip, draws on its complex psychological dynamic to perform analyses of three centuries of literary works:
published letters, biographies, Restoration drama, and novels. Her work,
I believe, immediately problematizes the practice of gossip as merely a
private mode of discourse, showing how traditional literary genres have
long relied on it to establish necessary connections between narrators
and readers. Her analyses reveal that what we normally think of as a private mode of talking is not all that simple or private. While we prefer to
distinguish still between the public and private realms, assigning gossip
to the private or "natural realm," this separation serves to occlude the
blurred and arbitrary lines we like to think of as separate. Feminist
analyses have long recognized these realms as fundamentally, unequally
interdependent. It is argued that the claims of civility—epitomized by
cosmopolitan, public behavior balanced against the claims of nature as
epitomized by the family—articulate the epistemic relations of a liberal
conception of freedom and equality, relations located squarely in the
male individualism constitutive of the public sphere. This specious
dichotomy—articulated in traditional conceptions of "personhood," "a
claimant before the law," "a citizen"—is now being challenged for its
gendered, exclusionary, hierarchical structuring of relations.

I use here Spacks's (1985) distinction of "serious gossip" to describe
conversations that take place in small groupings, usually at leisure, in
relations of trust, and that, I believe, provide a resource for the practice
of a number of activities: play, moral investigation, self-reflection, wonder, self-expression, discovery, the definition of ideas, the embodiment of
solidarity, and the circulation of information.

Gossip as Content

It is clear from objections voiced earlier that most thinkers, certainly the
philosophers mentioned, have focused on the avowed subject matter of

gossip to ground their condemnations. Their focus is embedded in a number of questionable assumptions, however. Important for our purpose is their view of language and the way it works. Heidegger (1962), for example, speaks of "Being-with," which "develops in listening to one another" (p. 206). He actually specifies the items constitutive of authentic discourse, namely, "what the discourse is about" (what is talked about); what is said-in-the-talk (the communication); and "the making known" (p. 206). His formulations, as do the others, suggest a passive role for the listener; at most, two or more people take turns listening to one another.

Communication here appears to involve transmission of ideas from mouth to ear, certainly not a *transaction* of exchange and mutual modification. In fact, Heidegger's worry is that in the transmission, stray utterances that are not imputable to a knowable origin will contaminate the space of internal, formal, private structures of a literary language. He wants to protect the purity of his language from external, referential, and public effects, establishing, in effect, a "rumor control center" for great thought (Ronell, 1988, p. 135). His view is also rooted in our now traditional view of a singular subject as the site of Being, knowledge, and virtue: the subject as *opposed* to the object or another subject. His view is also rooted in the idea that the subject matter unproblematically *determines* meaning. Meaning inheres in concepts and propositions that are transparent, merely expressing facts that need only to be laid out to be agreed upon, that is, if the speaker is "clear," exhibiting a communicative competence based on some universal standard for measuring discourse. This view of how ideas are *to be understood* at the very least flattens the relationship between language and participants. At its worst, it reinscribes and reinforces the complicity between discourse and normativity.

Foucault's (1972) commitment to unmasking this complicity leads him to pinpoint what feminists find as a most fertile contradiction of Western culture; namely, that because of its logocentric structure and the consequent value it attributes to scientific knowledge, it has actually become logophobic in that it fears spontaneous production of knowledge and is intent upon monitoring the extent and the kind of discourses that are allowed to circulate.

Of interest to us too is the attention Foucault draws to the discourses of law, medicine, and education as being major normative forms whose role has been infamous in the history of the regulation of women's bodies. What would seem politically desirable would be for a feminist to critically *resist* the modalities of power that structure those discourses. But from the treatment of language by our critics, all discourse, like all virtuous activities, should confine itself to "authentic" speech, the speech of the Father.

This "literalness" imposed on the listener by the speaker belies any series of complex relationships, consonances, and dissonances of meanings. It denies *active* understandings and the unexpectedly varied ways of seeing the world. It also reveals a desire for some magisterial "central intelligence" that can legitimately police the participants who may evoke implicitly the struggle to *assert* meaning in the face of competing assertions, actual or potential. To presuppose a certain content is to make the acceptance of that content a precondition for *further* dialogue. This is not merely a causal transformation tied to the fact that any enunciation influences the beliefs, desires, and interests of the listener. On the contrary, it is a juridical or institutional transformation (Deleuze & Guattari, 1987). Kierkegaard's and Heidegger's semantic efforts to define the "appropriate" content of dialogical discourse effectively erase difference and effectively hide the power relations embedded in the description. Their fierce efforts, like others', reveal a fear of the unleashing of impulse in language, its subversive possibilities, its openings that resist closing off or being shut down by the declarations of meaning by authorities interested in removing language from the terrain of contestation. Proposing serious gossip as a serious discourse helps us to illustrate and question those boundaries and dividing lines that make the normative prevailing discourses legitimate.

This is not to say that gossip as (an)other form of discourse is outside the play of forces that aim at both discipline and resistance in the production of subjectivity. There is no possible outside in a system of this sort because it invests the subject's corporeal field itself. What gossip as a discourse reveals instead is the polymorphous network of discursive production in which every thinking subject is caught. Gossip as a discursive production cannot, then, serve as a complete counterdiscourse, but, because it is on the margins of institutional discourse, it can help us to think otherwise about the prevailing norms. Its nomadic quality can be translated into a feminist problematic in philosophy that helps us address fundamental traits of the patriarchal theoretical system and that system's chronic inability to recognize a state of flow, fluidity, incompleteness, inconclusiveness, and the relational import of engagement, the *becoming* that emerges in the personal transaction of talking.

Indeed, I think that rumorological paranoia derives partially from the challenge to authorial control it presents—its incalculable scope. We can never know quite where it goes, whom it reaches, how it changes, how and by whom it is understood. In that way, it could prove to exemplify a Deleuzian rhizomatic network that would strangle the roots of that infamous tree of knowledge, the "arborescent" model of thought constructing "the proudly erect tree under whose spreading boughs laterday Platos discharge their function" (Massumi, 1993, p. 5). Taking gossip seriously gives substance to the idea that the personal is not only the political but also is the basis for the theoretical. As such, its exploration may also help us open out the traditional figures of philosophical discourse—for example, idea, presence, transcendental subjectivity, and absolute knowledge—to expose how these have been constructed from, yet have radically subverted the feminine, certainly submerging the idea of women's entitlement to theoretical subjectivity.

All gossip, as I see it, obviously, is not injurious or otherwise to be avoided. I would go further to suggest that usually the gossip that seeks to damage another—malicious gossip—is relatively rare. Even Bok (1989), who rather narrowly defines it as having four elements—it is (a) informal, (b) personal communication, (c) about persons who (d) are absent or excluded—finds nothing morally problematic about these elements in their own right (p. 69). Because the focus is usually on the havoc it can wreak, we have looked little at its harmless or supportive uses. Consider the talk about who is getting married, having a baby, moving to another town or job, needing work or help. Gossip, some of us would say, deals with what *matters* in human affairs.

It is certainly not one of the columns upon which the hegemonic political and theoretical order rests. Indeed, its value to subversive groups has been noted. Because gossip is hard to repress, it supplies a weapon for outsiders; it often reflects moral assumptions different from those of the dominant culture; it provides language and knowledge potentially disruptive to the state order but vital to individual and community life of subordinated classes. In these aspects, it provides oral histories for groups of people and/or nations who have been colonized by oppressors. "Loose" talk has been recognized as dangerous by the absolute state. Those oppressed by the state can use it to challenge the discourse of sovereign judgment, of stable subjectivity legislated by "good" sense, of "universal" truths and (white male) justice. In enactment, gossip is often about the importance of *not taking* everything at face value, the need to inquire, to learn from others' experiences: it is about the desire for the sort of knowledge that *goes against the grain* of "official" interpretations of people or events. It frequently leads us to go beneath the surface of what is said and done, to try to account for conflicting appearances of official institutional stories and then to test these contradictions, to evaluate them with others in conversations. Not so different from some current recommendations for critical pedagogical excellence, I think.

Gossip as Practice

What seems to have been overlooked by most is gossip's value as an activity in which all humans engage in ordinary life, one that I claimed earlier has a number of elements that speak to its power as a social mode of contracting relations. The settled practice of gossip can be analyzed as a form of *relating*, not one that involves participants' relation to ideas so much as to each other. It is this focus that I think may prove the most fruitful in our search for a way to understand differently notions of identity and subjectivity.

Gossiping can be understood as a relatively freeing activity standing quite consciously outside ordinary social inhibitions and established rules for discourse. As such, talkers often engage in a "non-sense" performance, exhibiting energy-filled manifestations of a sense of fun in an atmosphere of play and laughter. Indeed, one can wonder if our critics' admonitions stem from their realization of the intensity, unselfconscious impulses, creative imagination, and genuine satisfaction derived from this kind of interaction as opposed to the more "heroically profound" they have deemed essentially educational or important.

The often joyous and playful aspects of gossiping suggest compelling motives for friendly relations that incorporate a libidinal economy quite different from orgasmic orientation. In gossiping, there is no pretense to finality. Mind, affect, and body become defined uniquely in a circulation of states, a *play* of differences that produces meanings, though, of course, no guarantee of the same (or "right") kind. The latitude of free play in which parties engage can release the passionate substructures of thought and feeling in a space safe to wonder about or speculate on diverse forms of evidence about our/selves or others' humanness. At times, we "try on" different emotions, ideas, attitudes, attributes, or personas to feel how they "fit" or see what reactions they may elicit. To do this we rearticulate our personal myths where pain and hilarity blur, where anguish coexists with joy, and where sanity flirts with its opposite. We recall early memories, high points, low points, and turning points of our lives. We express in these our unique embrace of the facts and themes of the past, the strivings of the present and hopes for the future. In doing so, we reveal the values that have kept us vital. At its best, the emotional geography of engagement in this environment, like art, changes the way we look at the world.

The contrast between these relations and "polite," or what we might want to label "educational," conversation calls attention to all that the latter eliminates, particularly the neither-not yet of what we have come to call a "self" (Hardt, 1993, pp. 1–25). Unlike more didactic efforts, which often try too hard to *instill* meaning, these conversations become the treasures we remember. In them we find the setting up of relations that *preceded* the specific predicates others come to attribute to the substance they see as our "self." I am talking about finding an actual contextual mode of representation that better accounts for the creation and originality of a complex moment of self-relation—the being-to-come. I think, as a practice, gossiping shows us an alternative space in which to find the actual *conditions of possibility* for both the creation and examination of differences, in this case, a nondialectizable difference in a dynamic Bergson might call "indetermination" (Hardt, 1993). Importantly, we also observe the aim of a practice that is to help *un*burden: not to load life with the weight of higher values, but to create new values which are those *of* life, which make life "light and active." While (or perhaps because) gossip inhabits the borderlands of socially sanctioned oral discourse, it expresses the minutiae of relations that create the texture of life, the small "truths" like the "small" talk that infuse the *details of living* with meaning.

Conclusion

In case you are thinking that this has little to do with what *we* do or can do as academics, I would call your attention to that which we have already acknowledged as the kind of inquiry worthy of the most astute cultural historian or social science researcher. I suggest that the gossip's delight in narratives about events or about others is not so different from being thrust into exciting intimacy with those we don't know (reading oral history?), savoring secrets not intended for us (reading published letters?), and encountering aspects of others' experience not ordinarily or publicly divulged (reading qualitative research?).

Present-day "storytellers" are not exempt; they do much of the same work as gossips. An action-in-knowing inheres in both practices whether storytellers want to acknowledge it or not. My guess is that most men who pride themselves on being great storytellers will not much appreciate the analogy. But linking the two as loci of uncertainty, both being as they are fundamental interpretive activities often possessing the forms of certainty, reveals the artificiality of opposing activities of the "outer," "public," (male) realm to goings-on in the supposedly privatized realm most associated with women. It certainly serves to challenge the cherished distinctions we make and forces us to wonder why the one is an often admired and accepted social skill, while the other has gathered such censure. What is going on here?

Etymologically, gossip means "god-related" (Spacks, 1985, p. 25). What happened? How is the change in our views of the gossip related to the increasing pose of the subject who knows, the disdain of the body, and the public order of the masculine? In what ways does the practice of gossip both appropriate and undercut traditional representations of dialogue, stereotypical representations of women's talk and the everyday?

How does the paradox gossip presents force us out of our fixed categories, displacing polarities? And, a most important question of feminists—how can the focus on the relations constructed in our practice of ordinary talk help us in our effort toward living that which is no longer but cannot yet be, help us in the service of transition? "Inquiring minds want to know."

References

Alcoff, L. & Potter, E. (Eds.). (1993). *Feminist epistemologies*. New York: Routledge.

Aristotle. (1962). *Nicomachean ethics*. Cambridge, MA: Harvard University Press.

Baldewyn, W. (1556). *A treatise of morall phylosophye*. London: Edward Whitchurch.

Bok, S. (1989). *Secrets*. New York: Vintage Books.

Deleuze, G. (1986). *Foucault* (S. Hand, Trans.). Minneapolis: University of Minnesota Press.

Deleuze G. (1987). *Dialogues* (H. Tomlinson & B. Habberjam, Trans.). New York: Columbia University Press.

Deleuze, G. (1988a). *Bergsonism* (H. Tomlinson & B. Habberjam, Trans.). New York: Zone Books.

Deleuze, G. (1988b). *Spinoza: Practical philosophy* (R. Hurley, Trans.). San Francisco: City Lights.

Deleuze, G., & Guattari, F. (1983). *Anti-Oedipus: Capitalism and schizophrenia* (R. Hurley, M. Seem, & H. Lane, Trans.). Minneapolis: University of Minnesota Press.

Deleuze, G., & Guattari, F. (1987). *A thousand plateaus: Capitalism and schizophrenia*. Minneapolis: University of Minnesota Press.

Foucault, M. (1972). *The archaeology of knowledge*. New York: Random House.

Foucault, M. (1979). *Discipline and punish: The birth of the prison* (R. Howard, Trans.). New York: Vintage Books.

Foucault, M. (1980). *History of sexuality. Volume 1: An introduction*. New York: Vintage Books.

Foucault, M. (1988). *Technologies of the self* (L. Martin, H. Gutman, & P. Hutton, Trans.). Amherst: University of Massachusetts Press.

Gilman, C. P. (1914). *The man-made world, or Our androcentric culture*. New York: Charlton.

Hardt, M. (1993). *Gilles Deleuze: An apprenticeship in philosophy*. Minneapolis: University of Minnesota Press.

Heidegger, M. (1962). *Being and time* (J. Macquarrie & E. Robinson, Trans.). New York: Harper & Row.

Irigaray, L. (1985a). *Speculum of the other woman*. Ithaca, NY.: Cornell University Press.

Irigaray, L. (1985b). *This sex which is not one*. Ithaca, NY: Cornell University Press.

Irigaray, L. (1993). *An ethics of sexual difference*. Ithaca, NY: Cornell University Press.

Kierkegaard, S. (1962). *The present age*. New York: Harper & Row.

Krell, D. (1977). *Martin Heidegger, basic writings*. New York: Harper & Row.

Massumi, B. (1993). *A user's guide to* Capitalism and Schizophrenia. Cambridge, MA: MIT Press.

Ronell, A. (1988). Street talk. In E. Nägele (Ed.), *Benjamin's ground*. Detroit, MI: Wayne State University Press.

Spacks, P. (1985). *Gossip*. Chicago: University of Chicago Press.

Chapter 12

White Noise—the Sound of Epidemic: Reading/Writing a Climate of Intelligibility around the "Crisis" of Difference

Kate McCoy

With the current explosion of discourse representing cultural difference as a "problem" of epidemic proportions in politics, popular media, and education, what possibilities are there for analyses that reach toward new understandings of its constructions and implications? As an attempt toward new understandings, this chapter presents the theoretical framework I used and one resulting data display[1] in the form of a series of poems from a study of popular media and cultural difference I conducted in a 5-week course with preservice teachers in the summer of 1994. In this study, I used a combination of methodological approaches including cultural studies ethnography, Foucauldian genealogy (Foucault, 1984), and literary criticism to examine the ways preservice teachers' media analyses make use of available discourses to construct a network of intelligibility around cultural difference.

The idea of intelligibility is linked to the idea of the natural. The things that are most intelligible are the things that seem natural and, consequently, unquestionable. Barthes's (1972) conception of mythologies is helpful here for rethinking the seemingly natural. He speaks of mythologies as "types of speech chosen by history: [as speech that] cannot possibly evolve from the 'nature' of things" (p. 110); as economies of discourses [that] can no longer be "experienced as innocent speech" (p. 131) but as naturalized discourses that draw their power through "the pretension of transcending [themselves] into a factual system" (p. 134). Butler (1993) theorizes the process by which such mythologies might become "sedimented" into intelligible and hegemonic systems of meaning (p. 15)—i.e., discursive formations. She calls this process "performativity as citationality" (1993, p. 12), "a reiteration of a norm or set of norms" (1993, p. 12). This reiteration forms "regulatory schemas . . . [that are] historically revisable criteria of intelligibility" (1993, p. 14). Butler (1993) argues that sedimentation of discourse through citationality has material consequences, "establish[ing] normative conditions under which the materiality of the body is framed and formed" (p. 17).

Thus, intelligibility has consequences not only for what is sayable and understandable but also for what is doable. It helps create the conditions of possibility for both thought and action, not that these are easily or desirably separable things. The poems I present here, constructed from student journals and final papers, evoke a climate of intelligibility, suggesting ways that this climate makes possible, through the availability of discourses, certain ways of imagining cultural difference. To conclude, I discuss the possible implications of this approach to cultural criticism, one that positions future teachers as inquirers and strategizers, rather than as resistors to "liberatory" pedagogies.

The Difference Epidemic and Multicultural Education

> Multiculturalism includes all of us. . . . It is time for all educators to become concerned and, indeed, alarmed. Is there a more urgent educational problem before us today? (Garcia & Pugh, 1995, p. 40)

With schooling historically and currently upheld as a remedy for social ills (Perkinson, 1991; Tyack, 1990), it might be argued that an epidemic logic is set in motion, a logic, or force, which posits the modernist metaphor of the disease to be "cured" in the technocratic movement of a remedy. Singer (1993) argues:

> [I]n doing so, one not only engages in a kind of rhetorical inflation, but also mobilizes a certain apparatus and logic, a particular way of producing and organizing bodies politically. An epidemic is a phenomenon that in its very representation calls for, indeed, seems to demand some form of managerial response, some mobilized effort of control. (p. 27)

Singer explores the notion of epidemic logic in the context of AIDS, but she notes that "as metaphors of sickness and health come to dominate the representation of the social, we are confronted by an ever increasing number of cancers, viruses infecting the body politic through mechanisms of contagion and communicability" (1993, p. 27).

To begin my consideration of how multicultural education is positioned as an educational remedy for current social ills associated with cultural difference, I analyzed the 1994/1995 *Annual Editions: Multicul-*

tural Education published by the Dushkin Publishing Group. This volume, edited by Fred Schultz of the University of Akron, is an attempt to pull together current writings on multicultural education from a variety of journals "in which the knowledge bases for multicultural education are developed" (p. iv). I do not, however, think that the volume is a comprehensive or representative reflection of the academic discourse on multicultural education. I chose this collection, rather, because of the way it positions and packages itself as a "cure" for social/cultural problems to be addressed by multicultural education. I reviewed the edition, reading in a frame focused by Singer's (1993) articulation of epidemic logic, guided by the following question: "What 'problems' are to be addressed by multicultural education?" I found four types of problems that multicultural education is to address, problems defined in terms of (a) social realities; (b) psychosocial attributes of students, their families, and their teachers; (c) schooling; and (d) representation. Each of these ways of defining the problem to be addressed by multicultural education makes possible very different ways of imagining educational remedies. As Singer (1993) points out, epidemic logic does not have a

> singular origin or intentionality. . . . There may be tenuous consensus that the situation calls for changes, but the nature and direction of those changes are very much a site of contest and discord. . . . The polymorphous proliferation induced by the epidemic situation is a consequence of its destabilizing effects. . . . [It is] already a situation that is figured as out of control. . . . [There is a] recognition of the limits of existing responses. . . . [Such] a threat to the order of things [calls for] . . . immediate and dramatic responses to the situation at hand . . . [and] promote[s] the proliferation of opposing forms of response. (pp. 27–28)

My analysis of the 1994/1995 *Annual Editions: Multicultural Education* gave me a way to handle this "tenuous consensus" regarding cultural difference and "the proliferation of opposing forms of response" to it as it is perceived to be a "situation that is figured as out of control" (Singer, 1993, pp. 27–28).

At first I thought that looking in this way at the data I gathered in the ethnographic phase of my study might be fairly simple. I would just analyze how my students—through their journal reflections on media representation of cultural difference—articulated the problems multicultural education was supposed to address. Given these definitions of the problems, how would they conceive of possible solutions? I expected that such a focus would help me to narrow down and somehow "isolate" the discourses that are mobilized in deployment of such reasoning. As I got into the data, however, it became apparent that such a finely tuned focus was not possible. I was not prepared for the explosion of interpretive possibility presented by the data I gathered in the course of this project. The data, of course, exceeded the categorical treatment I had planned. I encountered a vast network of discourse and practice, veiny, rhizomatic, contradictory, yet one that I still had to find a way to map in order to say anything about it. I read multicultural education as a discursive formation, a dynamic and rhizomatic intertwining of discourse set in terms of an epidemic outbreak of information and "flurry of seemingly purposeful activity" (Katz, 1971, quoted in Robenstine, 1995, p. 80), an intense relay of forceful images, messages, inscriptions, and resistances that write bodies into particular and paradoxical ways of being.

White Noise: The Sound of Epidemic

I floundered for a while and started thinking maybe I should tell different stories. I could do that pedagogical tale of student receptivity and resistance: "The Thrill of Victory and the Agony of Defeat." I could do a reflexive methodological tale documenting the different ways I found myself reading the data and discuss those implications: "Sybil Speaks!" I went on and on, almost drowning in the possibilities presented by such a complex data set.

I attended a lecture one day that started pulling me back toward an analytic frame suggested by Singer's (1993) work via a detour, one that has presented both exhilarating possibility and overwhelming paralysis in the face of yet more possibility. The last thing I needed was more possibility. The lecturer was Linda Brodkey (1995). She was talking about her experiences teaching a composition course that required students to read and respond to "multicultural voices." She talked about the limitations of multicultural reform as a curricular issue—the addition of voices from the margins—noting, in particular, that unless the pedagogical question of how such voices might be read were addressed, students reading in traditional ways would not "hear the voices recently added to our courses, . . . because they are distracted by the White Noise that makes it nearly impossible to hear lyrics spoken in unfamiliar cadences" (Brodkey, 1995). In her opinion, the pedagogical endeavor becomes one of "reduc[ing] the volume of White Noise for those who cannot hear for the din of common sense" (Brodkey, 1995). Her lecture went on in important directions, and I will come back to it later, but what is important now is the figuration[2]—White Noise.

I remembered a novel I had read in the late 1980s, Don DeLillo's (1986) *White Noise*. I scribbled in my notebook. I remembered that popular media figured prominently in the novel, almost as a character, albeit a polymorphous one, in its own right. As I reread *White Noise*, I read it as staging a performance of the postmodern information explosion, a performance of the intricate mechanics of the creation, sustenance, and seduction of epidemic logic as a phenomenon both of information and discourse and of the embodied materiality of lived experience. I saw important parallels in the novel with the data I had collected. I began to understand why a simple explication according to the medical metaphor—documenting student efforts at rooting out causes, negating them with solutions, and arriving at desired outcomes—would not suffice.

Another work entitled *White Noise* came to my attention at about this same time—a 1991 album released by New York recording artists Cop Shoot Cop. The songs on this album connect the white noise figuration to consumer capitalism, urban anger, and the marketing of individuality and rebellion as desirable commodities. Both the lyrics and the music itself perform the white noise figuration in ways very similar to DeLillo's novel by presenting a layered pastiche of sampled material reproducing city noise and commercial media set in frantically paced, tightly executed compositions of driving bass lines, drum rhythms, alternately soothing and grating vocals, and keyboard and guitar-generated noise. It is the sound of urban emergency, the roar of the "American Death Machine" (Cop Shoot Cop, 1991), the angry man with a loaded gun and the consumer economy that produces his needs, desires, pleasures, and fears. Singer (1993) explains and theorizes the conditions that characterize and the representations that feed and sustain an epidemic climate, but DeLillo (1986) and Cop Shoot Cop (1991) enact these conditions in ways similar to the data I collected.

Preservice teachers are people with bodies positioned at a crucial juncture within what is represented in epidemic proportions as a crisis of cultural difference. If schooling is to serve as a remedy for what is characterized as a social illness arising from this crisis, then preservice teachers are charged with the responsibility for the cure, and perhaps teachers in the past could be blamed for the contagion. How does one negotiate this weighty positioning in an epidemic atmosphere? Clearly, I needed to consider in greater complexity the conditions that make epidemic logic possible in connection with multicultural issues, and with a gesture toward the awareness of particular, historical, embodied, yet fragmented subjectivities.

A Noisy Binary: Write or Be Written

Returning to Brodkey's (1995) analysis of student resistance to multicultural curriculum, she states that white noise refers to the "din of common sense . . . which cynically denies that difference matters, by dismissing it as superficial or maligning it as divisive," a distraction that "makes it nearly impossible to hear lyrics spoken in unfamiliar cadences." This distraction may even be something sought after in the noisy bombardment of postmodern lived experience. Consider this description of a product from the Sharper Image Catalog—the Heart and Sound Soother with Timer, $99.95, item #SI426:

> neutral White Noise screens out background noise
> use it as a stress relieving aid
> create a tranquil setting for sleep
> fall asleep to White Noise
> take a break from jarring noise
> escape . . . just by pushing a button

Compare this description with these lyrics from Cop Shoot Cop's "Discount Rebellion" (1991):

> Sit back! Relax!
> Allow yourself to believe . . .
> Conformity is sexy and productivity rules.
> Decision-making can be so taxing;
> why not let us express your feelings?
> Everything has been designed
> for your comfort and convenience.

In these depictions, White Noise is a comfort sound, convenient in its easy availability. The flip of a switch drowns out "annoying background noise" by providing a filter that focuses the stream in a soothing way—channeling belief, value, and desire amidst the threat of chaos.

The novel *White Noise* by Don DeLillo (1986) is set in the swirl of popular media inscription of fragmented subjectivities, foregrounding the bombardment of information in a consumer economy that generates fears, resentments, pleasures, and desires, largely in the interests of capital and governmental control. In the novel, characters are presented as composites. What DeLillo says of his characters in some of his other novels, Shapiro points out, is applicable to the characters in *White Noise:* "Some of the characters have a made up nature. They are pieces of jargon. They engage in wars of jargon with each other. There is a mechanical element, a kind of fragmented self-consciousness" (DeLillo, from an interview with LeClair, 1983, quoted in Shapiro, 1992, p. 131). This jargon takes the form of "revealing linguistic fragments, which reflect the fragmented nature of modern subjectivity" (Shapiro, 1992, p. 132). The narrative structure of *White Noise* is regularly interrupted "by emissions from postindustrial, consumer culture" (Shapiro, 1992, p. 135). Such a strategy performs the noisiness of the postmodern condition, in which the prevailing economic structure has shifted from "earlier stages of [production oriented] capitalism to the modern, information/consumer stage" (Shapiro, 1992, p. 129).

Hayles (1990) applies the term "parataxis"[3] to describe the tensions produced in postmodern culture when the body—theorized as an enduring, material, inscribed surface, yet able to be written and rewritten—is juxtaposed with information—theorized as ephemeral and "rapidly transmitt[able] from one surface to another" (p. 398):

> On the one hand, there is embodiment, materiality, replication; on the other, decontextualization, ephemerality, information. When the two come together, as they do in postmodern practices, the result is an explosive mixture with implications beyond the metaphorical. (Hayles, 1990, p. 398)

According to Hayles (1990), DeLillo's *White Noise* may be read as an exploration of the "polysemous and unstable" relation between embodiment and informatics (p. 398). "Lacking a coordinating structure," she says, "[this relation] is subject to appropriation, interpretation, and reinscription into different modalities" (p. 398). For example, Jack Gladney and his colleague Murray, two characters in DeLillo's *White Noise*, discuss, "in theory," killing and violence as the affirmation of life (DeLillo, 1986, p. 290). Jack takes this conversation seriously and sets out to kill the man with whom Babette, his wife, has been having sex in exchange for Dylar, a drug supposed to eradicate the fear of death. Jack is full of wonder at how alive he feels, how different everything looks and sounds as he attempts to carry out his revenge. Hayles (1990) reads this revenge-seeking as the "recuperation of embodiment through violence" (p. 411). Violence is seen as having the potential to return the body to unmediated mortality, rescuing it from mediation—appropriation and reinscription—through information technologies.

This parataxic tension is also present in Cop Shoot Cop's *White Noise* (1991). Songs from the perspective of the placating information/consumption hawkers such as "Discount Rebellion" and "Corporate Protopop" are juxtaposed with songs from the perspective of those living in urban anger and poverty, songs such as "Traitor/Martyr," "Heads I Win, Tails You Lose," and "Feel Good." The lyrics of "Discount Rebellion" and "Corporate Protopop," in particular, address consumerism's role in inscription:

> Our survey told us what you wanted:
> Rebellion at a low, low price.
> Be an individual through our product!
> Why jeopardize your life?

You can have it any way you want it
(if you really want it).
>   *(Cop Shoot Cop, 1991, "Discount Rebellion")*

The products you buy,
the programs you watch,
your job:
these are the things that define
you as an individual.
Without them, you have no identity,
no purpose, no reason to exist.
Greed. Hatred. They're not just good ideas,
they're the precepts this country
was founded on.
They're what keep you right where you are.
And we'd like to keep it that way.
>   *(Cop Shoot Cop, 1991, "Corporate Protopop")*

The songs mentioned above, "Heads I Win, Tails You Lose" and "Feel Good," can be read as featuring violence prominently cast as an attempt to recapture embodiment in the face of informatic and commodified mediation. "Feel Good" is a particularly good example of this tension. Hellbent on some unspecified revenge, the song's protagonist celebrates a breakthrough to embodiment in repeating the phrase "feel good" in between verses detailing his "mission" with a loaded gun, in a speeding car, in the wrong lane, refusing to compromise, true to his own cause—breaking with what has written him, writing himself in the process:

No more compromising;
There's a new sun and it's rising.
On a mission. This is *my* cause.
Breaking all chains. Fuck the damn law.
I feel good! Feel GOOD! FEEL GOOD!
Goddamn, I feel alright!

Parataxic tension is a struggle set in binary terms—write or be written. It is a tension that feeds particular readings of popular media and current events, readings that map onto an epidemic climate of intelligibility, a climate characterized by the generation of fear, the capitalist diffusion of rebellion, and the consequences of both refusing and taking up particular ways of being written—all this swirling in a complex, dynamic, and rhizomatic tangle of discourse and practice.

It is these thematic and performative aspects of the white noise figuration used in the work of Brodkey, DeLillo, and Cop Shoot Cop that I hope to move toward in my telling of the data stories that emerge from this study. I gesture toward styles of representation that acknowledge the " 'noise' of multidimensionality, historical variability, and subjectivity" (McCarthy & Crichlow, 1993, p. xviii), resisting the elimination of noise, while at the same time using the strategy of looking awry (Žižek, 1992) through epidemic logic to place the noise in a "centrifuge to separate out the many layers of codes, the maze constructing [the] facticity" that makes up the fragile intelligibility of cultural difference as it manifests in preservice teachers' embodied responses to popular media (Shapiro, 1992, p. 131).

The Epidemic Atmosphere: A Climate of Intelligibility

Epidemic logic fosters a certain climate of intelligibility. Some of the conditions that make an epidemic atmosphere possible are the characterization of a situation out of control through the articulation of symptoms, the search for a cause or for someone or something to blame, and the struggle to find a cure. Another related condition is the generation of fear about this loss of control, the

> perpetual revival of an anxiety it seeks to control, inciting a crisis of contagion that spreads to ever new sectors of cultural life which, in turn, justify and necessitate specific regulatory apparatus which then compensate—materially and symbolically—for the crisis it has produced. (Singer, 1993, p. 29)

DeLillo's novel (1986) and Cop Shoot Cop's album (1991), both entitled *White Noise*, perform this perpetual revival of anxiety by illustrating the ways that contemporary, fragmented, and embodied subjectivities map onto informatics in a capitalist society, in a polysemous explosion of disembodied knowledges, creating, sustaining, and commodifying what Shapiro (1992) terms a "politics of fear" through the staticky medium of white noise (p. 122). I aspire toward a kind of performance of this atmosphere in the series of poems that follow.

The words in these poems are quoted and/or paraphrased from 16 student journals and final papers. There were 2 white men, 13 white women,[4] and 1 black woman in this group. All names are pseudonyms. I have provided explanations of where the words in the poems come from in a footnote to each one. These footnotes may be read before or after reading each poem.

We Need to Do Something![5]

murder rape stealing
>It's mostly minority kids
>the ones with no support at home
>no fathers at home
>They're the ones who end up in gangs

crime murder drugs
>Why can't we set aside our differences
>for something much larger
>like the safety of our kids
>or the growth of our nation???

murder crime drugs suicide
>If it is true
>that there will be no racial
>majority in 50 years
>and the current social climate persists
>social and cultural fragmentation
>could result in
>sobering consequences

murder steal lie rape
>Everyone is vulnerable
>No one is completely safe . . .

Even Black Women Clutch Their Purses[6]

When a black man gets into an elevator
When he drives a nice car
>we think he deals drugs

When he goes into a store
>we think he's there to steal something

When a black man commits a crime
>we see it on the front page
>it's the lead story on the evening news

When an inner-city school deals with drugs and violence
>we see it on the front page
>it's the lead story on the evening news
>>One family controls the media in this city
>>Only one newspaper in this town

Even black women clutch their purses
When a black man gets into an elevator
>They think if no one calls me "nigger"
>They think if no one burns a cross in my yard
>I have nothing to complain about

Desegregation: Vidor, Texas—Then the World [7]

January 1994. Spent about 3 million dollars
to build that housing project
All to integrate this small town
in Texas.
Put the blacks in there—first one's in since the '20s
gave them protection
gave them buses for the grocery store
gave them motorized gates
We can't let our children walk to town
We can't walk to town
There haven't been any problems
Learning to live with this arrangement
Most everyone ignored the last KKK rally
We can't let our children walk to town
We can't walk to town
Going to build these communities
all over the world to end
racial
segregation

I Believe [8]

We have become hyper-sensitized   to EVERY cry
of discrimination that is leveled   by EVERY group
imaginable.
We are faced with competing victims
each trying to gain an advantage
based on an individual's ancestry
and injustices which have occurred   in the PAST
I do not discount the impact
on the present of historical events   of the PAST
However, I do believe
that it has become a MUCH too convenient crutch
to obtain a PERCEIVED level of equality
in the here and now
I believe
there is something VALUABLE to be learned   in DEALING WITH
failure
At the very least it prepares one   for DEALING WITH
the REAL world
If you believe the days of racism are over,
you are living in some kind of box!

Minor(ity) Adjustments [9]

talk white
act white
think white
everybody has to adjust
        it's a matter of situation
        it's a matter of respect
many black people make it big
plenty of white males live in poverty

PC Shopping List [10]

Multicultural Cosmetics
Multicultural Crayola Markers
Multicultural Construction Paper
Benetton and Unity
Ethnic music
Ethnic art
Ethnic jewelry
CDs by Rush and Seal

The New Independent Modern Woman [11]

Job and family got you runnin?
        Busy?
        Tired?
You don't have to look that way—
        Be Beautiful!
Johnson & Johnson Facial Cream for the
New Independent Modern Woman
NOT!

Brought to You by Our Sponsor [12]

What are little girls made of?
What are little girls made of?
Sugar and Spice and Everything Nice.
        Days of Our Lives
        Tucks, Cenerex, Calgon
        Take me away!

What are little boys made of?
What are little boys made of?
Snips and Snails and Puppy Dog Tails.
    Super Bowl Sunday
    Bud Lite, Bikinis, Lay-Z-Boy
    Get me a beer!
He Put Her In a Pumpkin Shell
There He Kept Her Very Well
    medicated
    dedicated

What Are These Poems Doing?

Richardson (1994) argues that "[p]oetry is . . . a *practical* and *powerful* method for analyzing social worlds" (p. 522). It involves "[s]ettling words together in new configurations [that let] us hear, see, and feel the world in new dimensions" (p. 522). Richardson quotes Frost, who said that a poem "is the shortest emotional distance between two points" (1994, pp. 521–22).

When I began to assemble the data I wanted to use in this section, I was unsure of how I could evoke the climate of epidemic that surrounds the crisis of difference. The thought of laying out a linear explication of the characteristics of that climate seemed tedious and artificial. Such explications tend to squeeze out emotion and urgency when the emotion and urgency of the epidemic climate, including the currents of rational and commodified response are specifically what I wanted to convey. I think of this swirl of emotion, urgency, rationality, and commodification as white noise. In order to discuss the effectivity of these poems, I want to disperse this swirl into the categories of crisis talk, crisis generation, sequestering fear, and free-market freedom.

I read the poem "We Need to Do Something!" as representing crisis talk, talk that generates fear related to cultural difference. The refrains—e.g., "murder rape stealing" and variations thereof—point toward a kind of diffuse fear—unfocused, yet urgent in its citational frequency. This diffusion of fear is also apparent in the unfocused concerns about cultural fragmentation, difference, as dangerous, and total vulnerability. Fear gets focused, however, by the characterization of minority children as future gang members. Situated as a critique, the poem "Even Black Women Clutch Their Purses" is an example of focusing fear—crisis generation—through the process of media representation that portrays black men as criminals. There is some hint of an agency at work behind this focusing through the mention of media ownership. The final two lines are a reaction against the idea that the only kind of racism is overt behavior, suggesting that media representation is a subtler and more insidious conduit. In their study of the discourse of resentment in TV news and film, McCarthy, Rodriguez, David, Godina, Supriya, and Wilson-Brown (1994) discuss

> suburban fear of encirclement by difference . . . [in which] the dangerous inner city and the world "outside" are brought into suburban homes through television and film creating both a desire for and a fear of the images viewed on the screen. (p. 5)

Brenda, whose final project was the source for "Even Black Women Clutch Their Purses," recognizes this desire: "People like to see drug busts and violence; but it is upsetting to a lot of whites to see the white criminals instead of white victims." Her recognition is borne out by the popularity of "true crime" shows such as *Cops*, in which the perpetrators of crime are overwhelmingly "minority" men. Jack Gladney in DeLillo's (1986) *White Noise* remarks: "Every disaster made us wish for more, for something bigger, grander, more sweeping" (p. 64). Shapiro (1992) suggests that danger is mediated through representation creating people who become "consumers of representations" (p. 128) of fear in order to "focus their fears effectively" (p. 128).

The poem "Desegregation: Vidor, Texas—Then the World" might be thought of as example of sequestering fear. The irony of racial containment in the name of racial integration speaks volumes about what Shapiro (1992) terms "sequestering . . . rather than confronting" fear. Glimpses of fear, however, leak out in the lines in italics about walking to town. I did not indicate whether it was the whites already living in Vidor who spoke those words or whether it was the black families behind the gates. I am not sure it matters.

I place both "I Believe" and "Minor(ity) Adjustments" under the category of free-market freedom. Both speak from positions of white privilege in which conformity to white norms means a cultural currency that buys freedom, with the attending merit, in a system imagined to reward situational appropriateness according to such norms. In different ways, the poems "PC Shopping List," "The New Independent Modern Woman," and "Brought to You by Our Sponsor" are also part of the free-market freedom category. "PC Shopping List" speaks to the commodification of difference in consumer products (which might also be thought of as a kind of sequestering of the fear of difference). Both "The New Independent Modern Woman" and "Brought to You by Our Sponsor" suggest consumer solutions to pathological gender inscription. The crisis facing women who juggle both family and career responsibility is medicalized and commodified. Apple (1993) argues:

> The citizen as "free" consumer has replaced the previously emerging citizen as situated in structurally generated relations of domination. Thus, the common good is now to be regulated exclusively by the laws of the market, free competition, private ownership, and profitability. In essence, the definitions of freedom and equality are no longer democratic, but *commercial*.[13] (p. 34)

I'd like to end this section with the following passage from DeLillo's (1986) *White Noise*, which pulls together issues of fear and commodification in a telling analysis of epidemic climate:

> Denise said the sun was a risk to a fair-skinned person. Her mother claimed the whole business was publicity for disease.
> "It's all a corporate tie-in," Babette said in summary, "The sunscreen, the marketing, the fear, the disease. You can't have one without the other." (p. 264)

From Student Resistance to Climate of Intelligibility: Pedagogical Implications

Cultural criticism, which ventures into the realm of representation, opens up the study of cultural difference to analytics that do not rely wholly on "the commitment to rationality" nor on "rational persuasion" (Britzman, Santiago-Válles, Jiménez-Múñoz, & Lamash, 1993, p. 197). Inquiry and pedagogy that focus on the "aesthetics and rhetorics" (Ellsworth, 1993, p. 202) and the "politics and poetics" (Britzman, et al., 1993, p. 189) of representation move cultural criticism in a direction that acknowledges the "'noise' of multidimensionality, historical variability, and subjectivity" (McCarthy & Crichlow, 1993, p. xviii). Attention to this "noise" allows for critique of hegemonic discourses that moves beyond analyses of logical or rational persuasion (*logos*) into the realm of emotional persuasion (*pathos*) and ethical appeal (*ethos*). Inquiry into the aesthetics of representation admits interrogation of embodied pleasure and desire that accompany the taking up of popular discourses (Eagleton, 1990), a perspective that takes into account human agency, rather than assuming a completely determined, falsely conscious subject. Such a configuration of analytics admits to the fluidity and polyvocality of discursive formations, providing avenues for analysis of power relations. Thus, the pedagogical move toward addressing the intelligibility of dominant and counterhegemonic discourses repositions students. Instead of characterizing them as irrational resistors, it admits emotionally charged engagement with explosive issues and takes into account that

> most students have been educated in contexts that do not address how social difference is fashioned by relations of power and how relations of power govern the self. Most have not had sanctioned opportunities to discuss subjects like feminism, gay and lesbian rights, anti-racist conduct, or what it means to construct one's own racial, sexual, and gendered identity. (Britzman, 1993, p. 9)

The absence of these kinds of opportunities make it difficult for students to hear what Brodkey (1995) calls "lyrics spoken in unfamiliar cadences." In other words, challenges to naturalized and commonsense discourses on difference are often not intelligible to students. In contrast to Brodkey, however, my pedagogical and analytic aims are not geared toward "reduc[ing] the volume of White Noise for those who cannot hear for the din of common sense" (Brodkey, 1995). Instead, my efforts have been focused toward foregrounding the noise, tracking and denaturalizing the climate of intelligibility, opening it up to interrogation. Pedagogical attention to issues of representation and intelligibility, then, has the potential to open up opportunities for critique that might otherwise be shut down when students' struggles are pathologized as irrational and resistant. Instead, students might be positioned as capable of interpreting and theorizing how a climate of intelligibility makes possible certain ways of thinking and acting—while it shuts down others, capable of reimagining how they might respond to the challenges of teaching within that climate. There are no prescriptions for such an endeavor: "We must begin *wherever we are*" (Derrida, 1976, p. 162) in experimental modes that defy our attachments to "tidy and efficient moments of learning" (Britzman et al., 1993, p. 195).

Notes

1. The other two data displays are entitled "Communication as Communicability or Performing Intelligibility" and "Articulable Cures and Discourse Breakdown." In a fairly conventional qualitative data display, the former explores how the students in my study performed the mobilization of sedimented, normalized discourses and what strategies were intelligible to them as they performed media analyses. The latter data display was re-presented in a two-column format that juxtaposed the "cures" students articulated most consistently with statements that interrupted the intelligibility of these cures.

2. "A figuration is not a graceful metaphor that provides coherency and unity to contradiction and disjunction" (St.Pierre, 1997, p. 280). Instead, it is more a

tool to be used in the "practice of failure" (Visweswaran, 1994, p. 99), the failure of linguistic and conceptual means of "fixing" reality. The use of white noise as a figuration in this paper provided a way to do "co-reading," to read data through something resembling more a prism than a lens, to employ a "splitting analytics," (McCoy, 1997, pp. 497–98), to "un-fix" that which is imagined as stable, to recognize and hone in on its leaky and contradictory spaces. See Elizabeth St.Pierre (1997), "An Introduction to Figurations—A Poststructural Practice of Inquiry," for a more thorough explanation of figurations and their uses.

3. Although Hayles does not mention the ancient Greek use of the term *parataxis*, I think it's worth noting here. Parataxis refers to a mode of argument and analysis characterized by the simple juxtaposition of ideas associated with preliterate orality. This mode is compared with a later development associated with literacy, a mode of expression called *hypotaxis*, the subordination of one idea to another in logical hierarchies. Parataxis is considered the lesser sophisticated of the two, subject to emotion and irrational appeals to authority, whereas hypotaxis makes use of the "higher" faculties of reason and the disinterested criticism of ideas (see Havelock, 1982). Hayles's (1990) point is that postmodern existence is parataxic in that it lacks stable and hierarchical coordinating structures between embodiment and informatics. Although it is beyond the scope of this paper to explore, I think that a parataxic analytic mode is an interesting way of thinking about recent movements in cultural criticism (see Žižek 1992, for example).

4. The anonymous demographic data I collected indicate that one woman in the class was Asian-American, but since I did not ask students to put their names on the demographic questionnaires and no one in my class "looked" Asian-American, I do not know if that student is part of this group.

5. The title comes from one of Michaela's journal entries, as does the refrain. The refrain is composed of four lines excerpted from four separate sentences in this entry. She was reflecting on the power of song lyrics to influence young people. The last two lines are from this journal entry as well. She is talking about AIDS here but in a very interesting juxtaposition with her lists of crimes. The first inset stanza is from one of Linda's journal entries. She is responding to an interview with Snoop Doggy Dogg. According to Linda, the rap artist helps her understand "why kids turn to the streets." The second inset stanza is from one of Randy's journal entries. He wonders this after attending a David Sanborn concert, which he describes as a harmonious multicultural event. The third inset stanza comes from one of Mike's journals. He is reflecting on a newspaper editorial by Joan Beck, in which she asserts that "we are preoccupied with ethnic diversity/multiculturalism" (quoted in Mike's journal without complete reference to the source).

6. I constructed this poem from excerpts of Brenda's final paper, in which she analyzes media construction of black males. The last three lines are paraphrased from one of her journals. She is reflecting on a situation in class when a white

male classmate complained that poor white males are harassed by police too. We had been discussing a newspaper article that someone brought in that talked about young black males being harassed by police.

7. I constructed this poem from a journal entry in which Trina reflects on a TV news broadcast on Vidor, Texas. She thinks it is good that integration is happening in such a positive manner. In her journal entry, she does not indicate just who built and who paid for this project. I remember flipping through channels and running across, if not this very story, then one quite like it. An architectural firm was hired by a city to create "secure neighborhoods." I remember these neighborhoods as being pretty much white and walled off in similar ways from other "communities." There were motorized gates, but no mention of buses that I remember. The show I saw almost looked like a paid "info-mercial," like the kind one might see for Hair Replacement Technologies.

8. This poem is constructed from excerpts out of two of Mike's journals. The first two sections come from his reflections on an editorial by Joan Beck, in which she asserts, "We are preoccupied with ethnic diversity/multiculturalism" (quoted in Mike's journal without complete reference to the source). The last section comes from his reflections on an editorial by William Raspberry on the success of a program for black students that sets high expectations instead of presuming a deficit model (quoted in Mike's journal without complete reference to the source). These last two lines come from one of Susan's journals. She is incredulous about a quote from one of our readings in which someone said they believed racism was a thing of the past.

9. This poem is constructed from excerpts of one of Trina's journals. She is reflecting on a small-group discussion in class. She notes that in the course of this discussion it was "insinuated" that the only people who lived in inner-city poverty were black. She also notes that someone in her group mentioned "that black people have to change their tones to the white people in order to succeed" and went on to say that "blacks can't talk to us the way they talk to their friends."

10. The first line comes from Anna and Karen, who reflect in their journals on an article that talks about Iman's line of cosmetics for women of color. Anna thinks that this article is good because it shows that a woman from "another culture" can be successful and that she not only thought about her own culture, but others' cultures too. Karen thinks that if "producers" stop catering solely to the white race, then perhaps "consumers" will change their attitudes toward different races. The next three items are from Susan's journals. She appreciates the Benetton ads for promoting unity across differences yet seems to speak with skepticism about the markers and construction paper, noting that she now thinks twice before she buys what the media tries to sell her. The next three items come from Lisa's journal in which she talks about the WOMAD Festival (World of Music Arts and Dance). She believes that such gatherings and the products sold at them are helping to build bridges across cultures. She adds this hesitation: "Why people are so accepting of other cultures' music and art (jewelry) and not

always of that culture's people is a good question. It could be that the 'mainstream' or 'normal' look at music and jewelry as status symbols." The final items come from one of Randy's journal entries. As he inspects his music collection, he finds that U.S. recording artists put out more racist messages than Canadian, British, and South American recording artists do. He mentions Rush (a Canadian group) and Seal (a South American artist) by name.

11. I constructed this poem disguised as advertising copy from excerpts of one of Sandy's journals in which she analyzes gender issues and advertising. She says: "The first underlining message that this ad sends us is that women should be worker and housewife, busy and tired. . . . The second message is that women, above everything, must look good."

12. The Mother Goose lines in this poem are from one of Betsy's journals. The power of nursery rhymes to shape gender roles in children was brought home to her one day as she watched children act out the rhymes on the playground at a preschool where she works. The product names and TV references come from an analysis by Michaela and Mandy of target marketing in TV programming.

13. On this last point regarding the commercialization of freedom and equality, Apple cites Stuart Hall (1986).

References

Apple, M. (1993). Between moral regulation and democracy: The cultural contradictions of the text. In C. Lankshear & P. McLaren (Eds.), *Critical literacy: Politics, praxis, and the postmodern* (pp. 193–216). Albany: State University of New York Press.

Barthes, R. (1972). *Mythologies* (A. Lavers, Trans.). New York: The Noonday Press.

Britzman, D. P. (1993). Beyond rolling models: Gender and multicultural education. In S. K. Biklin & D. Pollard (Eds.), *Gender and education: Ninety-second yearbook for the National Society for the Study of Education* (pp. 25–42). Chicago: University of Chicago Press.

Britzman, D. P., Santiago-Válles, K., Jiménez-Múñoz, G., & Lamash, L. M. (1993). Slips that show and tell: Fashioning multiculture as a problem of representation. In C. McCarthy & W. Crichlow (Eds.), *Race, identity, and representation in education* (pp. 188–200). New York: Routledge.

Brodkey, L. (1995, January). *Difference and a pedagogy of difference*. Paper presented at The Ohio State University, English Department Lecture series in Rhetoric and Composition, Columbus.

Butler, J. (1993). *Bodies that matter: On the discursive limits of "sex."* New York: Routledge.

Cop Shoot Cop. (1991). *White noise* [audio recording]. New York: Cat & Mouse Music.

DeLillo, D. (1986). *White noise*. New York: Penguin Books.

Derrida, J. (1976). *Of grammatology* (G. C. Spivak, Trans.). Baltimore: Johns Hopkins University Press.

Eagleton, T. (1990). *The ideology of the aesthetic.* Cambridge, MA: Basil Blackwell.

Ellsworth, E. (1993). I pledge allegiance: The politics of reading and using educational films. In C. McCarthy & W. Crichlow (Eds.), *Race, identity, and representation in education* (pp. 201–19). New York: Routledge.

Foucault, M. (1984). Nietzsche, genealogy, history. In P. Rabinow (Ed.), *The Foucault reader* (pp. 76–100). New York: Pantheon Books.

Garcia, J., & Pugh, S. (1995). Multicultural education in teacher education programs: A political or an educational concept. In F. Schultz (Ed.), *Annual editions: Multicultural education, 1994/1995* (pp. 36–40). Guilford, CT: Dushkin Publishing Group.

Hall, S. (1986). Popular culture and the state. In T. Bennet, C. Mercer, & J. Wollacoot (Eds.), *Popular culture and social relations* (pp. 22–49). Milton Keynes, UK: Open University Press.

Havelock, E. (1982). *The literate revolution in Greece and its cultural consequences.* Princeton, NJ: Princeton University Press.

Hayles, N. K. (1990). Postmodern parataxis: Embodied texts, weightless information. *American Literary History, 2*(3), 394–421.

Katz, M. (1971). *Class, bureaucracy, and schools.* New York: Praeger.

LeClair, T. (1983). An interview with Don DeLillo. In T. LeClair & L McCaffery (Eds.), *Anything can happen: Interviews with contemporary American novelists* (pp. 81–83). Urbana: University of Illinois Press.

McCarthy, C., & Crichlow, W. (Ed.). (1993). *Race, identity, and representation in education.* New York: Routledge.

McCarthy, C., Rodriguez, A., David, S., Godina, H., Supriya, K. E., & Wilson-Brown, C. (1994, April). *Danger in the safety zone: Notes on race, resentment, and the discourse of crime, violence, and suburban security.* Paper presented at the American Educational Research Association annual meeting, New Orleans, LA.

McCoy, K. (1997). Killing the father/becoming uncomfortable with the mother tongue: Rethinking the performative contradiction. *Educational Theory, 47*(4), 489–500.

Perkinson, H. (1991). *The imperfect panacea: American faith in education, 1865–1990* (2d ed.). New York: McGraw-Hill.

Richardson, L. (1994). Writing: A method of inquiry. In N. Denzin & Y. Lincoln (Eds.), *Handbook of qualitative research* (pp. 516–29). Newbury Park, CA: Sage.

Robenstine, C. (1995). The illusion of education reform: The educational system and at-risk students. In F. Schultz (Ed.), *Annual editions: Multicultural education 1994/1995* (pp. 73–81). Guilford, CT: Dushkin Publishing Group.

Shapiro, M. (1992). *Reading the postmodern polity: Political theory as textual practice.* Minneapolis: University of Minnesota Press.

Schultz, F. (Ed.). (1995). *Annual editions: Multicultural education, 1994/1995.* Guilford, CT: Dushkin Publishing Group.

Singer, L. (1993). *Erotic welfare: Sexual theory and politics in the age of epidemic.* New York: Routledge.

St.Pierre, E. A. (1997). An introduction to figurations—a poststructural practice of inquiry. *International Journal of Qualitative Studies in Education, 10*(3), 279–84.

Tyack, D. (1990). "Restructuring" in historical perspective: Tinkering toward Utopia. *Teachers College Record, 92*(2), 170–91.

Visweswaran, K. (1994). *Fictions of feminist ethnography.* Minneapolis: University of Minnesota Press

Žižek, S. (1992). *Looking awry.* Cambridge, MA: MIT Press.

Chapter 13

Nomadic Inquiry
in the Smooth
Spaces of the Field:
A Preface

Elizabeth A. St.Pierre

The problem of this essay is that I need to do some fieldwork but don't know where to go. For quite some time now I have been stalled in an ethnography—stopped, stuck, dead in the water. And since I am convinced that the technology called the essay can take me places I have been unable to imagine, I have decided to attempt a nomadic journey, to, in fact, travel in the thinking that writing produces in search of the field.[1] Nomadic inquiry[2] is quite appropriate for an armchair ethnographer unsure of her destination. Deleuze and Guattari (1980/1987) explain that nomads are not defined by movement as is commonly thought since they do not inhabit and hold space: "Of course, the nomad moves, but while seated, and he is only seated while moving [think of] (the Bedouin galloping, knees on the saddle, sitting on the soles of his upturned feet, 'a feat of balance')" (p. 381). Like the nomad, I intend to travel while seated, and this particular writing excursion commences with the story of an ethnography (St.Pierre, 1995) I began several years ago in Milton, a small town in Essex County[3] where I grew up, a deliciously beautiful and fertile portion of the southern Piedmont.

My project was designed to be a combination of an interview study with a group of older, white southern women who live in Essex County and an ethnography of that rural community where my family still lives. As I have grown older, I have become increasingly interested in how women construct their subjectivities within the limits and possibilities of the discourses and cultural practices that are available to them. I have also become intrigued with Foucault's (1984, 1985/1984, 1986/1984) ethical analysis, care of the self, that focuses on the arts of existence, or technologies of the self, that people use to create themselves as the ethical subjects of their actions. Since it was the older women of Essex

County who taught me how to be a woman, I believe that their practices of the self have sedimented out in my own subjectivity. I study them and their community because I am curious about who they are now in the last years of their lives (Who will I be?) and about what they have done and continue to do every day that makes them who they are (Do I still do those things and, if so, do I want to continue to do them?). My question for the rest of my life is what "small supplies of significance and subjectification" (Deleuze & Guattari, 1987/1980, p. 160) must I keep as I continue, journey proud, until the end? What part of myself must I maintain in order to subvert myself?

Thus, my research is not motivated by the desire to produce knowledge for knowledge's sake. I urgently need to hear what these women tell me about thinking and doing; in fact, during our interviews 2 years ago, I often sat on the edge of my chair waiting for their responses to my questions. And even though I left Milton and Essex County 20 years before the study began, I have learned that I am much attached to the place itself, to the land, which I now understand will always serve as the literal "ground of my consciousness" (Conway, 1989, p. 198), the mental and physical map against which all other places collide. "Some are born in their place, some find it, some realize after long searching that the place they left is the one they have been searching for" (Stegner, 1992, p. 201). What is the meaning of our attachment to certain places; why do we return to them over and over again? Why do I need to do fieldwork in this particular place, in Essex County?

Welty (1956) writes that we attach ourselves to places because they have a more lasting identity than we do and that "we unswervingly tend to attach ourselves to identity" (p. 59). De Certeau (1984) writes:

> places are fragmentary and inward-turning histories, pasts that others are not allowed to read, accumulated times that can be unfolded but like stories held in reserve, remaining in an enigmatic state, symbolizations encysted in the pain or pleasure of the body. (p. 108)

An examination of our attachment to places, our histories, is not done "for safety's sake" (Welty, 1956, p. 70). On the contrary, as Welty (1956) reports, it is a risky business, but "no art ever came out of not risking your neck. And risk—experiment—is a considerable part of the joy of doing" (p. 70). An attachment to a place then—a particular and fleeting convergence of ideological, cultural, historical, and emotional relays—does not necessarily produce permanence or peace, for even the materiality of a place may shift. Familiar and beloved landscapes—woods, beaches, hilltops—may be altered by flood or hurricane or earthquake, since, as Deleuze and Guattari (1987/1980) explain, "the earth itself asserts its own powers of deterritorialization, its lines of flight, its smooth spaces that live and blaze their way for a new earth" (p. 423). The possibilities of that "new earth," that different place, can only be imagined from a particular location and requires risking the loss of the positivities that have coalesced and rooted themselves there.

The point here about attachment to places, and our histories in them, is that home is not a haven; identity can never be a refuge. A consolation derived from an authentic, stable essence is no more possible in places than in subjectivities. Both are performances accomplished within relations, and both, for the sake of ethics, require persistent critique. The purpose, then, of fieldwork in our "growing-up places" (Pratt, 1984, p. 17), places like Essex County, as well as in the field of a text such as this one, is to confront the constraining framework of one's past and thereby "to learn to what extent the effort to think one's own history can free thought from what it silently thinks, and so enable it to think differently" (Foucault, 1985/1984, p. 9). As one's past becomes a place (Dainotto, 1996, p. 496), it is no longer an absent, out-of-date, or empty space (Serres & Latour, 1995/1990, p. 48) but a very present, up-to-date, and busy site of agency, a productive location from which to practice Butler's (1995/1994) "subversive citation"[4] (p. 135), Pratt's (1984) "negative self-identity" (p. 46), and Spivak's (1993) "deidentification" (p. 6).

With Welty (1956), I believe that "it is by knowing where you stand that you are able to judge where you are" (p. 67) and then, perhaps, think of where you might rather be. Braidotti (1994a), along the same lines, writes that, since "identity is retrospective" (p. 35), one must be placed for a time in order to remap one's cartography. The construction and subversion of identity that Butler, Pratt, Spivak, and Braidotti describe, however, is hardly ever deliberate or intentional; rather, it most often seems accidental and even capricious. It is the outside that folds us into identity, and we can never control the forces of the outside. I believe the forces in certain places provides especially fertile conditions, exquisitely dynamic intensities, that make us "available to a transformation of who we are, a contestation which compels us to rethink ourselves, a reconfiguration of our 'place' and our 'ground'" (Butler, 1995/1994, p. 131). If we wish to practice identity improvisation, attention to places may be required.

For this reason, I constantly return to my continuing history in that place in fragile, fleeting junkets no matter where my feet are rooted; but when my feet do land on the red clay of Essex County, my body pauses, settles, and readies itself for another motionless voyage that always seems to involve painful desubjectification, joyful disarticulation. Stewart's (1989) words about fieldwork could be mine:

For myself, fieldwork was not to be an encounter with any primitive, or yet again, even foreigners. The "other" in my field was
heavily constituted out of a tension between my own memory of
an earlier time, and the recognizable changes of my return: out of
the memory of how I used to be, and the inadequacy of my new
cultural reflexes. (p. 15)[5]

This risky business, "homework" (Visweswaran, 1994, p. 101), the disturbance of the saturation of identity in places, may create an overflow
that produces those tiny explosions of the self that refuse to repeat the
same I—great, shattering revolutions, in fact.

As a result, I refuse to valorize homelessness, "a certain placelessness"
(Visweswaran, 1994, p. 111) or "being a citizen of the world" (Braidotti,
1994a, p. 21), over home, thereby "mythologizing exile" (Quinby, 1991,
p. 148), since that practice sounds too much like Haraway's (1988) "god
tricks promising vision from everywhere and nowhere equally and fully"
(p. 584). I also object, with Ann Game (1991), to those who confound
the desire for a place with the nostalgic search for origins. Like
Visweswaran (1994), I see "home as the site of theory" (p. 111). Like
Game (1991), I am interested in the "practices of space" (p. 148), the
"practices a place makes possible, or closes off" (Game, 1991, p. 183). So
I go home to do my homework, to practice fieldwork and head work
(Van Maanen, 1995) and identity work.

Nor have I neglected my text work about Essex County. I have written and written about my research there in a dissertation (St.Pierre,
1995), but the writing was not happy. I mourned as the dissertation
became a palimpsest that relentlessly overwrote the very different book
I had been writing in my head about the women of Essex County. Text
intruded upon text in rude and raucous ways. And unlike this essay that
I am already thinking of as a joyful and playful rhizome,[6] that very long
essay employed an arborescent, circular architecture (Foucault,
1979/1975, Deleuze & Guattari, 1987/1980) and lumbered along under
a fairly benign disciplinary gaze dutifully tracking the prescribed grid. I
did resist. First, I found I could not write a proper introduction to the dissertation since I could find no beginning to describe; later, I resisted writing an ending, since I did not know how to end something that had had
no beginning.

I was not surprised by my inability to perform a conclusion, for I had
not yet finished. Indeed, I wondered whether I could ever finish. I felt
trapped in the clarity of the simple tenses edging the path I was expected
to trace, a straight path from beginning to end, when I suspected that it
was the incomprehensible future anterior[7] in which I often worked. I felt
trapped by the "careless habits of accuracy" (Kermode, 1966, p. 43) of

the overdetermined plotting I was expected to reproduce, an accuracy that focuses on the facile comfort of a beginning and an end and slips carelessly over the spectacular trajectories in the middle[8] that demand our most rigorous attention. Why would I ever want to end?

Another reason for my failure to conclude was then and remains a problem many feminist ethnographers confront (Behar, 1995; Gordon, 1995; Mascia-Lees, Sharpe, & Cohen, 1989; Stacey, 1988; Strathern, 1987; Visweswaran, 1994) and has to do with the "burden of authorship" (Geertz, 1988, p. 138) that becomes heavier once we admit that we are not only inventing but then "speaking for others" (Alcoff, 1991, p. 5) in our descriptions. The dilemma this burden produces is "finding somewhere to stand in a text that is supposed to be at one and the same time an intimate view and a cool assessment" (Geertz, 1988, p. 10). Abiding by that inside/outside binary is bound to produce failure. How do we, rather, escape that binary to negotiate in praxis and represent in text the never-ending contradictions that stymie, the looping folds that shift us into some different pause from which we try to make a more tentative sense, or the last interpretation that is always presumptuous and often violent?

Complications such as these have contributed to my failure to end, and, since I am so anxious to return to the field to think some more and then write a different text, I have troubled these problems in mental spaces and am now trying to write my way into them in this textual space. However, poised on the edge of the field in this preface, I have discovered another complication as well—it's not just that I don't know where the field is, I don't know *when* it is either. My study has been peculiar in many ways, but perhaps most unsettling (at first, but not now) has been my inability to separate space and time; after all, I have been studying this community since I moved to the South from Yankee country as a child of 5. I have not been able to separate unofficial data that I collected all my life about these women and their community from data collected during the official course of my research project.

Nor am I able to stop thinking about what this community, my home-place, will be like when my subjects are gone, for I am now collecting obituary data. My mother, who still lives in this community, sends me narrow columns of insufficient words, skinny life histories, announcing the deaths of my participants, my friends. I add a death date to the top of a file folder, I reread an interview transcript (I dare not listen to the tape), and I think about the empty place on the pew at the Baptist church, the empty place at the women's lunch table at the Holiday Inn, the empty house the children have sorted through, and I wonder where all that intensity has gone. I mourn and envision a community empty of these women, a very different place. I find I have far too many "memor[ies] of the future" (Deleuze, 1988/1986, p. 107). As Derrida

(1996) writes, it is "the undeniable anticipation of mourning that constitutes friendship. It reveals the truth of its topology and tropology" (p.
188). I do fieldwork in mourning and in the anticipation of mourning,
and the data from my work in that field-to-come surely feed all my
inscriptions.

So a tremulous simultaneity of pasts and presents and futures that will
have been have produced a different ontological status for this ethnographer, a position that has kept her plunging through time at breakneck
speed, so that a place, the field, has simply become a pause in time (Tuan,
1977, p. 161), some time, any time. The ethnographic present, a welcome simulacra, has become a time to catch my breath and rest a bit
before the bottom drops out of the field again. If ethnography depends
not just on methodology but also on "being there" (Geertz, 1988, p. 1),
on "spatial practices" (Clifford, 1988, p. 13; Clifford, 1992, p. 97), what
and when is "there"?

I have begun to suspect that this morass of confusion about time and
place and beginnings and endings, this "cognitive failure" (Spivak, cited
in Visweswaran, 1994, p. 98), is a signpost to some unexplored field of
ethnography, one of those fields of red clay just down the road a piece
that I can never find because of poor directions. I am beginning to understand that I will have to give up on asking directions, take some risks,
and use the "practice of failure" (Lather, 1996, p. 3) enabled by nomadic
inquiry to transform "impossibility into possibility where a failed account
occasions new kinds of positionings" (Lather, 1996, p. 3). To find that
new position in some field of ethnography to which I have not yet trav-
eled is my desire.

Convinced that I will need all the help I can get on this expedition, I
have latched onto an image described by Deleuze and Guattari
(1987/1980),[9] that of a nomad deterritorializing striated space, space that
has been carefully and conscientiously timed and placed. Deleuze and
Guattari (1987/1980, see pp. 352–53, pp. 474–500) differentiate
between "striated space" and "smooth space."[10] They explain that striated space is sedentary space, space that is coded, defined, bounded, and
limited. Think of the spaces of the game of chess and the chess pieces
themselves that are defined by a coded interiority. Chess pieces are like
subjects who have an intrinsic agency, and their movement in space is
defined in advance. The relationship between chess pieces and space is
thus structural and, as Deleuze and Guattari (1987/1980) say, the point
of the game of chess is a "question of arranging a closed space for oneself" (p. 353), an impenetrable space.

On the other hand, think of the smooth nomad space of the game of
Go. Go pieces have no intrinsic properties, only situational ones. They
are anonymous, collective, and nonsubjective with no inherent agency.

They have no coded interiority, only a milieu of exteriority, and rather than moving from one closed space to another, they array themselves in an open space and may spring up anywhere on the board at any time. Their movement is "perpetual, without aim or destination, without departure or arrival" (Deleuze & Guattari, 1987/1980, p. 353). They know no closed space.

Thus, chess pieces code and decode striated space; they regulate space, define points within it, and ascribe traits to it, whereas Go pieces territorialize and then deterritorialize space without ascribing it features or locking it into binding patterns. Smooth space and striated space do not exist in opposition but in mixture: "smooth space is constantly being translated, transversed into a striated space; striated space is constantly being reversed, returned to a smooth space" (Deleuze & Guattari, 1987/1980, p. 474). It is important to remember, however, that

> smooth spaces are not in themselves liberatory. But the struggle is changed or displaced in them, and life reconstitutes its stakes, confronts new obstacles, invents new paces, switches adversaries. Never believe that a smooth space will suffice to save us. (Deleuze & Guattari, 1987/1980, p. 500)

Still, smooth space "always possesses a greater power of deterritorialization than the striated" (Deleuze & Guattari, 1987/1980, p. 480). A smooth space (like the desert, the steppe, the sea, the air) "gnaws, and tends to grow, in all directions" (Deleuze & Guattari, 1987/1980, p. 382). And nomads, who are like Go pieces, settle in smooth spaces. The nomad's relation to the earth is deterritorialization to such a degree that the "nomad reterritorializes on deterritorialization itself" (Deleuze & Guattari, 1987/1980, p. 381).

How might this figuration of the nomad deterritorializing striated space inform ethnography, which, of course, is all about inscribing some space, some place, some field? A nomadic ethnographer[11] might, for instance, appear in one local space and then another without defining transitions and paths to connect those points into a fiercely ordered grid of striations. A nomadic ethnographer speeding within connections and conduits and multiplicities might gnaw a smooth space to extend her territory (the field grows). She might indulge in the "transformations, deformations, passages to the limit" (Deleuze & Guattari, 1987/1980, p. 362) produced by the itineration of problematics, rather than settle for the iteration of theorematics. She might be more interested in the surprising intensity of an event than in the familiar serenity of essence. If she has been stalled for quite a while in the heavy, cloying sedimentation that has shored up ethnography, she might be rather desperate for an image like that of the nomad deterritorializing striated space to get her unstuck so that she can do more fieldwork.[12]

How to begin this journey of writing beyond an ending that failed (Behar, 1995), of unlearning the old ethnography (Spivak, 1993), that enabling aporia that more often than not signals a "project that may no longer be attempted, or at least not on the same terms" (Visweswaran, 1994, p. 100)? In this preface to more fieldwork, I have chosen to get myself unstuck by writing and thinking once more about some of the places and spaces in which I have already worked. It's time to get specific about where I've been so that I can think of where to go next, for, as Van Maanen (1995) explains about the state of ethnography in a postfoundational world, "With no fixed, natural, objective, or universal criteria to guide ethnography up to the mountain top, there is no alternative but to get down to the specific studies that make up the field(s) and acknowledge that ethnographic values, criteria, and perspectives spring from the specific interests and histories of ethnographic writers" (p. 31). I hope this rhizomatic rendering of the smooth spaces of my research will produce a fruitful "line of flight"[13] for this nomadic ethnographer who finds mucking around in the field about as exciting as it gets—confusing, nerve-wracking, even terrifying, but thrilling nonetheless.

■■■

Aside: I thought about writing an elaborate arrival trope here to announce the beginning of this return to the field, but, as I said before, nomadic ethnographers travel "without departure or arrival" (Deleuze & Guattari, 1980/1987, p. 353). Like Go pieces, they are unpredictable and are likely to spring up anywhere. (A touch of that old "rough and ready" quality that early ethnographers espoused may, in fact, be called for.)

At any rate, I doubt that I will be able to maintain the kind of order such tropes represent during this adventure. I can't even write that helpful paragraph that you expect in an essay and may have been impatient to read, the one that points the way through the text that is to come by explaining that I will first discuss this and then that and then the other. I have no idea where I am going, except that I am moving toward the outside. The "outside is not another site, but rather an off-site that erodes and dissolves all other sites . . . the outside is never exhausted; every attempt to capture it generates an excess or supplement, which in turn feeds anew the flows of deterritorialization and releases new lines of flight" (Boundas, 1994, pp. 114–15). In that offsite, I intend to grab hold of some of those dazzling, dizzying lines of flight and see where they take me. So we will just have to see what happens. I may have to write harder, and you may have to read harder. I hope that you don't mind too much.

■■■

Stopover—a Smooth Mental Space

In my reading of late, I have observed that many posthumanist writers invoke what Lefebvre (1991/1974) calls an extra-ideological "mental space" (p. 6). In the philosophy of humanism, space has generally been thought of as an "empty area" (Lefebvre, 1991/1974, p. 1), an area that is "in opposition to the doctrine of categories" (Lefebvre, 1991/1974, p. 3). We use this notion of mental space as we theorize about "literary space, ideological spaces, the space of the dream, psychoanalytic topologies, and so on and so forth" (Lefebvre, 1991/1974, p. 3). We read much about a space between this and that, the space of the unthought, the gaps in which such and such might occur, the interstices between two overcoded concepts. It seems we "cannot not want" (Spivak, 1993, p. 46) this smooth mental space where, as Holland (1991) writes, "anything could happen to anyone because nothing yet has and no one is there. . . . Nothing has taken place but the place" (p. 61).

Is this the "transparent space" (Blunt & Rose, 1994, p. 5) outside language, ideology, and cultural practice that we long for? If what "we cannot imagine stands guard over everything we must/can do, think, live" (Spivak, 1993, p. 22), is this uncoded space the space of rigorous imagination, the space of the unintelligible unthought, the space we must move into if we are to deterritorialize the "grid of spatial practices" (Harvey, 1989, p. 227) produced by the *logos*? Is such a free, natural, uninscribed, and empty space possible?

I fear that this space is always already inscribed by what it is possible to imagine and that once we imagine the possibility of this space, we fix it, locate something within it, if only our desire for freedom. How can we escape the "politics of space" (Harvey, 1989, p. 257), the inevitable striation of mapping? As Deleuze and Guattari (1987/1980) remind us, liberation is impossible even in smooth space; but within it we might at least find different fluxes and trajectories and the possibility of further deterritorialization. So we continue to talk about those gaps and interstices and intervals, the smooth spaces we need to rupture the sovereignty of metaphysics.

I, for one, will not give up on the possibility of such mental spaces nor on the practices of deterritorialization that might produce them. With Bachelard (1994/1958), I like to think of this mental space as "*felicitous space*" (p. xxxv), intimate space, since "space that has been seized upon by the imagination cannot remain indifferent space . . . it has been lived in, not in its positivity, but with all the partiality of the imagination" (Bachelard, 1958/1994, p. xxxvi). This mental space cannot be absent or present but is both at once and neither. It seems barely possible but then impossibly obvious. It is an affirmative, joyous space, perhaps the most thrilling of all the fields in which we work.

I surely sought this smooth mental space in my own work several years ago. I often found myself moving into it as I took my early morning walks down littered sidewalks, priming my body and mind for the day's writing; or when I wrote myself into some new understanding, watching words appear on the computer screen that I did not quite understand but knew I must stick with and worry about; or, when in conversation with friends about some trying dilemma, I heard myself speak an answer I had never thought of; or when I gave up on thinking entirely and went outside to kneel and work among my flowers on the longest, hottest summer afternoons.

I do not understand how this happens. I do not understand how to find this smooth mental space except to give it up, to let it go. It seems entirely accidental. I have certainly found it by writing and talking, but I have also come upon it within some physical activity, within the distraction of some mundane, physical chore; and, in the doing then, I am able to "to produce space" (Lefebvre, 1991/1974, p. 73), to explode data (St.Pierre, 1997), to disrupt the field. I have called this phenomenon the "physicality of theorizing" (St.Pierre, 1997) but expect that the "physicality of problematics" is more apt. Tackling problematics may require a tumultuous flurry of molecular intensities within the vortex of the movement and mixture of mind *and* body. The temptation to maintain the mind/body dualism and privilege mind over body may prevent us from understanding that action of all kinds might be required in deterritorialization.

I did work in this smooth mental space. I found it occasionally if only momentarily, and I would like to return there to do more fieldwork. I am there now sometimes as I write this, and that is encouraging for one who likes to speed along across the steppes, galloping willy-nilly, hooting back at the deep, somber warnings pulsing from the *logos*.

■ ■ ■

Aside: I have been to Milton since I last wrote. I returned to collect more data, to get a "feel" for the place, so that I could refresh and deploy my ethnographic authority in this aside, my warrant for credibility that Clifford (1988) describes as an "accumulated savvy and a sense of the style of a people or a place" (p. 35). I wanted to look around again and listen to the women talk so that I could write with what Geertz (in Olson, 1991, p. 191) describes as that "sense of circumstantiality and of power in reserve (if an anecdote or an example doesn't sound strained but sounds like you've got fifty others and this is the best one you chose)." I know, however, that I am always an "unreliable narrator" (Visweswaran, 1994, p. 62) and can never produce a traditional authoritative account. Nevertheless, I might manage to construct some semblance of Essex County women for you in this space.

During my days there, I was much concerned about this telling and rehearsed first one story and then another and composed bits of text in my head as I tried once again to put myself in the dubious scientific position of participant-observer. I am just about ready to give up on that signifier, since I am always sucked right into the middle of things, barely able to maintain the status of fieldworker, once more just Bettie Adams, come home to celebrate her mother's birthday.

Actually, one of the purposes of my visit, other than that birthday, was to see whether my dissertation was finally on the shelf in the Essex County room of the public library next to the other dissertations and theses that have been written about that place. It was, and that made me both proud and anxious. I looked at that particular shelf of research and wondered what it is about this place that makes so many of us want to write about it. Why do we dote on it so? It must be the peculiar intersections of relationships that have produced Essex County, relationships that have, to a great extent, been managed by women like my participants and their mothers before them. Ah, they are wondrous women, these women of Essex County, and their practices of place "enlarge the sense of how life can go" (Geertz, 1988, p. 139). Yet even as I celebrate the place they have constructed, which has, in turn, constructed them, I find much about it very worrisome — terrible, in fact. Nothing is innocent, particularly places striated from centuries of patriarchy and racial prejudice and unremarked poverty.

Still, I did what I usually do when I go home. For one thing, I went to church with my mother on Sunday morning. The Milton Baptist Church is big and sunny, with two scarlet-carpeted aisles, cream and gold paneled walls and pews, and exquisite stained-glass windows; and it sits on a prominent corner right downtown across from the post office and the public library. There's a wide, steep flight of steps from the Main Street sidewalk to the narrow front portico framing the main entrance to the sanctuary; members who can't manage those steps use the side entrance.

Since we hadn't gone to Sunday School, we arrived early to visit with anyone else who might also be there. We sat in Mother's pew near the back of the church, and my aunt sat in front of us. I don't know why these sisters don't sit together, but there are some long-term understandings, unspoken striations, about who sits where on what pew. Sitting in the wrong place is a chancy proposition since it would disrupt lives and be a topic of conversation for days.

As people always sit in the same place, it's easy to see who's missing. Even I could see that some were missing. The parents of a school friend of mine have always sat to our right in this pew, but only the husband was there that morning. His wife had died since I last went to church in

Milton. I kept seeing her there anyway, smiling and leaning across the pew to take my hand and ask me how long I could stay with my mother this time. He looked very lonely but smiled and greeted me, a bit confused about which of his daughters I had been friends with. His wife, of course, would have known.

We sang hymns that I have never sung before. My mother says the Baptists have a new hymnal and that "What a Friend We Have in Jesus," "Love Lifted Me," and "The Old Rugged Cross" are not in vogue. My aunt's lovely alto soared out over the other voices in the back of the church.

I missed the clear soprano of one of my participants who used to sing in the choir, who taught my Sunday School classes when I was a child, and who made us learn a Bible verse every week. (Of course, the first verse we all memorized for recitation was the shortest we could find, "Jesus wept.") My interview with her was inspiring and joyful and rock-bottom hard. She was dying then, carrying her oxygen from room to room in her house as she searched for pictures of her favorite teacher about whom she said, "She came to my college graduation. She came to see me and my husband after we were married. She was the kind that followed through." Lots of good people were missing.

The preacher preached about the need to be open to God's call, about finding our authentic voices, about listening for specific orders from God, about burdens that don't go away. As I sat there, responding to the familiar rhythms of the church service, observing the patriarchal overtones of the sermon, the music, and even the lovely windows, I wondered what it was about the practices of this place that still seduce me. I thought about the articulation of relationships that have been produced here for me as well as for my participants. I thought about all the Sunday mornings that long-dead members of my family have risen from pews at 11:55 to sing the Doxology, "Praise God from whom all blessings flow. Praise him all creatures here below. Praise him above, ye Heavenly Hosts. Praise Father, Son, and Holy Ghost." Amen.

Though the code of Christianity with its foundations entangled in patriarchy defines religious practices in Essex County, women there have nevertheless invented their own smooth spaces and lines of flight. They have broken barriers in some churches by becoming deacons and even preachers. They take issue with patriarchal practices the church continues to enforce and subvert them in small ways. They may dismiss the teachings of Paul, refuse to teach Sunday School lessons that condemn abortion, and vote against particularly heinous Southern Baptist proposals. They work within and against. I should say that some do, because some don't, of course. In any case, most of my participants find solace, companionship, and spiritual nourishment from the church. They speak in ordinary conversation of "saying a little prayer," of turning their wills over to God, and of following the Golden Rule. I have come to believe that their relationship with their God is a smooth mental space, the likes of which their daughters may never know.

The friendship relations within which my participants construct their subjectivities are anchored in the county's churches. (I particularly love the little white clapboard country churches, often sitting in a clearing on top of a hill, with a graveyard on one side and a shelter and picnic tables off to the other side for covered-dish dinners after church. I can almost smell the fried chicken and taste the country ham biscuits and slaw and chess pie and sweet iced tea served up during revivals.) These older women are the pillars of their churches, since they are the ones who have time to do the work that needs to be done. It is in the Sunday School classroom that they organize to take care of each other. From that site, they keep track of lives. They identify local needs and address them and visit the sick and the shut-ins. They tithe. They pray for everyone else.

What are the effects of so much soul service? One woman said that all this work might be good for the church, but that it produced a very restrictive life, that you could spend all your extra time at church and have nothing left for yourself. Most, however, do not give up on their churches. After all, they have been baptized as girls and married as young women in their churches. They have sat in a front pew and watched their husbands escort their daughters down the aisle to be married. They have celebrated their grandchildren's christenings and baptisms. They have sat in a front pew and stared at their husbands' caskets. They have found the strength—"God gives you the strength to do what you must do"—to come to church and face everyone all alone the Sunday after their husbands' deaths. They say that when things are bad, there's always somebody at church to help you out.

I stew about all this religion every time I go to church in Milton. It may be another way of reading the abyss, but its commands to accept, rather than protest, to maintain order, rather than question it, and to be so certain of the truth make me very nervous. All alternatives are dangerous, but the effects of the positivities of this one often seem so cruel to women that I have become testy and impatient with its allure. Its smooth spaces seem so small to me, and I wonder how long it will take for them to gnaw away at the dense, massive striations, the religious practices of place that keep these women in their place.

But who am I to judge those who pray over me so sweetly? Who am I to desire a different life for them? Who am I to question the smooth spiritual spaces they slip into for comfort with such a practiced ease? And what is my task as a researcher?

I can't make any sense of this, and I fear getting myself trapped between censure and empathy. Practicing homework is too hard. Yet, in the end, I believe that it is here in Essex County, rather than in some other place where the attachments might be looser, and I might not be so fearful of the effects of my interpretation that I must grapple with the issues that plague research in a postmodern world. It is here that I must confront the "burdens that don't go away." I will just have to keep working at it and talk with these women again and read some more and think harder about thinking differently. I need to find different smooth mental spaces for my homework, for the fieldwork that never ends.

■ ■ ■

Stopover—the Smooth Space of the Text

Writing about our research is, of course, only one of a variety of ways to make sense of it. Brave and gifted researchers are opting for different forms of representation such as painting, dance, theater, music, and so on. However, I call myself a writer, and I refuse to give up on writing. Unfortunately, there remain many sites where the academic essay is the only legitimate text available to a researcher. In addition to the politics of academic publishing, Peters (1996) notes the "conventions that comprise the present economy of writing and publishing based on the organization and standardization of writing space" (p. xiii). Any writing space, any form of writing, becomes standardized and normalized and constrains content, but the dissertation format is so heavily striated that I railed against it and searched for some smooth textual space where I might play. I learned from my resistance that easily identifiable limits can often be more easily subverted. I also remembered that writers have always created smooth textual spaces and that there are many writerly technologies waiting to be appropriated by science writers.

Distressed that I could not present the women of Essex County until chapter 4 of my dissertation, I decided to use the "aside," a centuries-old theatrical convention, as a textual space where they might perform too soon. *The Random House Unabridged Dictionary* defines the "aside" as a "part of the actor's lines supposedly not heard by others on the stage and intended only for the audience." In my dissertation, I used the aside to speak to the reader without the rest of the text hearing me. At least that's the way I thought about it then, as nomad space that might encroach on the authoritative, legitimate, and ponderous text that surrounded it. In the "folding of one text onto another" (Deleuze & Guattari, 1987/1980, p. 6), I found relief from the need to write with citational authority, and I was able to use that writing breather for fieldwork and homework.

Never one to work alone for long, I began to hear others speak around my imaginings of this writing space, and I wrote the following bit of poetry that is thick with their words. This poem is inspired by Benjamin's (see Arendt, 1968a) conception of a text "consisting entirely of quotations" (p. 47). I, too, found pleasure in "tearing fragments out of their context and arranging them afresh in such a way that they illustrated one another and were able to prove their raison d'être in a free-floating state, as it were" (Arendt, 1968a, p. 47). Here are their words.

The Aside

I see the space of the aside in this performance as a pleat in the text where the outside and inside fold upon each other, a space for "what Blanchot called 'the passion of the outside,' a force that tends towards the outside only because the outside itself has become 'intimacy,' 'intrusion'" (Deleuze, 1988/1986, p. 120).

The space of the aside might be a "movement of play, permitted by the lack or absence of a center or origin . . . a supplementarity" (Derrida, 1970/1966, p. 260). It is the excess, the overflow.

The space of the aside toys with the "rage for unity" (Spivak, 1974, p. xvi) demanded by a leveled humanist construct such as the academic essay. It encourages "subversive repetition" (Butler, 1990, p. 147) and interrupts form for meaning's sake.

The space of the aside is a parergon—an embellishment, an accessory to confusion, a space for play and fancy.

The space of the aside is a space of doubling, a site of enunciation that evokes the thrill and the threat of discourse (Bhabha, 1987, p. 8).

The space of the aside is post-history, a ruin where "the events of history shrivel up and become absorbed in the setting" (Benjamin, 1977/1963, p. 179).

The aside is a space of "sheer happenings" (Arendt, 1968b, p. 104) which might present "those unassimiliable fragments of experience that refuse to be woven into a neat tale, the unspeakable, what literally cannot be talked about" (Linden, 1993, p. 17).

The space of the aside might create a "new form of reflexive and transgressive verisimilitude" where the text's authority becomes self-referential (Denzin, 1994, p. 304).

In the space of the aside, one textual space might incite another textual space to discourse (Lather, 1993, p. 673) in a collision of heteroglossia (Bakhktin, 1975/1981, p. 428). Text intrudes upon text in an "enabling disruption" (Butler, 1993, p. 23).

The aside is a space for nomads, "those emigrant thinkers who deterritorialize accepted notions of space" (Conley, 1988/1993, p.
xv).

The aside is a space "*to be other and to move toward the other*" (De
Certeau, 1984, p. 110). It is a "space-off" (de Lauretis, 1987,
p. 25), a spatial practice.

The space of the aside is a place, a pause in textual space (Tuan, 1977,
p. 6).

And so on.

The space of the aside contains more data, if you will; but data that
may escape the violent coercion of manipulation, narration,
and interpretation—but only if you wish it to.

The aside is the field.

You might like to add your own verses to this poem about the possibilities of smooth textual spaces, spaces where nomads try to deterritorialize economies of writing that no longer suffice. I have found that I need
all sorts of writing spaces for textwork, fieldwork, and headwork (Van
Maanen, 1995) as I think about Essex County women, and I believe that
spaces like the aside emerge from the desires of particular writers situated in specific projects that demand nomadic inquiry.

Stopover—the Smooth Space of Theory

Deborah Britzman (1995) mentions what she calls a "messy problem" (p.
236) that I too have struggled with in my study: the paradox of a
researcher who leans toward a poststructural feminism interpreting the
lives of women who, if they had the words, would likely describe themselves as humanists. (I think, by the way, that only a very few of my participants would call themselves feminists.) I have struggled mightily with
the violence of interpretation, but this particular complexity has floored
me.

How in the world can I presume to continue to interpret the lives of
my participants, lives they have lived for decades within one theoretical
description of the world, using another theoretical description that is
committed to the persistent critique of all claims to truth, including the
truth of their lives, the Truth of the *logos*? What does this mean? What
kind of ethnographer am I? What kind of feminist am I? I suppose I could
say that my interpretation of the field is just another description. I suppose I could say that this is a case of alternate realities existing in the same
place—either "mutually exclusive or simply parallel worlds that barely or
rarely intersect" (Hufford, 1992, p. 250), but that seems to let me off the
hook too easily since those worlds are certainly intersecting in this text.

I remember how out-of-place I felt as I talked with my participants. The language of humanism roiled in our conversations, and I found myself slipping back into the familiar traps of its cadences as I assumed the subject position I was offered as the younger woman come home to gather wisdom from her elders. In order to have a conversation, I almost had to talk the talk of humanism and assume the world its language produces. I found I often wanted to deploy my own descriptions of the world, to stop and explain and theorize and teach. It was very, very difficult sometimes not to give in to this desire and all the arrogance it assumes.

To illustrate, I am reminded of my conversation with a woman in her late 80s who worked very, very hard during our interview to put the events of her life in order, to explain the significance of those events, and to describe as many joys as sorrows. She had had so many disappointments, and I could feel her moving into sad, keening places as she described loss after loss. With each painful remembrance, she pulled herself out of the sorrow by talking about her recovery, about how she had had to keep on going no matter what, about how she had had to work harder and go to church and do the right things and be a better person. Her community does not condone women who rail at the world or question rampant patriarchy, nor is resistance to practices that keep women in their place commonplace.

Yet the piling up of sorrow in the retelling of her life did produce resistance in this case. She said to me:

> I believe that things work out for good. I believe the Lord will take care of you if you just hand it over to him. I have prayed that prayer many a time. It's hard and I don't know whether you can *see* that things work out. I've had many disappointments and, you know, I just don't see yet how they worked out.

In the revelation of those last words she looked at me and said:

> You know the only thing that hasn't been taken away from me, Bettie? My education. My granddaddy was right. He said, "They'll never be able to take your education away." He was right! You tell those girls they *must* get an education.

At this point she lifted her frail arms in the air and shook her fists and said, "That's the *only thing* that hasn't been taken away from me! I don't understand how it worked out! I don't understand!"

I was devastated and couldn't say a thing. Shocked at this last-minute doubt and horrified that my questions had helped to trigger it, I was paralyzed by the futility of any facile comfort I might offer. She collected herself after a moment and sighed and then laughed a bit to smooth over her lapse. It was then that I found myself clinging to the necessary fiction of liberation that persists in my personal narrative, and I wanted to give her new language to understand her life. I wanted desperately to give her feminist theory and poststructural theory, anything, any other way of making sense of what had happened to her. I thought that if she could just see it all differently, maybe it wouldn't be so hard.

I wondered how well that education that hadn't been taken away from her had served her. The theory that undergirds her education and mine is devastating to women, particularly "good" women who always try to please and do the right thing. The breach of that theory in her momentary and desperate protest drove into my bones Foucault's (see Racevskis, 1987) point that philosophy must matter to the nonphilosopher. "The *point* of doing philosophy is to occasion new ways of thinking about the forms of experience around which there exist controversy or protest" (Rajchman, 1985, pp. 97–98). Did her education encourage her to think differently about her place in the world? I doubt it.

And then I wondered whether poststructuralism or feminism or any other theory is any more useful than humanism when we are too close to the wrong side of that most material of binaries, life/death. Does it matter then? I'm not sure. But how about all that living in the middle? Might those theories have been tools for this woman to use in rupturing the fierce structures that bound her so tightly within the very material effects of humanism? What practices of place did our homeplace of Essex County define in advance for her? Did her education enable her to think it might be possible to construct different practices and thereby "possible to constitute a new politics of truth" (Foucault, 1977, p. 14)? I don't think so.

In the end, I don't know what to make of the implications of the disjunction between the theory of the researcher and the theory of her participants. Surely, this disjunction gnaws at the research project, opens it up in some way, and demands a different science. How does theory influence what counts as data, i.e., what data become incoherent and what intelligible? What kind of knowledge is produced in this ricochet of theories? What are the ethical issues involved in doing fieldwork in relationships that produce this kind of disjunction? What will nomadic inquiry allow us to think about this paradox?

I expect that each researcher will have to struggle in this unintelligible space, taking note of the features of the landscape in order to tell us about the spikes and chasms and rhizomes of the map that precedes her territory. All I can say is that even though disjunction is a place of discomfort, it is also a site of affirmation, since there is the possibility of living differently. Thus, I cannot give up thinking about how one might reterritorialize on deterritorialization itself since, next time, I would like to be able to follow some line of flight that I could not think of during the conversation I have described here. Then, again, I may have to be content with that silent space I could not exit; nomadic inquiry may also involve practices of silence I haven't yet explored.

Stopover—the Smooth Space of Endings

Massumi (1992) writes of "how hard it is to keep a text in departure from taking leave of itself" (p. 9), and I understand his difficulty since I could quite easily continue this journey in search of the field. I did not know where this preface to more fieldwork would take me when I began, and I see now that I have revisited only three of the smooth spaces in which I have already worked: mental space, textual space, and theoretical space. Returning to these spaces is treacherous, because there is still no grid to follow and because the spaces themselves have ballooned and mutated since I last wrote about them. Of course, I did return to Essex County. I must always go to Essex County, since it is there that I am propelled into the middle of things and am forced to look for smooth spaces that might erode the topologies of its thick, dense codes.

And even as I write this ending, which, of course, is not an ending but still a preface, I know that I have barely begun to explore a postfoundational ethnography, one that is a site of passage, rather than a cumbersome spatial history of power and knowledge. No longer transparent, ethnography must always be a provisional space, one coded as soon as it is imagined, yet mobile, nomadic—always a mixture of the striated and the smooth. Happily, there are endless fields in which to do fieldwork once the old ethnography falls apart. The practices of place made available by that failure are intoxicating, and it is not so unusual to speed along among the fragments of a center that could not hold. In this tumultuous vortex of potentialities, science must enlist the scandalous, the outrageous, and the forbidden to stay alive.

Holding tight to the possibilities of nomadic inquiry, I am off to Essex County once more. This nomadic writing journey, this administrative review of some of the smooth spaces in which I have worked, has been both grueling and exhilarating, and I am now eager to collect response data (St.Pierre, 1977), to talk again with the women of Essex County, and to think once more about that book I lost, the one about their practices of place, the things they do every day that make them who they are. Essex County is still there, and my participants practice care of the self even as I write and you read. This story has no beginning and no end but has always been, and I slip into it over and over again in different places, and it is as if I too have always been there.

Acknowledgments

I am very grateful for the careful readings of earlier drafts of this paper by Donna Alvermann, Steve Kogan, Mary Leach, Kate McCoy, Wanda Pillow, Laurel Richardson, and the members of my writing group: Eurydice Bauer, Michelle Commeyras, Peg Graham, Joan Hall, and Linda Harklau.

Notes

1. I am taking Laurel Richardson (1994) at her word and using writing as a method of inquiry, nomadic inquiry at that.

2. Deleuze and Guattari (1987/1980) describe nomad science as an "eccentric" (p. 361) science, one that is about flux, becoming, and heterogeneity, "as opposed to the stable, the eternal, the identical, the constant" (p. 361). "It operates in an open space throughout which things-flows are distributed, rather than plotting out a closed space for linear and solid things" (Deleuze & Guattari, 1987/1980, p. 361). Nomad science is also problematic, rather than theorematic, and involves "all kinds of deformations, transmutations, passages to the limit, operations in which each figure designates an 'event' much more than an essence" (Deleuze & Guattari, 1987/1980, p. 362). It is opposed to "State science" (Deleuze & Guattari, 1987/1980, p. 362) that tries to limit, appropriate, and transform it.

3. I have changed the names of places in this essay.

4. Judith Butler (1993) explains that discourse produces the effects it names by citation, by the reiteration of a performance (such as the performance of gender) until it becomes recognizable, even a norm (p. 2). However, she goes on to explain that it is this "repeated process, an iterable procedure, [that] is *precisely* the condition of agency within discourse" (Butler, 1995/1994, p. 135). Agency occurs by refusing to reproduce or repeat the performance. "If a subject were constituted once and for all, there would be no possibility of a reiteration of those constituting conventions or norms. That the subject is that which must be constituted again and again implies that it is open to formations that are not fully constrained in advance" (Butler, 1995/1994, p. 135). "Interruptions" or "inadvertent convergences with other networks" (Butler, 1995/1994, p. 135) thus might produce "subversive citation" (Butler, 1995/1994, p. 135) that disrupts the *"sedimented iterability"* of subjectivity (Butler, 1995/1994, p. 134). In an earlier work, Butler (1990) refers to this view of agency as "subversive repetition" (p. 147).

5. Thanks to Laurel Richardson to pointing me to Stewart's (1989) work on "homework."

6. According to Deleuze and Guattari (1987/1980), rhizomes are not like trees or their roots, which provide grounding and structure, but rather are like crab-

grass that "connects any point to any other point" (p. 21). Rhizomes encourage deterritorialization; they penetrate what *is* rooted and put it to "strange new uses" (p. 15). Also, a rhizome is like a *"map and not a tracing* . . . The map has to do with performance, whereas the tracing always involves an alleged 'competence'" (pp. 12–13). In Judith Butler's (1995/1994) terms, a tracing is about citation, whereas a map or rhizome is about "subversive citation" (p. 135).

7. Lyotard (1984/1979) writes the following about the future anterior and poststructural practice: "A postmodern artist or writer is in the position of a philosopher: the text he writes, the work he produces are not in principle governed by preestablished rules, and they cannot be judged according to a determining judgment, by applying familiar categories to the text or to the work. Those rules and categories are what the work of art itself is looking for. The artist and the writer, then, are working without rules in order to formulate the rules of what *will have been done*. Hence the fact that work and text have the characters of an *event*; hence also, they always come too late for their author, or, what amounts to the same thing, their being put into work, their realization (*mise en oeuvre*) always begin too soon. *Post modern* would have to be understood according to the paradox of the future (*post*) anterior (*modo*)" (p. 81).

8. Deleuze and Guattari's (1987/1980) image of the "middle" is helpful in disrupting the linearity produced by beginnings and endings. One fails to follow a tangent if one works on the line. The middle is the site of passage, the place of passage "where things pick up speed" (Deleuze & Guattari, 1987/1980, p. 25). To work in the middle is to "establish a logic of the AND, overthrow ontology, do away with foundations, nullify endings and beginnings" (Deleuze & Guattari, 1987/1980, p. 25).

9. Appropriating an image from Deleuze and Guattari is quite in line with their nomadic thought. Brian Massumi (1992), who has translated their work, writes the following: "Most of all, the reader is invited to lift a dynamism out of the book and incarnate it in a foreign medium, whether painting or politics. Deleuze and Guattari delight in stealing from other disciplines, and they are more than happy to return the favor" (p. 8).

10. The terms *smooth space* and *striated space* were actually coined by Pierre Boulez. See note 22, p. 518, of Deleuze & Guattari's (1987/1980) *A Thousand Plateaus: Capitalism and Schizophrenia.*

11. James Clifford (1992) prefers the translation term "travel" to "nomadism," which he speculates might be a "postmodern primitivism" (p. 110) that too easily appropriates non-Western experiences. However, "travel" seems pretty tame to me and implies tickets and destinations and direction and, of course, baggage. Anyway, language is up for grabs, and, as Clifford (1992) points out, translation terms like "travel" and "nomadism" "get us some distance *and* fall apart" (p. 11).

12. Images and figurations can be used to help us think differently by breaking down the dualism between thinking and doing. Given that there is always a

lack of fit between theory and practice such that we can seldom adequately perform our theories (see Deleuze and Foucault, 1977/1972; Gramsci 1971, p. 365), figurations provide connections and detours that fold theory and practice into some space outside logocentricism. Spivak (1993) explains that this lack of fit is not about failure, but is "the new making-visible of a 'success' that does not conceal or bracket problems" (p. 28). Rosi Braidotti (1994b) writes, "Figurations are not pretty metaphors. They are politically informed maps, which play a crucial role at this point in the cartography of feminist corporeal materialism in that they are redesigning female subjectivity. They are relational images; they are rhizomes. In this respect, the more figurations are disclosed in this phase of feminist practice, the better" (p. 181).

13. Deleuze and Parnet (1987/1977) say that both individuals and groups are made up of a tangle of three kinds of lines: (a) lines of rigid segmentarity (sedentary lines like family, school, profession, etc.); (b) more supple lines of molecular segmentarity (migrant lines that operate at the same time as rigid lines but confound their rigidity, e.g., the hidden or mad things that happen within families or schools or professions); and (c) lines of flight (nomadic lines of creativity, lines that are always in the middle, lines of flux—not synthesis—that disrupt dualisms with complementarity) (pp. 124–147). This discussion also appears in *The Deleuze Reader* (1993) edited by C. V. Boundas, pp. 225–56, and in Deleuze and Parnet's essay "Politics" in *On the Line* (1983) published by Semiotext(e), pp. 69–114. As for lines of flight, Todd May (1991) explains that they "break both the axioms and the codes of a given society in order to create new forms of life that are subversive to the repressions of that society. They do not flow along regulated pathways, but are instead 'transversal' to them, cutting across them and using elements from them in the process of producing something new, different, and most important, alive" (p. 32). There is no escape through lines of flight, Deleuze and Parnet (1987/1977) write, "The great and only error lines [*sic*] in thinking that a line of flight consists in fleeing from life; the flight into the imaginary, or into art. On the contrary, to flee is produce the real, to create life, to find a weapon" (p. 49).

References

Alcoff, L. (1991). The problem of speaking for others. *Cultural Critique, 20* (winter), 5–32.

Arendt, H. (1968a). Introduction. In W. Benjamin *Illuminations* (pp. 1–55). (H. Zohn, Trans.). New York: Schocken Books.

Arendt, H. (1968b). *Men in dark times.* San Diego, CA: Harcourt, Brace, & Company.

Bachelard, G. (1994). *The poetics of space* (M. Jolas, Trans.). Boston: Beacon Press. (Original work published 1958)

Bakhtin, M. M. (1981). *The dialogic imagination: Four essays* (M. Holquist, Ed.) (C. Emerson & M. Holquist, Trans.). Austin: University of Texas Press. (Original work published 1975)

Behar, R. (1995). Introduction: Out of exile. In R. Behar & D. A. Gordon (Eds.), *Women writing culture* (pp. 1–29). Berkeley and Los Angeles: University of California Press.

Benjamin, W. (1977). *The origin of German tragic drama* (J. Osborne, Trans.). London: Verso. (Original work published 1963)

Bhabha, H. K. (1987). Interrogating identity. In L. Appignanesi (Ed.), *Identity documents* (pp. 5–11). London: Institute of Contemporary Art.

Blunt, A., & Rose, G. (1994). Introduction: Women's colonial and postcolonial geographies. In A. Blunt & G. Rose (Eds.), *Writing women and space: Colonial and postcolonial geographies*. New York: Guilford Press.

Boundas, C. V. (Ed.). (1993). *The Deleuze reader*. New York: Columbia University Press.

Boundas, C. V. (1994). Deleuze: Serialization and subject-formation. In C. V. Boundas & D. Olkowski (Eds.), *Gilles Deleuze and the theater of philosophy* (pp. 99–116). New York: Routledge.

Braidotti, R. (1994a). *Nomadic subjects: Embodiment and sexual difference in contemporary feminist theory*. New York: Columbia University Press.

Braidotti, R. (1994b). Toward a new nomadism: Feminist Deleuzian tracks; or, metaphysics and metabolism. In C. V. Boundas & D. Olkowski (Eds.), *Gilles Deleuze and the theater of philosophy* (pp. 159-86). New York: Routledge.

Britzman, D. (1995). "The question of belief": Writing poststructural ethnography. *International Journal of Qualitative Studies in Education, 8*(3), 229–38.

Butler, J. (1990). *Gender trouble: Feminism and the subversion of identity*. New York: Routledge.

Butler, J. (1993). *Bodies that matter: On the discursive limits of "sex."* New York: Routledge.

Butler, J. (1995). For a careful reading. In S. Benhabib, J. Butler, D. Cornell, & N. Fraser, *Feminist contentions: A philosophical exchange* (pp. 127–43). New York: Routledge. (Essay dated 1994)

Clifford, J. (1988). *The predicament of culture: Twentieth-century ethnography, literature, and art*. Cambridge, MA: Harvard University Press.

Clifford, J. (1992). Traveling cultures. In L. Grossberg, C. Nelson, & P. A. Treichler (Eds.), *Cultural studies* (pp. 96–116). New York: Routledge.

Conley, T. (1993). Translator's foreword: A plea for Leibniz. In G. Deleuze *The fold: Leibniz and the Baroque* (T. Conley, Trans.) (pp. ix–xx). Minneapolis: University of Minnesota Press. (Original work published 1988)

Conway, J. K. (1989). *The road from Coorain*. New York: Vintage Books.

Dainotto, R. M. (1996). "All the regions do smilingly revolt": The literature of place and region. *Critical Inquiry, 22*(3), 486–505.

De Certeau, M. (1984). *The practice of everyday life* (S. Rendall, Trans.). Berkeley and Los Angeles: University of California Press.

de Lauretis, T. (1987). *Technologies of gender: Essays on theory, film, and fiction.* Bloomington: Indiana University Press.

Deleuze, G. (1988). *Foucault* (S. Hand, Ed. & Trans.). Minneapolis: University of Minnesota Press. (Original work published 1986)

Deleuze, G., & Foucault, M. (1977). Intellectuals and power. In D. F. Bouchard (Ed.), *Language, counter-memory, practice: Selected essays and interviews* (D. F. Bouchard & S. Simon, Trans.)(pp. 205–17). Ithaca, NY: Cornell University Press. (Discussion recorded March 4, 1972 and reprinted from *L'Arc*, no date, *49*, 3–10)

Deleuze, G., & Guattari, F. (1987). *A thousand plateaus: Capitalism and schizophrenia* (B. Massumi, Trans.). Minneapolis: University of Minnesota Press. (Original work published 1980)

Deleuze, G., & Parnet, C. (1987). *Dialogues.* (H. Tomlinson & B. Habberjam, Trans.). New York: Columbia University Press. (Original work published 1977)

Deleuze, G., & Parnet, C. (1983). Politics. In *On the line* (pp. 69–114). New York: Semiotext(e).

Denzin, N. K. (1994). Evaluating qualitative research in the poststructural moment: The lessons James Joyce teaches us. *International Journal of Qualitative Studies in Education, 7*(4), 295–308.

Derrida, J. (1970). Structure, sign and play in the discourse of the human sciences. [Lecture delivered October 1966]. In R. Macksey & E. Donato (Eds.), *The structuralist controversy* (pp. 247–72). Baltimore: Johns Hopkins University Press.

Derrida, J. (1996). By force of mourning. *Critical Inquiry, 22* (Winter), 171–92.

Foucault, M. (1977). The political function of the intellectual. *Radical Philosophy, 17*, 12–14.

Foucault, M. (1979). *Discipline and punish: The birth of the prison* (A. Sheridan, Trans.). New York: Vintage Books. (Original work published 1975)

Foucault, M. (1984). On the genealogy of ethics: An overview of work in progress. In P. Rabinow (Ed.), *The Foucault reader* (pp. 340–72). New York: Pantheon Books.

Foucault, M. (1985). *History of sexuality, Volume 2: The use of pleasure* (R. Hurley, Trans.). New York: Vintage Books. (Original work published 1984)

Foucault, M. (1986). *History of sexuality, Volume 3: The care of the self.* (R. Hurley, Trans.). New York: Vintage Books. (Original work published 1984)

Game, A. (1991). *Undoing the social: Towards a deconstructive sociology.* Toronto: University of Toronto Press.

Geertz, C. (1988). *Works and lives: The anthropologist as author.* Stanford, CA: Stanford University Press.

Gordon, D. A. (1995). Conclusion: Culture writing women: Inscribing feminist anthropology. In R. Behar & D. A. Gordon (Eds.), *Women writing culture* (pp. 429–41). Berkeley and Los Angeles: University of California Press.

Gramsci, A. (1971). *Selections from the prison notebooks of Antonio Gramsci* (Q. Horae & G. N. Smith, Eds. & Trans.). New York: International Publishers.

Haraway, D. (1988). Situated knowledges: The science question in feminism and the privilege of partial perspective. *Feminist Studies, 14*(3), 575–99.

Harvey, D. (1989). *The condition of postmodernity: An enquiry into the origins of cultural change.* Cambridge, MA: Blackwell.

Holland, E. (1991). Deterritorializing "deterritorialization"—From the *Anti-Oedipus* to *A thousand plateaus. SubStance, 66,* 55–65.

Hufford, M. (1992). Thresholds to an alternate realm: Mapping the Chaseworld in New Jersey's pine barrens. In I. Altman & S. M. Low (Eds.), *Place attachment* (pp. 231–52). New York: Plenum Press.

Kermode, F. (1966). *The sense of an ending: Studies in the theory of fiction.* New York: Oxford University Press.

Lather, P. (1993). Fertile obsession: Validity after poststructuralism. *Sociological Quarterly, 34(4),* 673–93.

Lather, P. (1996, April). *Methodology as subversive repetition: Practices toward a feminist double science.* Paper presented at the annual meeting of the American Educational Research Association, New York City.

Lefebvre, H. (1991). *The production of space* (D. Nicholson-Smith, Trans.). Cambridge, MA: Blackwell. (Original work published 1974)

Linden, R. (1993). *Making stories, making selves: Feminist reflections on the holocaust.* Columbus: Ohio State University Press.

Lyotard, J.-F. (1984). *The postmodern condition: A report on knowledge* (G. Bennington & B. Massumi, Trans.). Minneapolis: University of Minnesota Press. (Original work published 1979)

Mascia-Lees, F. E., Sharpe, P., & Cohen, C. B. (1989). The postmodernist turn in anthropology: Cautions from a feminist perspective. *Signs: Journal of Women in Culture and Society, 15*(1), 7–33.

Massumi, B. (1992). *A user's guide to* Capitalism and Schizophrenia*: Deviations from Deleuze and Guattari.* Cambridge, MA: MIT Press.

May, Todd G. (1991). The politics of life in the thought of Gilles Deleuze. *SubStance, 66,* 24–35.

Olson, G. A. (1991). The social scientist as author: Clifford Geertz on ethnography and social construction [Interview with Clifford Geertz]. In G. A. Olson & I. Gale (Eds.), *(Inter)views: Cross-disciplinary perspectives on rhetoric and literacy.* Carbondale: Southern Illinois University Press.

Peters, M. (1996). *Poststructuralism, politics, and education.* Westport, CT: Bergin & Garvey.

Pratt, M. B. (1984). Identity: Skin, blood, heart. In E. Bulkin, M. B. Pratt, & B. Smith (Eds.), *Yours in struggle: Three feminist perspectives on anti-semitism and racism* (pp. 11–63). Ithaca, NY: Firebrand Books.

Quinby, L. (1991). *Freedom, Foucault, and the subject of America.* Boston: Northeastern University Press.

Racevskis, Karlis. (1987). Michel Foucault, Rameau's nephew, and the question of identity. In James Bernauer & David Rasmussen (Eds.), *The final Foucault* (pp. 21–32). Cambridge, MA: MIT Press.

Rajchman, J. (1985). *Michel Foucault: The freedom of philosophy*. New York: Columbia University Press.

Richardson, L. (1994). Writing: A method of inquiry. In N. K. Denzin & Y. S. Lincoln (Eds.), *Handbook of qualitative inquiry* (pp. 516–29). Thousand Oaks, CA: Sage Publications.

Serres, M., & Latour, B. (1995). *Conversations on science, culture, and time* (R. Lapidus, Trans.). Ann Arbor: University of Michigan Press. (Original work published 1990)

Spivak, G. C. (1974). Translator's preface. In J. Derrida, *Of grammatology* (G. Spivak, Trans.) (pp. ix–xc). Baltimore: Johns Hopkins University Press.

Spivak, G. C. (1993). *Outside in the teaching machine*. New York: Routledge.

Stacey, J. (1988). Can there be a feminist ethnography? *Women's Studies International Forum 11*(1), 21–27.

Stegner, W. (1992). *Where the bluebird sings to the lemonade springs: Living and writing in the west*. New York: Penguin Books.

Stewart, J. O. (1989). *Drinkers, drummers, and decent folk: Ethnographic narratives of village Trinidad*. Albany: State University of New York Press.

St.Pierre, E. A. (1995). *Arts of existence: The construction of subjectivity in older white southern women*. Unpublished doctoral dissertation, The Ohio State University, Columbus.

St.Pierre, E. A. (1997). Methodology in the fold and the irruption of transgressive data. *International Journal of Qualitative Studies in Education, 10*(2), 175–89.

Strathern, M. (1987). An awkward relationship: The case of feminism and anthropology. *Signs: Journal of women in culture and society 12*(2), 276–92.

Tuan, Y-F. (1977). *Space and place: The perspective of experience*. Minneapolis: University of Minnesota Press.

Van Maanen, J. (1995). An end to innocence: The ethnography of ethnography. In J. Van Maanen (Ed.), *Representation in ethnography* (pp. 1–35). Thousand Oaks, CA: Sage Publications.

Visweswaran, K. (1994). *Fictions of feminist ethnography*. Minneapolis: University of Minnesota Press.

Welty, E. (1956). Place in fiction. *South Atlantic Quarterly, 55*(January), 57–72.

Chapter 14

Drawing the Line at Angels: Working the Ruins of Feminist Ethnography

Patti Lather

The title of this paper comes from a meeting of an interdisciplinary theory group at my university where one of the presenters, speaking of his "tentative engagement" with Walter Benjamin, said that he "drew the line at angels" in his inquiry into the construction of historical consciousness in fascist Italy.[1] In contrast, Dick Hebdige (1988) argues "the multiple enablements of living on the line, toward more fluid categories" (p. 231). For Hebdige, living on the line is about being positioned between ways of thinking about language, meaning, and "the real" that no longer offer purchase on contemporary conditions and the "not yet" of new concepts. Here the task is to begin presenting such concepts in the cracks created by the loss of mastery of the old concepts.

In what follows, I take up this task, using Walter Benjamin, among others, to argue the usefulness of angels in breaking out of the Hegelian enclosure that so shapes late-twentieth-century critical thought and practice. I ground my comments in the efforts of my collaborator, Chris Smithies, and myself to write a book, *Troubling the Angels: Women Living with HIV/AIDS* (1997). We desktop published an early version in the fall of 1995 in order to get feedback from the 25 women we had interviewed and to solicit publishers toward what the women call a "KMart book," widely available to women like themselves, their families, and friends, as well as a more general audience. Additionally, Chris and I needed some sort of "first-draft" approach in order to take a step toward letting go of this "text of responsibility" (Derrida, 1994; see also, Spivak, 1994). As indicated by the title of the book, angels have played no small part in this project. Hence, it is precisely the work of the angels in the textual and the interpretive moves of the book that I focus on in this paper. Beginning with some background on the project and an overview of the book that foregrounds the various angel inter texts, I use the instructive complications of this project to sketch ephemeral interpretive and textual strategies, "micro-becomings" (Deleuze & Guattari, 1983) p. 70), toward a less comfortable social science.

Background: Troubling the Angels

> One makes oneself accountable by an engagement that selects, interprets, and orients. In a practical and performative manner, and by a decision that begins by getting caught up, like a responsibility, in the snares of an injunction that is already multiple, heterogeneous, contradictory, divided. (Derrida, 1994, p. 93)

Troubling the Angels grew out of interviews conducted from 1992 to 1995 with 25 women living with HIV/AIDS, largely in meetings with women and AIDS support groups in four major cities in Ohio. But also, as is not atypical of even quasi-ethnographic work, we met at holiday and birthday parties, camping trips, retreats, hospital rooms, funerals, baby showers, and picnics. Invited in as a feminist qualitative researcher, my job was "to be of use" (Piercy, 1973) to support group members motivated to open up their lives for scrutiny in order to help create the book they wished had existed when they were first diagnosed. Benefiting greatly from my co-researcher's already established networking and rapport with the women,[2] my major role in the project was to design the study and the resulting book and, particularly, to get the book published in a way that would make it widely available.

Situated in a feminist poststructural problematic of accountability to stories that belong to others, my sense of task was how to tell such stories in a way that attends to the crisis of representation. Working in the ruins of an earlier moment of a feminist ethnography assumed "innocent" in its desire to give voice to the voiceless (Visweswaran, 1994), Chris and I have attempted a text that both reaches toward a generally accessible public horizon and yet denies the "comfort text" that maps easily onto our usual ways of making sense. We wanted to create a "messy text" (Marcus, 1994) while still honoring our charge of producing a book that would do the work the women wanted. We wanted to use the ruins of feminist ethnography as the very site of possibility for movement from a "realist" to an "interrogative" text that reflects back at its readers the problems of inquiry at the same time an inquiry is conducted. Such a text strikes the epistemological paradox of knowing through not knowing, knowing both too little and too much, addressing the question, "How does one act knowing what one does?" (Visweswaran, 1994, p. 80).

Aimed at a popular audience, *Troubling the Angels* traces the patterns and changes of how the women make sense of HIV/AIDS in their lives. The book begins with two prefaces, the first introducing the book and the second the women, many of whom have written their own introductions. The heart of the book consists of a series of short chapters that narrate the interview data around topics on the day-to-day realities of living with the disease: relationships, efforts to make sense of the disease in their lives, death and dying issues, and the role of support groups. The titles were chosen from the words of the women themselves, including "If I didn't have HIV I'd be dead" and "It's taken me years to get here," the latter dealing with the support groups. In sidebars, references are made to such things as further resources for dealing with HIV/AIDS in the deaf community, information on gynecological signs of HIV infection in women, and the demographics of AIDS as a global crisis, with references for those who want further information.

Interspersed with these short data chapters are angel inter texts and illustrations that use the reemergence of angels in popular culture, especially AIDS discourses, to function both as "breathers" between the themes and emotions of the women's stories and as shifts from the women's testimony to short engagements with history, poetry, and sociology around AIDS issues. Running across the bottom is a subtext commentary where Chris and I, as co-researchers, spin out our tales of doing the research. This subtext provides background for the study and researcher efforts to make sense of the "data" and the study and the larger context in which the AIDS crisis is such a cultural marker. Scattered throughout the book are some of the women's own writings in the form of poems, letters, speeches, and e-mails. Finally, the book concludes with an epilogue that updates the reader on each of the women and the support groups and includes their reactions to the desktop published version of the book. What follows is an overview and excerpts from the angel inter texts.

The Angel Inter Texts

There are five angel inter texts in the book, following each of the five clusters of "story series" that are based on transcribed tapes of support group meetings. Each angel inter text is followed by an angel image that ranges from Paul Klee to the work of contemporary artists. Inter text 1 is designed as a series of floating boxes, drawn from both "high culture" and popular culture sources, that surveys the way angels have been portrayed across the sweep of angelology from pagan, early Jewish and Christian traditions, the Angelic Doctor, St. Thomas Aquinas, through contemporary millennialism. Rilke's "terrible angel," Valery's broken angel, Klee's 50 angel drawings and paintings, Benjamin's Angel of History, Laurie

Anderson and Tony Kushner's updating of Benjamin's angel, Irigaray's angels—all are evoked (as cited in Lather & Smithies, 1997). Finally, the use of angels in contemporary AIDS discourses is surveyed. What follows are excerpts from the prelude, the "angel boxes," and the subtext of inter text 1, which delineates my autobiographical interest in the topic.

Prelude: The Work of the Angels in This Book[3]

READER: Why the emphasis on angels in a book on women living with HIV/AIDS?

AUTHORS: Traditionally, angels serve as messengers, and these women have a keen sense of wanting to get their story out to help other women like themselves. They also want to reach a larger audience about the work of living with HIV/AIDS. As writers, we were looking for a way to organize the book that would provide both a "breather" from the intensity of the women's stories and a way to situate their stories in the larger cultural context of the AIDS pandemic. . . . Believing that HIV/AIDS exceeds our ability to "master" it through knowledge, we wanted a book that used a "flood" of too much too fast, data flows of trauma, shock, and everydayness juxtaposed with asides of angel breathers to break down the usual codes we bring to reading. Hence the book "works" by not working the way we expect a book to work: a linear unfolding of information that builds toward a sense of "being on top" of a situation through knowledge . . .

READER: Before getting on to things quite so scholarly, I wonder whether you could provide me with a key, in order to make it easier for me to read your book.

AUTHORS: The angels provide many keys. As this project began, they were intended to provide a reversal of the "demonizing" attitudes that many have toward people with HIV/AIDS who are often treated like lepers. Instead, the angels are used to situate these women as messengers who trouble any easy sense we might have that the AIDS crisis is "out there," unrelated to each of us. As the project developed, the angels assumed the weight of researcher interpretation in the study. Instead of analyzing the women's stories, we wanted to give pride of place to those stories, uninterrupted by our coming in and saying what the women's words "really meant," as is typical of academic research. So the angel inter texts provided a place where we could bring to bear the sociological and historical layers of the AIDS crisis on the women's stories, without having to insert those layers directly into their stories.

READER: But isn't there a danger that the angels will take over the women's stories?

AUTHORS: Yes, the risk of the angels is that they will displace the "real" with a mythos. Intended to mark what Rilke called "generous spaces" that "passed far beyond us" (1989, p. 191), they may, in fact, be an error. But it seemed a greater risk to tell a "simple" tale, a "realist" tale about the AIDS pandemic that so challenges our usual ways of making sense of crisis. We take the risk in order to make the point that there is no "simple" way to tell the story of women living with HIV/AIDS, that having to negotiate layers of constantly changing, often contradictory information is a hallmark of the pandemic. By mobilizing the familiar icon of the angel and then "troubling" any easy reading of it, we want to underscore how our usual ways of making sense of crisis are inadequate in the face of AIDS.

READER: Were the angels your idea or did they come from the women?

AUTHORS: The angels were very much Patti's idea. Everyone else, Chris included, expected a much more straight-ahead story. Somewhat obsessed with angels as a means to trouble familiar categories and logics, Patti wanted to work against the "comfort text" that would provide the consolations of certain meaning and knowing, the romance of knowledge as cure . . . . The hope is that the very fragmentation of the book, it detours and delays, will unsettle readers into a sort of stammering knowing about the work of living with HIV/AIDS, a knowing not so sure of itself.

READER: Well, I guess I'll just have to see for myself how this works as I still don't exactly understand what you are about here.

AUTHORS: Our hope is that each reader will work through the accumulating layers of information in the book and decide for themselves how it all comes together. Or, more exactly, how the various layers of information about HIV/AIDS, researcher reflections, and the women's stories interrupt one another into some place of not making any easy sense. At some level, the book is about getting lost across these various layers and registers, about not finding one's way into making a sense that maps easily onto our usual ways of making sense. Here we all get lost: the women, the researchers, the readers, the angels, in order to open up present frames of knowing to the possibilities of thinking differently.

READER: But why would you WANT a reader to get lost and disoriented in reading the book?

AUTHORS: AIDS is not the only crisis in our times, and we all face death. But AIDS combines sex, blood, and untimely death within a particular moment in history. Instead of the comfort text that maps easily onto our usual way of making sense of crisis, this book is written out of a kind of knowing through not knowing, knowing both too little and too much about that historical situation. . . . In a time when the need to chronicle the world seems to outstrip our capacity to make sense of it, the angels add a layer that works to trouble formerly comfortable holds on making meaning. Such trickster angels are a register of ruin, unable to make whole what has been smashed in a book involved in telling other people's stories in the shadow places of history as loss.

PATTI: It is important to note that everything I've learned about angels in the last few years was all new to me. I didn't even know

---

The gnosis of angels

"The angelic world, whether it be metaphor or reality, is a giant image in which we may see and study ourselves, even as we move towards what may be the end of our time." (Bloom, 1996, p. 11). Harold Bloom's book on angels, dreams, and the millennium complicates the New Age revival of angels by focusing on angel menace, power, and otherness. Bloom bases his arguments on Talmudic, Gnostic, and Mormon ideas and argues that we debase this tradition when we do not know the long history of angels. Angels become insipid, "pressed into service as philosophy or prophecy," by "angel enthusiasts."[4]

Klee's angels

German painter Paul Klee (1879–1940) used angels more than any other major twentieth-century artist, producing drawings and paintings of angels that carry such names as *Unfinished Angel, Forgetful Angel, Angel Still Female, Angel Still Groping, Angel As Yet Untrained in Walking,* and *Angel Delivering a Light Breakfast.* With changing forms and meanings, from the dawn of creation to birth and death and other states of becoming or intermediate zones, Klee's angels were more about an ironic reflection of facing the ordinary terrors of the here and now than about an afterlife. Hopeful but uncertain, his angels occupy a position between life and death, the poignancy of departures, the mysteries and vagaries of life, and the possibilities of transformation within a context of human frailties.

Fisher, M. (1994). *Sleep with the Angels: A Mother Challenges AIDS*. London: Moyer Bell.

Glaser, E., & Palmer, L. (1991). *In the Absence of Angels: A Hollywood Family's Courageous Story*. New York: Berkeley Books.

Philip Kayal's (1993) book, *Bearing Witness: Gay Men's Health Crisis and the Politics of AIDS*, was originally entitled *Angels at War*. Boulder, CO: Westview Press.

the word angelology, the long time study of angels in Talmudic, Gnostic, Christian, and Islamic traditions.

I did not expect to get into such a vast and diversified esoterics when I began this project on women and HIV/AIDS. As was pointed out to me at a small research retreat in Wisconsin, the metaphor of angel is so excessive that it raises red flags of caution. What we came to call there "angelizing" is dangerous business, tied to romanticizing and otherwising as it is, resonant with images of vacuous cherubs. But I seek different angels, angels who exceed our categories of angels as I struggle to know what I want from and bring to my encounters with these women with/for/to whom I am doing this inquiry.

Angels came into this project at the "Women and HIV/AIDS" retreat where I was introduced to many of the women. At the closing "sistercelebration" where we were lighting candles for those who had died from AIDS, one group of women ended up all crying together in a configuration that looked like the statue of Iwo Jima. I remember a particularly small woman looked HUGE to me as she circled the group of four with her arms. Some angel image jarred in my mind, some image from my own Catholic past and present post-Wiccan spiritual sensibility. Across multiple differences of race, class, age, and health, the women seemed angels in their care for one another and in their wanting to be "messengers" to other women about HIV/AIDS. Not too much later, as I puzzled over how to situate myself in relation to the women, the concept of "standing with" impressed itself upon me, which segued into standing with angels—and a world opened up. Chris had told me to expect a spiritual experience in this work, but I had not expected it to announce itself in the form of angels, angels who troubled any comfortable familiarity with their very availability.

Inter text 2 focuses on Walter Benjamin's angel of history as a way to negotiate AIDS as a global crisis. After sketching Benjamin's philosophy of history as a "permanent emergency," the global dimensions of the AIDS crisis are outlined (Benjamin, 1968a). What follows are scattered excerpts from that inter text.

Inter Text 2—The Angel of History: AIDS as a Global Crisis

> Thus ... there is an infinite amount of hope, but not for us.
>
> (Benjamin, 1994, p. 565)

Why the upsurge of interest in angels in late-twentieth-century American culture, especially in writing and thinking about AIDS? While a respect for the spiritual in a time of plague and danger is by no means new, some possibilities quite contrary to the more common Hallmark angels are suggested by Walter Benjamin's "angel of history" (1968b). Based on 20 years of contemplating Paul Klee's small watercolor entitled *Angelus Novus*, Benjamin's angel of history was marked by his experience of a Europe that had erupted into the war that would cause him to take his own life in 1940 at the age of 48, fleeing from the Nazis. In his "Theses on the Philosophy of History" (1968a), Benjamin writes of the angel of history as no longer singing, melancholy if not desperate given the debris of history, an angel unsure of fulfilling its angelic mission. Seemingly at the end of historical "progress," the angel is both witness and guide to the wreckage of human history where the millennium has come too soon and the air seems thick with danger. History is full of scandal and unacceptable worlds, a situation Benjamin terms history as "a permanent emergency." In this emergency of AIDS, where is hope? How are we to think about the future? Will the disease become a manageable chronic condition? What relations is it structuring across multiple differences and cultural practices, locally and globally? An epidemic among sex workers in Bangkok, the decimation of African villages and gay male communities in the Unites States, the steady increases among heterosexuals in the United States largely via IV drug users, particularly hard-hitting for people of color, the scourge of hemophiliacs worldwide: across our differences, we face a disease that defies belief in the endless capacities of modern science to save us. Prevention effectiveness has become central, given the capacity of the virus to mutate, making treatment difficult. But while education was successful among gay men and their reduction in cases in the late 1980s, the number of cases among young gay men is on the rise again. In what is called the "second wave" of AIDS, minorities and women are at particular risk.[5] Concepts of blame and otherness stymie effective AIDS education. To shift from blaming individuals requires taking into account the national and international order that has contributed to the transmission and spread of the pandemic.

How are we to think our way into such a global situation? As both witness and guide, the angel of history is about learning to find our way into a future that is always in the making, bereft of the fictions of certain knowledge that supported past generations as they wrestled with the scandals of their own historical time. In Bill Haver's book on our sense of history in the time of AIDS (1996), he argues that serious engagement with the questions of AIDS leads to a "shock" of recognition that we will not be saved by any of the familiar ways of making sense of crisis: god, heroic science, the dialectic of history, education. Our task, Haver argues, is to use AIDS to think what it is impossible to think, by refusing the consolations and easy evasions of habituated knowing in order to think the ruins of our ways of making sense as the condition of possibility for movement toward a different kind of future. It is the capacity of AIDS to shock us into a different relation with the future that is of interest here. As Haver notes, in our present historical moment of struggle where we all live and die "in AIDS," as earlier generations lived and died "in religion" regardless of personal belief (Haver, 1996), we have to live "somehow." What help can do us any good?

Inter text 3 is a history of angelology that traces the ways angels have been studied over the centuries, from pagan myths, Jewish, Christian, and Islamic early writings, and canonical texts of the Middle Ages through contemporary efforts to link angels with space aliens and the New Age revival, including multicultural dimensions. This is juxtaposed with an overview of the way AIDS has been studied during the last decade, raising issues about how our practices of studying and knowing are deeply shaped by culture and history. The following is a scattering of excerpts.

Inter Text 3—Angelology: A History of Truths

> But angels are supposed to be immortal, so even if the
> plague did claim them as victims they couldn't actually
> have died. So if they emptied the old mansions of
> Heaven where did they go? And where are they now?
>
> (Godwin, 1990, p. 183)

Over the centuries, interest in angels has waxed and waned. Until the reign of science, they were considered to be the overseers of the cosmos, guiding everything from time and space to the particulars of each human life. The scholarship of the Middle Ages was full of controversy regarding whether angels had wings or not, what their number and essence was, and the nature of their link with humans. The erosion of faith in angels, both their ability to serve as intermediaries between humans and a higher power and their very existence, began with the plagues of the fourteenth century and was exacerbated by the Age of Reason ushered in by the scientific revolution of the sixteenth century.

While angels have suffered some displacement over time, they are reentering the popular imagination in the United States, particularly via New Age interest in angels as mediators between worlds. As Mortimer Adler (1982) points out, for centuries angels were all we knew of superhuman intelligence. Now we have cyborgs and UFOs as part of the grammar of available possibilities. *Angels and Aliens* (1991) by Keith Thompson posits a link between all of this. Primarily about UFOs, the book surveys various myths and mystical beliefs from shamanism to angels to undergird his arguments.

Like angels, how something such as AIDS is thought about over time and what this might mean socially and politically raises questions about how ideas are produced, framed, and sustained. For example, to look at the intersection of AIDS, Africa, and race moves AIDS to "AIDS," where "AIDS" becomes a creation of the audience/media interaction. This is not to deny that AIDS kills people. It is, however, to focus on how the burden of signification is a cultural event that has a profound shaping influence on how this disease gets lived. Whether angels or "AIDS," phenomena are always socially defined. Whether from churches or doctors, knowledge systems of religion or science, filtered through information media from books to television, we construct the world we live in by how we make meaning of it.

Is AIDS but the first of many viruses we will see rise up, decimate populations, and be outside the limits of science to control?[6]

Will some people develop genetic resistance as a form of survival of the fittest over eons? Will educational programs about safer sex and not sharing needles take effect? Will governments develop the will to deal with the crisis in a timely fashion? How will the answer to these questions be shaped by the very ways knowledge about HIV/AIDS is constructed?

Inter text 4 explores the theme of claiming life in the face of death by juxtaposing the poetry of Rainer Maria Rilke with the AIDS angel by artist Benjamin Jones, a papier mâché sculpture about rage in the face of governmental neglect. It follows in its entirety.

Inter Text 4—Death Makes Angels of Us All

> They are waiting to take us into
> the severed garden
> Do you know how pale & wanton thrillful
> comes death on a strange hour
> unannounced, unplanned for
> like a scaring over-friendly guest you've
> brought to bed
> Death makes angels of us all
> and gives us wings
> where we had shoulders
> smooth as raven's
> claws
>
> (Jim Morrison, quoted in Mu, n.d., p. 134)

The German poet Rilke (1989) wrote about the hard-to-grasp parts of life, what he termed the Too Big, especially how to live in a world marked by death. He tried to bring such knowings to words in a way that created a widened space that was about the oneness of life and death. What Rilke called the "work of the heart" posits the Angel as about living without certain belief and truth. In essence, Rilke's "assenting Angels" are about the paradox of affirming from negation, about overcoming the lack of hope that comes when life is "teaching its most desperate lessons." For Rilke, the test of living was a kind of alchemy that used pain and suffering in order to earn hope in a hard world. His Angels are TERRIBLE ANGELS, annihilators of images we have built up "fondly and lazily," in our delusions of some higher order. Shatterers, great undeceivers, this is "the angelic terror" where we have to learn to live without redemption, no longer sheltered by the ruins of Christianity. Here the Angel is about saying yes to life in the face of disaster, sickness, murder, cruelty, and senseless death. Sixty years after Rilke's terrible angels is Benjamin Jones's papier mâché AIDS Angel. Names cover the angel's body in a roll-call of accountability for governmental neglect and ignorance. "Fuck George Bush" screams across the angel's belly. Slash marks and names track the dead. Dollar and cent signs on the angel's feet underscore the fiscal bottom line. Reminding one of a piñata, each whack would be like the women at the Women and AIDS retreat whacking a softball and shouting out objects of their anger, from the government to "bisexual men who lie." This is the angel as an exorcism of rage. Part of an art show in Cleveland in the spring of 1994, "Creating in Crisis: Making Art in the Age of AIDS," the AIDS Angel addresses the emptiness of words, trying to overcome that few are listening, trying to say something more, to find a new way of getting the same old message across, trying to inspire the strength to keep on fighting, working under and through the shadow of the virus, trying to address death which makes no distinctions between sexes, races, or classes, the great leveler, the ultimate common denominator.

Not knowing how to act, being caught unaware, inadequate, without resources, is almost a mark of facing the Too Big. In an economy so marked by loss as the place of AIDS, is the angel what the poet Wallace Stevens (1982) terms "necessary angels"? Necessary angels are about our need to create and believe in what we can hardly avoid suspecting are fictions. In this move to "trouble" angels, no longer so smitten with them, the "necessary" move locates the angel as a ruin/rune, shot through with inadequacies, a perverted and deflated angel, witness to the human capacity to carry on and even sing in the midst of anguish, an audience of astonished angels, come down to earth to learn about living in a historical time of permanent emergency.

Inter text 5 raises some of the sociological issues involved in AIDS and women's lives by probing the human cost and benefit of varied institutional practices. What follows are scattered excerpts.

Inter Text 5—An Ache of Wings: The Social Challenge of AIDS

> And how bewildered is any womb-born creature that
> has to fly. As if terrified and fleeing from itself, it zigzags
> through the air, the way a crack runs through a teacup
>
> (Rilke, 1989, p. 195)

This final angel inter text is a moment of determined sociology in this book on HIV/AIDS and women's lives that foregrounds the certain power that outside forces have over our lives. It is also a moment of determined policy talk, a moment of what it is that can be done.

AIDS intensifies social problems. The list of social programs needed by PWAs includes: increased funding for research, extended insurance benefits, housing, emotional support, support for children, hospital and medical services, hospice care, and increased educational programs in safer sex practices. Culturally sensitive education in safer sex is needed among communities at risk for HIV: men who have sex with men, intravenous drug users, and their sexual partners, particularly in communities of color. As the incidence of AIDS continues to spiral among injection drug users, prevention and treatment programs, and harm-reduction efforts, especially needle exchange programs, become key. Sexuality education for girls and women needs to be about much more than promoting the use of condoms that often leaves sexual relations of power intact in not dealing with the constraints on women's negotiation of their sexuality. Women continue to be underdiagnosed and misdiagnosed. Women also live differently with AIDS than men, especially around issues involving pregnancy and child rearing. In the United States, all of these services are especially needed in culturally sensitive forms and among the poor whose access to public services is limited. And all of these services are global needs.

CR talked at a lakeside retreat of how, since having AIDS, she has the social services she has needed all her life: adequate housing and medical care, community support, even, speaking of Chris, "her own personal psychologist." One thinks of the story of young Cubans deliberately infecting themselves with HIV in order to gain better social services. One thinks of the story Chris tells of "HIV impostors" who create an HIV identity in order to access social services. One wonders what such stories have to say about how people get their needs met in a social order increasingly marked by the maldistribution of social resources and the erosion of the welfare state.[7]

Linda Singer (1993) writes of AIDS as a "world transforming moment" as we face the limits of our present systems (p. 31). The everyday looks different; fantasies of salvation fall apart. Rather than quick fixes, great crusades or grand gestures, our task begins to look like a long haul toward a different kind of power and pleasure in building communities built on recognition of the limits of present logics of response. Here, in the ruins of our historical space, the complications deflect any magic bullet of some one solution in the face of the very proliferation of AIDS, its noncontainment, its roots in the mix of racism, misogyny, heteronormativity and global politics that so determine AIDS policies. Here, we live out a complexity of "the pure too little, the empty too much" (Komar, 1987, p. 89), an ache of wings.

Working an Angel Economy

> Work: that which makes for a work . . . indeed, that which works—and works to open . . . insofar as it engenders, produces, and brings to light . . . all work is also the work of mourning.
>
> (Derrida, 1996, p. 171)

From the beginning of this project, the women's vision was of a book marketed like Magic Johnson's book on AIDS. They wanted to see it at supermarket checkout stands and KMarts, an easily available reaching out to those, especially women, dealing with HIV/AIDS in their lives. Combining this with my gnomic, abstruse ways of knowing has been a source of both energy and paralysis. The angels have become the site of this struggle, and so it is to an exploration of how they help me locate myself in the problematic of the book that I turn.

In order to probe the workings of my angel economy, I mobilize four thematics: displacement/dispersal/deferral, translation as betrayal, rhizomatics, and feminist ethnography as a ruin/rune. Rather than discrete categories, each is positioned as a plateau, with various effects of opening up and closing down in delineating the interpretive and textual practices in *Troubling the Angels*. My interest here is in a reading of the work of the angels that produces, rather than protects. My intent is to not protect the angel as a monument but to situate it, rather, as a trickster, following its adventures through the text, noting its concealments and its not knowings. Given Derrida's (1996) caution regarding the need to protect from every ontology, from the authority of ontology, this move is toward the angel as a concept that owes it to itself not to be, an image that annuls its representative presence. In this effort, what follows rehearses plateaus that are multiple, simultaneous, and in flux toward a reading productive of strategically underdetermined conceptual assemblages that oscillate between rigorous and inexact, inventing new tools for thinking, connecting one's work to becomings (Deleuze & Guattari, 1983).

Each of the "plateaus" is prefaced by a quote from a group of students who previewed *Troubling the Angels* in a course on AIDS taught in the Stanford anthropology department in early 1996.[8] This sort of "fold"

(Deleuze, 1993) of "response data" (St. Pierre, 1996) is presented within an argument that moments of failure are particularly important in tracing the kind of work that something does. Derrida calls this the work of mourning "that would have to fail in order to succeed. In order to succeed, it would have to fail well . . . a work that would have to work at renouncing force, its own force, a work that would have to work at failure, and thus at mourning and getting over force, a work working at its own unproductivity" (1996, pp. 173–74).

Displacement/Dispersal/Deferral: Under the Sign of Benjamin

> I couldn't follow along regarding the women's identities . . . divided pages . . . and angels . . . unsettling. . . . I wanted to find out about the women, but I felt like there was always something in my way: either random boxes, lines across the page, or angels floating by.
>
> All most people expect is a kind of voyeurism into lives usually unseen . . . book kept my attention. I did struggle with the format, but it was survivable. I found myself pondering the points made in the angel inter texts. . . . It may be that I am not being sufficiently postmodern when I see the need to connect the layers of meaning. If struggling with the text is the entire point, point taken!
>
> . . . frustrated . . . angry, at the structure and some of the content of the book. . . . I had tried to actually KNOW who each of the women is. . . . However this aspiration to understand who each woman is was perhaps stifled. . . . Maybe we aren't supposed to form attachments to the individual women, to imply that they are merely representatives of the thousands of women living with HIV/AIDS, but I don't find this as effective as portraying them as whole and real people.

Drawn to the possibilities afforded by such a project to address the politics of knowing and being known in a postrealist time, I saw an opportunity to wrestle across the "deconstructive excesses and extreme forms of social constructionism "characteristic of some postmodernisms" via a feminist responsibility to "real bodies and political rage" (Stockton, 1992, pp. 114, 117). My discovery of the work of Walter Benjamin was key in my negotiation of the effacement of the referent in postmodern culture, an effacement that has made "the real" such contested territory and created anxieties about narrative will and interpretive weight.[9]

Concerned with the problems of representation, Benjamin's goal was practices that allow some "handle on the ungraspable" (Shiff, 1992, p. 98), some historical materialism that is more about traces than certainties, but which refuses to give up on "the stubborn presence of the real" (Eagleton, 1981, p. 92). Against subjectivism and objectivism, relativism and romanticism, rather than writing to persuade, Benjamin wrote for brooding, against both himself and conventional ways of relating to subject matter. Practicing dispersal/deferral as a way to get closer to the thing itself, in all its unrepresentability, the real that always eludes us, he searched for the most adequate form of critical thought in a post-Enlightenment world. This resulted in a body of work that plays with rhetorical and poetic effects in order "to incite all manner of irrational states: fascination, enchantment, melancholy, frustration, distraction" (Cohen, 1993, p. 252).

Paul de Man (1986) writes of Benjamin's tendency to display "the inability of trope to be adequate to its meaning" (p. 92). By both using familiar tropes and displacing them, Benjamin used images in order to signal the all-too-human appeal that they make to us. He particularly used messianic appeals toward displacing, destabilizing, and translating beyond the object of his inquiry. Writing in such a way as to keep his object of interest in circulation, he foregrounded disjunctions, disruptions, accommodations, weaknesses, cheatings, conventions. "By using symbols which are particularly convincing, which are particularly seductive" (de Man, 1986, p. 98), perverse images that undo the claim that is associated with them, Benjamin works toward what he termed "profane illumination": a secularized truth content that the material world offers to those who can hear and see beyond conventional regimes of meaning.

Functioning as a displacement device, at a moment when material forces overwhelm the shock defenses, perhaps the angel marks what it is that I, like Benjamin, want "to articulate but cannot produce from within the Enlightenment horizon of [my] thought" (Cohen, 1993, p. 219). To be beguiled by an angel like Benjamin's that is rigorously unsentimental, unpretentious, and situated is to make its "fiction a constant contemplation of its own perplexing meanings" (Alter, 1991, p. 76). Troubling the production of meaning-effects, the angel enacts an ironic mode of reference by foregrounding how we make sense within codes that are sedimented in past productions of meaning. Both courting and then trapping the reader in an ironic recoding of angels which troubles our very sense of angels, such "dizzying reversals and perverse appropriations" (Holland, 1993, p. 16) work to trouble the referential function of discourse. Concerned with undecidables, limits, paradoxes, and complexities, the angel works as a deceptive code, situated within present frames of intelligibility only to disrupt them.

Refusing to deliver the women to the reader in a linear, tidy narrative, the book uses the angels to block and displace easy identifications and sentimentalizing empathy. Benjamin (1968a) rejected empathy as an "indolence of the heart" (p. 256) that keeps intact history as the victor's story, a triumphalist narrative. Eschewing sentimentality, empathy, and subjectivism, his historical and sociological impulses underwrote Chris and my efforts to construct a book where the reader comes to know through discontinuous bits and multiples of the women's stories.

> Renouncing directed argument, Benjamin relies upon the ideas through language to produce their own cross-meanings: his arrangements are material for contemplation, they force the reader . . . to draw the meaning from the resonances of the ideas, from the perspectives created by the order of sentences. (Rosen, 1977, p. 35)[10]

Such textual dispersal works against easy categories of us and them, where "us" is the concerned and voyeuristic and "them" are the objects of our pity, fear, and fascination. Breaking our practices of scrutiny that invoke the cruelty of the pitying gaze, our usual critical voice of abjectifying, triumphant unmasking (Fuss, 1996), such practices of textual dispersal work, instead, toward the impossible tense out of time of these women who look back at the "us" who listen to and read their stories in a way that points us to ourselves. Through a different organization of space and visibility, the usual idealization and consumption of some other as what Derrida (1996) calls "the mourning-object" (p. 187) is interrupted. Living in mourning, learning "how to transfigure the work of death into a work that gives and gives something to be seen" (p. 187), not waiting to know that death is marked out in everything and then to go on living: this is no small part of the work of living with HIV/AIDS. Derrida (1996) writes, "I was thus read, I said to myself, and staged by what I read" via a topology of a mourning that inverts the gaze, "an inversion of dissymmetry that can be interiorized only by exceeding, fracturing, wounding, injuring, traumatizing the interiority" that it inhabits (pp. 188–189).

To think topographically rather than ontologically, the angel is a place of use, a mechanism for a pragmatics of dissemination to gradually build up by partial pictures the idiom of our history. Evoking between-spaces, the angel works as a displacement device that links local to global. This is a fold versus a depth model, a fold designed to disrupt the conditioned responses of the modernist reader, particularly sentimental empathy with its "transference and narcissistic cathexis" (Nagele, 1991, p. 137). Fragmenting the story lines and intercutting them with seemingly unrelated segments, the text works to elicit an experience of the object through the very failures of its representation, setting up a different economy of exchange in order to interrupt voyeurism.

Translation as Betrayal

> I did not at all understand the significant of the angels . . . they really were in no way related to most of the book. Sadly enough, the angel chapters seemed to resemble commercials. I started to flip the pages as one would flip the channel. . . . The work was supposed to be on women speaking their minds in support groups, but before you know it, we're introduced to the personal lives of the authors and sit in on conversations during car rides.
>
> [It was] quite difficult for me to stay focused on any one aspect of the book . . . my attention was never fully where it should be.

Benjamin's (1968b) articulation of translation situates the translator as lost from the beginning, given the necessary failure of bearing witness to the original. To situate the witness as translator opens toward a practice that begins to grasp what Felman, in her study of Holocaust survivors, refers to as "the nonsimplicity of reference in the shadow of the trauma of contemporary history" (Felman & Laub, 1992, p. 164). Both validating the absolute necessity of speaking AND radically invalidating all parameters of reference, the task is doubled: breaking silence and simultaneously shattering any given discourse. Translator to those who have witnessed history as outrage, Felman proceeds via a performance not about what the Holocaust is "but to gain new insights into what not knowing means, to grasp the ways in which erasure is itself a part of the functioning of our history" (p. 253).

As a translator bearing witness, one becomes a witness to "questions we do not own and do not yet understand, but which summon and beseech us" (Felman & Laub, 1992, p. xiii). Brought in as a chronicler, situated so that, like Felman in her study of Holocaust survivors, "[m]y attempt as interviewer and listener was precisely to respect—not to upset, not to trespass—the subtle balance between what the woman knew and what she did not, or could not, know" (p. 61). Such a position is about ways of listening that worry less about historical truth and more about what is being performed in the telling of not knowing too much, "the place of the greatest density of silence" (p. 64), given the price of speaking.

In order to explore the textual possibilities for telling stories that situate researchers not so much as experts "saying what things mean" in terms of "data," our text situates the researcher as witness giving testimony to the lives of others, with subtextual and intertextual practices that displace direct commentary on such testimony. Britzman (1995) raises the dangers of the posture of researcher as witness: the reification of experience and identity, agency and voice, and unmediated access to some "real." There is no exit from the lack of innocence in discursive stagings of knowledge, she notes, even when the goal is to work against some reversion to humanist pathos, empathic caring, and a longing for transcendence, some way out, in the face of human struggle.

Felman (Felman & Laub, 1992) writes of the inevitable failure and betrayal of the witness and predicts that "to look at history from hell" (pp. 176–78) will issue in a failure to march toward the future, a failure of the prophetic gesture, a deconstruction of the very ideology of salvation, of prophetic Marxism. This is about some breaching of congealed discourses, critical as well as dominant, some refusal to situate the researcher as the "Great Emancipator," saying what things mean, some way to use theory to incite questions and context, rather than to interpret, reduce, fix. But I remain haunted by the task of doing justice to the women's words.

"Easy to spot the problem, hard to supply the ethic!" Serres (1995, p. 101) writes, in addressing a code of practice for messengers. His answer is quite useful here, in all its density: that the task of the translator is to fade out behind the message, once the incomprehensibility of the message is communicated, once philosophy herself appears, in the flesh. Becoming visible as an intermediary, the task becomes to empty out the channel while still foregrounding the productive and distorting effects of the channel, a kind of presence, and absence, and presence again. The only way to break free is to invent new channels, which will soon become blocked again as messengers derive importance from the channels created, but the goal is to disappear in delivering the word of the something else that the word signals and gestures toward.

Rhizomatics

The poignant and richly informative [stories in the book are] about women and AIDS for women with AIDS, [but the text] violated my traditional reading patterns. The layers of meaning and detail were simultaneously literal and metaphorical . . . intentionally simultaneous . . . esoteric but at the same time wildly interesting . . . [where] I found myself getting lost in those levels of discourse all too often.

. . . angel concept seems kind of out there for me . . . but by the end it did make the ending of the work more meaningful and beautiful . . . tie it all together for us . . . there were so many little meanings around, that I couldn't figure out which one I was supposed to apply here. And maybe that's the point.

. . . like any other college student, [I] read it all the night before we were to discuss it in class. And while this reading style would have worked for any other book, it was difficult to do for this book.

The difficulty arose in part due to the fragmentary style of the book, but mostly from the trouble I had trying to refrain from stopping and thinking about what I had just read.

Deleuze and Guattari (1983) delineate the rhizome as an open trajectory of loose resonating aggregates as a way to trace how the space of knowledge has changed its contours. Altering the way we organize and communicate knowledge, rhizomatic practices question taxonomies and construct interconnected networks where readers jump from one assemblage to another (Saper, 1991). Delineating a rhizomatics of proliferations, crossings, and overlaps, all without underlying structures or deeply rooted connections, information in *Troubling the Angels* is organized like a hypermedia environment, a mapping of potential assemblages, a storing, retrieving, and linking well beyond a tracing of descriptive information. The fragmentary nature of the book invites multiple entry, multiple readings. Does one read each data story and then go back and read the researchers' running subtext? Does one assume connections between upper and lower page? Does one read only the angel inter texts or, quite the converse, only the "data" stories? Networking across the interviews, the angel breathers, the running subtext that moves between autobiography and academic encoding of methodology and theoretical analysis, the "factoid" boxes, and the women's writing scattered throughout the text, the rhizome moves outside of formerly comfortable holds on sense making. Trying to unsettle from within, it taps some underground in movement toward a text that provides multiple openings, networks, and complexities of problematics. This practice produces indirection, obliquity, and irony through the multiplication of endless layers of meaning in a text designed to foreground what it means to know more than we are able to know and to write toward what we do not understand.

Here the angel functions as a "line of flight." Lines of flight are part of the plethora of conceptual assemblages that Deleuze and Guattari (1983) build up in their efforts to devise an open system of philosophy capable of tracking intensities, flux, and movement. Molar and molecular lines explain how we become fixed and unfixed; lines of flight are about pull and velocity, being carried away by something that comes from elsewhere to disturb our binaries (Leach & Bolen, 1998). As a line of flight, that which is the crack in the teacup that resonates and accumulates with other cracks, the angel interrupts salvation narratives of science and rationality. Presented as a detour, the angel is positioned as the ghost of unassailable otherness that haunts Western ideas of reason, self-reflexive subjectivity, and historical continuity (Nagele, 1991). This is an economy of displacements and substitutions that gestures toward a force other than individualized and psychologized motivations. Here the angel is a multiple line of effect/affect that permeates and helps organize a much broader, less-bounded space where we do what we can while leaving a place for what we cannot envision to emerge.

Working the Ruins of Feminist Ethnography

> AIDS and being infected with HIV is a real problem which affects real people who are in many ways best situated to speak about how the disease influences their lives. Yes, this book has done that very admirably, but in other ways it has also heightened how narrative represents the disease and hence constructs the effect of HIV as something distant and discordant from reality. It has taken over from reality, rather than depicting it.
>
> I felt lost. . . . I actually feel this is a disservice to all the women who participated in this book . . . intellectualized and theorized. . . . I had many expectations that were not met and were actually contradicted.

What does it mean to situate this project as a ruin/rune, permeated by limits and error, where much is refused, including abandoning the project to such a moment (Haver, 1996)? Against the grain of research traditions that fabricate inquiry as a triumphal continuity, I look for breaks and jagged edges as a place from which to read the practices that my co-researcher and I have devised. Here inquiry is a rune from which we might draw useful knowledge for the shaping of practices of feminist inquiry.

Judith Butler's (1993a) address to the American Historical Association suggests what opens up when inquiry is situated as a ruin by drawing on Walter Benjamin's "Theses on the Philosophy of History." Butler argues that the failure of teleological history, whether Marxist, messianic, or, in its most contemporary formulation, the triumph of Western democracy (e.g., Fukuyama), is the very ground for a different set of social relations, a certain opening up of a field of contestatory possibilities. It is the ruins of progressivist history, naive realism, and transparent language that allow us to see what beliefs have sustained these concepts; only now, at their end, Butler argues, does their unsustainability become clear. Hiroshima, Auschwitz, Mai Lai, AIDS, for example, make belief in history's linear unfolding forwardness unsustainable.

Butler's point is that, in such a time and place, terms understood as no longer fulfilling their promise do not become useless. On the contrary, their very failures become provisional grounds and new uses are derived. The claim of universality, for example, "will no longer be separable from the antagonism by which it is continually contested," as a possibility for moving toward a configuration of ethics and sociality that is other to the

Hegelian dream of a reconciliation that absorbs difference into the same (Butler, 1993a, p. 6). Butler terms this "the ethical vitalization" (p. 7) of the failure of certain kind of ideals, a Nietzschean transvaluation of working the pathos of the ruins of such ideas as the very ground of post-foundational practices that contribute to struggles for social justice.

Moving across levels of the particular and the abstract, trying to avoid a transcendent purchase on the object of study, we set ourselves up for necessary failure in order to learn how to find our way into post-foundational possibilities. The task becomes to throw ourselves against the stubborn materiality of others, willing to risk loss, relishing the power of others to constrain our interpretive "will to power," saving us from narcissism and its melancholy through the very positivities that cannot be exhausted by us, by the otherness that always exceeds us. To situate inquiry as a ruin/rune is to foreground the limits and necessary misfirings of a project, problematizing the researcher as "the one who knows." Placed outside of mastery and victory narratives, inquiry is a kind of self-wounding laboratory for discovering the rules by which truth is produced. Here we attempt to be accountable to complexity. Thinking the limit becomes our task and much opens up in terms of ways to proceed for those who know both too much and too little.

In addressing where Chris and I began, what we encountered, and how we moved as we engaged in "fieldwork, textwork and headwork" (Van Maanen, 1995), it was, as Deborah Gordon (1995b) argues, a situation where "[w]riting is about history coursing its way through us" (p. 429). Western feminist ethnographic traditions of romantic aspirations about giving voice to the voiceless are much troubled in the face of the manipulation, violation, and betrayal inherent in ethnographic representation. Working the limits of intelligibility, *Troubling the Angels* mixes sociological, political-economic, and historical analysis with policy recommendations along with the privileging of ethnographic voice in constructing an audience with ears to hear.[11] This was Chris and my task in this text of responsibility as we live out the ambivalent failure of the uses of research toward something more productive of an enabling violation of its disciplining effects. Inhabiting the practices of its rearticulation, "citing, twisting, queering," to use Judith Butler's words (1993b, p. 237), we occupy the very space opened up by the ruins of the concept of ethnographic representation.

Refusing much in an effort to signal the size and complexity of the changes involved in the move away from modernist metaphysics of presence, assured interiority, and the valorization of transformative interest, the book is written out of a kind of "rigorous confusion." Such confusion displaces the heroic modernist imaginary in turning toward otherness, being responsible to it, listening in its shadow, confused by its complexities.[12] Here "the participant witness" (Gordon, 1995a, p. 383) tells and translates so that something might be seen regarding the registers in which we live out what Serres (1995) terms "the weight of hard-borne history" (p. 293) in evoking an ethical force that is directed at the heart of the present.

Conclusion

In this account of strategies risked, the preceding plateaus are offered as a means to track the levels of failure in *Troubling the Angels*, a text positioned as a general field of failure in order to begin to theorize those failures. Within such a field, perhaps the angel is the sort of writing out of failure that Blanchot (1986) speaks of in *The Writing of the Disaster*. "Falling beneath Disastrous necessity" (p. 11), writing "in failure's intensity . . . when history takes fire and meaning is swallowed up" (p. 47), Blanchot separates himself from that which is mastery and power as he strives toward a language "where the unrepresentable is present in the representation which it exceeds" (p. 111).

In a context where AIDS is overburdened with representations (Treichler, 1988), here is yet another. Circulating among many questions, sharpening problems, making insufficiencies pressing, and clarifying the limits of any easy resolutions, the angel works to make the text say more and other about something as absurd and complicated as dying in the prime of life of a disease of global proportions. Via a path of detours and delays, in an alchemy beyond conscious intentionality, the angel gains a new and unsettling valance as Chris and I search for

> something other than to entertain in the key of sentimental optimism . . . some fusion of kitsch and death that is adequate to the topic it engages in a form that defies our narrative urge to make sense of, to impose order on the discontinuity and otherness of historical experience. (Hansen, 1996, p. 298)

In an economy so marked by loss as the place of AIDS, the text undercuts any immediate or total grasp via layers of point-of-view patterns. In a space where untroubled witnessing will not do, the angel functions somewhere "between theory and embarrassment" (Ellison, 1996, p. 368), some space-time of turbulence and passages of relational bodies "where the most fragile bring the new and have to do with the future" (Serres & Latour, 1995, p. 123). Even as we are suspicious of "the mystifying ends to which enchantment can be put" (Cohen, 1993, p. 259), the angels work to reject sentimentality and devise a hopefully resonant spectacle in the crucible of lives lived in historical time. Hence, the very dangers of angels may signal their usefulness in Chris and my search for a multiply layered way of telling stories that are not ours.

Dick Hebdige (1988) states that postmodern closings should be anti-climactic, down to earth, grounded in learning our place in time which requires us to "draw the line" between the limits of the situations inside of which we live and attention to what is gathering beyond, "to yearn responsibly across it towards the other side" (p. 244). Grounded in Chris and my study of women living with HIV/AIDS, I have sought the possibilities of research that makes a difference in struggles for social justice while working against the humanist romance of knowledge as cure within a philosophy of consciousness. My investment is, rather, to work toward innovations leading to new forms, negotiation with enabling violence attentive to frame narratives that works within and against the terrain of controllable knowledge (Spivak, 1993). Positioned on the line of demarcation between materialism and idealism, the angels mark the incomplete rupture with philosophies of the subject and consciousness that undergird the continued dream of doing history's work. Thinking the thought of the limit of the saturated humanist logics, which determine the protocols through which we know, I put the angels to work as a line of flight in regard to our enabling aporias as we move toward practices of academic writing that are responsible to what is arising out of both becoming and passing away.

Notes

1. Anxieties regarding what "drawing the line at angels" might mean are suggested in Richard Wolin's (1995) delineation of Heidegger's "crossing over the line" that separates falsifiable from nonfalsifiable claims to truth and the consequent "politicized science" of the universities under Hitler where philosophy and ideology became inextricably commingled. For Wolin, "crossing the line" means "the failure to separate warranted philosophical assertion from unverifiable, ex cathedra pronouncements" (p. 132). Wolin's arguments are underwritten by particular notions of truth and verifiability, with the threat of totalitarianism thrown in for good measure in the face of the "irrationalism" of postmodernism.

2. Chris has been involved in facilitating women and HIV/AIDS support groups and retreats since 1988.

3. This prelude is modeled after Michel Serres's (1995) *Angels: A Modern Myth*, where, at the end of the book about science and the philosophy of history, Serres has a dialogue between "The Reader" and "The Author" that begins with, "Why should we be interested in angels nowadays?" (p. 293).

4. Harold Bloom (1996).

5. According to the June 1996 *HIV/AIDS Surveillance Report* put out by the Centers for Disease Control, in the U.S. the total number of AIDS cases among women increased from 15,495 in 1990 to 27,485 in 1992 and then to 78,654 in 1996, with the majority of these being Hispanic (22%) and African-American (53%) women who combined make up 75% of AIDS cases. Globally, the World Health Organization estimates that by the year 2000 as many as 40 million people worldwide will have been infected with HIV, with more than 70% of HIV infections occurring through heterosexual transmission. In addition, more than half of newly infected adults worldwide will be women. Of the 226 million affected by HIV worldwide, 14 million are Africans (Purvis, 1997, p.78).

6. See Laurie Garrett (1994), *The Coming Plague*, about the bureaucratic infighting, drug-company indifference, environmental degradation, and population explosion upon which she posits a world health crisis that includes but goes beyond AIDS. HIV/AIDS and other previously unknown diseases, such as Ebola fever, which is more than 97% fatal, baffle medical science. There is no cure. Killer viruses and bacteria, unfazed by antiseptic conditions, adapt faster than they can be documented, classified, and studied, let alone stopped.

7. Several Cuban youth deliberately infected themselves with HIV in order to access the higher standard of living available at the quarantined AIDS sanitorium set up by the government. In a video smuggled out of Cuba, 80 young people are said to have shot up infected blood between 1989 and 1991. Sanitarium life offers far more comfort than most Cubans ever see: three full meals a day, air conditioning, no power outages, and the absence of police (Katel, 1994, p. 42).

8. "Constructing HIV/AIDS: The Epidemic's Second Decade," a course taught by Dr. Ruth Linden, Stanford University, Anthropology Department, Winter 1996.

9. Art historian Stephen Melville complicates the issue of ontology in the postmodern in "Color Has Not Yet Been Named: Objectivity in Deconstruction," published in Jeremy Gilbert-Rolfe and Stephen Melville (1996).

10. Regarding Benjamin's textual practice of juxtaposing quotations from seemingly incompatible theories, "Benjamin tears individual sentences or sentence-fragments from their original context and accumulates them into series, so that . . . they form clusters, then adds his own thought to them, without binding all these elements into a continuum" (Witte, 1991, p. 81). "[In his] critical strategy of citation . . . the quotation summons the word by its name, wrenches it from its context and, in doing so, calls it back to its origin. . . . In the word thus emancipated is mirrored the language of the angels" (Witte, 1991, p. 217).

11. The question of audience for *Troubling the Angels* is addressed in Lather (1996).

12. From a talk by Dick Hebdige (1996, January) part of a series, "Style: From Subculture to High Culture," sponsored by the Center for Interdisciplinary Studies in Art and Design, Wexner Center for the Arts, Ohio State University.

References

Adler, M. (1982). *The angels and us.* New York: Macmillan.

Alter, R. (1991). *Necessary angels: Tradition and modernity in Kafka, Benjamin, and Scholem.* Cambridge, MA: Harvard University Press.

Benjamin, W. (1968a). Theses on the philosophy of history. In H. Arendt (Ed.), *Illuminations* (pp. 253–64). New York: Schocken.

Benjamin, W. (1968b). The task of the translator. In H. Arendt (Ed.), *Illuminations* (pp. 69–82). New York: Schocken.

Benjamin, W. (1994). *The correspondence of Walter Benjamin 1910-1940.* (G. Scholem & T. Adorno, Eds.; M. Jacobson & E. Jacobson, Trans.) Chicago: University of Chicago Press.

Blanchot, M. (1986). *The writing of the disaster* (A. Smock, Trans.). Lincoln: University of Nebraska Press.

Bloom, H. (1996). *Omens of millennium: The gnosis of angels, dreams, and resurrection.* New York: Riverhead Books.

Britzman, D. (1995). "The question of belief": Writing poststructural ethnography. *International Journal of Qualitative Studies in Education, 8*(3), 233–42.

Butler, J. (1993a). Poststructuralism and postmarxism. *Diacritics 23*(4), 3–11.

Butler, J. (1993b). *Bodies that matter: On the discursive limits of "sex."* New York: Routledge.

Centers for Disease Control. (1996). HIV/AIDS Surveillance Report. Atlanta, GA: National Center for HIV, STD, and TB Prevention.

Cohen, M. (1993). *Profane illumination: Walter Benjamin and the Pais of surrealist revolution.* Berkeley and Los Angeles: University of California Press.

Deleuze, G. (1993). *The fold: Leibniz and the Baroque* (T. Conley, Trans.). Minneapolis: University of Minnesota Press.

Deleuze, G., & Guattari, F. (1983). *On the line* (J. Johnston, Trans.). New York: Semiotext(e).

de Man, P. (1986). *The resistance to theory.* Minneapolis: University of Minnesota Press.

Derrida, J. (1994). *Specters of Marx.* New York: Routledge.

Derrida, J. (1996). By force of mourning. *Critical Inquiry, 22*(2), 171–92.

Eagleton, T. (1981). *Walter Benjamin or towards a revolutionary critique.* London: Verso.

Ellison, J. (1996). A short history of liberal guilt. *Critical Inquiry, 22*(2), 344–71.

Felman, S., & Laub, D. (1992). *Testimony: Crises of witnessing literature, psychoanalysis, and history.* New York: Routledge.

Fisher, M. (1994). *Sleep with the angels: A mother challenges AIDS.* London: Moyer Bell.

Fuss, D. (1996). Look who's talking, or if looks could kill. *Critical Inquiry, 22*(2), 383–92.

Garrett, L. (1994). *The coming plague.* New York: Farrar Straus Giroux.

Gilbert-Rolfe, J., & Melville, S. (1996). *Seams: Art as a philosophical context*. Amsterdam: G & B Arts.

Glaser, E., & Palmer, L. (1991). *In the absence of angels*. New York: Berkeley Books.

Godwin, M. (1990). *Angels: An endangered species*. New York: Simon & Schuster.

Gordon, D. (1995a). Border work: Feminist ethnography and the dissemination of literacy. In R. Behar & D. Gordon (Eds.), *Women writing culture* (pp. 373–89). Berkeley and Los Angeles: University of California Press.

Gordon, D. (1995b). Conclusion: Culture writing women: Inscribing feminist ethnography. In R. Behar & D Gordon (Eds.), *Women writing culture* (pp. 429–41). Berkeley and Los Angeles: University of California Press.

Hansen, M. (1996). Schindler's list is not Shoah. *Critical Inquiry, 22*(2), 292–312.

Haver, W. (1996). *The body of this death: Historicity and sociality in the time of AIDS*. Stanford, CA: Stanford University Press.

Hebdige, D. (1988). *Hiding in the light: On images and things*. London: Routledge.

Holland, E. (1993). Deterritorializing "deterritorialization"—from *Anti-Oedipus* to *A Thousand Plateaus*. *Substance, 20*(3), 55–65.

Katel, P. (1994, May 16). Choosing to die. *Newsweek*, 42.

Kayal, P. (1993). *Bearing witness*. Boulder, CO: Westview Press.

Komar, K. (1987). *Transcending angels: Rainer Maria Rilke's Duino Elegies*. Lincoln: University of Nebraska Press.

Lather, P. (1996). Troubling clarity: The politics of accessible language. *Harvard Educational Review, 66*(3), 525–45.

Lather, P., & Smithies, C. (1997). *Troubling the angels: Women living with HIV/AIDS*. Boulder, CO: Westview.

Leach, M., & Bolen, M. (1998). Gilles Deleuze: Practicing education through flight and gossip. In M. Peters (Ed.), *Naming the multiple: Poststructuralism and education*. South Hadley, MA: Bergin & Garvey.

Marcus, G. (1994). What comes (just) after "post"?: The case of ethnography. In N. Denzin & Y. Lincoln (Eds.), *Handbook of qualitative research* (pp. 563–74). Thousand Oaks, CA: Sage.

Mu, Q. (n.d.) Orpheus in the Maelstrom. *Mondo 2000,4*, 134.

Nagele, R. (1991). *Theatre, theory, speculation: Walter Benjamin and the scenes of modernity*. Baltimore: Johns Hopkins University Press.

Piercy, M. (1973). *To be of use: Collected poems*. Garden City, NY: Doubleday.

Purvis, A. (1996/1997, December-January). The global epidemic. *Time*, 76–78.

Rilke, R. (1989). *The selected poems of Rainer Maria Rilke* (S. Mitchell, Ed. & Trans.). New York: Vintage International.

Rosen, C. (1977, October 27 and November 10). The ruins of Walter Benjamin. [Review of *The Origin of German Tragic Drama*]. *The New York Review of Books*, pp. 31–40.

Saper, C. (1991). Electronic media studies: From video art to artificial invention. *SubStance, 20*(3), 114–34.

Serres, M. (1995). *Angels: A modern myth* (F. Cowper, Trans.). Paris: Flammarion. (Original work published 1993)

Serres, M., & Latour, B. (1995). *Conversations on science, culture, and time* (R. Lapidus, Trans.). Ann Arbor: University of Michigan Press. (Original work published 1990)

Shiff, R. (1992). Handling shocks: On the representation of experience in Walter Benjamin's analogies. *Oxford Art Journal, 15*(2), 88–103.

Singer, L. (1993). *Erotic welfare: Sexual theory and politics in the age of epidemic.* New York: Routledge.

Spivak, G. (1993). *Outside in the teaching machine.* New York: Routledge.

Spivak, G. (1994). Responsibility. *Boundary 2, 21*(3), 19–64.

St.Pierre, E. A. (1996, April). *Methodology in the fold and the irruption of transgressive data.* Paper presented at the annual meeting of the American Educational Research Association, New York City.

Stevens, W. (1982). *The collected poems of Wallace Stevens.* New York: Alfred A. Knopf.

Stockton, K. B. (1992). Bodies and god: Poststructural feminists return to the fold of spiritual materialism. *Boundary 2, 19*(2), 113–49.

Thompson, K. (1991). *Angels and aliens.* New York: Fawcett Columbine.

Treichler, P. (1988). AIDS, homophobia, and biomedical discourse: An epidemic of signification. *October, 43,* 31–71.

Van Maanen, J. (1995). An end to innocence: The ethnography of ethnography. In J. Van Maanen (Ed.), *Representation in ethnography* (pp. 1–35). Thousand Oaks, CA: Sage.

Visweswaran, K, (1994). *Fictions of feminist ethnography.* Minneapolis: University of Minnesota Press.

Witte, B. (1991). *Walter Benjamin: An intellectual biography* (J. Rolleston, Trans.). Detroit, MI: Wayne State University Press.

Wolin, R. (1995). *Labyrinths: Explorations in the critical history of ideas.* Amherst: University of Massachusetts Press.

CONTRIBUTORS

Donna E. Alvermann is Research Professor of Reading Education at the University of Georgia in Athens, Georgia, where she teaches courses in content literacy and literacy research. Her recent work focuses on exploring the potential of feminist pedagogy and poststructural theories for teaching and learning literacy in middle and high school classrooms. She is currently co-chairing the International Reading Association's Adolescent Literacy Commission and is a past president of the National Reading Conference. In the last 2 years, Dr. Alvermann was awarded the Oscar S. Causey Award for Outstanding Contributions to Reading Research and the William A. Owens Award for creative research. Currently, she is the recipient of a Spencer Foundation grant to study critical media literacy and popular culture texts in an after-school program for adolescents in public libraries.

Deborah P. Britzman is author of *Lost Subjects, Contested Objects: Toward a Psychoanalytic Inquiry of Learning* (Albany: State University of New York Press, 1998) and *Practice Makes Practice: A Critical Study of Learning to Teach* (Albany: State University of New York Press, 1991). She is Associate Professor in the Faculty of Education at York University, Toronto, Canada.

Lubna Nazir Chaudhry received her Ph.D. from the University of California at Davis in 1995. Earlier, she received a master's degree from the University of Punjab, Lahore, Pakistan, and from the University of Hawai'i at Manoa. Currently, she is on leave from the University of Georgia in Athens, Georgia, where she holds a joint appointment in Women's Studies and in Social Foundations of Education.

Patricia Hill Collins, the Charles Phelps Taft Professor of Sociology in the Department of African-American Studies at the University of Cincinnati, Ohio, is the first female in the University of Cincinnati's history to hold this title. While

Collins's specialties in sociology are diverse, her research and scholarly interests deal primarily with issues of gender, race, and social class, specifically related to African-American women. She has published many articles in professional journals and edited volumes. Her first book, *Black Feminist Thought: Knowledge, Consciousness, and the Politics of Empowerment* (New York: Routledge, 1990) has won many awards, and her second book, *Race, Class, & Gender: An Anthology*, edited with Margaret Anderson, is in its second edition (Belmont, CA: Wadsworth Publishing, 1998) Collins's latest book is *Fighting Words/Black Women and the Search for Justice* (Minneapolis: University of Minnesota Press, 1998).

Bronwyn Davies is a Professor in Education at James Cook University (Queensland, Australia). Her published research involves analyzing the ways in which individual and collective gendered identities are constructed through text and talk. She works with teachers and students at all levels of schooling and uses a number of research methodologies including poststructuralist analysis of texts, autobiography, and collective biography. Her work seeks to find ways to deconstruct current knowledge structures and identity structures with a particular focus on the male-female binary. Her current work will be published by Alta Mira Press in a book entitled *(In)scribing Body/Landscape Relations*. Previous books include *Power/Knowledge/Desire: Changing School Organization and Management Practices* (Canberra, Australia: Department of Employment, Education, Training, and Youth Affairs, 1996); *Shards of Glass: Children Reading and Writing Beyond Gendered Identities* (Cresskill, NJ: Hampton Press, 1993); *Frogs and Snails and Feminist Tales: Preschool Children and Gender* (North Sydney, Australia: Allen & Unwin, 1989); and *Life in the Classroom and Playground: The Accounts of Primary School Children* (London: Routledge, 1982).

Patti Lather is a Professor in the School of Educational Policy and Leadership at The Ohio State University, Columbus, Ohio, where she teaches qualitative research. Her work includes *Getting Smart: Feminist Research and Pedagogy With/in the Postmodern* (New York: Routledge, 1991) and *Troubling the Angels: Women Living With HIV/AIDS* (with Chris Smithies, Boulder, CO: Westview, 1997). Recent journal articles have appeared in the *Harvard Educational Review, International Journal of Qualitative Studies in Education*, and *Qualitative Inquiry* on issues of critical and poststructural theories, feminist methodology, and practices of educational research. Distinctions include a Fulbright to New Zealand and a visiting appointment at Goteborg University in Sweden.

Mary Leach is Associate Professor of Cultural Studies in Education at The Ohio State University, College of Education, Columbus, Ohio. Her interests include educational theory, cultural foundations of education, and feminist theory as it applies to gender theories of education.

Kate McCoy has a Ph.D. in Cultural Studies in Education from The Ohio State University. Since 1997, she has served as research associate on an ethnographic study with heroin users in New York City funded by the National Institute on Drug Abuse entitled "Heroin in the 21st Century." She is an Adjunct Assistant Professor of Anthropology at John Jay College of Criminal Justice, City University of New York. She is beginning work as a consultant on "A Qualitative Study of the Accessibility and Acceptability of HIV Care for People Who Inject Drugs or Use Crack Cocaine," a project with the New York Academy of Medicine funded by the New York City Mayor's Office for AIDS Policy Coordination. She has published articles in *Educational Researcher, International Journal of Qualitative Studies in Education*, and the *Journal of Psychoactive Drugs*. Her area of academic interest is critical/cultural studies, with emphases in qualitative research methodology, critical and poststructural theories, and literary and rhetorical criticism.

Erica McWilliam is Associate Professor (Associate Chair) in the School of Cultural and Policy Studies, Faculty of Education at the Queensland University of Technology, Queensland, Australia. She is widely published in the area of pedagogical studies, bringing poststructuralist theorizing to bear on a range of developments in the field, such as the professional development of teachers, changing academic practices, new technologies, new feminisms, and new modes of inquiry in educational research.

Wendy Morgan is a Senior Lecturer in the School of Language and Literacy Education at the Queensland University of Technology, Queensland, Australia. Her overlapping research interests include poststructuralist feminist research writing and its hypertextual reinscription, unconventional fictional writing and its effects on readers' understanding of the nature of texts and reading, poststructuralist and critical literacy theories, and technologized literacy. She has recently completed "Choose Your Own Adventure: English as Interactive Hypertext," a multigeneric hypertext on hypertexts in secondary English education.

Wanda S. Pillow is Assistant Professor in Educational Policy Studies at the University of Illinois at Urbana-Champaign and teaches courses in qualitative theory and methods, policy analysis, and feminist theories. Her theoretical, research, and lived interests focus on critical theories of cultural and political representation. Her research interests focus on gender, race, class, mothering, and sexuality; she is completing a 2-year project tracing social and policy discourse surrounding teen pregnancy from the passage of Title IX to the 1980s. However, she has recently been distracted by Ken Burn's documentary habits, which has led to an interest in Sacagawea, the Shoshone Indian woman who accompanied Lewis and Clark on their "Corps of Discovery," and a paper, "Sacagawea: The Making of a Colonial Heroine Subject" (*Qualitative Inquiry*, in press).

Laurel Richardson is Professor Emerita of Sociology, Professor of Cultural Studies in the College of Education, and Graduate Professor of Women's Studies at The Ohio State University Columbus, Ohio. She has written extensively on qualitative research methods, ethics, and issues of representation. She is the author of seven books, including *Fields of Play: Constructing an Academic Life* (New Brunswick, NJ: Rutgers, 1997), which was honored with the C. H. Cooley award for the 1998 Best Book in symbolic interaction. Currently, she is interested in the relationships between conceptual and personal constructions of "timeplaces," narratives of the self, and knowledge practices.

Elizabeth A. St.Pierre is Assistant Professor in the Language Education Department at the University of Georgia at Athens, Georgia. Her teaching and research focus on critical and poststructural theory, feminist and qualitative methodology, and how these inform the reading/writing/language theories of secondary English Education. She has published several articles about her on-going study of subjectivity with the older, southern women of her hometown in *International Journal of Qualitative Studies in Education, Qualitative Inquiry*, and *Journal of Contemporary Ethnography*. Currently, she and Donna Alvermann are collaborating on a study of how expert readers read texts that are too hard to read.

Sofia Villenas is Assistant Professor in the Department of Educational Studies and in the Ethnic Studies Program at the University of Utah at Salt Lake City, Utah. Her research centers on investigating Latino home and community education within the dynamics of racial/cultural community politics, as well as exploring positionality and location in qualitative research. Her publications include "The Colonizer/Colonized Chicana Ethnographer: Identity, Marginalization and Co-optation in the Field" in *Harvard Educational Review* [Vol. 66(4), 1996] and a co-edited book with Laurence Parker and Donna Deyhle, *Race Is . . . Race Isn't: Critical Race Theory and Qualitative Studies in Education* (Boulder, CO: Westview Press, in press).

INDEX